Value Maps

Value Maps

**VALUATION TOOLS THAT
UNLOCK BUSINESS WEALTH**

Warren D. Miller
CFA, ASA, CPA

WILEY

For general information on our other products and services or for technical support, please contact our Customer Care Department within the United States at (800) 762-2974, outside the United States at (317) 572-3993 or fax (317) 572-4002.

Wiley also publishes its books in a variety of electronic formats. Some content that appears in print may not be available in electronic books. For more information about Wiley products, visit our web site at www.wiley.com.

Library of Congress Cataloging-in-Publication Data:

Miller, Warren D., 1943-
  Value maps : valuation tools that unlock business wealth / Warren D. Miller.
    p. cm.
  Includes index.
  ISBN 978-0-470-43756-8 (cloth)
  1. Business enterprises–Valuation.   2. Corporations–Valuation.   I. Title.
  HG4028.V3.M55 2010
  658.15′5–dc22   2010004696

To my bride and loving spouse, Dorothy Beckert

Contents

Preface

From conception to publication, this book had a gestation period of almost 17 years. Not until August 2005 did it finally begin to take on a life of its own. Even then, another three years of rethinking, reanalyzing, and reframing went by before I decided I was ready to commit to writing this. For me, book-writing includes, in roughly equal parts, aspects of writing valuation reports, giving birth, and mud-wrestling. (I can only imagine the giving-birth experience, of course.) Those who have written a book know that it is a nontrivial undertaking. It is harder and takes longer than the first-time author expects. So it was with me.

The Journey

Like some in this field, I came to valuation by accident. After a checkered career as an internal auditor (Union Pacific Corporation), staff accountant (Borg-Warner Corporation), and chief financial officer (United Video Satellite Group, then United Video Inc.), I did a five-year stint as an academic in strategic management at Oklahoma State University (OSU) and the University of Oklahoma. I completed all of my Ph.D. coursework at OSU. Like marriage and children, doctoral programs change participants' lives, and I was no exception. Among other changes in my perspective, I became a visceral opponent of the existence of undergraduate business education, despite the fact that my undergrad degree is in business. With rare exceptions—the McIntire School of Commerce at the University of Virginia is one—undergraduate business curricula have too little education and too much training.

The problem that creates is that training does not teach one how to think, only how to do. Done right, education teaches thinking skills. So, if the economic world changes and business no longer has a need for as many, say, accountants as it used to need, those who have been doing accounting for 10, 20, or 30 years and have never thought about anything else are up a creek. Think of the displaced auto workers in Michigan and former steelworkers in Pennsylvania.

The doctoral courses I took were game-changers for me. My dim view of economics changed when I was introduced to industrial organization (IO).

I also had an unwarranted and unrealistic perception of the value of accounting's contribution to enterprise, doubtless because I had done a lot of it. Graduate school taught me that strategy and economics mattered a whole lot more.

If I had to boil down my incomplete Ph.D. experience into two take-aways, they are:

1. After tens of thousands of published research papers from hardworking scholars doing difficult and demanding work, we still know very little about how companies do what they do. Evidence of this shows up in the low R^2s from hypothesis-testing. After all, $1 - R^2$ is the percentage of variance *not* explained by the variables in the test. I have seen highly rated dissertations with R^2s of .25. That means that three-quarters of the variance was unexplained.
2. For anyone doing complex or interdisciplinary work in the non-academic world, there is no substitute for good theory. Confirmation of this lies in the repeating question that few valuation reports can answer: **Why? Why** is the subject company's inventory turnover one-quarter (or twice) the industry average? **Why** does the client company assert that its employees are its most important asset, yet in its most recent year it issued 134 W-2s for jobs done by its full complement of 35 employees? At a company that's been in business for over 20 years, **why** is every payday an administrative train wreck?

The reports don't explain why because their authors don't know why. One reason they don't is that they rely on traditional valuation tools. Another is that some in our field confuse theory with a half-baked idea. "Well, that's thuh thee-ree," they snort, contempt dripping from every syllable. They seem not to understand that valuing a company for whose securities there are no active markets is a damnably difficult undertaking. Colleagues who have valued both public and private companies tell me that valuing private equity is several magnitudes more difficult. I believe them.

While some knowledge of finance and accounting is essential, I quickly concluded that even an encyclopedic grasp of those topics was inadequate. I also saw that in valuing small and medium-sized enterprises (SMEs), getting my arms around unsystematic risk was going to consume the lion's share of my time. We had some size-premium data from Ibbotson, but that was all. The valuation community had no other data because we had no framework around which to gather it. Without data, there can be no hypothesis-testing. Without such testing, we lack for good theory.

Recognizing the need for a framework that gave me a baseline series of questions to ask about unsystematic risk, I immediately combined the

General Electric four-sided model (see Chapter 8) with Porter's five-forces framework (see Chapter 9). That gave me a way to organize my thinking about external influences on a company's performance. These constituted my first iteration of the "OT" of SWOT (strengths, weaknesses, opportunities, threats) analysis. The challenge was to find (or create) the "SW" piece for the framework.

About 90 minutes into the first day of my first valuation course from the American Society of Appraisers, an instructor put up an overhead transparency (not much PowerPoint in use then)—the Porter framework. I almost fell out of my chair. Five long, stressful, miserable, poverty-stricken years as a Ph.D. student flashed before me. That moment confirmed that I was on the right track: There was a place for strategic management, IO, and organization theory in valuation. I later found that two other disciplines within economics also offered useful tools for valuation professionals: evolutionary economics and Austrian economics.

Valuing private equity offered ample opportunity to use much of the nonvaluation knowledge I already had in order to get at underlying causes of why a company did some things really well or really badly. I believed from the beginning that, if I couldn't explain why, then I was unlikely to get a reasonable valuation estimate, except through dumb luck. Even then, my report would lack the credibility essential for a valuation craftsman.

Later in my search for the "SW" component, I immersed myself in evolutionary economics with Nelson and Winter's classic, *An Evolutionary Theory of Economic Change.* I had had some exposure to it in one of my doctoral courses, but I had not given the book the time and energy it deserved. A few years later I read "The 'Austrian' School of Strategy."[1] That paper led me to Austrian economics, which connected most of the random dots that traditional economics had left floating around in my head.[2]

I still did not have the "SW" piece, though. I reviewed each of my own valuation reports and those I had done in collaboration with others. I made a list of the various causes that I had found that underpinned the effects (metrics and ratios) of financial performance. I looked for patterns in the causes and saw a few. I stayed after it and, in summer 2005, was able to classify the causes into a five-part framework that, after some what-iffing, became SPARC (**s**trategy, **p**eople, **a**rchitecture, **r**outines, **c**ulture). In the meantime, the four-sided GE model of the macroenvironment had become hexagonal, as had the framework for domain analysis. On September 26, 2005, on the back of a cocktail napkin at Mr. K's, a first-rate Chinese

---

[1] Jacobson, "The 'Austrian' School of Strategy."

[2] I will have much more to say about the deficiencies of equilibrium-based economics in Chapter 3.

restaurant at 51st and Lexington Avenue in midtown Manhattan, I drew two concentric hexagons with a triangle inside circumscribing five SPARC blocks, labeled them, and handed the napkin to Jim Travis, a colleague from Chicago.

"How's that look?" I asked.

"Cool. What is it?" he said.

As I explained, he nodded. What I drew that night has changed only slightly since then. It is a robust framework that we use in every engagement. It is no exaggeration to say that we would be lost without it. It would probably take me two or three times as long to do a valuation half as good if I did not have that framework.

About This Book

If you are a valuation professional or consultant with an interest in helping SMEs increase their value, this book is for you. If you are anyone else,   welcome. The book might be for you, too, but you can make that call.

The 21 chapters contained herein are divided into four parts. Part One, *Cornerstones*, leads off with a chapter that makes the case for why a new approach to valuation is needed. Chapters 2 through 6 are devoted to discussing tools from the five disciplines that undergird the new approach: strategic management, industrial organization, organization theory, evolutionary economics, and Austrian economics.

In Part Two, *Pouring the Foundation*, we begin the move from theory to practice. The part leads with a chapter on valuation drivers, a much-misunderstood topic in the valuation community. Chapters on assessing risk in the macroenvironment and the domain follow. Chapter 10, "Getting to Why," covers analyses, composites, and on-site interviews. Chapter 11 is, in my view, the most important chapter in the book because its focus is the company. The part closes with a short chapter about SPARC archetypes. These chapters are the how-tos.

Part Three is entitled *Tales from the Firing Line*. The five chapters here comprise 22 vignettes taken from actual valuation and consulting engagements. These are disguised stories, of course. But they are real, and they happened. Any seasoned valuation professional will swear that Hollywood scriptwriters could never make up the stuff we see and hear, and these vignettes are further proof of that if any were needed.

Part Four is called *Practice Management*. In my view, this area is an understudied, underexplicated topic. The chapters here deal with the engagement process, working with clients in value-mapping engagements, and an international perspective on value maps. The part and the book end with a chapter that examines the future of value enhancement services.

Software and Web Site

John Wiley & Sons provides a Web site on which purchasers of this book can access the proprietary Excel templates that take you through the value-mapping process. These templates have some set (i.e., unchangeable) features, but they have some flexibility, too. After all, valuation is about "facts and circumstances," so a degree of customization capability is essential. See the About the Web Site section for more information.

Acknowledgements

The debt I owe to colleagues, mentors, friends, and family is enormous. The support and encouragement of one's colleagues is high praise, as any recipient will attest. Gary M. Karlitz, ASA, and Mandeep Sihota, CFA (both of Citrin Cooperman & Company, LLP), Don M. Drysdale (Drysdale Valuation, LLC), Ed Moran (now retired from Horne, LLP), and Sarah von Helfenstein, AVA (Braver and Company, LLP), have been especially helpful, upbeat, and supportive. The many professionals who have attended classes I've taught, listened to presentations I've made at conferences, and responded to articles I've written are too numerous to mention, but each is appreciated and saluted here.

One does not learn about good theory without good scholars as mentors. I am especially blessed to be a student and friend of Professor Ben Oviatt, now retired from Georgia State University. Ben and I go back 26 years. He and his spouse, Judy, have put Dorothy and me up in their home. Ben was my first strategy professor. He is a wonderful teacher and sterling human being. He has also listened to my ideas and raised substantive questions that forced me to improve on them. Without Ben's patient guidance and friendship, I doubt this book would have ever seen the light of day.

Professor Joe Mahoney of the University of Illinois, Urbana-Champaign, is a model for many young scholars and at least one old one. He is a man whose work I have admired for almost two decades. If there is a book that Joe has not read, I have never discovered it. And I don't mean just books on strategy and economics. I mean *books*. The man is a mobile branch of the Library of Congress and a source of bountiful insights, thoughtful perspectives, understated humor, and infinite patience. He and I have spent many hours on the telephone discussing papers, constructs, and the craft of research. Joe and his bride, Professor Jeanne Connell, are the loveliest and most generous of people. Dorothy and I are fortunate to have them as friends.

Professor Peter Klein, blogger without peer[1] and associate director of the Contracting and Organizations Research Institute at the University of

---

[1] Don't miss http://organizationsandmarkets.com, *the* best blog for strategy and economics anywhere on the Net.

xix

Missouri, Columbia, is a dear friend, stunning intellect, and unbelievable reservoir of erudition and good sense. I "met" Peter by sending him an e-mail when I became a serious student of Austrian economics. He has been unfailingly generous with his time and ideas. Peter has read and commented on my abstracts and other writing. I am also fortunate that he has signed on as an occasional subcontractor for Beckmill Research, LLC. Who else among us can claim a subcontractor with a Nobel laureate as the chair of his dissertation committee? (Oliver Williamson, 2009 co-winner, chaired Peter's.) What I most admire about Peter is his commitment to Austrian economics, despite the toll taken on his career at the hands of "traditional" microeconomists who couldn't tell a production function from a real company. Come to think of it, *of course* they can't: They think they're synonymous.

Last, but certainly not least, is Professor Tom Box of Pittsburg State University. Tom and I are Marines.[2] Tom is also a former union steward and construction foreman. He got his undergraduate degree in math when he was almost 40, his MBA in operations research after that, and his Ph.D. in strategic management in his fifties. He is a great colleague, close friend, and sometime consulting and literary collaborator. Tom and I are gruff, serious men devoted to country and family. We met when Oklahoma State offered its first MBA classes in Tulsa in January 1983. We have been fast friends ever since.

And then there are the friends I am so lucky to have. First among equals is Bob Kimmel, semiretired CEO of the Elliot Companies, Roanoke, Virginia. I first met Bob in 1976 when I was a junior auditor at Union Pacific and he was director of accounting operations at its Champlin Petroleum subsidiary. Not quite eight years later he and his lovely bride, Fran, moved in next door to some good friends of mine in Tulsa. Bob and I have been thick as thieves ever since. The four of us have spent many wonderful hours together solving the world's problems (several times, at least). Bob is also the wisest man I know. I would never play poker with him. It would be far more fun to just write him a check and forgo the humiliation.

Right alongside Bob is Alfred M. King, vice chairman of valuation firm Marshall & Stevens Inc. Al is a friend, colleague, collaborator, coauthor, sounding board, encyclopedia of institutional knowledge, and like-minded troublemaker. He and I see politics, ethics, and valuation almost identically. He is a relentlessly upbeat, high-energy man who, at an age when many guys are playing too much golf and drinking too much whiskey, continues to pursue with passion the work he loves.

---

[2] There is no such thing as an ex-Marine.

I have also received encouragement from Jay B. Abrams, Dorothy Alford, Parnell Black, Vicki and James Breech, Byrlan Cass-Shively, Professor Russ Coff, Don and Maggie Cunningham, Tony Eastmond, Jim Edge, David Foster, James A. Hale Jr., Professor Emeritus John Harris, John B. Hennis, Brien Jones, Michael Kalashian, Chris Kean, Professor Michael Leiblein, Tom Lincoln, Lucretia Lyons, Professor Rich Makadok, John Markel, Professor Cathy Maritan, Michael J. Mattson, Maureen McNamee, Professor Tom Moliterno, Bill Rister, Susan M. Saidens, Margaret Schlachter, Dale Shepherd, and Dan Vance. Thanks to all of you. Any omissions are inadvertent and unintended.

My editor at John Wiley & Sons, Sheck Cho, is the best. He is a gentle man with a wonderful sense of humor who understands writers and our demons. Al King recommended Sheck to me early. Without him, a wonderful mix of carrot and stick, the book would be yet unfinished.

My go-to software guy, Russell Hudson of StrategeMetrix, LLC, is a talented and hardworking professional whom I met at the annual Strategic Management Society conference in San Diego in 2007. He congratulated me after a session in which I had asked some especially difficult questions. We talked for a while and agreed to follow up by phone after the conference. During one of those conversations, I suggested to Russ that he consider enrolling in the curriculum leading to the Chartered Financial Analyst designation. With his DBA in strategic management, I thought that having the CFA charter would open a world of valuation and consulting to him. He said that he would look into it.

I got an e-mail from him 19 months later in June 2009. He wrote to say he had sat for Level 2 of the CFA exam two days before. I picked up the phone and called him. I was looking for an Excel expert with some strategy knowledge. I asked him to rank his Excel skills on a scale of 1 to 7. I'll never forget his response: "I'm about a 5.5, but I'm surrounded by 9s." He undersold himself. He is a first-rate colleague who will make a world-class valuation professional. He did a great job asking me tough follow-up questions that produced a terrific and easy-to-understand Excel tool to go with this book.

Last, but certainly not least, is my family. My daughter, Seana Roubinek, and my grandson, Jordan T. Roubinek, have been inspirations to me when they didn't know it. My stepsons, Jim and Paul Beckert, give their mom the respect and affirmation she richly deserves. Paul's wife, Janie, is a continuing source of good humor, hilarious e-mails, great photographs, and insightful commentary on life's events.

A key member of my family is no longer with us: Grandmother Miller. She was a third-generation college graduate, Cal/Berkeley, Class of 1912. She worked until she was 99 and lived to be 106. She was upbeat, positive, and forward-looking. She is my model for aging with grace. I know that she would be delighted with the publication of her only grandson's first book.

My bride and loving spouse, Dorothy Beckert, to whom this book is dedicated, is the source of all things good in my life. She has taught me everything I know about love, respect, and family. There is not a kinder, sweeter, dearer, more steadfast, more patient, or tougher woman on this earth, and I am the beneficiary of all of that. She knows I love her with all my heart and soul because I tell her at least a dozen times every day.

I have received insightful comments, wonderful advice, and recommended changes from many I have named here. They are far smarter than I, which is one of many ways that I benefit from knowing them. In most cases, I took their advice. In some cases, I did not. In those instances and others, no doubt, I have erred. Those mistakes are mine and mine alone.

About The Web Site

Congratulations! With your purchase of this book, you also gain access to a special Web site: www.wiley.com/go/valuemaps. There you will find sample questions for on-site interviews (Chapter 10) and Excel templates to help you quantify non-size unsystematic risk: macroenvironment (Chapter 8), domain (Chapter 9), and company (Chapter 11). There is also another Excel sheet, which gives you a graphical representation of the archetype to which your client company is closest, based on how you responded to scaled questions related to Chapter 11. Inconsistencies in a client's SPARC profile present opportunities for value enhancement.

In addition to these goodies, we have included graphics of the trilevel unsystematic risk framework and its three components. You are welcome to use these in your reports so long as you agree to attribute them to Beckmill Research, LLC. We include suggested wording for a footnote or end note.

Please revisit the site on occasion. From time to time, we will add materials to support your work in helping client companies enhance value.

The password for the Web site is: value

Don't hesitate to contact us via SPARC@beckmill.com with ideas and suggestions for what we can do better. We also encourage you to syndicate our blog. It is on our Web site, www.beckmill.com. While you're there, please register at www.beckmill.com/register.asp.

List of Acronyms

CAPM   Capital asset pricing model; the modified version that includes elements of unsytematic risk is used here.

CEO   Chief executive officer.

CFO   Chief financial officer.

CPA   Certified public accountant; similar to the CA (chartered accountant) designation used outside the United States.

DCF   Discounted cash flow. Unlike net income, DCF measures changes in cash from the perspective of either the company or the shareholders. These are often labeled FCFF (free cash flow to the firm) and FCFE (free cash flow to equity).

FTC   Federal Trade Commission. In the United States, a federal agency charged with consumer protection and with encouraging greater competition.

FTEs   Full-time-equivalent employees.

GM   General manager.

GE   General Electric Company.

HR   Human relations (a.k.a., personnel). The department or the professionals that oversee that function within a company.

IO   Industrial organization. Within economics, a field that is concerned with the structure, conduct, and performance of industries and also with antitrust policy and enforcement.

IRS   Internal Revenue Service. In the United States, the federal agency responsible for collecting taxes and administering the Internal Revenue Code (IRC), now over 65,000 pages long.

LBO   Leveraged buy-out. Entity-level financing technique that favors debt over equity.

NAICS   North American Industry Classification System. Governmental numerical scheme for classifying business activities in the United States, Canada, and Mexico; in the United States, it replaces SIC codes (see entry).

OT   Organization theory. Within management, an academic discipline concerned with the structure, processes, and culture of an organization and its relationship with its external environment.

PDPs   Personal development programs. These are goals, usually annual, to which employees commit to increase their knowledge and skillsets. Such programs are essential in high-growth companies, or else the scope of the company will quickly outstrip the management ability of those running it. Tell-tale sign: rising revenues and falling profits.

R&D   Research and development. Sometimes called R&E (research and experimentation) outside the United States.

RBV   Resource-based view of the firm. This theory has two key assumptions: (1) the resource endowment of a company is unique, and (2) resources are nonportable.

S-C-P   Structure-conduct-performance paradigm that is widely used by IO scholars.

SIC   Standard Industrial Classification. A numerical scheme devised by the United States Bureau of the Census in the 1930s to classify business activities; it is being replaced by NAICS (see entry).

SKU   Stock-keeping unit (unique item of inventory). More SKUs mean greater complexity, which requires more investment in infrastructure and increases the likelihood of error and rework.

SME   Small and medium-sized enterprises. There is no consensus on what the upper and lower limits of SMEs are, but, in this book, we use SME to describe an organization that is bigger than one-person or "mom-and-pop" business and has annual revenues below $250 million.

SPARC   **S**trategy, **P**eople, **A**rchitecture, **R**outines, **C**ulture. The central analytical framework of this book; it contains the universe of company-level causes of aberrant metrics (those that are well above or well below industry or domain norms).

VRIO   A framework devised by Ohio State's Jay Barney to gain insight into the durability of a capability; VRIO asks four questions: (1) Is the capability **v**aluable? (2) Is it **r**are? (3) Is it **i**nimitable? (4) Is it **o**rganizationally aligned?

Value Maps

PART I

CORNERSTONES

Why a New Approach Is Needed

At the conclusion of a valuation engagement, the professional should have value-enhancing insights into the client's business that the client does not have. This is true even in projects in the rapidly growing niche, valuation for financial reporting. If the analyst does not have such insights, then he or she did not do the job right. That is a strong statement, I know. But I am with Dizzy Dean, the supremely self-confident pitcher from the 1930s, who liked to say "If you can do it, it ain't braggin'."

The valuation field is growing fast. The general absence of barriers to entry in our arena, however, invites opportunists, charlatans, incompetents, low-ballers, and rip-off artists to eviscerate pricing and destroy the opportunities that serious practitioners can have to create value for clients. At Beckmill Research, LLC, we are about value creation. That comes from my experience before I became a valuation guy. I had held various jobs as a financial professional, but the game-changer—life-changer, really—was the half-decade I spent as a Ph.D. student in strategic management in the mid-1980s. As the word 'strategic' suggests, it is management for the long term as seen from the top of the organization. The focus is on the creation and retention of value. We—my wife, Dorothy, and I—launched our firm in 1991 as a strategy boutique. I "discovered" valuation in 1993. As I dove into the field devouring books and everyother piece of information I could find, I was struck by the huge disparity in rates of return among firms of different size in the Ibbotson dataset. Frustrated by the insufficiency of tools from finance and accounting to explain such disparities, I began experimenting, first with tools from strategy. I found that they had considerable utility. I then added other tools from industrial organization and organization theory, two other disciplines I had encountered in my Ph.D. coursework.

At a valuation seminar sponsored by the American Society of Appraisers (ASA) in 1995, one of the instructors introduced Porter's five-forces framework. My jaw dropped, and I almost fell out of my chair. I had the empirical confirmation that I needed that I was on the right track.

Not surprisingly, we see the world differently from most of our colleagues. For starters, we do not believe that valuation has much to do with accounting. Now, before all my accounting colleagues take aim at me, please hold your fire and allow me to explain. For starters, I am a Certified Public Accountant (CPA) and a Certified Management Accountant, as well as a former controller and chief financial officer (CFO). But, if accounting knowledge were essential in this line of work, we would see CPAs on what remains of Wall Street and working for buy-side institutions. Few are there. Labor markets are telling us something.

Don't misunderstand. I'm glad I know, understand, and can do accounting. I'm a better valuation professional because of that knowledge and experience. But I suffer from no delusions that valuation should be seen through the lens of accounting. It shouldn't, and here's why: Valuation is about the future, and accounting is about the past.[1] It's that simple.

Like most who have worked in this emerging field for a while, I didn't start out here. Near the end of cramming four years of undergraduate education into 14, I had 54 on-campus job interviews, got 53 rejection letters (including eight in one day, which surely must be a record), and received one job offer. That lifeline was to become an internal auditor at Union Pacific Corporation (UP).

Next to what I do now, that job was the most fun I ever had professionally. The staff at "Uncle Pete," as we called it, was run in the mid-1970s by former members of the "traveling audit staff" at General Electric. My two years there were a career-changing experience that stands me in good stead to this day.

For one thing, the idea of paying our way was hammered into us. We were obsessed with finding ways to reduce costs, eliminate inefficiencies, and help processes work better in our operational audits of various functions within the far-flung UP empire. The late Charlie Billingsley, then the general auditor for UP, oversaw the staff. It was a preschooler, barely five years old when I joined it. We spent only a quarter of our time on financial audits; that was to keep the fees of the outside auditors down. The other nine months of the year, we did operational auditing, long before such audits became all the rage in U.S. industry.

We had audit programs, of course, but Charlie liked to say: "At the end of the day we have a three-word audit program around here: 'Do something smart.'" That is because operational audits, like business valuations, are very much about "facts and circumstances."

---

[1] Section 3.03, Revenue Ruling 59-60: "Valuation of securities is, in essence, *a prophecy as to the future* [italics added] and must be based on facts available at the required date of appraisal."

As I did when I started out in 1975, today I still go where the facts and the circumstances lead me. If that makes the client happy, terrific. If it makes the client unhappy, well, I'm sorry. We want clients to be happy but their happiness is not part of our engagement letter. It doesn't change anything we do. In the inimitable characterization by the late Senator Paul Tsongas, valuation professionals cannot be "pander bears." Those who are—and there are many of them these days—mislead and disrespect clients. In the process, they undermine the hard work and credibility of the rest of us.

Valuation as Craft[2]

We often hear colleagues bantering back and forth over the question, "Is valuation an art or a science?" Some claim to know the answer. Others take an unambiguous position straddling the fence, muttering that it is some of each. We believe that, like adherents to traditional microeconomics, what they are debating is about the pinhead-dancing of angels.

Valuation is craft. It is not science because it lacks precision and certainty. It is not art because it has utility and economic dimensions. The word "craft" summons images of objects made by hand—by masons, carpenters, weavers, silversmiths, sculptors, and potters. But such one-off work products also come from surgeons, writers, dentists, basic researchers—and valuation professionals. In a craft, neophytes serve apprenticeships under the supervision of a journeyman (or journeywoman). She or he is experienced in the craft and is older, wiser, and more knowledgeable. In a craft, experience dominates because only through experience can one acquire the necessary knowledge of nuance and technique that enables the delivery of a top-flight product.

When craftspeople talk with clients, we speak as weavers, masons, silversmiths, carpenters . . . or analysts. When we speak to one another, however, we speak as craftspeople. We understand the use of every tool in our toolbox. That understanding, combined with our experience, gives dignity to our work product.

Each craftsman creates a body of work that grows, evolves, and improves with experience. Each creation is unique. Each is personal. Each is a stand-alone statement by and about the craftswoman. Improvement comes only from repeated ventures into the craft, pushing the envelope, extending knowledge, expanding reach, and explaining meaning. Craft that does not explain has not meaning and is not craft.

None of these aesthetics, sensory experiences, or nuances afflict charlatans masquerading as craftsmen. They think only of power, prestige, and

---

[2] This section draws from my article of the same title, which appeared in the Winter 2008 issue of *Business Valuation Review*.

money. We think only of preserving and enhancing our craft. If we do right by our craft, money and the rest of it takes care of itself.

Done right, every valuation—like every surgery, every piece of hand-made furniture, every rock wall, and every silver-and-turquoise belt buckle—is different, not at the margin but in substance. There *is* a process, of course, and we must respect and follow it wherever it leads us, regardless of how the client feels; if she feels strongly enough, she can fire us. So be it. But, that is why "facts and circumstances" are so important in our craft. It is also why one-size-fits-all doesn't work any better in valuation than it does in haberdashery.

The State of Our Craft

Academic scholars are craftspeople, too. Every paper, whether published or not, gives them new knowledge, new understanding, and insights that they didn't have before. Some business professionals disparage the primacy, at least at larger institutions, of research. Before I spent five years in a doctoral program, I did, too. I learned there, though, that research keeps professors, especially the tenured ones, current in their knowledge. I have seen faculty members at colleges without a research emphasis, and what they know—and what they teach, of course—is often out of date. But 19-year-olds will never know until it's too late.

Besides keeping professors' knowledge current, I believe there is an even stronger argument for a research component: Those in the business of disseminating knowledge should also be about the business of creating some. Similarly, those of us in the business of assessing value should be about the business of knowing how to create it. And if we know how to create it, then opportunities present themselves to do great work helping clients increase the value of their life's work.

The literature of business valuation today is resoundingly mute on the issue of value creation. The major reference books—by Shannon Pratt; George Hawkins and Michael Paschall; Chris Mercer; McKinsey's Tim Koller and his colleagues; and by those who contributed chapters to Jim Hitchner's edited volume[3]—all come from serious professionals with financial backgrounds. Such backgrounds can be limiting; I know because I started out that way. In none of these books, for instance, is there any discussion about value-creating mechanisms, their durability, and the ability of current or would-be competitors to replicate or imitate them. There is nothing about how to analyze and assess such mechanisms. Most important, they are silent on the issue of how to create value.

---

[3] Pratt, *Valuing a Business*; Hawkins and Paschall, *Business Valuation Guide*; Mercer and Harms, *Business Valuation*; Koller, et al., *Valuation*; Hitchner, *Financial Valuation*.

I'm reminded of the famous words of Supreme Court Justice Potter Stewart in a 1964 pornography case:

> I shall not today attempt further to define the kinds of material I understand to be embraced within that shorthand description [of pornography]; and perhaps I could never succeed in intelligibly doing so. But I know it when I see it.[4]

Business valuation is more than numbers. It is about cause-and-effect relationships and how or if a firm creates value. We need an approach to valuation and a framework that enables us to identify causal relationships and that takes us to how value is created, how to assess the durability of value-creating mechanisms, and how to make replication and imitation by competitors more difficult and impossible if possible. This book advances such an approach and such a framework.

Cause and Effect: What *and* Why

The data archives and ratio analysis tell us what. The published research tells us where. But neither tells us *why*. The view taken here is that *why matters*. In our experience, it is all too common in a valuation report to read a paragraph like this:

> The Company's inventory turnover, which is Cost of Goods Sold divided by average inventory, is ½ the industry average. That means that the Company is not selling what it has on hand as fast as the rest of the industry is. Days' sales outstanding is. . . .

We have only one question: **Why** is inventory turn half the industry average? The expanding literature of valuation teems with "tools of the what," especially ratio analysis. Unfortunately, it offers few tools that help us get at "the why." Yet if a valuation professional cannot explain why a certain metric is notably above or notably below where competitors' performance is, then the probability is overwhelming that the analyst does not understand the business that she or he purports to value. And without that understanding, the valuation will be on point only by chance.

To be sure, a blind hog can find an acorn every now and then. But it is not something I'd want to bet the farm on every day of the week.

Explaining why not only enhances the quality of the analysis, it also increases the credibility of the analyst. Put yourself in the role of a judge and

---

[4] *Jacobellis v. Ohio*, 378 U.S. 184 (1964).

ask yourself who you would think is more credible: a professional who can explain why or one who cannot. It never ceases to amaze us that so few valuation reports really explain the why. They don't explain why because their authors don't know why, yet understanding why is the key to sound valuation practice as well as to unlocking business wealth.

Multidisciplinary Tools for Analyzing Value Creation

Many of our valuation colleagues—hardworking, honest, well-intended people, all—have one "deep" specialty. It might be accounting or finance. Or it could be expertise in a domain—for example, healthcare. We believe that valuation, especially of closely held companies for whose securities there are no active markets, is difficult and complicated. It is also multifaceted. Therefore, we cannot get by with knowing a little about a lot or a lot about a little. To serve clients and do right by our profession, we must know a lot . . . about a lot.

As a craft, our work is multifaceted. The absence of active securities markets requires us to be able to look at a situation from different angles, with different perspectives, and through different lenses. In our shop, we have an arsenal of tools that we use in almost every valuation. These tools— mental, but no less cutting edge than a surgeon's scalpel—come from a panoply of disciplines that we have learned to use over the years.

First and foremost is **strategic management**. Before "discovering" business valuation in 1993, I spent a half-decade as a Ph.D. student in strategy. Almost from the beginning of my valuation journey, I saw overlap in the basic questions underpinning these two fields:

- **Strategy.** Why do some companies perform much better than others for long periods of time?
- **Valuation.** Why is this company worth what I say it is worth?

It is all about why. I knew that finance and accounting knowledge was not going to be enough. I also saw that some key ideas from strategic management could be deployed in valuation. Strategy-based notions such as distinctive advantage, strategic intent, and generic competitive strategies had roles to play in business valuation. We elaborate at length on these in Chapter 2.

The second field on which we rely for understanding and explaining value creation is a branch of economics, **industrial organization** (IO). IO itself has two subfields: antitrust and industry studies. We focus on the tools of industry studies. In IO, the unit of analysis (i.e., what the analyst examines) is *not* the individual company. It is the domain: the group of firms in the valuation entity's competitive arena. The 1974 Ph.D. of strategy guru

Michael Porter was in IO. It was thus no accident that he rose to prominence through his "five-forces framework" (which we have expanded to six).[5] Chapter 3 is about IO's applications to valuation.

The third field from which we draw our perspective about creating value is **organization theory** (OT). OT deals with the multidimensional relationship between organizational structure and company performance. It also considers external influences (macroenvironment and domain) on the available choices for structuring and designing an organization. Phrases such as "span of control," "boundary scanning," and "policies and procedures" are prominent in the OT lexicon. Prominent OT scholars include Barney and Ouchi, Daft, and Galbraith.[6] We devote Chapter 4 to a discussion of the use of OT tools in business valuation.

The fourth piece of our multidisciplinary puzzle is **evolutionary economics**. The connection between evolution and economics originated with UCLA's Armen Alchian.[7] Building on Alchian and on the behavioral theory of firms,[8] *An Evolutionary Theory of Economic Change* brought evolutionary economics to the fore.[9] The gist of this book is the importance of "routines" in determining firms' behaviors and decision making, the economic analog of genes embedded in firms' behaviors, the effects of technological innovation on economic growth, and the selection processes by which firms grow and survive . . . or don't grow and don't survive.

Somewhat parallel to the work of Alchian was Edith Penrose's seminal contribution, *A Theory of the Growth of the Firm.*[10] Penrose was the first to identify the constraints imposed by managerial knowledge and a firm's resources on its ability to grow. Her work laid the foundation for what became, 25 years later, the *resource-based view of the firm* (RBV).[11]

The RBV posits that firms have unique resource endowments, which are due in no small part to the uniqueness of the people working inside companies, and that those resource endowments ultimately become embedded in routines and thus are nonportable from one firm to another. In part, this explains why imitation can never explain superior performance. It also explains why firms that try to purloin the capabilities of competitors by hiring their key people invariably come up short. The only way to appropriate

---

[5] Porter, *Competitive Strategy.* See also Porter, "Competitive Forces". An update of this article appeared in 2008.

[6] See, for instance, Williamson, *The Mechanisms of Governance;* Barney and Ouchi, *Organizational Economics;* Daft, *Organization Theory and Design;* Galbraith, *The Customer-Centric Organization.*

[7] Alchian, "Uncertainty, Evolution, and Economic Theory,"

[8] Cyert and March, *A Behavioral Theory.*

[9] Nelson and Winter, *An Evolutionary Theory.*

[10] Penrose, *Growth of the Firm.*

[11] Wernerfelt, "The Resource-Based View."

those capabilities is to buy the entire rival. Even then, it probably won't work, however, because most acquirers cannot leave well enough alone and insist on meddling and changing the prize they bought. That is a major reason why over three-quarters of acquisitions fail to earn back their cost of capital: Firms overpay and then cannot deliver. Evolutionary economics is the subject of Chapter 5.

Given my criticism of traditional microeconomics, readers will not be surprised that I have a different perspective: **Austrian economics**. It has two central tenets: (1) value is subjective and (2) human action is purposeful. But for Hitler's rampage against Jews, it is likely that the legislatures and central banks of the free world would have seen economics from an Austrian perspective for the last 70 years. The key debate in economics in the 1930s was, after all, between John Maynard Keynes and Friedrich von Hayek. But Jewish economists, including Hayek, Ludwig von Mises, Ludwig Lachmann, and Fritz Machlup, had to flee Vienna to elude the coming Nazi murder machine. The resulting geographic dispersion of these scholars snuffed out the synergy of intellectual firepower that occurs when brilliant people gather daily to argue, theorize, criticize, and innovate. We elaborate on these and other aspects of the Austrian School in Chapter 6.

Our focus on these five disciplines does *not* mean that they are the only ones that matter. Certainly an in-depth knowledge of finance—the capital asset pricing model (CAPM) and hedging—is essential. A good grasp of marketing, anthropology, and operations management is likewise helpful. Each has its own vernacular, which valuation professionals should be able to speak. But we zero in on these five other fields because they comprise the cornerstones of the new approach to valuation that is the subject of this chapter and of this book.

Parameters of Valuation

The value of an equity interest depends on a company's expected free cash flow, expected growth in discretionary cash, and the risk of the business in which the interest is held. Expressed in terms of these three variables, the relationship is:

$$V \propto EFCF, EG, 1/R \qquad (1.1)$$

where:

$$\begin{aligned}
\mathbf{V} &= \text{value} \\
\boldsymbol{\alpha} &= \text{``varies with''} \\
\mathbf{EFCF} &= \text{expected free cash flow} \\
\mathbf{EG} &= \text{expected growth in free cash flow} \\
\mathbf{R} &= \text{risk}
\end{aligned}$$

This equation means that as expected growth or free cash flow increases, value should also increase. However, value varies *inversely* with risk (i.e., as risk increases, value decreases). We see it every day in bond markets: Interest rates [risk] rise (fall), bond prices [value] fall (rise). We know from statistics that there are outliers in any large distribution, but the exceptions serve to prove the rule.

In our experience working for and with owners of smaller businesses for the last 30 years, we have yet to meet one who has been advised to increase the value of his business by reducing its risk. They have all heard that they should grow the business, though growth seems to focus on the top line only. They have all heard that, to increase the value of their business, they should "increase profit." However, few of them have understood why there is a substantial difference between "net income" and "free cash flow" in growing businesses. In fact, many owners judge the health of their business by how much cash they have in the bank.

Rapid growth is risky. It has impoverished—and sometimes bankrupted—many more businesses than it has ever enriched. We subscribe to the adage, "If you're going to grow the business, you'd better grow the people *and* the infrastructure *first.*" Otherwise, a $20 million business ends up perched on a $2 million infrastructure while it's run by people with $2 million skill sets. The data from Morningstar and Duff & Phelps persuade us that reducing risk is a gigantic slice of the valuation pie for most owners and chief executive officers (CEOs) of nonpublic businesses.

What We Know about Risk

From the data sets of Morningstar and Duff & Phelps, we know that, on balance, smaller companies are far riskier than larger ones. What those data do not tell us, however, is *why.* Are smaller enterprises riskier because they're smaller, or smaller because they're riskier? We subscribe to the former because most firms become less risky as they grow larger.

What those data sets do not tell us, however, is where the risk of smaller companies comes from. For that, we turn to the literature of strategic management. From 1991 through 2007, nine papers published in top-tier "A" journals found that, on average, variation in rate of return was 2.9 times as great at the company level as it was at the domain (i.e., industry) level. Let's think through the implications of those findings for valuation professionals.

- Companies *within* a domain are more different than domains themselves. That notion of "competitive heterogeneity" flies in the face of traditional microeconomic models, which ignore innovation, exclude the effects of entrepreneurship, disregard differentiation, are silent about causality, assert that the actions of no competitor affect the actions or profitability of any other, and assume that a domain's output is a commodity where the only question is price. Such assumptions make for elegant mathematics, but little else.

- Domain definition is essential because it provides the constraints that enable the facts and circumstances of a given valuation situation to be analyzed in context.
- The research findings also suggest that the variation which has enabled humans to evolve and survive for millions of years is found in economics, too. Imitation is not the way to fame and fortune. Superior performance comes from doing differently.
- Competitors have different beliefs about what is important, different views about how things work, different resources, and different ways of doing things (called "routines") that lead to different levels of performance.
- These differences highlight disparities in the value of assets because of disparities in how companies deploy them and the rates of return the assets would bring. The farther one goes down the balance sheet, the more disparate these views become.

Components of Risk

From the capital asset pricing model, we know that risk comes in two flavors: systematic and unsystematic. Systematic risk is "market risk," also known as undiversifiable risk. Using modern portfolio theory, finance scholars assume away the problem of unsystematic risk by positing that rational investors hold fully diversified portfolios. That is sound investment counsel, of course, but it is a nonstarter for most owners of closely held businesses. To paraphrase the late football coach Vince Lombardi, for them, "Unsystematic risk isn't everything. It's the only thing." But exactly what do we mean by *unsystematic risk?*

Let's begin with the standard build-up method for estimating the cost of capital for a nonpublic business:

$$E(R_a) = R_f + (R_m - R_f) + U_a \qquad (1.2)$$

where:

$E(R_a)$ = required rate of return on security a
R_f = risk-free rate of return (typically the yield to maturity on a Treasury security, short-, medium, or long-term, depending on facts and circumstances)
R_m = market rate of return for large-cap stocks
U_a = unsystematic risk associated with security a

As we have previously noted, longitudinal data from Morningstar and from Duff & Phelps confirm that size (however measured) and rate of return are negatively correlated. However, both data sets take us only as far as the size premium. Therefore, let's list the components of nonsize unsystematic risk:

- **Macroenvironment.** Six forces.
- **Competitive domain** (industry or strategic group). Six forces.
- **Company.** Firm-level risk is a function of alignment and of the durability of value-creating mechanisms.

Expressed mathematically, then, unsystematic risk looks like this:

$$U_a = RP_{size} + RP_{mac} + RP_{dom} + RP_{co} \qquad (1.3)$$

where:

$$U_a = \text{total unsystematic risk for firm } a$$
$$RP_{size} = \text{risk premium for size}$$
$$RP_{mac} = \text{macroenvironmental risk in } \textit{the industry/strategic group}$$
$$RP_{dom} = \text{domain (i.e., industry or strategic group) risk}$$
$$RP_{co} = \text{company-specific risk}$$

Now, expanding equation 1.2, we get:

$$E(R_a) = R_f + (R_m - R_f) + RP_{size} + RP_{mac} + RP_{dom} + RP_{co}$$

And, since $(\mathbf{R_m - R_f})$ = the equity risk premium (ERP), the equation simplifies to:

$$E(R_a) = R_f + ERP + RP_{size} + RP_{mac} + RP_{dom} + RP_{co} \qquad (1.4)$$

Solid data are available for the first three terms but not for the rest. It is these latter factors that complicate the analysis and valuation of smaller companies. That is why an analytical framework is so important. Done right, the process endows us with insights and a comprehensive understanding of the business(es) of the subject company. One cannot understand a smaller firm's business—*really* understand it—without an in-depth grasp of its unsystematic risk.

A Framework for Unsystematic Risk

Small and medium-sized enterprises (SMEs) are the sweet spot in the market for valuation services. Finance scholars assume away unsystematic risk,

	Firm Infrastructure			
	Human Resource Management			
	Technology Development			
	Procurement			
Inbound Logistics	Operations	Outbound Logistics	Marketing and Sales	Service

Support Activities

Margin

Margin

Primary Activities

Exhibit 1.1   Value Chain

yet these are the companies that have most of it. There are few data for non-size components—macroenvironment, domain, and company. Morning-star/Ibbotson publishes industry risk premiums, but these are of little use to most professionals, as we shall see in Chapter 9. Before we can gather data, create hypotheses, and test them, however, we need a framework to guide us toward that data. We wrestled with the problem for a dozen years, beginning with Porter's value chain (see Exhibit 1.1).[12]

SME clients found it convoluted, unintuitive, and hard to use. We next tried McKinsey's "7-S Framework" (see Exhibit 1.2).[13]

This had the appeal of being alliterative, which McKinsey did intentionally to make for ease of recall. But it ignored such organizational facets as

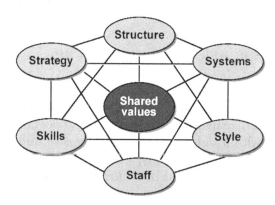

Exhibit 1.2   McKinsey's 7-S Framework

---

[12] See Porter, *Competitive Advantage*, 37.

[13] See Peters and Waterman Jr., *In Search of Excellence*, 10.

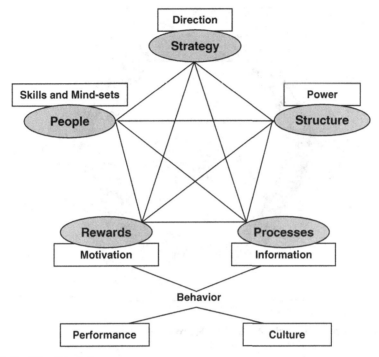

Exhibit 1.3   Star Model

culture. And all the interacting variables, as represented by the lines in 7-S lines, made it visibly "busy," both for SME clients and for us.

We next tried something from Jay Galbraith. His field is OT, and that is evident in his model (see Exhibit 1.3).[14]

Truth be told, we liked the star model. But we believed that culture should be an integral part of any model, not an afterthought, as the exhibit seems to suggest. We also had the problem with all three models—Porter's, McKinsey's, and Galbraith's—of how to make it work inside a graphic representation of the other two nonsize components of unsystematic risk, macro-environment, and domain.

Borrowing from strategic management, industrial organization, OT, evolutionary economics, and Austrian economics, we created a trilevel unsystematic risk framework (see Exhibit 1.4).

The framework resonated with clients when we first used it in 2005. For valuation professionals, it is easy to remember (two hexagons + SPARC) and easy to work with. In our shop, we also use it as a kind of mental filing cabinet as we gather information, do research, conduct

---

[14] Galbraith, *Designing Organizations*, 15.

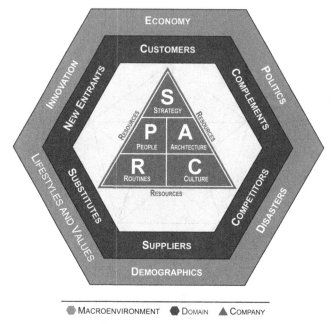

Exhibit 1.4   Trilevel Unsystematic Risk Framework

interviews, and work through the analysis and performance metrics in valuing a client company.

Most important from our standpoint, we now have a framework that enables valuation professionals to explain **why**. At the company level, there are five components. SPARC has been back-tested in more than 400 valuations and advisory engagements over the last 17 years. In every case, its elements—**s**trategy, **p**eople, **a**rchitecture, **r**outines, **c**ulture—explained, sometimes in combination with one another, the aberrant metrics at the company level.

Unlocking Business Wealth

Using the framework and tools in this book, valuation professionals will have opportunities for add-on consulting work. In our shop, for instance, we often combine "calculations engagements" with a value-enhancement phase. Most often this combination occurs in the initial stages of exit planning, buy-ins by one or more new internal owners, or an overarching desire by an owner or chief executive to enhance business value. No valuation report is necessary at that point. Besides getting a range of value of the business, the client also gets a "value map" that points the way to increasing the value of the business as it goes through the fix-up stage prior to being put on the market or sold to known buyers.

SPARC is the linchpin of the add-on deliverable. Understanding the why is the essence of SPARC. And once we have our arms around the why, we can, with additional research *and* an in-depth understanding of the routines and capabilities of the client company, make detailed recommendations under the SPARC aegis to reduce risk, boost cash flow, and increase the expected rate of growth in free cash flow. This process adds real value for clients.

To be sure, it does not happen overnight. Lead time of 18 to 36 months provides the kind of window necessary to do the work to get the value up, identify and contact potential buyers, and conduct the auction that fetches top dollar for the seller. It is a natural extension of the work the valuation professional has already done for her to be the outside quarterback in the value-enhancement phase. Besides leading to a far bigger payday for the client, the work—which can be done on a contingency basis, but with a hefty retainer—is lucrative for the professional. Routing it through a separate entity where one does not run afoul of provisions that restrict or prohibit contingency pricing, especially for CPAs, can be useful, as can teaming up with a boutique investment banking firm. In contingency-fee engagements, however, one must be careful to avoid holding oneself out as, for instance, a CPA or as having any other credential whose sponsoring organization takes a dim view of "success fees."

Summary

In this chapter we made the case for a new approach to business valuation, one that uncovers cause-and-effect relationships to enable professionals to explain *why*. If we cannot explain the *why* causing the *what*, then presenting only the naked what makes us like the emperor and his new suit of clothes. We also argued that tools for analyzing the creation of value come from at least five nontraditional disciplines. We provided a brief overview of the "risk archives" from Morningstar and Duff & Phelps, which led into an extensive discussion of risk. We presented the graphic of a trilevel framework for analyzing and understanding unsystematic risk; it is the key to understanding SMEs and why the valuation is what it is. We also noted that such understanding will lead to opportunities for professionals to provide add-on consulting services and offered some caveats about doing that.

Additional Reading

Kerr, Steven. "On the Folly of Rewarding A, While Hoping for B." *Academy of Management Journal* 18, No. 4 (Fall 1975): 769–783.
Teller, Edward. *The Pursuit of Simplicity*. Malibu, Calif.: Pepperdine University Press, 1980.
Weick, Karl E. *Making Sense of the Organization*. Malden, Mass.: Blackwell Publishing, 2001.

CHAPTER 2

Tools from Strategic Management

The meaning of the Greek word *stratego* is "to plan the destruction of one's enemies through effective use of resources."[1] The early writing of such giants as Homer (c. 800 B.C.) and Euripides (480–406 B.C.) discussed basic strategy principles. More from Bracker:

> One of the first known applications of strategy to business occurred when Socrates consoled Nichomachides, a Greek militarist who lost an election [for] the position of general to Antisthenes, a Greek businessman. Socrates compared the duties of a general and a businessman and showed Nichomachides that in either case, one plans the use of one's resources to meet objectives. This viewpoint was lost, for all practical purposes, with the fall of the Greek city-states and was not to rise again until after the Industrial Revolution.[2]

History

Later, such writers as Shakespeare, Clausewitz, and Tolstoy dealt with strategy in military or political contexts . . . or both. The idea of strategy in a business context appears to have first surfaced in 1912 at the Harvard Business School in a course called business policy taught by Arch Wilkinson Shaw.[3] The course focused on the business as seen from the perspective of its general manager (GM). Shaw's intention was to help students integrate the lessons of functional courses by adopting the vantage point of the upper-level manager. To do this, Shaw asked a number of company presidents to visit the class, talk about the most critical problems facing their firms, and engage students in discussions about what could be done.[4]

---

[1] Bracker, "The Strategic Management Concept."
[2] Ibid.
[3] http://institutionalmemory.hbs.edu/timeline.
[4] Montgomery, "Diamonds and Rust," 253.

Four years later, Shaw wrote *An Approach to Business Problems.*[5] The intellectual connection between strategy and business first did not emerge until nearly 30 years later with the publication of the now-classic *Theory of Games and Economic Behavior.*[6] It applied game theory to business. It was a collaboration between a leading mathematician (von Neumann) and a prominent economist (Morgenstern). Economics would later provide the intellectual underpinnings for the strategy field.

One of the most influential strategy books ever published was Barnard's *The Functions of the Executive.*[7] Barnard was the CEO of New Jersey Bell Telephone Co. when he wrote his seminal book. He was concerned about the relatively short life of most enterprises. At the time, the only organization that he could cite that was really old was the Catholic Church. He maintained that organizations failed to survive because of their inability to be both effective (doing the right thing) and efficient, which he defined as satisfying the motives of the individuals in them. This book is widely viewed as the best and most insightful one ever written by a CEO.

In the 1960s, the strategy field began to come of age. First, business historian Alfred Chandler published *Strategy and Structure: Chapters in the History of the American Industrial Enterprise.*[8] This monumental study of four American corporations—DuPont, General Motors (GM), Standard Oil of New Jersey (now ExxonMobil), and Sears, Roebuck—had two notable findings. The first was that all four of these companies, independently of one another, had established decentralized organization structures as they implemented strategies of diversification. The second was to become a topic that remains hotly debated to the present time: Structure follows strategy.

The first attempt at making "business policy" something other than the case studies did not occur until 1965. That is when the first edition of *Business Policy: Text and Cases* was published;[9] the third edition of this book had just 80 pages of "text" (i.e., theory)—all of it written by Ken Andrews—and 925 pages of cases.[10] *Organization and Environment: Managing Differentiation and Integration* followed in 1967.[11] This book examined structural mechanisms for organizing work and their effect on performance. Defining integration as collaboration among departments and differentiation as

---

[5] Shaw, *Approach to Business Problems.* At the time, he was also the editor of a magazine called *System;* it later became *BusinessWeek.*

[6] von Neumann and Morgenstern, *Theory of Games.*

[7] Barnard, *The Functions of the Executive.*

[8] Chandler, *Strategy and Structure.*

[9] Learned, et al. *Business Policy.*

[10] Christensen, et al.

[11] Lawrence and Lorsch, *Organization and Environment.*

the need for different departments with different time orientations and levels of formality, Lawrence and Lorsch found that, in most organizations, these mechanisms were substitutes for one another, except in the highest-performing firms, where they were complements. We'll have much more to say about complements and their utility in wealth creation later in this book.

Managing the Resource Allocation Process: A Study of Corporate Planning and Investment[12] was an in-depth study of how four multibusiness companies prepared budgets and allocated capital. Bower found:

> Individual planning and investment decisions are made by managers at many levels of the firm; each idea is shaped as it proceeds up managerial levels until it emerges fully packaged as a request for capital or a business plan for consideration by corporate management. At the same time, each level of management influences the ones above and below it.[13]

In 1971 Kenneth Andrews wrote *The Concept of Corporate Strategy*.[14] Here, for the first time, an underlying theory of strategy began to emerge. It included a discussion of the need for successful GMs to align their companies' strengths and weaknesses with the opportunities and risks in the external environment. It also spelled out three levels of strategy: *corporate*—for diversified multiline companies; *business*—for single-line companies or divisions of diversified enterprises; and *functional*—for individual departments within a single-line firm or division. With some exceptions, our focus in this book will be on business strategy because most SMEs are not widely diversified.

Andrews's book was the catalyst for a series of rapid intellectual developments as "business policy" morphed into "strategic management." In 1972, Michael Hunt completed his Harvard dissertation focusing on the U.S. home appliance industry; in it, he originated the notion of strategic groups. In 1973, Richard Rumelt finished his Harvard dissertation; we'll have more to say about the findings of his seminal research in the "Diversification" section of this chapter. A longitudinal study of diversification in U.S. business, it later emerged in book form as *Strategy, Structure, and Economic Performance*.[15] In 1974, Michael Porter received his

---

[12] Bower, *The Resource Allocation Process.*

[13] Ibid., 19–20.

[14] Andrews, *The Concept of Corporate Strategy.*

[15] Rumelt, *Strategy, Structure.*

doctorate from Harvard in industrial organization; much of Chapter 3 focuses on his work.

Porter's seminal 1979 paper in the *Harvard Business Review*, "How Competitive Forces Shape Strategy,"[16] is the all-time best-selling article from the *Review*'s archive. His seminal book came out the following year[17] and gave legitimacy and respectability to the "new" field of strategic management. The year 1980 was also when Purdue's Dan Schendel launched the leading journal of the discipline, *Strategic Management Journal*. Since then, strategic management has become a full-fledged and respectable academic field. With over 5,300 members, the Business Policy and Strategy division is the second-largest group within the Academy of Management.

Perspective

Strategic management sees the world through the eyes of the CEO or division GM. In most closely held businesses, we're talking about the owner. While this individual is responsible for the performance of the organization as a whole, she must also be looking outside the enterprise most of the time. That is consistent with the fact that, as one moves up in an organization's hierarchy, he spends relatively more time on external matters and relatively less on internal ones. That should be as true in closely helds as it is in public companies, but it seldom is.

The essence of strategy is patterns, intended or unintended, in a stream of major decisions by a company. For the valuation professional, the ability to spot patterns and connect seemingly unrelated "dots" is a major asset in getting at "the why." For the strategy advisor, that ability is a major resource for adding value for SMEs. For the CEO, dot-connecting requires a broad intellectual span of control (i.e., command of both "direct reports" and a variety of disciplines, including the five that underlie our new approach to valuing businesses).

It is important to emphasize the role of economics in strategic management. It cannot be overstated. Therefore, a firm grasp of economics, including price theory, is extremely helpful in understanding strategy-oriented tools as well as those from the other four disciplines comprising our new approach. The importance of economics will be evident as this book unfolds.

Valuation Tools

We turn now to eight tools from strategic management that professionals will find useful in their valuation and consulting work with clients. Readers

---

[16] Porter, "Competitive Forces."

[17] Porter, *Competitive Strategy*.

should not infer the importance we place on any of these tools from the order in which they are arrayed next. They appear simply in a sequence that makes sense to us.

1. Strategic intent
2. Generic competitive strategies
3. Resources
4. Competitive analysis
5. Distinctive versus sustained competitive advantage
6. VRIO (valuable, rare, imperfectly imitable, organizationally aligned with incentives and culture)
7. Customer satisfaction surveys
8. Diversification

Strategic Intent

This concept originated in the 1989 article of the same name in *Harvard Business Review* by Hamel and Prahalad.[18] They defined "strategic intent" as "an obsession with winning at all levels of the organization and then sustain [ing] that obsession over [a] 10- to 20-year quest for global leadership."[19] While this definition sounds as if it excludes SMEs, if we strike "global," then it includes them. Some might say that strategic intent is nothing more than what some call a company's "vision." We disagree.

By putting its emphasis on "an obsession with winning at all levels of the organization," Hamel and Prahalad emphasized the need to communicate a message that employees enthusiastically buy into and inculcate into everything they do and how they do it. They pointed to the Japanese as the exemplars of motivating this level of commitment from employees. They detailed how Canon set about dislodging Xerox from its number-one position in the copier industry, not by cutting costs but by setting for its engineers a target price of $1,000 for a home copier, this when the least-expensive home copier cost about $3,000. This required the engineers to start over. They succeeded. The article also describes how Komatsu overtook Caterpillar.

Herewith some excerpts from this McKinsey Award–winning article:

> [S]trategic intent is more than simply unfettered ambition. The concept also encompasses an active management process that includes: focusing the organization's attention on the essence of winning;

---

[18] Hamel and Prahalad, "Strategic Intent."
[19] Ibid., 66.

motivating people by communicating the value of the target; leaving room for individual and team contributions; sustaining enthusiasm by providing new operational definitions as circumstances change; and using intent consistently to guide resource allocations. (p. 66)

For a challenge to be effective, individuals and teams throughout the organization must understand it and see its implications for their own jobs. Companies that set corporate challenges to create new competitive advantages quickly discover that engaging the entire organization requires top management to do the following:

- Create a sense of urgency
- Develop a competitor focus at every level through widespread use of competitive intelligence
- Provide employees with the skills they need to work effectively
- Give the organization time to digest one challenge before launching another
- Establish clear milestones and review mechanisms (p. 69)

The essence of strategy lies in creating tomorrow's competitive advantages faster than competitors mimic the ones you possess today. (p. 70)

To achieve a strategic intent, a company must usually take on larger, better financed competitors. That means carefully managing competitive engagements so that scarce resources are conserved. Managers cannot do that simply by playing the same game better—making marginal improvements to competitors' technology and business practices. Instead, they must fundamentally change the game in ways that disadvantage incumbents—devising novel approaches to market entry, advantage building, and competitive warfare. For smart competitors, the goal is not competitive imitation but competitive innovation, the art of containing competitive risks within manageable proportions. (p. 70)

The strategist's goal is not to find a niche with the existing industry space but to create new space that is uniquely suited to the company's own strengths, space that is off the [industry's] map. (p. 73)

Almost every strategic management theory and nearly every corporate planning system is premised on a strategy hierarchy in which corporate goals guide business unit strategies and business unit strategies guide functional tactics. In this hierarchy, senior management makes strategy and lower levels execute it. The dichotomy between formulation and implementation is familiar and widely accepted. But the strategy hierarchy undermines competitiveness by fostering an elitist view of management that tends to disenfranchise most of the organization. Employees fail to identify with corporate goals or involve themselves deeply in the work of becoming more competitive. (p. 75)

Unfortunately, a threat that everyone perceives but no one talks about creates more anxiety than a threat that has been clearly identified and made the focal point for the problem-solving efforts of the entire company. That is one reason [that] honesty and humility on the part of top management may be the first prerequisite of revitalization. (p. 75)

Where strategy formulation is an elitist activity it is also difficult to produce truly creative strategies. For one thing, there are not enough heads and points of view to challenge conventional wisdom. For another, creative strategies seldom emerge from the annual planning ritual. (p. 76).

Returning to the critical importance of the on-site interview, an analyst can ask such questions as:

- Where will this company be 10 or 20 years from now?
- On a scale of 1 (minimum) to 7 (maximum):
  - How explicitly does this company identify and communicate to employees at all levels external threats to their jobs?
  - How well does the enterprise create a sense of urgency?
  - To what extent does it help employees get the skills, knowledge, and tools they need to do their jobs to the best of their ability?
  - How rigid is the company in how it sees the world?
  - How rigid in terms of its own flexibility?
  - How well does it explain who the main competitors are and why they're a threat to all of us?

We are particularly fond of asking scaled questions. For one thing, it gives employees flexibility in how to answer. For another, employees have never shied away from expressing their perceptions using a scale. But be sure that (1) the scale is not too wide (e.g., 1 to 10); (2) it has an odd number of points (so a midpoint is distinct); and (3) responses are in integers only. Asking a set of the same scaled questions of every interviewee also allows computation of means, medians, and standard deviations.

And what if the responses to the questions above are uniformly low? We increase the discount rate because we doubt that the company can change enough to remain in business over the long term.

Generic Competitive Strategies

Porter argues that there are but three ways to compete:[20]

1. **Cost leadership.** Usually the industry's market leader because lowest cost comes only from highest output volume. Lowest cost leads to lowest price. Caveat: There can be but one cost leader in an industry. For example: Toyota, Dell, Black & Decker, DuPont, Intel, McDonald's, Wal-Mart.

2. **Differentiation.** This means "perceived uniqueness." After the cost leader, all other savvy competitors use the form of differentiation that best suits their resource base and their customers. The sources of differentiation are limited only by managers' imaginations and customers' willingness to pay. Differentiators charge more than cost leaders, but customers buy because they perceive more value. Exemplar differentiators: Estée Lauder, Mitchum, Palm, BlackBerry, Ben & Jerry's, Godiva, Wild Turkey, Cole Haan.

3. **Focus.** This strategy, which can be either cost leadership or differentiation, occurs only in a segment of an industry, not industry-wide. Rarely have we seen situations where an SME should be anything other than a focus-type player. Examples of successful focus competitors include Lexus, Four Seasons, Oxxford, Mont Blanc, Mercedes, Saint John, and Martin Brower (a food distributor whose only customer is McDonald's).

There is a fourth strategy, one that leads to failure: "stuck in the middle." This is the strategy of competitors that refuse to commit to cost leadership, differentiation, or focus. Instead, they try to be all things to all customers. It won't work. However, those doing stuck-in-the-middle can be highly disruptive competitors, especially with low-ball pricing, until they finally close their doors. "Stuck in the middle" is a mistake many smaller businesses and start-ups make.

The odds favor a normative strategy of focus/differentiation for an SME.[21] That is because (a) few SMEs compete industry-wide, and (b) even within an industry segment, the only-one-cost-leader reality remains.

We get a first inkling of what the competitive strategy should be when the client company begins providing us with documents, data, and financial history. As soon as we have financial statements, we prepare a quick, rough-cut guideline public company (GPC) analysis. Our GPC template

---

[20] Porter, *Competitive Strategy*, 34–46.
[21] By "normative," we mean what the strategy *should be*. Whether it is or not reveals itself during the engagement.

automatically size-adjusts valuation multiples depending on the size measure we choose: Ibbotson's market capitalization of equity or one of the eight measures in the Duff & Phelps data set. This approach to multiples enables us to use many more GPCs than would otherwise be the case. More GPCs equals more "degrees of freedom," as statisticians call it, and that reduces the likelihood of substantial error. In most valuations, even those of companies with only $2 million or $3 million in annual revenues, our GPC analysis will include anywhere from 12 to 30 GPCs and sometimes more. This rough-cut analysis enables us to get a quick look at the gross and operating margins of our client company. We compare those with the GPCs. Our client company's margins are usually lower, so we infer, at least for the time being, that the strategy should be focus/differentiation.

The type of competitive strategy—cost leadership or differentiation, either industry-wide or within a segment—has implications for how a company is managed. Cost leaders, for instance, tend to have these characteristics:

- Mantra of low cost permeates the organization
- State-of-the-art, efficient-scale facilities
- Tight control of costs
- Many reports
- Many measurements
- Low incidence of marginal customers
- Big-league process engineering skills
- Low complexity–simple products/services
- Limited number of choices in product/service portfolio
- Related products/services are likely complements
- Tight supervision
- Emphasis on scale
- Centralized decision-making
- Targeted spending on research and development (R&D), service, sales force
- No variation in repetitive tasks

Cost leadership helps insulate a firm against:

- **Competitors.** Its lowest-cost structure enables it to build market share.
- **Suppliers.** It has flexibility to deal with cost hikes.
- **Customers.** They are unlikely to push it to reduce price because it already has the lowest one.
- **New entrants.** By creating a barrier to entry through economies of scale.

Risks of cost leadership:

- Industry blind spots
- Inflation in costs over which it has no control
- Disruptive innovation that blindsides it

The cost leader's challenge is not to be *so* cost-driven that it ignores industry evolution. Ask Sears, now just a shadow of its former self, about Wal-Mart.

The characteristics of successful differentiators, whether industry-wide or focus players, differ from those of cost leaders:

- Costs are *not* the primary target.
- Major commitments to innovation.
- Lots of amenities to attract highly skilled, creative people.
- Heavy pressure to introduce new products and services.
- Prices are higher than the cost leader's.
- Customer care is high—customers expect to be coddled.
- Decision-making is typically decentralized.
- Lots of personal freedom.
- Emphasis is on margin, not scale.
- Marketing and advertising outlays are usually significant.
- Major R&D spending.
- Incentives to generate significant revenues from new products or services.

Risks of differentiation include:

- Customers become better informed and redefine their needs.
- Imitators and knock-offs confuse customers.
- R&D becomes unproductive.

The differentiator's challenge is to ensure that the price disparity between it and the cost leader does not become unacceptable to customers. It aims to achieve this through innovation and frequent customer surveys.

As with strategic intent, the on-site interviews offer opportunities to identify the causes behind strengths and weaknesses in the strategy arena:

- Why do customers buy from this company and not from its competitors?
- What does this company do better than its competitors?
- How is that capability (or those capabilities) measured?
- What is the firm's competitive strategy?

- Has the strategy changed in recent years? If so, why? How?
- What, if anything, does this enterprise do or believe differently from its rivals?
- What competitor is the most troublesome? Why?
- What is this company doing about it?
- What additional capabilities is the company designing to evolve its strategy?

Focus competitors are different. As we indicated a few pages back, they do not compete industry-wide but in an industry segment. In the strategy literature, these segments are called "strategic groups" (see Chapter 3). But suffice to say that there are different ways to define an industry segment—by distribution channel, for instance, or buyer group, subset of the product/service portfolio, or, as is usually the case in private equity, geographic market. However the segment is defined, the focuser's goal is to serve it well.

Focus strategies abound in such highly segmented industries as public accounting, lodging, publishing, and restaurants. By choosing a focus strategy, a company is deliberately limiting its sales volume in hopes of achieving higher profitability at lower risk over a smaller scale. Such a choice has inherent risks, however:

- Competitors, either within the focus group or industry-wide, locate segments within the segment and out-focus the focuser.
- Boundaries between the focus segment and the industry as a whole blur, and customers don't perceive a difference.
- The differential, either in cost or in differentiation, between industry-wide rivals and focusers widen so much that the advantage of the focus strategy disappears.

Resources

As will be seen in Chapter 11, the notion of *resources* is so broad that having a schema within which to organize one's thinking about them is not just helpful but essential. We have adapted such a framework (see Exhibit 2.1).[22]

We added the metrics to Barney's examples of resources to further buttress the fact that not all measures that matter come from financial statements. In our work with SMEs, we have found these nonfinancial metrics to be especially illuminating:

---

[22] Barney, *Competitive Advantage*, 134.

Exhibit 2.1   Four Types of Resources

❑ **financial capital** = funds from investors and lenders

Financial Capital

Examples of Resources	Measures
Borrowing capacity	1. Debt ratio versus industry average 2. Debt-equity ratio versus industry average 3. Net cash flow to Total Invested Capital
Liquidity	1. Quick ratio 2. Current ratio 3. DSO versus industry average. 4. Inventory turnover versus industry average 5. Credit rating 6. Gross cash flow $\div$ net cash flow to equity
Ability to raise equity capital	1. ROE versus industry average 2. Net profit margin versus industry average
Sustainable growth rate	1. ROE $\times$ (1 – dividend payout ratio)

❑ **physical capital** = the physical endowments a firm requires

Physical Capital

Examples of Resources	Measures
Productive capacity	1. Annual revenues $\div$ FTE employees 2. Annual revenues $\div$ production square feet 3. "Line" square feet $\div$ as a % of total square feet
Investment service	1. CapEx versus depreciation expense 2. Accumulated depreciation $\div$ gross fixed assets
Dedication to maintenance	1. Maintenance expense/revenues versus industry average
Flexibility of fixed assets	1. Market value of equipment $\div$ book value
Technological commitment	1. Average RAM per computer 2. Average age of PCs 3. Average age of software applications 4. Number of computers $\div$ FTE employees
Access to suppliers	1. Weighted average distance from which goods are received

❏ **human capital** = resources of **the individuals** who comprise the firm (knowledge, education, training, insights, intelligence, etc.)

Human Capital

Examples of Resources	Measures
Education	1. Σ years of education ÷ FTE employees
Training	1. training hours/year ÷ FTE employees
Knowledge	1. Σ educational reimbursement ÷ FTE employees
Employee commitment	1. % of absentee days versus industry average 2. Σ sick leave taken ÷ Σ sick leave available
Leadership ability	1. Weighted average manager rating by FTEs
Trust	1. Annual number of workplace thefts 2. Number of complaints to HR (or ombudsman)
Experience	1. Σ years **with Company** ÷ FTE employees

❏ **organizational capital** = attributes of the people comprising **the firm** (teamwork, reputation, speed, etc.)

Organizational Capital

Examples of Resources	Measures
Loyalty	1. Employee turnover versus industry average
Teamwork	1. $ cost of rework ÷ FTE employees 2. Σ years with company ÷ number of managers 3. Performance of company's sports teams
Reputation	1. Overall customer satisfaction 2. % of revenue from repeat customers 3. Average length of customer relationship
Product innovation	1. Σ # of patents 2. Revenues from patents and copyrights 3. R&D $ ÷ revenues versus industry average
Process innovation	1. % of employees making suggestions/year
Speed	1. Number of organizational levels

Source: Jay B. Barney, *Gaining and Sustaining Competitive Advantage,* 3rd ed. (Upper Saddle River, N.J.: Pearson/Prentice-Hall, 2007).

- **Physical capital.** Productive capacity (annual revenues ÷ full- time employees [FTEs]); investment service; technological commitment.
- **Human capital.** Training; knowledge; commitment; experience.
- **Organizational capital.** Loyalty, teamwork, reputation, speed.

To be sure, many SMEs don't monitor many of these measures. They should, though, and that's the point. The essential starting place is financial statements, but there is more to measurement than what's on them.

Competitive Analysis

We never cease to be amazed by the valuation reports we review that are silent, or nearly so, on the subject of competitors—who they are, where they are, how big they are, the shared values of each, what each believes, how fast each is growing, the major strengths and weaknesses of each competitor, and, especially, the estimated market share of each. No general would lead troops into battle without a plan that focused heavily on matching up troops' strengths with enemies' weaknesses. And let's face it: Much of the early thinking and literature in the strategy field came from military circumstances. One wag described it this way: "Business is war without bloodshed. Sometimes bleeding would be less painful." Yet, if we didn't know better, we'd conclude that competitors' actions, size, and market share have no impact on the performance of client companies.

In his 1980 book, Porter devotes Chapter 3 ("A Framework for Competitor Analysis") to the subject. He lists four key components of a competitor profile.[23] He notes, too, that these can be part of a company's self-analysis:

1. **Future goals.** What are its financial goals, its attitude toward risk, its values and beliefs, its organizational structure, its control and incentive systems (especially incentives; see Chapter 6), its accounting system and conventions, the kinds of managers in its leadership, the degree of consensus among its leadership about future direction, the composition of its board, its goal-constraining contractual commitments, and regulatory/government/social constraints on its behavior?

2. **Assumptions (i.e., how things work).** About itself, its competitive domain, and its rivals. Here is how Porter puts it:

   Every firm operates on a set of assumptions about its own situation. For example, it may see itself as a socially conscious firm, as the

---

[23] Porter, *Competitive Strategy*, 48.

industry leader, as the low-cost producer, as having the best sales force, and so on. These assumptions about its own situation will guide the way the firm behaves and the way it reacts to events. If it sees itself as the low-cost producer, for instance, it may try to discipline a price[-]cutter with price cuts of its own.

A competitor's assumptions about its own situation may or may not be accurate. Where they are not, this provides an intriguing strategic lever. If a competitor believes it has the greatest customer loyalty in the market and it does not, for example, a provocative price cut may be a good way to gain position. The competitor might well refuse to match the price cut believing that it will have little impact on its share, only to find that it loses significant market position before it recognizes the error in its assumption.

Just as each competitor holds assumptions about itself, every firm also operates on assumptions about its industry and competitors. These also may or may not be correct.[24]

> And:

Examining assumptions of all types can identify biases or *blind spots* that may creep into the way managers perceive their environment. The blind spots are areas where a competitor will either not see the significance of events (such as a strategic move) at all, will perceive them incorrectly, or will perceive them only very slowly. Rooting out these blind spots will help the firm identify moves with a lower probability of immediate retaliation and identify moves were retaliation, once it comes, is not effective.[25]

A famous blind spot was Sears's resolute indifference to the head of steam that Wal-Mart was building up as it rolled through smaller cities and towns in the United States during the 1970s, even as it stayed out of metropolitan areas. As late as 1984, Wal-Mart wasn't even mentioned in Sears's annual report. By the time Sears decided that Wal-Mart might be a serious threat, the fate of the decades-long market leader in department store retailing was sealed.

3. **Current strategy.** How each rival competes.
4. **Capabilities.** Porter lists "strengths and weaknesses" after "capabilities" in his book. We define capabilities elsewhere in this volume as "resources." Since the Porter book was published, the word

---

[24] Ibid., 58.
[25] Ibid., 59.

"capabilities" has come to carry a new meaning, which we'll explore in depth in Chapter 5. For now, let's think of capabilities as the value-creating (revenue-enhancing and/or cost-minimizing and/or rivals-disrupting) activities that a company does better than its competitors.

While a valuation report need not, in our view, get overly granular about a competitor's resources, it should certainly zero in on the rival's weaknesses, why customers do business with it, and its estimated market share. Most in our professional community ignore share. We believe that is a huge mistake. The key insight to be gleaned from rivals' market shares is a snapshot view of the industry's (or, more likely, the strategic group's) market structure. There are four of these: Monopoly is at one end, perfect competition is at the other, and oligopoly and monopolistic competition are in between. We will have much to say about these structures, especially oligopolies, in Chapter 3.

In our shop, our standard document request list requests a brief narrative about each of the client company's major competitors. Sometimes we receive it; more often, we don't. In the latter case, we talk with the owner or CEO, get anecdotal information, and confirm it with spot-checking. The information gathered in these four key areas can then be combined into a brief profile of each of the client company's major rivals. This adds significant credibility to the analyst's report. It also opens the door to value-enhancing work later on.

Distinctive versus Sustained Competitive Advantage

The central research question that bedevils strategy scholars—Why do some companies outperform others over long periods of time?—can create buzzwords among nonacademics, consultants, and business executives. Foremost among those is "sustained competitive advantage."

In all of the consultant- and biz-speak we hear, there is probably no phrase that is as misunderstood, misused, and abused as that one. Start with "sustained." It sounds, well, if not permanent, then certainly long-lasting. And "advantage"? Wow. What business doesn't want to have an honest and durable advantage? As for competitive, well, it's the perfect bridge between the other two. In other words, we're gonna whup our rivals and keep that whupping going for a good long time.

Simple as that. Sprinkle a little magic dust here and there, and *voila*! Where is the tooth fairy when we need her?

This much-ballyhooed phrase is a hoax. Here's why.

First, it's fair to say that strategy consultants—strategists generally, in fact—tend to be optimists. They want to help clients and employers be successful. How better to do that than by emulating the perceived behaviors of successful companies? Upbeat helps. Put yourself in the place of the owner of your client company: Would you want to hire a negative, bad-news consultant to tell you your company's going down the tubes and there's not a thing you can do about it? You might refer such a consultant to your competitors but certainly not to your friends who own businesses.

Second, the strategic management field tends to ignore not-successful companies. Again, it goes back to that basic research question. The field doesn't look much at failure. Even when it does, though, successful turnarounds are invariably the subject. Shades of Lake Wobegon: All the companies are successful, all the turnarounds work, and all the performance is above average.

Third, strategy research has a survivorship bias. That is, the data that scholars analyze are from live companies, not dead ones. That is consistent with the research question, but also with the persona of most strategy scholars, many of whom are friends and acquaintances of mine. I don't know a pessimist in the group.

There's a major problem with all of this: data. With few exceptions, the data don't much affirm long-term success. Many of the "excellent companies" in Peters and Waterman's *In Search of Excellence* barely a quarter century ago no longer exist as independent companies or have struggled for survival. Turnover in the Fortune 500 companies continues to be brisk. Nearly half of the Fortune 20 twenty years ago no longer exist. Of the 51 largest companies in the United States in 1909, barely 7 are recognizable today. Of those 7, only 3—General Electric (GE), Sears, and ExxonMobil (né Standard Oil)—were in the top 51 in the 2008 Fortune 500. DuPont was 81st, International Paper was 114th, U.S. Steel was 146th, and Eastman Kodak was 238th.

This is all consistent with Joseph Schumpeter's inimitable phrase, "creative destruction": Capitalism revitalizes itself through renewal with new companies, new technologies, and new ways of doing things. We will see more about this renewal process in Chapter 5. This notion of birth, death, and rebirth has a distinct biological ring to it. Implicit within it is turnover, but of a more permanent variety than just personnel. That suggests that sustainable competitive advantage is (1) not sustainable indefinitely and (2) not an advantage forever. The obvious question is: How long?

In a presentation at the 2003 annual conference of the Strategic Management Society meeting in Baltimore, UCLA's Dick Rumelt said that he had studied competitive advantage and concluded that it *might* last for ten years, but probably not any longer than that. He defined competitive *advantage* as organizational performance significantly above a company's industry peers. Of course, he was speaking in terms of a "normal distribution," which means there will be exceptions. One that comes to mind is Procter & Gamble (P&G). But P&G is the exception that proves the rule.

Government, however, is no exception. While the political motivation behind the 22nd Amendment limiting a president to two full elected terms was anti-FDR (Franklin D. Roosevelt), it has worked out to be sensible and, indeed, desirable. Without it, Reagan could have run for a third term and likely been elected, even though just six years after leaving office he went public that he had Alzheimer's. Perhaps Bill Clinton could have won a third term, too, though that is less certain. The fine print in this amendment makes it possible for a U.S. president to serve ten years—two years as a vice president succeeding to the Oval Office and then two full elected terms.

The last limb on this three-legged stool is a paper by McGill University strategy scholar Danny Miller.[26] He found that firms with CEOs serving longer than ten years had less "fit" between their organizations and their external environment and, therefore, lower performance.

These three sources have a single point of agreement in terms of both performance and CEO tenure: ten years. This is a simple and instructive measure. If the CEO of your client company has run it for more than ten years, declining performance is often evident.

Therefore, rather than sustained competitive advantage (which is a false combination of words) or even competitive advantage (because it implies homogeneity among strategies), we look for *distinctive advantage*. This emphasizes that being different trumps being better. It reinforces the essential competitive strategy of differentiation in SMEs. It is consistent with the notion of heterogeneous competitors, which we'll encounter in Chapter 5. If a company is merely better than its rivals, it will always feel them breathing down its neck. If, instead, it is different—think *distinctive*—then it will have a niche all or mostly to itself. Another name for this is "blue ocean strategy," after the book of the same name, but *distinctive advantage* is a far more descriptive term, in our view. It also dovetails perfectly with the SPARC framework that is the linchpin of this book.

Unlike the "traditional" view of sustained competitive advantage—that only bigger companies have it, that it requires huge amounts of resources to create and maintain, and so forth—distinctive advantage is available to any firm, large or small. It requires a company to analyze its unique bundle of

---

[26] Miller, "Stale in the Saddle."

resources. And make no mistake about it: Every firm's resource bundle is different from every other firm's. The challenge for those running the business is to configure those resources into routines—rote ways of doing things—and then combine routines into unique capabilities that attract customers. Uniqueness begets differentiation, higher profits, and few competitors, at least temporarily.

VRIO

Jay Barney's seminal research and writing about the resource-based view of the firm (see Chapter 5) brought him to an essential question for practicing managers: what are the characteristics of capabilities that really matter? Out of that came *VRIO* (**v**aluable, **r**are, **i**mperfectly imitable, **o**rganizationally aligned with incentives and culture). Four simple yes/no questions comprise the VRIO framework:

1. **Question of Value.** Is the capability valuable? In other words, does it result in higher revenues, lower costs, or a combination of thereof?
2. **Question of Rarity.** Is the capability rare? A monopoly on it is not necessary, but it needs to be scarce and not widely available.
3. **Question of Imperfect Imitability.** Is the capability imperfectly imitable by competitors? By "imperfect," Barney means that it can be neither replicated, except at great expense or major disruption to rivals' existing businesses, nor substituted against, except imperfectly. This is why imitation is not the path to fame and fortune: One company is always playing by another's rules. That someone can change them at any time. Imitation is a perpetual game of catch-up.
4. **Question of Organization.** Are the company's incentives, structure, and culture organizationally aligned to encourage its people to exploit resources and create new capabilities?

The questions should be asked in the above sequence. If there is a "No," stop. You're done with the particular capability. Exhibit 2.2 spells out the competitive and economic implications of the response.

We will have more to say about VRIO in Chapter 11. In the meantime, remember that in free markets, things change. Success is always a moving target. So a capability that offers distinctive advantage must also be tweaked and adjusted to keep up with the pace of evolution in the competitive domain. The best way to get ideas about what to do is through customer satisfaction surveys. Those are next.

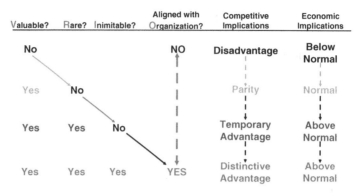

Valuable?	Rare?	Inimitable?	Aligned with Organization?	Competitive Implications	Economic Implications
No			NO	Disadvantage	Below Normal
Yes	No			Parity	Normal
Yes	Yes	No		Temporary Advantage	Above Normal
Yes	Yes	Yes	YES	Distinctive Advantage	Above Normal

Exhibit 2.2   VRIO Assessment Tool

Source: "Beyond that *What*: Using SPARC to Determine the *Why* and Add Value for Clients," at NACVA's 2008 15th Annual Consultants' Conference, June 11, 2008, in Las Vegas. Used with permission. Beckmill Research, LLC © 2008.

Customer Satisfaction Surveys

In our 19 years in business, we have received, read online, and created many such surveys. There is the right way to do it, and there are all the other ways, including three shortcomings we often see. First, seldom is the survey designed with an eye toward rigorous statistical analysis of the results. By "rigorous statistical analysis," we mean much more than averages, medians, and measures of dispersion. We mean dependent and independent variables, thoughtfully designed, pretested on a focus group, and later analyzed through multiple regression or factor analysis, with low correlations among the independent variables.

The second mistake is that scales are often too wide (e.g., 1 to 10), or are too narrow (1 to 3 or 1 to 5), or have an even number of choices in the scale (4, 6, etc.). The optimal width is 7. It is an odd number, which means there is a midpoint: 4. It is wide enough to have precision but not so wide that identical perceptions by different people will produce noticeably different results.

The third shortcoming is that the instrument almost never asks *how important* a given activity, characteristic, design, or other aspect of the product or service is to the customer. For instance, if an activity is unimportant to the customer and is not required by law or business prudence, why is the company doing it? Well-designed survey instruments measure satisfaction and its correlates, but they also have the potential for identifying ways that a company can increase its profits.

Survey results can produce impressive performance gains. We relate an anecdote in Chapter 4 about how we helped one small manufacturer double its sales in 90 days using recommendations we made based on a survey we designed and tested on a small focus group before it went to the company's customers. Surveys don't double sales every time, of course. But the value of a well-designed survey that incorporates sophisticated statistical procedures cannot be overstated. And these days, with the technology to conduct, tabulate, and crunch the statistical numbers using online distribution, it's much less expensive than it was in the "bad old days."

Diversification

At some point, the ability of smaller companies to continue to grow rapidly in their current domains tapers off. To restart the growth engine, at least on the top line, managers have two choices: market development (taking the same products/services to new groups of customers) or product development (selling additional products/services to the same group of customers). Regardless of how they choose, they face a second fork in the road: how to grow, organically or by acquisition. Buying other companies is faster and more expensive, but it is also riskier. Organic growth is slower. Though success is not assured—developing new products/services can be dicey, as can expanding into new markets—it also tends to be much less expensive. And if organic growth fails, the blowback should be far less disruptive that an overpriced acquisition (most are) that doesn't work out.

A scholar whom we've previously mentioned, Dick Rumelt, did seminal research in diversification. His Harvard thesis became a now-out-of-print book, *Strategy, Structure, and Economic Performance.*[27] Rumelt conducted that rare study, a longitudinal one (i.e., it went through time, 1949–1969). Most strategy research is cross-sectional—as of a single point in time. Longitudinal studies allow insights into long-run performance effects of observed phenomena.

In the Rumelt study, the phenomenon was diversification. He divided acquirers into nine types falling into four categories (single business, dominant, related, unrelated). He was able to classify the firms in his sample using three measures:

1. The specialization ratio is "the portion of a firm's revenues that can be attributed to its largest single business in a given year."[28] Building on the work of Wrigley,[29] he used 0.7 as the dividing line between Dominant (>.7) and Related or Unrelated (< 0.7).
2. The related ratio is "the proportion of a firm's revenues attributable to its largest group of related businesses."[30] Again, 0.7 was the divider, this time between Related and Unrelated.

---

[27] Rumelt, *Strategy, Structure.*
[28] Ibid., 14.
[29] Wrigley, *Divisional Autonomy and Diversification.*
[30] Rumelt, *Strategy, Structure,* 16.

3. The vertical ratio is "the proportion of a firm's revenues that arise from all byproducts, intermediate products, and end products of a vertically integrated sequence of processing activities."[31]

Here is how that plays out in Rumelt's four categories:[32]

Vertical ratio ≥ 0.7
    Single Business if SR ≥ 0.95
    Dominant Business if SR < 0.95
Vertical ratio < 0.7
    Related Business if RR ≥ 0.7
    Unrelated Business if RR < 0.7

The most important findings were that (1) "constrained" diversification (i.e., diversifying into domains that added to or extended existing core competence) was most profitable, whether the category was Dominant or Related; (2) vertical integration (current examples: integrated oil companies, investor-owned utilities) performed worse than average, contrary to what television talking heads would have us believe; and (3) so-called conglomerate diversification (collections of unrelated businesses) are not, despite what portfolio theory might suggest to the contrary, the path to prosperity. Here are three quick examples of what has worked and what hasn't.

Constrained diversification has worked very well for such companies as Procter & Gamble. In the last 25 years, it has acquired Richardson-Vicks (ethical pharmaceuticals), Iams (dog food), and Gillette (branded consumer products). The textbook examples of constrained diversification, however, occurred in the cigarette-manufacturing companies.[33]

In the wake of the U.S. Surgeon General's report in 1964 excoriating the dangers of cigarettes, both Philip Morris and R.J. Reynolds made astute moves into food processing and distribution. Philip Morris turned the brewing industry, then dominated by such venerable names as Falstaff and Schlitz, upside down when it bought Miller Brewing and quickly rolled out Miller Lite (targeting calorie-conscious beer drinkers) and Miller in 8-ounce cans (aiming at the distaff market). Brewing promptly became a consolidating industry, and many old-line brewers either went by the

---

[31] Ibid., 23.
[32] Ibid.
[33] Miles and Cameron, *Coffin Nails.*

wayside or shrank to a fraction of their former size. Philip Morris went on to buy Kraft and General Foods. Similarly, R.J. Reynolds snapped up Nabisco.

These acquisitions were insightful and valuable. They leveraged the core competence of both companies—segmented marketing, product development, and distribution—and reduced the risk posed by a public policy campaign underwritten by the federal government. These combinations enabled both companies to use process manufacturing to create goods shipped through existing distribution channels to the same target market (grocery stores, convenience stores, and pharmacy retailers).

The next example comes from a conversation I had in 1995 with the then-CEO of Arizona Public Service Company. It is the investor-owned utility (IOU) serving the populous areas of that state. Mark DeMichele was trained as a lawyer and had not spent his entire career inside the utility industry. That enabled him to see the industry more clearly than any other utility executive I've ever met.

For one thing, he understood the dangers of his domain's insularity. Low turnover in IOUs produces very parochial views of how things not only do work but *should* work. Soon after he arrived, he directed his human resources (HR) staff to hire only people from outside the utility industry, except when a position called for engineering or operational expertise.

He also understood that the state of vertical integration in the industry—power generation, transmission, and distribution—resulted *only* from the regulator apparatus overseeing monopoly utilities. Regulators based their rate-making activities, not on net profit margins, but on return on assets (ROA). Therefore, to get ROA down, managers had to expand their asset bases. That alone will take most companies into businesses unrelated to what they know how to do. But ROA has another effect: capitalize every expense that can possibly be capitalized. With a twinkle in his eye, DeMichele looked at me and said, "You know, Warren, this is a great business. It's the only one I've ever been in where I can redecorate my office and increase my bonus. It's a great country!"

The third example of diversification is the old Beatrice Foods Company. That name might not ring a bell with younger professionals today, but some of its product lines will: Day-Timers, Tropicana Orange Juice, Peter Pan, Wesson Oil, Altoids, Krispy Crème, Samsonite luggage, Play-Tex, Culligan, Avis, and Airstream. The question is one of relatedness: What do Day-Timers, food, luggage, undergarments, auto rentals, water treatments, and high-end house trailers have in common? Not much. As securities markets became more efficient when information technology (IT) began to improve in leaps and bounds in the mid-1980s, conglomerates such as Beatrice found their stock prices discounted due to what became known as the conglomerate discount. That discount arose because, if an investor wanted to buy into Beatrice because it was a food-processing behemoth, she also found that she owned pieces of a whole bunch of non-food-processing companies that she might not want. Investors bid the price down. Leveraged buyout firm KKR bought Beatrice in 1985, sold off the pieces to different buyers, and made a fortune.

Conglomerates are not much in evidence these days because of market efficiency. The only two that have survived and thrived are GE and Berkshire Hathaway. The performance of GE's stock since Jack Welch rode off into the sunset in 2001 raises questions about whether GE can survive as an amalgamation of unrelated businesses (lighting, health insurance, business lending, airplane engines, power turbines, household appliances, consumer electronics, consumer finance, media [NBC], security devices, diesel locomotives, and water treatments, to name just a few).

Berkshire Hathaway (B-H) under CEO Warren Buffett has achieved similarly iconic status. Its businesses are pretty humdrum; a partial list: Dairy Queen, Geico (insurance), Clayton Homes (manufactured housing), Nebraska Furniture Mart, Borsheim's (jewelry and china), NetJets (partial ownership in commercial jets), See's Candies, Pampered Chef (kitchen tools), Benjamin Moore (paint), Helzberg's (diamond jewelry), Cort (furniture rental), MidAmerican Energy (public utility), Kirby (vacuum cleaners), World Book (encyclopedias), Northern Natural Gas, and Shaw Industries (flooring). B-H's companies employ over 200,000 people . . . with an Omaha headquarters staff of 19 and a CEO whose base pay is $100,000 a year (as it has been for many years). Though Buffett assures one and all that he has successors groomed and ready to go, one wonders how well his company will fare after he's gone, especially considering the post-Welch example at GE.

Unlocking Business Wealth

These eight tools, singularly or in combination, offer the professional powerful vehicles for insights during a valuation or its aftermath. Each is a distinctly nontraditional weapon in the securities analyst's arsenal. Strategic intent gives one a quick-hit view of whether the client company sees reality with even faint clarity. Generic competitive strategies give the lie to price-based competition for all but the most powerful (or reckless) SMEs. Resources are the linchpin around which routines, capabilities, and, eventually, strategy are built. Competitive analysis helps managers anticipate what a competitor will do through understanding what it can do and how it is likely to react to threats on its turf. Distinctive advantage has it all over sustained competitive advantage because it reinforces differentiation while communicating that nothing is forever. VRIO is a simple yet powerful tool for assessing a company's capabilities and their potential for contributing to economic performance. Customer satisfaction surveys have the potential to reshape a company, grow it, and dramatically enhance its profitability, but one has to understand statistics and be able to sell the benefits to the client. Depending on how a company does it, diversification can be a great friend or a horrible enemy. The key, as Peters and Waterman[34] pointed out so many years ago, is to "stick to the knitting"—stay with what you know or, as longtime Texas Longhorn football coach Darrell Royal used to say, "We're gonna dance with who brung us."

Summary

This chapter is long, but necessarily so. The eight tools detailed here are indispensable in uncovering new valuation insights, advising clients about how to grow, keeping the firm aligned with an ever-moving external environment, and understanding competition in a way that perhaps was not the case before. We have never seen any of these tools in any valuation textbook. They are nontraditional but also helpful. We need not be parochial in our approach to our work. We need to be better at what we do, though, and looking outside the "usual suspects" for new ways to understand companies and serve clients is always a good idea.

There is a close link between strategic management and industrial organization, which is the focus of Chapter 3. In fact, there is proximity with strategy and economics generally. But none of these disciplines will help the professional who cannot, or will not, see the world clearly and communicate what he sees to the client in simple English. That is a much taller order than it appears to be. The biggest reason is that reluctance we cited in the section on strategic intent: "a threat that everyone perceives but no one talks about." Beware the emperor who is naked as a jay bird.

Additional Reading

Besanko, David, David Dranove, Mark Shanley, and Scott Schaefer. *Economics of Strategy*, 4th ed. Hoboken, NJ: John Wiley & Sons, 2006.
Buffett, Warren E. Berkshire Hathaway's Annual Shareholder Letter (1997– 2007). Available at www.berkshirehathaway.com/letters/letters.html.

[34] Peters and Waterman, *In Search of Excellence.*

Dillman, Don A. *Mail and Internet Surveys: The Tailored Design Method,* 2nd ed. Hoboken, NJ: John Wiley & Sons, 2007.

Faulkner, David O., and Andrew Campbell, eds. *The Oxford Handbook of Strategy: Volume 1: A Strategy Overview and Competitive Strategy.* New York: Oxford University Press, 2003.

Grant, Robert M. *Contemporary Strategy Analysis,* 6th ed. Hoboken, NJ: Wiley-Blackwell, 2007.

Maister, David. *Strategy and the Fat Smoker.* Boston: Spangle Press, 2008.

3

Tools from Industrial Organization

ndustrial organization is a branch of economics. It focuses on competition (which drives free markets and raises standards of living) and monopoly power (which distorts the beneficial outcomes of competition). IO also has policy implications in deregulation and antitrust issues.

Like other fields in economics, IO got started in the 1870s. It began to come to the fore in 1890 with the enactment of the Sherman Antitrust Act. The act was a response to the legal machinations of Standard Oil Company through "trust agreements" (hence the term "antitrust"). Although Standard Oil inspired the act, it was first used in 1894 against a labor organization, the American Railway Union, during a strike against the Pullman Company. President Theodore Roosevelt relied heavily on the Sherman Act to break up industrial monopolies.[1] His successor, William Howard Taft, invoked it to split the American Tobacco Company.

Many Americans would be surprised to learn that a monopoly achieved on merit is legal. However, one created or maintained by overt collusion or market manipulation is not.

As valuation professionals, we are seldom concerned with antitrust and related policy issues. In fact, in only two valuations since 1993 have we had to deal with antitrust. I doubt that we are unique in that respect. When President Reagan came to power in 1981, approaches by governments at all levels to antitrust enforcement changed from one rooted in politics to one based on economics, especially the Herfindahl-Hirschman Index, about which we will have more to say in the "Concentration Ratios" section later in this chapter.

---

[1] In 1902, he moved against Northern Securities Company, a railroad trust that owned the Northern Pacific, Great Northern, and Burlington railroads. By the time the Supreme Court issued its decision two years later, 318 trusts held over 5,300 U.S. businesses, an average of about 17 companies per trust (www.encyclopedia.com/doc/1G2-3468300044.html). Roosevelt's administration filed 45 antitrust actions.

The competition side of IO focuses on the structure, conduct, and performance of *industries*. A working definition of this branch of IO is the study of the structures and performance of industries and of the nature of competition within them. This is the economics of *imperfect competition*, which is where the real money is made.

By "industry," we mean groups of companies engaged in similar business activities. The federal government has devised numeric schemes with which to classify these activities. There are Standard Industrial Classification (SIC) codes, for instance. Created by the Bureau of the Census in the 1930s, SIC codes are slowly being phased out and replaced by those of the North American Industry Classification System (NAICS, pronounced "nakes"). In transactional databases such as Pratt's Stats, for instance, both SIC and NAICS codes appear. However, in Securities and Exchange Commission (SEC) filings, SIC codes still govern.

In the United States, IO advanced during the first half of the twentieth century as a result of research conducted by Edward S. Mason of Harvard and his student Joe S. Bain (1912–1991) of the University of California, Berkeley. Bain is often called the "father of modern industrial organization." Later, Harvard's Richard E. Caves studied under Mason. Caves, in turn, supervised the dissertations of Michael E. Porter and Anita M. McGahan. We will have much more to say about McGahan later in the "Domain Evolution" section of this chapter.

Perspective

Industrial organization's "unit of analysis"—the lens through which what it seeks to analyze is viewed—is the *industry*. The unfortunate follow-up phrase, "industry analysis," leads valuation professionals to make such ill-advised choices as buying off-the-shelf industry "profiles" from well-meaning vendors such as Integra. These profiles can lead the analyst of SMEs astray. Think about a purchased industry analysis for grocery stores, when your client is a small independent grocer serving a constrained market area. Of what use would replicating an analysis of an industry dominated by the likes of Kroger and Wal-Mart be in the context of a valuation of your client?

Defining an industry—a more precise term is "domain"—is a crucial aspect of valuation. Yet analysts often give it short shrift. They fail to conduct their analyses in the context of the domain in which their client company competes. This matters because domain structures at local and regional levels often differ in major respects from the structures of their industry counterparts nationally.

Therefore, define the domain *first*. If you can do it before you even get the engagement, so much the better. That will enable you to take a quick look at the would-be client's world prior to meeting its owner or president. You can then ask relevant questions about that domain, not only to learn for yourself but also to see how the owner or president responds.

Except for discussing market share in the context of domain concentration, avoid talking about individual companies when writing a domain analysis. Speaking of which, if the domain is the unit of analysis, it follows that external risk premiums *are the same for all players within a domain.* After all, each faces the same set of threats and opportunities, does it not? Why would their external risk premiums not be equal?

Do not confuse domain analysis with how your client company deals with those opportunities and threats. Save the latter for the company level of your analysis. That is where its strengths (how it takes advantage of external opportunities, how it creates unique sources of distinctive advantage, etc.) and weaknesses (its inability to reduce its exposure to external threats, its weak system of internal controls, major audit adjustments, etc.) show up.

Tenets

On the competition side of industrial organization, the central tenet is the structure-conduct-performance (S-C-P) paradigm. That is, (domain) structure drives (domain competitors') conduct, which drives (the domain's) performance. There are feedback loops from performance to structure and conduct and from conduct to structure (see Exhibit 3.1).

The feedback loops reflect the dynamic nature of markets: They are always evolving—quickly, slowly, or irregularly. Evolution and change are constant. That is why success in free markets is a moving target.

Any football coach will attest that it is a lot easier to *become* number one than it is to *remain* number one. Let us put that in a business context: Assume that your employer has become phenomenally successful. Money is raining on officers and employees alike. The *last* thing anyone in that situation wants to do is change *anything.* It is human nature to let Mother Nature continue to drench everyone with torrents of cash. That is why most successful companies, and most of those within them, resist any change. They want

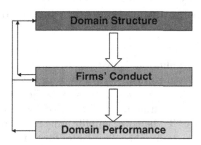

Exhibit 3.1   Structure-Conduct-Performance Model

the deluge of greenbacks into their bank accounts to continue unabated *ad infinitum*. They want the adoring press and envious neighbors to remain adoring and envious. That is not reality in free markets. Competition will not permit it. What worked yesterday might not work today, and what gets top-flight performance today might not get it tomorrow. The capitalistic system of creative destruction can be a not-fun system—markets can melt down, and home prices can fall. It is an unforgiving system, no matter how much politicians and policy makers try to hide reality from angry voters.

For every company that does change, evolve, and remain on top, there are thousands that do not. For every Nucor, there are a myriad of Jones & Laughlins, U.S. Steels, and Bethlehem Steels. For every GE, there are scads of GTEs. For every Southwest Airlines, there is a pile of Braniffs, PanAms, and Easterns.

The exceptions prove the rule. Those that do survive, adjust, and continue to succeed have the capacity to change *with* their domain and sometimes even to shape that change in ways that play to their own strengths. Ask Sears about Wal-Mart or Microsoft about Google.

Individuals are apt to have different perspectives on this branch of IO, depending on the lens they use:

- **Economist.** "Does the structure of this industry lead to efficient outcomes?"
- **Regulator.** "Does the structure of this industry mean that firms can engage in anticompetitive behavior at customers' expense?"
- **Business owner/CEO.** "How does the structure of this domain affect our ability to create distinctive advantage?"
- **Valuation professional.** "What is the risk profile of this domain's underlying structure?"

As professionals, our concern is with, first, the economic infrastructure of the domain. Later on, we will talk about structure and distinctive advantage, the concerns of business owners and CEOs in middle-market companies.

A key tenet of IO is equilibrium analysis. We do not find such analysis useful in the world of valuation.[2] That said, despite the fact that the S-C-P

---

[2] The problem we have with equilibrium is that it is an end state and an undesirable one, at that, at least for our clients. What company wants to be in a domain and earn only "normal profits," which is about the same rate of profit as its rivals? Besides, how can a mechanism as complex and multifaceted as a $14 trillion economy in an advanced industrial nation *ever* be "in balance" in the first place? To be sure, equilibrium-related research produces elegant mathematics and, by extension, tenured professorships for those who do it. However, it is not much use to business owners or to those of us who advise them.

Exhibit 3.2   Basic Domain Structures

paradigm comes out of the equilibrium context, it remains a useful platform for thinking about domain dynamics.

A second IO tenet is that industry structure has an impact on the conduct of individual companies. Now, when we say "conduct," readers should think "strategy." We're talking behavior here and in a branch of economics, no less. Exhibit 3.2 shows the four basic states of domain structure, according to traditional economics. They lie along a continuum of competitive intensity.

Monopolists do not have to ponder competitors, but they must, except in "natural" monopolies, consider regulators and politicians (think public utilities and cable TV companies). At the other end of the spectrum, hypercompetitors do not worry much about regulators, but they do think about their rivals. The irony is that, in those intensely competitive states, players' performance is hardly affected by rivals' choices. But the really interesting structure, and one that occurs often in local and regional contexts, is the oligopoly. We will have plenty to say about that configuration later in this chapter in the subsection called "Behavior in Oligopolies."

The key for valuation professionals is to understand that domain structure affects firms' conduct, which affects performance. Strategy feeds back to structure, and performance feeds back to both structure and conduct. From those relationships, we have identified six tools in the IO arsenal:

1. Domain analysis
2. Strategic groups
3. Domain evolution
4. Concentration ratios
5. Behavior in oligopolies
6. Price discrimination

In certain contexts, which we will identify, each is useful for analysts.

Tools

As we said leading off the section about strategy tools in Chapter 2, we ask that readers not infer relative importance from the sequence in which the following discussions appear. The sequence is just one that makes sense to me, and I hope it will to you, too.

Domain Analysis

What others call "industry analysis" we call "domain analysis." That is because few clients in middle-market valuations are industry-wide competitors. Because they are not, canned industry overviews from such firms as Integra and First Research are seldom useful. Of necessity, those overviews are one-size-fits-all. Their economics do not allow them to focus on subtle nuances in regional and local contexts.

Still, whether the analysis is industry-wide or not, the process is the same. It involves six forces:

1. The threat of new entrants
2. Rivalry among incumbent firms
3. Bargaining power of customers
4. Bargaining power of suppliers
5. The threat of substitutes
6. The power of complements

Expanding the middle level of the trilevel unsystematic risk framework introduced in Chapter 1, in Exhibit 3.3 we have positioned each force opposite its obverse, in hopes of facilitating ease of recall.

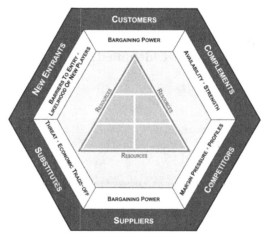

Exhibit 3.3 Six Forces of Domain Analysis

Source: Adapted from Michael E. Porter, *Competitive Strategy: Techniques for Analyzing Industries and Competitors* (New York: Free Press, 1980).

To repeat: We can analyze the forces in Exhibit 3.3 by looking through either an industry-wide lens or one that focuses locally or regionally. Those "subindustries" are the subject of the next section.

Strategic Groups

Domains that are less than industry-wide are called "strategic groups." Appearing originally in a 1972 Harvard dissertation,[3] strategic groups came to the fore in 1978 with the publication of a paper advancing a new term, "mobility barriers."[4] They are the strategic-group equivalent of barriers to entry at the industry level.

Each group has its own target market. Within a group, business models tend to be similar. Their sharing of certain attributes makes them rivals. Those may include, for instance, target market, distribution channel, product/service portfolio, competitive strategy deployed, and/or geographic reach. In our experience, geography is often a primary determinant for defining a strategic group (i.e., the domain) in middle-market engagements.

Why Strategic Groups Matter.   These subunits are important because few SMEs have the resources to compete industry-wide. Instead, they focus where they think they are most likely to succeed—in a segment of the industry. Most valuation professionals should be analyzing strategic groups, not entire industries, because groups are where their client companies compete.

Examples of Strategic Groups.   A group's members tend *not* to compete with firms in other groups due to the aforementioned mobility barriers. One example of such a group is the cadre of nonnational accounting firms offering traditional services in a metropolitan statistical area. Yes, the "Big Four" firms might also be there, but these behemoths do not encroach on the turf of the smaller firms because their cost structure makes them uneconomic for small engagements. Below the Goliaths lie regional firms, large locals, multi-partner (but not large) locals, and sole practitioners. Each of these is a strategic group defined by geography and target market.

Another example is new-car retailing. Again, the groups within this broad domain run the gamut: luxury, subluxury, sports car, moderate-priced sedans, low-priced sedans, convertibles, large sport utility vehicles (SUVs), small SUVs, and crossovers. If, instead of "new cars," we said "new

---

[3] This term originated with Michael S. Hunt in his unpublished 1972 Harvard dissertation, "Competition in the Major Home Appliance Industry, 1960–1970."
[4] Caves and Porter, "Mobility Barriers."

vehicles," then the list of strategic groups would include vans and several different types of pickup trucks.

Our final example comes from the lodging industry. It has many strategic groups: full-service/expensive, full-service/moderate, extended stay, budget, bed-and-breakfasts, luxury, and resorts. These groups may be divided further along geographical lines, of course. And within these groups are others. Resorts, for instance, come in two flavors: those catering to families and those targeting businesses. Between the two, the amenities, ambience, entertainment, and price points differ hugely. The competitive dynamics of each group are also different. That is why, for instance, you may see a full-service Marriot next to a Courtyard by Marriott, which might share a boundary with a Fairfield Inn, on the other side of which might be a Residence Inn. Each is part of the Marriott brand, but each targets different customers with different price points and different needs.

Domain Evolution

Domains change. That is the nature of the capitalist system. Evolution may come rapidly (e.g., consumer electronics). It may occur slowly (e.g., pallet manufacturing). But domains are in a state of constant change. That is why valuation firms that have annuity relationships with certain clients for planned gifting or employee stock ownership plan appraisals, for instance, might be skating on thin ice when they copy and paste from last year's report.

The more narrowly you define your client's competitive domain, the more relevant your report will be *and* the more understanding you will have of your client's business and why the value is what you say it is. The "why" is an often-overlooked aspect of valuation. It comes in handy if you ever have to testify.

On the first page of her classic book, *How Industries Evolve*, Anita McGahan writes:

> The central purpose of this book is to help you achieve and sustain superior performance in your organization by adhering to two principles. The first is to avoid the unnecessary risks and costs that arise from a strategy that breaks the rules of industry change. The goal is to make sure that the strategy you envision for a business can succeed given the specific conditions in your industry today and in the future. The second principle involves recognizing and then capitalizing on the lasting opportunities for developing advantage in your business that arise from industry change. The challenge here is to see the implications of

structural change before your competitors see them, and to use your existing strengths to achieve an enduring competitive advantage.[5]

She identifies four "exhaustive" industry "trajectories." Which one an industry or domain falls under depends on the extent to which innovation in products or processes threatens its core assets (by "accelerating their rate of real depreciation") and its core activities (either by causing suppliers to be less willing to sell to the industry or by reducing the willingness of buyers to pay for the industry's output).[6] McGahan defines an asset or activity as being "core" if its owner cannot replace it within 12 months without disruption to profitability. By an industry being "threatened" or "not threatened" on the two dimensions (core activities and core assets), a 2 × 2 matrix results that defines the four types of trajectories can be built:

1. **Progressive** (43% of industries, she estimates). Neither core activities nor core assets is threatened; industry performance is steady, if unspectacular; exemplars: discount retailing, long-haul trucking.
2. **Intermediating** (32%). Activities are threatened, assets are not; performance is volatile and declines over time; exemplars: auto dealerships, fine arts auctions.
3. **Radical** (19%). Both activities and assets are threatened; performance is high until the transformation takes place, when profitability nosedives; exemplars: landline telephone manufacturing, typewriter manufacturing.
4. **Creative** (6%). Assets are threatened, activities are not; bimodal distribution (big profits or huge losses) of performance outcomes due to high likelihood of failure; exemplars: pharmaceuticals, motion picture production.

Before an in-depth discussion of each of the trajectories, McGahan implores analysts and strategists to remember four guiding principles:

1. Every industry *has* but one trajectory.
2. Each industry *follows* but one trajectory.
3. Shifts between trajectories are *infrequent.*
4. Change in the underlying economic structure of an industry *can be significant* even when the industry faces no threat of obsolescence.[7]

---

[5] McGahan, *How Industries Evolve*, 1.
[6] Ibid., 12.
[7] Ibid., 27–28.

McGahan also proposes ten rules of evolutionary change. She puts them into three categories:

Defining rules
1. Robustness of core assets
2. Robustness of core activities

Corollaries
3. Industry boundaries
4. Operational effectiveness
5. Locus of innovation

Guidelines
6. Buyer power
7. Supplier power
8. Threat of substitution
9. Intensity of rivalry
10. Threat of entry[8]

Domain matters. Those wanting to help clients unlock wealth can find major value-added opportunities in McGahan's work and her book. Others will do well to consider what type of evolutionary trajectory their client companies' domains fall under because that is a crucial determination in assessing unsystematic risk at the domain level.

Concentration Ratios

Every five years the U.S. Bureau of the Census collects and publishes volumes of industry data showing levels of concentration by SIC code, called "concentration ratios" (CRs). It calculates them for the largest 4, 8, 20, and 50 firms in an industry at the two-, three-, and four-digit level. A concentration ratio is the aggregate market share, expressed as a whole number, of the 4, 8, 20, or 50 biggest firms in an industry. But these ratios tell us nothing about how market share is distributed *among* the 4 (i.e., CR4), 8 (CR8), 20 (CR20), or 50 (CR50) firms comprising a concentration ratio. So, a CR4 = 100 could mean market shares of 25%–25%–25%–25%. But it could also mean 40%–30%–20%–10% or 97%–1%–1%–1%. In the latter case, of course, the smaller three firms are "price takers."

---

[8] Ibid., 40–42.

Beginning in the Reagan administration, the Herfindahl-Hirschman Index (HHI) became the measuring stick for whether a merger would be challenged.[9] It carries more information than CRs because, by squaring the share of *every* competitor, disparities among them become evident. Let us start with a monopoly: share = 100%, so HHI = 10,000. That is the maximum HHI.

In the first example two paragraphs earlier, HHI = 2,500 ($25^2+25^2+25^2+25^2$). The 40%–30%–20%–10% structure's HHI = 3,000 ($40^2+30^2+20^2+10^2$). The last structure, 97%–1%–1%–1%, has an HHI = 9,412 ($97^2+1^2+1^2+1^2$). Note that the HHI takes quantum leaps when the share of the largest firm increases. Domains in which HHI is greater than 1,800 are said to be "concentrated." Domains with HHIs between 1,000 and 1,800 are viewed as "moderately concentrated" by antitrust authorities.

Regardless of the method used to estimate concentration, the underlying economic structures of most strategic groups tend to differ from that of industry-wide players. For example, the oligopoly that offers auditing services for publicly held companies vaporizes when firms target closely held concerns. In fact, the Federal Trade Commission (FTC) has found major differences in within-industry strategic group structures, depending on geography. Of interest to valuation professionals, the FTC says that the incidence of oligopoly is much higher locally and regionally than it is nationally.

The question arises: Why should a valuation professional care about domain concentration? Well, if the analyst could get *firm-level* data, she could get insights into relative market share. That would start to tell her something about where on the concentration continuum the particular domain might fall. Problem is, few closely helds disclose their financial statements to outsiders other than the Internal Revenue Service (IRS), lenders, and regulators. Data for sales and units of output are, therefore, unavailable.

More concentrated industries are usually (but not always) more profitable than less concentrated ones. Regardless, concentration bears on valuation. The temptation is to extrapolate from the Census data and assume that national concentration levels are the same locally or regionally.

Bad idea. For one thing, the FTC data show that that would be a mistake. For another, the Census data are not published until several years (at least) after their effective date.

But why is share important in the first place? Well, if concentration is an indicator of market share, and share helps define structure, then we are trying to get at the first leg of the structure-conduct-performance graphic

---

[9] For a short but clear, discussion of HHI, see www.usdoj.gov/atr/public/testimony/hhi.htm.

we talked about earlier in this chapter. But share is also alluded to in Revenue Ruling 59-60. Without coming right out and using the phrase "market share," the IRS seems to call for it:

> It is important to know that the company is more or less successful than its competitors in the same industry, or that it is maintaining a stable position with respect to competitors.[10]

We use headcount as a proxy for output. Besides being one of the eight size measures in the Duff & Phelps data set, headcount figures are easily accessed. Think about it: If you go up to the owner of a thriving business and ask her what her company's revenues were last year, she is apt to look at you as if you just came to town and fell off a turnip truck. But ask her how many jobs she has created for the community, and she cannot get that number out of her mouth fast enough. Luckily for us in valuation, headcount figures are readily available through chambers of commerce, companies themselves, and at least one database.[11]

Within a domain, there is some level of correlation between headcount and revenues. There has to be, or else some firms could not compete against others. That correlation will vary from company to company depending on its efficiency, management savvy, view of how the business works, technology, and so on, but, because an industry's economic underpinnings create the same domain risk profile for all players in the domain, the relationship between sales and people on the payroll must hold. It is not perfect, of course, but little in the valuation arena is.[12]

We ask the people running the valuation entity what they estimate their own market share to be, as well as those of their closest competitors.[13] Then we use available data to estimate total employment in the strategic group we have defined. We estimate a company's market share based on its number of full-time-equivalent employees as a percentage of total employment in the domain.

The sum of the four headcount-based market shares is a proxy for the CR4. Anytime that number gets north of 45 or so, our antennae go up. We might be looking at an oligopoly. If we are, things get even more interesting.

---

[10] Section 4.02(b), Revenue Ruling 59-60.

[11] www.zapdata.com.

[12] In valuation, being a valuation professional is kind of like being in the Marine Corps: Marines and private-equity analysts do a lot of improvising.

[13] For reasons we have never been able to understand, most owners have uncanny perceptions about share, their own and their competitors'.

Behavior in Oligopolies

An oligopoly is a domain with few sellers. How few? Economists disagree. Many believe that a domain with a CR4 ≥ 50 *and* with no dominant player qualifies as an oligopoly. What is the maximum number of relevant players in a well-functioning oligopoly? Economists' views seem to converge around 8.

What makes oligopolies different? One implication of having few sellers is that such sellers are interdependent. That is, what one does affects the fortunes of the others. As a result, word travels fast in oligopolies. A strategy of differentiation, either focus or industry-wide, is the norm for an oligopolist. Members of oligopolies often advertise and promote heavily, the better to differentiate their product or service offering. Thus, a well-functioning oligopoly can also be highly profitable for all players.

Domains with few rivals have implications for competitors' behavior.

- The first five rules of the oligopolist in good standing with its rivals are never, <u>never</u>, **never**, NEVER, **NEVER** *compete on the basis of price.* Never. I know we said that a few pages back, but it bears repeating. Often.
- Firms' fortunes—and their profits—depend on *interdependence.* That is, their destiny depends on one another. So they keep close tabs on each other, but *not* through overt collusion.
- Some domains—airlines, for instance—tend to observe *rigid pricing,* even if they practice price discrimination (covered in the next section of this chapter). In such arenas, competitors are likely to match price cuts, but not price increases. Only in 2007–2008 did the U.S. airline industry's repeated attempts to raise prices finally gain traction as all players suffered under the burden of skyrocketing oil prices and their own inability to hedge those prices.
- Firms cannot collude overtly to set prices, but there is nothing to keep them from engaging in *tacit collusion.* Such collusion, in fact, is one of the hallmarks of well-functioning oligopolies. Overt collusion is illegal in the United States, but we see it internationally in cartels of oil (Organization of Petroleum Exporting Countries), sugar, and diamonds (DeBeers).
- Oligopoly is a market structure found in mature domains, so the only way to grow at any pace other than that of a snail is through *mergers.* Those eliminate competition, of course, but can become a public policy issue if antitrust regulators in either the U.S. Department of Justice or the FTC perceive a merger as anticompetitive. In fact, all mergers are anticompetitive. The only question is how anticompetitive.

Competing on price also makes the buying decision a no-brainer for customers. Worse, within a domain, there can be only one—count 'em, one—cost leader. Everyone else is playing a game of catch-up, only they are playing it by the leader's rules, which can change at any time.

Sometimes, though, even in concentrated industries and strategic groups, price competition prevails. In the 1990s, we saw that in audit services where the sole emphasis in the service offering was compliance rather than adding value; in many firms, that is still the case. Compliance is essential, of course, but there is more to auditing than square-peg/square-hole, tick-and-tie routines.[14]

As noted earlier in this chapter, monopoly (ultimate concentration) lies at one end of the domain-structure spectrum. At the other is perfect competition (ultimate fragmentation). Oligopoly is somewhere in between. For instance, the CR4 in tobacco manufacturing (NAICS 312221) is 95.3; the comparable figure in pallet manufacturing (NAICS 32192) is 6.9. Highly concentrated industries sometimes have highly differentiated products. That combination makes price a much less important consideration in their purchase. Fragmented industries, including most agricultural products, are often characterized by so-called commodity outputs where price is the primary, and often the only, consideration in the buying decision.

The notion of *interdependence* means that a firm's pricing decisions should not be made with merely its own self-interests in mind but, instead, the interests of the group (i.e., the oligopoly). The good (or ill) fortunes of one oligopolist likely reflect the good (or ill) fortunes of all. This is not the case in a commodity-type business.

I am sometimes asked where fragmentation stops and oligopoly begins. As with so many valuation issues that frustrate those with a low tolerance for ambiguity, there is no specific answer. In the first study done on the subject, Bain found that firms in industries with CR4s above 50 were more profitable than those below 50.[15]

Further, says a prominent industrial-organization expert:

> [After Bain,] studies of U.S. data also have found such a "critical level" of concentration for CR4 between 45 and 60; that is, there is little evidence that increases in seller concentration to CR4 levels below 50 have any effect on [relative] profitability.[16]

---

[14] By not figuring out a way to convey valuable information in the management letter, auditors might be missing an opportunity to add value, differentiate what they do, and increase prices (and margins).

[15] Bain, "Industry Concentration."

[16] Scherer and Ross, *Industrial Market Structure,* 423.

This assumes, of course, that relative shares are not unduly skewed to the point where one firm is dominant (i.e., has market share > 40%). In dominant-firm domains, competitors, suppliers, and customers tiptoe around "the big gorilla."[17] Everyone other than the lead dog is a "price-taker" —they follow the big mutt's lead.

At the national level, trustbusters and competition have significantly, if not wholly, reduced the incidence of oligopoly. In the 1950s, the three major television broadcasting companies—ABC, CBS, NBC—enjoyed a combined market share north of 90%; today it is below 40% and sinking fast, thanks to the advent of cable and satellite technologies. The Big Three Detroit automakers used to rule the world. Now, having made fools of themselves taking separate private jets to Washington while asking for a $25 billion bailout from the federal government even as their CEOs resolutely refused to take pay cuts, the question is whether any of them can survive, not only this economy but also the onslaught of high-quality cars from non-U.S. competitors and a major cost disadvantage caused, at least in part, by huge obligations for retiree healthcare borne by the domestic car makers.

Our favorite example of a national oligopoly that still persists is ready-to-eat (RTE) breakfast cereals. Lest any reader doubt the pricing power of a well-functioning oligopoly, the next time you are in a large grocery story, go to the RTE cereal section. Pick up a box that weighs little more than a feather, and ask yourself: "How *do* these people get four bucks for this?" In fact, shelf space is at such a premium that grocery stores, long known as businesses with paper-thin margins, discovered "slotting fees" in the 1980s.[18] In essence, suppliers "rent" shelf space based on its relation to eye level. In RTE cereals, the combination of slotting fees and brand proliferation (to ensure there is no space for new entrants) makes for an air-tight oligopoly.

In local and regional segments, however, regulators seldom intervene.[19] Oligopoly is alive and well locally and regionally. And, so long as competitors understand the "rules of engagement," they can be highly profitable.

Through the combined efforts of the antitrust professionals at the FTC and at the Department of Justice, the incidence of national oligopoly is low.

---

[17] For a recent example, see the transcript of the recent antitrust action against Microsoft. Giants in industries outside Microsoft's bailiwick—operating systems—cowered. Those include such well-known companies as IBM, Compaq, and Hewlett-Packard. Only Oracle and Sun Microsystems (which was later acquired by Oracle) remained consistently and resolutely antagonistic toward Microsoft.

[18] See Therrien, "Want Shelf Space."

[19] We are aware of two such situations, but there are probably more. These tend not to attract much attention, so are not particularly newsworthy.

However, it occurs often in local and regional markets. That has implications for valuation professionals because of the tacit collusion present in well-functioning oligopolies. That makes possible a sustained period of stable profitability, which reduces the cost of capital in such domains.

Price Discrimination

The definition of "price discrimination" is charging different customers different prices for the same product or service. Unless a set price is mandated by law, price discrimination is legal. If valuation is price- and circumstances-dependent, why do valuation firms not charge different prices for what we do? Some do. But most, especially bigger firms, do not. We have never understood why.

IO defines three types of price discrimination: first, second, and third degree. *First-degree* price discrimination is a matter of charging each customer the maximum price that he or she is willing to pay. Monopolists prefer to practice first-degree discrimination wherever possible.

Before it made legal peace with the U.S. Department of Justice in 2002, Microsoft practiced first-degree price discrimination with computer assemblers. At that time, each Microsoft patent license for its operating system was individually negotiated for two years. Microsoft required a negotiated fee with each assembler for a minimum number of licenses. In the typical case, the "minimum" was at least the number of computer shipments the assembler expected to make, whether with Microsoft-based systems or not; sometimes the minimum was greater. If the maker shipped fewer than the minimum number, it still paid for the minimum number. And if it shipped more, it paid an additional royalty per unit shipped, regardless of whether the unit was Microsoft-based or not.[20]

But Microsoft carried it much further. An assembler was allowed to carry over unused licenses from Year 1 to Year 2. That made for an incentive for the assembler to install Windows on Year 2's machines. But Microsoft also slapped penalties on assemblers for their shipments of non-Microsoft systems. An assembler shipping a large number of such systems, for instance, might not be allowed to carry forward unused credits from previous years. Or Microsoft might withhold technical support or require the aberrant assembler to buy a higher minimum number of licenses in future years. It was a well-known "secret" that Microsoft also increased the price of Windows to firms installing non–MS-DOS operating systems on some of their personal computers.

---

[20] Scherer, "Technological Innovation and Monopolization."

In *second-degree* price discrimination, a company offers all customers the same price schedule. Customers then self-select themselves into different price categories. Airlines, pizza retailers, and couponing businesses all practice second-degree discrimination. The airlines do it on the basis of how far in advance a passenger books his ticket, where the passenger is going, how long he will stay at his destination, and whether he leaves the destination and comes back to the point of origin or goes elsewhere. A pizza parlor might charge $12 for one large pizza and $6 for a second one. Thus a person buying one pizza pays $12/pizza, while the customer buying two pays $9. As for coupons, well, in 2003, businesses offered $250 billion of coupons, and customers used $3 billion, a "hit" rate of 1.2 percent. The disposition of a customer to use a coupon depends, first, on how much value the customer puts on her time. A secondary consideration is how big the discount is. In 2003, the average coupon was worth 85 cents.[21]

Although the coupons are of equal value to all customers, those with lower opportunity costs of time are more apt to use them. One study found that unemployed people and people with kids under six were more likely to use coupons for consumer products than those with jobs or without children under six.[22]

Firms that practice *third-degree* price discrimination are able to divide customers into two or more groups, something that second-degree practitioners cannot do. In contrast to the situation with second-degree discrimination, customers encountering third-degree price discrimination cannot determine which group they will join. The manufacturer or retailer puts them in a group according to the company's preconceived idea of the customer's price elasticity of demand (i.e., price sensitivity). The more elastic the demand, the lower the price.

The first time we encountered third-degree price discrimination, we were not even aware of the phrase. We end the book with the details of that experience, which happened during a break from undergraduate school in May 1974.

There is far more to price discrimination than we can cover in this book (e.g., in-state versus nonresidential prices; tariffs; frequent-buyer programs). We urge readers to get a good basic textbook on industrial organization; if it does not have a chapter devoted to price discrimination, pass it up. With sophisticated information technology available at affordable prices, even middle-market companies can and should entertain the idea of price discrimination. To do so, of course, they need knowledge and data

---

[21] Waldman and Jensen, *Industrial Organization*, 520.
[22] See Blattberg, et al., "Deal-Prone Segment."

about their customers, individually and in segments. They also need to have a good grasp of the buying patterns of those customers. Price discrimination is a potentially powerful tool for savvy manufacturers, retailers, and service providers.

Unlocking Business Wealth

These six tools make for a potent arsenal for the professional focusing on domain issues. Done well, the analysis of those issues will identify potential opportunities and threats in the domain. During the on-site interviews that accompany value enhancement engagements, the analyst can then zero in on whether the client company is taking advantage of the opportunities and trying to avoid the threats. She can also assess what, and how well, senior managers at the client are doing to shape the evolution of industry forces in ways that play to the strengths of their company.

The only one of the six tools discussed in this chapter that we have ever encountered in a valuation report other than our own is domain analysis, but with two differences: (1) every one was called an "industry analysis," and (2) most used "canned" industry overviews. We will have much more to say about that framework in Chapter 9.

Analysts can expect to use domain analysis, concentration ratios, and domain evolution on the road to unlocking business wealth. Middle-market valuation professionals will find strategic groups an especially helpful tool. Because of their unique behavior aspects, the potential presence of an oligopoly-like structure must be examined. And price discrimination can be a powerful tool in increasing revenues, profits, and cash flow, all real pluses where boosting wealth is concerned.

Summary

This chapter discussed six tools available to analysts from the arsenal of industrial organization:

1. Domain analysis
2. Strategic groups
3. Domain evolution
4. Concentration ratios
5. Oligopolies
6. Price discrimination

Each affords the analyst a way to glean additional insights and understanding about the client, its competitive domain, how things work in that domain, and, above all, *why* they work the way they do.

Additional Reading

Brock, James. *The Structure of American Industry*, 12th ed. Upper Saddle River, NJ: Prentice Hall, 2008.

Cabral, Luís M.B. *Introduction to Industrial Organization*. Cambridge, MA: MIT Press, 2000.

Carlton, Dennis W., and Jeffrey M. Perloff. *Modern Industrial Organization*, 4th ed. Boston: Addison-Wesley, 2004.

Carroll, Glenn R., and Michael T. Hannan. *Organizations in Industry*. New York: Oxford University Press, 1995.

Ferguson, Paul R., and Glenys J. Ferguson. *Industrial Economics: Issues and Perspectives*, 2nd ed. New York: New York University Press, 1994.

Tirole, Jean. *The Theory of Industrial Organization*. Cambridge, MA: MIT Press, 1988.

Tools from Organization Theory

Organization theory (OT) sees the firm through its structure. In the OT view, that structure constrains the firm's goals, its activities, and, thereby, its profitability. OT also does not buy into the economic notion of profit maximization. Average profits will do just fine, according to OT.

Some see the publication in 1532 of Niccoló Machiavelli's classic, *The Prince*, with its focus on organizational politics and power as laying the foundation for what later became OT. Adam Smith's *An Inquiry into the Nature and Causes of the Wealth of Nations* 144 years ago focused on the importance of the division of labor as a source of nations' wealth. A little over a century later, Frederick Taylor began the "scientific management movement" with his studies of piece rates and efficiency; his book *The Principles of Scientific Management* was published in 1911.

At about the same time, German sociologist Max Weber wrote about three types of political domination: *charismatic, familial,* and *legal;* he argued that all relationships between rulers and those they govern can be studied with the underpinnings of this three-legged stool. It was Weber, of course, who also brought us the idea of *bureaucracy,*[1] which he envisioned as the ultimate and unbiased rational-legal structure free of politics. The public choice school of economics for which James Buchanan won the Nobel Prize in 1986 has since proved otherwise: Bureaucrats and politicians are human beings with the same wants, needs, and motivations as the rest of us.

On the heels of Weber's book came the empirical work of researcher Elton Mayo and his colleagues at Western Electric Company's Hawthorne plant outside Chicago. Their work found that a slight improvement in workplace lighting improved worker productivity significantly, but only temporarily. The work of Mayo and his colleagues launched what became known in the OT literature as the human relations movement.

---

[1] His classic, *Economy and Society,* was published in 1922, two years after he died.

In 1938, the CEO of New Jersey Bell Telephone Company, Chester Barnard, wrote *The Functions of the Executive*.[2] In the words of contemporary management scholar Joe Mahoney of the University of Illinois, "This book is the most high-powered intellectual contribution to organization or economic theory ever written by a practicing manager."[3] Barnard saw executives as having three essential responsibilities:

1. Promoting and facilitating communication among members of their organization.
2. Maintaining organizational cohesiveness and stability of authority as underpinnings to the willingness of employees and external stakeholders to serve the organization.
3. Creating a tone of "personal integrity, self-respect, and independent choice."[4]

Mahoney continues:

> Barnard maintains that successful cooperation in or by formal organizations is the abnormal, not the normal, condition. We observe from day to day the successful survivors among innumerable organization failures. Failure to cooperate, failure of cooperation, failure of organization, disorganization, dis-integration, destruction of organization—and re-organization—are the characteristic facts of human history.

> The executive is critical. Executives inculcate belief in a common purpose. More concretely, executives synthesize the actions of contradictory forces and reconcile conflicting instincts, interests, conditions, positions, and ideals.[5]

Barnard's singular focus on executives is the reason that, in our own work advising owners and CEOs of middle-market companies, we are stern judges of how they do what they do and why they do it. It starts at the top. If those people do not get it right, no one else in the organization will, either. This is one dimension of organization that is top down. For all the bottom-up factors to work as they should, the few top-down forces have to be hitting on all cylinders.

Other scholars followed Barnard. Herbert Simon, a psychologist and cofounder of the so-called Carnegie School of Management, won his Nobel

---

[2] Barnard, *Functions of the Executive*.
[3] Mahoney, *Economic Foundations of Strategy*, 3.
[4] Ibid.
[5] Ibid., 3–4.

Prize in economics but much of his work was in OT.[6] He was a prodigiously productive researcher, churning out, either by himself or with a coauthor, such classics as *Administrative Behavior* (1947) and *Organizations* (1958, with James G. March). He was an authority—some would argue *the* authority—on artificial intelligence and decision-making. He gave us such memorable phrases as "bounded rationality" and "satisficing." He refuted the neo-classical view that individuals always maximize. Simon said that people do not have enough time to do that, so they select the first workable solution they can find; he calls that "satisficing."

Two other books merit mention in the OT literature. The first is *A Behavioral Theory of the Firm*.[7] Like the work of Simon, this book confronted the firm-as-profit-maximizing-production-function construct of neoclassical economics and, at least in my view, sent it packing because it looked at how organizations actually function.

The second, *Organizations in Action*,[8] was written by the late James Thompson. His death at an early age (53) makes his work underappreciated, in my view. But I inhaled his book while I was in the Ph.D. program in strategic management at Oklahoma State, and it continues to have great influence on our work with clients. I tried to inhale Barnard, too, but came down with a terrible case of intellectual indigestion. Thompson was the driving force behind the founding of the preeminent OT journal today, *Administrative Science Quarterly*. It is a great publication, one that is quite comprehensible to nonacademics. The only thing that is predictable about this quarterly publication is that every issue will have at least one paper that is riveting. It also carries great book reviews.

One of the central contributions of *Organizations in Action* was the notion that organizations will buffer their "technical core" from environmental uncertainty. That is, they will do whatever they have to do to protect their primary distinctive capabilities from being disrupted. Thompson's thrust was to reduce risk by removing uncertainty. Funny thing. He was way ahead of the valuation community. He couched the argument in the context of asserting three distinct levels of responsibilities and control within enterprises: the *technical*, the *managerial*, and the *institutional*. The managerial level is the liaison between the technical core, its outputs, and the inputs it needs, while the institutional level obtains legitimacy for the organization and its goals from its external environment.

---

[6] For a sense of this remarkable man, see www.acm.org/crossroads/dayinlife/bios/herbert_simon.html and http://nobelprize.org/nobel_prizes/economics/laureates/1978/simon-autobio.html

[7] Cyert and March, *Behavioral Theory*.

[8] Thompson, *Organizations in Action*.

Thompson also brought us the crucial concept of organizational boundaries—what should be done inside (critical technologies) and what should be outsourced (almost everything else). Most organizations do too much inside (think accounting firms building their own Web sites), outsource the wrong processes (think hotels and Internet connections), and, once they outsource it, tend to ignore it (think "pooled" airline mechanics at smaller U.S. airports these days). Thompson's thinking also foreshadowed strategic alliances, the resource-based view of the firm, and the "new" institutional economics. Forty years later, in our own work advising clients on organizational design issues, his book is at the forefront of my thinking.

Prominent OT scholars today are Oliver E. Williamson (University of California, Berkeley), Jeff Pfeffer (Stanford), Jim March (Stanford), Gareth Morgan (York University), Howard Aldrich (University of North Carolina, Chapel Hill), Dick Daft (Vanderbilt), and Henry Mintzberg (McGill University). After appearing for years in lists of prospective Nobel laureates in economics, Williamson won in 2009. March remains a prime candidate.

Perspective

OT sees companies as *open systems*. In contrast to *closed systems*, open ones interact with and depend on their external environments. As a result, they must continually change, evolve, and adapt. Open systems can be complex. Complexity can impede efficiency, and that is sometimes a major obstacle. Because companies depend on their environments, their functioning is susceptible to external disturbances and uncertainty. Through it all, however, companies depend on their environments to provide them with inputs (a form of resources) and to buy their outputs. The interdependency and the threats that can arise from outside means that those inside must cooperate and find ways to work together.

OT comes in two flavors: micro and macro. On the micro side, the unit of analysis is often the company itself, but it could be a group or department within the enterprise, depending on the situation and the problems being addressed.

OT at the micro level sees organizations through two lenses:

1. **Contextual dimensions**
   - **Size.** How many people does this organization employ?
   - **External environment.** How do outside forces affect the firm?
   - **Goals.** What makes this outfit different from all the others?
   - **Technology.** What is the nature of primary process by which organizational inputs are converted into outputs? In professional

services firms, it is organizing knowledge and information. On college campuses, it is classrooms. In a manufacturing plant, it is the production line. In distribution, it is purchasing and logistics.

2. **Structural dimensions**
   - **Centralization.** At what level are most day-to-day decisions made?
   - **Complexity.** How many activities, locations, or departments comprise the firm? *Vertical* complexity means how many levels there are in the organization. *Horizontal* complexity is the number of departments that are shown laterally across the company. *Spatial* complexity is the number of geographic locations a company has. If any one of these increases, so does complexity.
   - **Formalization.** How many pages of documentation are there about the organization, and how it should work? More documentation leads to greater formalization (think military procurement).
   - **Standardization.** Is work performed the same way in most organizational subsystems? Or is it situation-dependent and fluid?
   - **Specialization.** How much division of labor is there within the company? In other words, does each employee do only a narrow range of tasks, or does each do a broad range?
   - **Hierarchy.** How "steep" or "flat" is the shape of the organization chart? This reflects its "span of control."
   - **Configuration.** What are the various personnel ratios? For instance, what is the *administrative ratio* (the number of FTEs doing administrative tasks ÷ total people on the payroll)?
   - **Professionalism.** How much education and training is necessary for the average employee? This is most often measured by years of education.

These 12 variables can and should be analyzed by valuation professionals. Consistent with the simplicity of the preceding variables, the analysis is neither time-consuming nor complicated. We come away with insights and enhanced understanding of why the company is the way it is. There is that word again: *Why?*

On the macro side of OT, we have the relationships between the company and its external environment. Chapter 3 dealt with forces in the company's competitive *domain*. OT brings us a crucial set of forces called the *macroenvironment*. As with the industry/strategic group, the *unit of analysis* in the macroenvironment is the domain itself. Every player within a domain will have the same macroenvironment risk premium. Does that mean that the opportunities and threats from the macroenvironment *affect* every player the same way? No. How a given player is affected depends on its own *internal* strengths and weaknesses. It does mean that the macroenvironmental risk profile for every player in a given domain is identical. That is something that bears repeating.

Tenets

Within OT today, the major tenet is the notion of *contingency*. Many organizational issues can be solved in similar fashion across companies and domains. But many cannot because, at some level, every organization is different from every other one. That makes for contingency relationships, which means that one characteristic depends on another, which depends on another, which depends on another, and so forth. As in business valuation, the answer to many specific questions about a given organization "depends" on the facts and circumstances of that company. There are no one-size-fits-all sure-fire set of principles that will apply to every organization. So most organization variables, including the five that make up SPARC are contingent ones.

Not surprisingly, OT research focuses on contingencies. Scholars aim to determine and measure relationships between key variables so that they can better understand which features help firms deal successfully with certain conditions in the external environment. The environment itself and its size and technology are key contingent variables.

Understanding the configuration of a company's contingent relationships is essential to unlocking business wealth. That is why cookie-cutter approaches to valuation and value enhancement not only cannot work but also, in our view, constitute professional malpractice. Valuation is damnably complicated, multidisciplinary, ambiguous, and demanding work. We need all the tools we can find in whatever quarters we can find them. Not even the wide-ranging arsenal of tools in this book is complete. No toolkit ever can be. That is the nature of the organizational beast.

Tools

Organization theory has a set of tools that differs in substantial ways from those in the other disciplines in this book. For one thing, several of them—organization structure, distinctive competence, and culture—will already be familiar to most readers. It is crucial, however, to use these and other tools as organization theorists use them: to be able to recommend solutions to company problems based on the relationships among variables. That is the essence of the contingency school of OT.

Macroenvironment

Boundaries

Organization structure

Distinctive competence

Integration and differentiation

Organization archetypes

Culture

Macroenvironment

The most remote set of forces that affect performance reside in the macro-environment. As the domain level, the unit of analysis here is the industry or strategic group. Forces in the macroenvironment are generally exogenous (i.e., companies exert almost no control over them). Exhibit 4.1 shows six forces comprising the macroenvironment.

The inner band of each dimension elaborates on the meaning or the dimensions of the outer band. We place the organization's triangle inside the graphic so that we keep in mind that a key responsibility of senior management is to procure the resources that allow the company to insulate itself from threats and to position itself to seize opportunities. Managers do this by keeping weaknesses from being fatal and by cultivating strengths that create distinctive advantage.

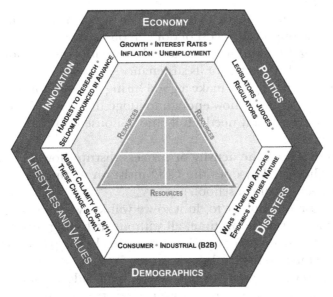

Exhibit 4.1   The Macroenvironment

Boundaries

As suggested earlier in this chapter, the boundaries question revolves around which activities the firm will do for itself and which it will outsource. Core processes, of course, stay inside because they require the control of the company. The harder question is what "noncore" processes to keep inside.

Many middle-market enterprises do far too much inside. They build their own Web sites. They prepare their own payrolls. They design their own ads and place their own advertising. Some of them even, heaven forbid, write their own computer code for applications and processes for which off-the-shelf software is easily and economically available.

Ask them why they do all this, and they will tell you, without a hint of doubt, "Because we can't afford to pay someone else to do it." If you press them, sooner or later you will hear, "You don't understand. Our business is different." *Our business is different.* We have heard that so often we made an acronym out of it: OBID. When we hear OBID, we know it is their last line of defense for doing something they should not be doing, or vice versa.

What factors drive the decision to outsource or insource a given process or activity? In no particular order, they include:

- How important is it to the daily functioning of our business? In other words, how *valuable* is it? (Do we really need someone inside who is an HR expert?)
- How often do we need to have it done? (Corporate income tax returns?)
- Do we have the expertise to do it? (Write our own advertising?)
- What is the opportunity cost of doing it ourselves? (How much revenue could we generate if we outsourced Web site construction to a company that did Web sites for its sustenance?)
- Do we know enough to make a good hiring decision for someone to do it inside, and do we know enough to judge that person's performance? (Does our firm really need a full-time in-house information technology [IT] staffer?)
- How much does the activity or process disrupt how we make money around here? (Why does the CEO insist on writing legal documents without benefit of law school?)
- Can we use technology to do it so we will know it got done, got done right, and got done on time, all without us having to invest a ton of time in a learning curve? (Why write checks for payroll tax deposits and take them to the bank?)
- If we know we are going to have to bring it inside sooner or later, does it make sense to do so now, so we can learn while the cost of learning

is not astronomical? (How big do we have to be to justify doing our own accounting rather than having our accounting firm do it?)

Few business owners in our stable have ever heard the phrase "opportunity cost." We believe that is one of the most important considerations in deciding what to outsource. It is just as important, however, in deciding what to keep inside.

For instance, Beckmill Research is hell-bent on differentiating what we do and how we do it. The most durable way we leave the message of differentiation in a client's mind is the appearance of our finished work product. Some valuation professionals have their own administrative staffers proof and edit the report, and then take a CD-ROM out to print and bind the written document. Even then, typos remain in the report, and the binding can appear, well, cheesy.

Every report in our shop is read at least three times—twice silently and once aloud. I can hear it now: "You read your report *aloud?*" Yup. We do that because our ears hear things our eyes will never see, especially when they have been over and over and over the same written document dozens of times. If we use the same 50-cent word four times in two sentences, we will pick that up in the read-aloud. At least, we better!

We also have a color laser printer. Not just any color laser, but a *solid ink* printer that prints *duplex.* Why solid ink? Well, the ink reflects light. Clients love the colors. Why duplex? Any knucklehead can print a one-sided report. Few can do two sides without disrupting their processes and taking forever.

Differentiation? You bet.

What else do we do inside that is unusual? Well, we have our own server in-house, two of them, in fact. We host our own e-mail. We write most of the copy that is on our Web site. We have just launched a quarterly newsletter entitled *Valuation at the Bar.*

Living as we do in the Virginia countryside, we have had to make significant investments in infrastructure. For instance, we have a T-1 line coming into our large home office. After a three-day power outage a couple of years ago, we bit the bullet and invested in 20-kilowatt propane-powered generator that comes on automatically whenever there is a hiccup in our electrical service. It seemed that every outage occurred when we were on deadline. We also have a dedicated exercise room (treadmill, elliptical, strength machine, TV with TiVo) that helps when the business gets stressful, as it does on occasion.

What do we not do ourselves? Well, we do not do our own advertising, lay out our own business cards, design our own brochure, or host our own Web site. We do not do our own lawyering, prepare our own tax returns, or manage our own management of retirement funds. We are not do-it-ourselvers when it comes to protecting our firm's intellectual property. We outsource IT monitoring and maintenance, which is provided to us 24/7.

Organization Structure

Most of us think of structure in terms of "org charts." Those can be helpful, depending on what they contain. We like to see not just the name of a department or function but also who is in charge of it and how many people she oversees. That gives us insights into "span of control" (how many direct reports?) and also into the design of the organization itself. Structure is part of design, which is a broader concept that includes, among other things, incentives and boundaries.

Many smaller companies devote little attention and even less energy to structure. They think it is for "big corporations." We disagree. We once saw a 32-person company that had more layers in its org chart than Toyota!

Then again, there are org charts, and then there are org charts. There is the formal one, and there is the informal one. If your client hands you one, ask which it is and how the informal one differs. If you are told, "There is no difference," duck.

Org charts come in different configurations. The most basic structure is the *simple* (entrepreneurial) one: Everyone reports to the founder. (We once saw that in a 44-employee company whose owner wondered why he was working 20 hours a day.) Once headcount gets out of single digits, and sometimes sooner, it is time to move up the food chain, probably to a *functional* structure. We say "probably" because, if the company has more than one physical location, functional is likely not the best choice.

In a functional structure, organization is by division of labor. For instance, there might be an operations department, a sales department, and an accounting department, to name just three. Each has someone in charge, and that someone oversees subordinates and usually reports to the president or owner. This is the first stage of *delegation* of authority. Some entrepreneurs never get there because they would rather be in control than be rich. That is why many small companies stay that way. Delegating can be a tall emotional order.

Functional structures tend to promote silos. That is, if the issue is not in "my department," it is not "my problem." It also encourages specialization. That is not all bad—specialization usually increases productivity. But it does so at the cost of perspective.

If the company decides to open up a second office, then things get really interesting. If the second location is the first one in a different place, then the question is whether it is time to move up to the next rung of the org-structure ladder: the *divisional* structure (i.e., "the M-form"). A general manager (GM) heads a division, which comprises at least Operations and Sales, whether for a geographical area, a product line, or a market segment. The GM usually has "P&L responsibility," which means that he is responsible for his location's income statement. Unfortunately, there is seldom also a balance sheet, which means that the GM is never exposed to managing assets, to understanding the internal controls governing those assets, or to earning a return on them. Even if each location has its own balance sheet, it will rarely have its own bank account. Even so, a balance sheet is a useful tool for management learning, besides helping with internal controls.

"Line" activities (e.g., operations and sales) are usually decentralized, but most "staff" functions (accounting, HR, etc.) are centralized. That is because the scale economies to be had in staff functions are hard to realize if those activities are geographically dispersed. Line functions tend to deliver higher performance when they are closer to the customers. That matters less with staff slots.

Every now and then, a truly one-off situation lands on our radar screen. A niche manufacturing client several years ago had part of its manufacturing at its headquarters location and another part about 27 miles away. The off-site plant did the first and last stages of production, while all the rest of the work was done at the main facility. It was a process manufacturer, so big 18-wheelers continually shuttled back and forth between the two facilities. Sometimes employees in one place did not have anything to do as they awaited the arrival of a truck from the other place. It was foolish and expensive. Ultimately, the majority shareholder had to sell out for a pittance.

Distinctive Competence

The phrase "distinctive competence" originated in a classic OT book about the Tennessee Valley Authority.[9] Trained as a sociologist, he and Simon were the preeminent organization theorists of the 1940s. Simon attached primacy to "distinctive competence" in his classic *Leadership in Administration*.[10] He wrote:

> We shall stress that the task of building special values and a distinctive competence into the organization is a prime function of leadership.[11]

---

[9] Selznick, *TVA.*
[10] Simon, *Leadership in Administration.*
[11] Ibid., 27.

"Distinctive competence" is sometimes used interchangeably with "core competence."[12] That is not wrong, but we much prefer Selznick's term, and for a simple reason: It connotes uniqueness, the essence of differentiation.

We ask the following question early on in our relationship with a client: "Why do customers do business with your company instead of with your closest competitor?" We are looking for what the enterprise sees as its unique attribute. Our follow-up, of course, is: "How do you measure that?"

A client in the mid-1990s made a gadget that had the potential to inflict major damage on demand for commercial solid-waste-hauling services. In our visit preceding the launch of the engagement, we asked the CEO those two questions. His answers were "Customer service," and "We talk to our customers," respectively. I looked him in the eye and said, "You know, John, the plural of anecdote is data. Where's your data?" After much oral fencing back and forth, he confessed his company had none.

We were impressed with the company's product. However, the firm was staggering, lurching from cash crisis to cash crisis. The majority owners had other business interests and decided they wanted to get this particular headache out of their lives. They contacted us to get a preliminary idea of what the company might be worth. When the CEO confessed to having no data, we said that we thought his company would be far better served by a customer satisfaction survey that had a multiple regression statistical design built into it. We said we might find out that his company's customer service either was not all he thought it was or, more likely, was not what drew customers into the fold in the first place. He went for it.

The company had seven key selling points for its $8,000 contraption. Its target market was fast-food stores, cafeterias, and nursing homes. Its sales force was having trouble closing sales. Worse, those doing the selling could not make as many sales calls as the price point required in order to realize sufficient revenue. The scaled survey instrument we designed for its 700+ customers asked (1) how important each of the company's seven selling points was to that customer, and (2) how well the firm performed on each point. Five of the seven, including customer service, turned out to be unimportant.[13]

Based on our interviews with the salespeople, we concluded that they could sell only between the hours of 9 and 11 a.m. and 1 and 4 p.m. The rest of the time, the manager to whom they would make their pitch was

---

[12] Prahalad and Hamel, "Core Competence."

[13] Customer service did not matter because the gizmo was so well designed that it failed only when it was not properly maintained. Maintenance was basic, simple, and inexpensive.

too busy to see them. Clearly every minute in those two sales windows was valuable.

We recommended the hiring of a college student to "dial for dollars"—call geographical clusters of prospective customers and set up sales appointments an hour apart. That would be 25 per week per sales person. We also advised the company to get rid of the five irrelevant selling points. Besides, we said, "A fast-food store manager doesn't have the attention span to sit still for a seven-item sales pitch." What happened as a result of this double-barreled approach of a telemarketer making appointments and of simplifying the sales pitch? As we noted in Chapter 2, revenues doubled in 90 days. Ownership remains intact.

Integration and Differentiation

The twin notions of integration and differentiation[14] represent a different view of organization structure. They are two of the linchpins of the contingency approach to understanding organizations. They came to the fore in 1967 through the research of two scholars at the Harvard Business School, Paul Lawrence and Jay Lorsch. Their book, *Organization and Environment: Managing Integration and Differentiation,* is another classic in the OT literature. A brief overview follows.

The functions within an organization are different ("differentiated") from each other, but they must also cooperate in order to achieve organizational objectives. The cooperation requires "integration" mechanisms. More specifically, *differentiation* in an OT context is about interdepartmental differences in time horizons, formality, goals, and interpersonal norms. Lawrence and Lorsch found that greater task certainty correlates with greater formality and greater centralization. Hence, an accounting department would have high formality, high centralization, and short-term goals (e.g., close the books on time and accurately each month). The nature of the work in a research and development (R&D) department, in contrast, makes for high uncertainty. Therefore, it would be characterized by greater informality, more collegiality, and more individual responsibility for decision making. *The greater the differentiation among departments, the greater are the levels of integration they require.* Integrative tools include hierarchy, rules, integrating individuals, and entire integrating departments.

The contingency factor that drives the required organizational structure (read "differentiation and integration") is the rate of change—in products, markets, and process technology—in the external environment. The lower the rate of change, the lower the uncertainty. That means greater

---

[14] Differentiation in an OT context is not the same as a strategy of differentiation.

centralization, more formality, and lower need for R&D. It also reduces differentiation, which suggests that hierarchy and rules will likely do the job as integrating mechanisms.

Lawrence and Lorsch made their inferences from studying, first, six companies that developed, made, and marketed plastics. They later extended their observations to two container companies and two food-processing firms. Neither the external environment nor internal integration/differentiation was measured directly. Instead, these forces were characterized by executives' responses to extensive questionnaires. Thus the inferences were drawn from perceptions, not from direct measurements.

A key finding of their research was that, in situations involving high integration, the "integrators" (people or departments) could not use power or evasiveness to resolve conflicts. Instead, conflicts needed to be confronted by facing facts. In fact, confronting turned out to be the best way to resolve conflict in all the companies studied. Therefore, it is not a contingency tool but a "universalistic" one. That is, it can be used in all situations without regard for specific circumstances. But keeping the focus on facts, not personalities, is the key.

Organization Archetypes

Organization archetypes[15] differ from the organization structures we discussed earlier in this chapter. The archetypes herein derive from the kind of work done and how it is coordinated. Those we discuss briefly here are, in truth, *configurations*. That means interlocking components, not silhouettes or perimeters (e.g., "steep" or "flat"). The visual differences between configurations and structures are striking. We will get to them shortly.

Thirty years ago, scholar Henry Mintzberg conducted an exhaustive study of the literature about organizational design. His key finding, which was most unexpected: "Five" really matters. He even wrote a book about it, *Structure in Fives: Designing Effective Organizations.*[16] His findings have held up for over 25 years. He found five of each of the these:

- Basic organizational "configurations"
  Simple
  Machine bureaucracy
  Professional bureaucracy

---

[15] Not to be confused with the SPARC archetypes that are the subject of Chapter 12.
[16] Mintzberg, *"Structure in 5's."*

Divisionalized form

Adhocracy

- Basic parts of any organization

   Operating core. Those producing the basic outputs

   Middle line. Those between the core and the apex

   Technostructure. Analysts, accountants, schedulers, planners

   Support staff. Indirect support (payroll, legal, HR, etc.)

   Strategic apex. Senior managers

- Basic coordinating mechanisms

   Mutual adjustment. Individuals coordinate their own work

   Direct supervision. Hovering-type oversight

   Standardization of work processes. Orders, rules, procedures

   Standardization of outputs. Output specs/performance measures

   Standardization of skills. Internalized knowledge and skills

- Contingency factors of organization

   Age

   Size

   Technical system

   Environment

   Power

Mintzberg wrote:[17]

> Each of the five configurations relies on one of the five coordinating mechanisms and tends to favor one of the five [basic] parts. In Simple Structure, the key part is the strategic apex, which coordinates by direct supervision; the structure is minimally elaborated and highly centralized; it is associated with simple, dynamic environments and strong leaders, and tends to be found in smaller, younger organizations or those facing severe crises.

> The Machine Bureaucracy coordinates primarily by the imposition of work standards from the technostructure; jobs are highly specialized and formalized, units functional and very large (at the operating level), power centralized vertically at the strategic apex with limited horizontal decentralization to the technostructure; this structure tends to be found

---

[17] Ibid.

in simple, stable environments, and is often associated with older, larger organizations, sometimes externally controlled, and mass production technical systems.

The Professional Bureaucracy relies on the standardization of skills in its operating core for coordination; jobs are highly specialized but minimally formalized, training is extensive, and grouping is on a concurrent functional and market basis, with large-sized operating units, and decentralization is extensive in both the vertical and horizontal dimensions; this structure is typically found in complex but stable environments, with technical systems that are simple and non-regulating.

In the Divisionalized Form, a good deal of power is delegated to market-based units in the middle line (limited vertical decentralization), whose efforts are coordination by the standardization of outputs, through the extensive use of performance control systems; such structures are typically found in very large, mature organizations, above all, operating in diversified markets.

Adhocracy coordinates primarily by mutual adjustment among all of its parts, calling especially for the collaboration of its support staff; jobs are specialized, involving extensive training but little formalization, units are small and combine functional and market bases in matrix structures, liaison devices are used extensively, and the structure is decentralized selectively in both the vertical and horizontal dimensions; these structures are found in complex, dynamic environments, and are often associated with highly sophisticated and automated technical systems.

As valuation professionals, we are in the business of diagnosing what is right and not-so-right in client organizations. A key aspect of that—and one that is easy to do early on—is to see if the archetype, its key part, and its major coordinating mechanism are in sync. If they are not, well, company-specific risk probably just went up again.

Culture

Arguably the most underappreciated explanatory variable in understanding why an organization is the way it is is its *culture*. Definitions abound, but we like one we read in *Fortune* in 1983:[18]

---

[18] Uttal, "The Corporate Culture Vultures."

A system of shared values (what is important) and beliefs (how things work) that interact with a company's people, structure, and control systems to produce behavioral norms (how we do things around here)

MIT's Edgar Schein, arguably the country's preeminent authority on the subject, asserts that organizational culture rests on a three-legged stool:

1. **Artifacts.** Observable to outsiders but without revealing the underlying logic. Examples: architecture; technology; behavior patterns.
2. **Values and beliefs.** These determine what constitutes acceptable behavior within a given organization. Grasping these helps us understand the rationale for that behavior, which is sometimes off-the-charts goofy.
3. **Basic underlying assumptions.** For longtime organization members, these are nearly subconscious because they are taken for granted. These define the thoughts, perceptions, and even the feelings of those members.

Every company has a culture. It has its roots in the values, beliefs, and behaviors of the founder. The older the company, the more ingrained the culture . . . and the harder it is to change. Ask General Motors. The political obstacles to cultural transformation in a company that has been around for a while, even if it has only a few dozen employees, are daunting. A critic of a culture is often relegated to the same class as one who would say to the proud parents of a newborn, "Wow. Your baby is really ugly."

Moreover, the prospect of cultural transformation affects employees' status, power, feelings of self-worth, and, indeed, bank accounts. How they are perceived inside the company is often the root of their identity. It has much to do with how they are seen outside it, too. It has put their kids through college, paid for the big house in the upscale neighborhood, and created a position of respect and probity in the larger community in which they live.

Therefore, longtime employees, especially, will fight like alligators, though usually covertly, to preserve the status quo. Why not? What do they have to lose? To them, it is kill or be killed. Again, the sad case of General Motors is instructive. It could not change if it wanted to, and it does not, no matter what ex-CEOs Rick Wagner and Fritz Henderson and everyone else says.

Another example is Russia. When Mikhail Gorbachev came to power in the old Soviet Union in 1985, many in the West gushed because he had an American Express card and his wife wore Gucci. But in what kind of organizational *culture* had Gorbachev been successful? It was the same one that produced Stalin, Trotsky, and Lenin.

The inability to change cultures probably explains much of the organizational mortality that characterizes capitalism. Recall Schumpeter's "creative destruction." For every Google, there are 100 Compaqs, Digital Equipments, Commodores, and Altairs. At one point early in the twentieth century, there were over 100 automobile manufacturers in the United States. Remember the Peerless? The Duryea? The Stearns? The Winton? The Hupp? The Jordan? The Baker? No? And those were just the car makers in *Cleveland!*[19]

Unlocking Business Wealth

With the exception of organization structure and culture, both of which command some ink in the business press, few tools on the OT workbench are much appreciated. Fewer still are used by valuation professionals. The power of OT tools lies in their ability to help us understand *why*, usually in a contingency context. Their power is diagnostic, not firm-changing. But if we cannot explain why the company is where it is, performing as it is, then we cannot devise a value map that will show the way to where it can be. OT tools are essential, if not glamorous.

When a new managing partner tries to run an accounting firm or law firm like a machine bureaucracy, we can safely predict that trouble lies ahead. Unless, of course, the firm was *always* run on the machine bureaucracy model, in which case those who work there think it is perfectly normal. We know of a venerable accounting firm like that in Tulsa. It mistreated its people, but it had a slew of longtime employees nonetheless. To them, that culture must have seemed normal; to us, it looked austere and abusive. But the firm is still around today and has several dozen employees.

In the second half of this book, we have a lot more to say about the deployment of OT tools and how they can contribute to the wealth-unlocking process. They are vital, as you will see.

Summary

In this chapter, we discussed organization theory—its history, perspective, and tenets. It is a useful discipline with a lot to offer those of us in the valuation and value-enhancing niche. We hope readers agree.

We also presented seven tools from OT. Some—structure and culture, for example—were probably familiar. Others—such as differentiation/integration and archetypes—might be new. Each is powerful. Each has a role to

---

[19] www.jcu.edu/chemistry/naosmm/2007/AutoCapital.html (accessed on January 13, 2009).

play in the diagnosis of the company's current situation. We will also see them in the value-mapping process.

Additional Reading

Aldrich, Howard, and Martin Ruef. *Organizations Evolving*, 2nd ed., Newbury Park, CA: Sage, 2006.

Allison, Graham T. *The Essence of Decision: Explaining the Cuban Missile Crisis.* Boston: Little, Brown, 1971. (In 1999, Allison, with Philip Zelikow, staff director of the 9/11 Commission, wrote a second edition.)

March, James G., Martin Schulz, and Xueguang Zhou. *The Dynamics of Rules: Change in Written Organization Codes.* Stanford, CA: Stanford University Press, 2000.

Miller, Danny, and Peter H. Friesen. *Organizations: A Quantum View.* Englewood Cliffs, NJ: Prentice Hall, 1984.

Morgan, Gareth. *Images of Organization: Executive Edition.* San Francisco: Berrett-Koehler, 1998.

Pfeffer, Jeffrey. *New Directions for Organization Theory: Problems and Prospects.* New York: Oxford University Press, 1997.

Williamson, Oliver E. *Markets and Hierarchies: Analysis and Antitrust Implications, a Study in the Economics of Internal Organization.* New York: Free Press, 1975.

Williamson, Oliver E. *The Mechanisms of Governance.* New York: Oxford University Press, 1996.

CHAPTER 5

Tools from Evolutionary Economics

Like many readers of this book, I suspect, I struggled through my first two undergraduate economics courses. The macro stuff was so abstract that it flew right over me. IS/LM curves made my eyes cross and my head hurt. The idea that anyone could predict economic futures with accuracy struck me as farfetched, at best. It made me wonder what the study of astrology might be like.

Micro did not treat me much better. As in macro, drawing and interpreting graphs based on fact patterns whose variables the instructor would then change had me thinking I was graphs-challenged and maybe downright dyslexic where economics was concerned. One thing I was sure of, though: The microeconomic view of the world I was being force-fed did not comport with anything I had seen, read, or experienced in my checkered and generally unsuccessful life outside the university. In particular, the assumptions underpinning microeconomics struck me as silly: Consumers had perfect information, companies *always* maximized profits (begging the question of what the definition of "maximized" was), there were no barriers to entry and no taxes, and there was no such thing as interdependency among competitors because, by definition, the actions of a single player had no impact on the actions or performance of any other.

I mean, we all know that any theory of human behavior is slimmed down and simplified. It has to be because we humans are complex mechanisms. Slimmed down and simplified is one thing, but ridiculous is quite another. And I found that the assumptions underpinning microeconomics undermined what I was being taught. Granted, I've not done Ph.D. work in economics. Maybe that would change my view.

The problem with the traditional approaches to economics, macro and micro, is that they deal with idealized "end states" of how the world *should* work, not how it *does* work.[1] I have no objection to idealism, of course, but I wish those dispensing it would identify it as such.

---

[1] This coulda-woulda-shoulda view is called the "normative" perspective.

So-called mainstream economists are resolutely silent on what happens between here and there—the process, if you will. If someone shows me pictures of a big trout she caught in a remote stream in Idaho but refuses to tell me how to get there or what kind of fly she fished with, well, I just come away frustrated. Traditional approaches to economics say nothing about "how to get there."

Many years later, as a Texan and Ph.D. student at Oklahoma State, I was sure that economics would never be my friend, much less a subject I took seriously. That all changed when I took two courses in industrial organization. The first focused on antitrust and regulatory economics. I found it interesting and even comprehensible, although, as in undergraduate school, the graphs still made my stomach twitch. Being required to read Bork's classic, *The Antitrust Paradox*, however, was pure joy. I understood why not one of the 80+ opinions he wrote as a sitting judge on the D.C. Circuit Court of Appeals was overturned by a then-leaning-left Supreme Court.

My intellectual fire lit up with the second course: IO as the study of industries. It was a wonderful course in the economics that I described in Chapter 3. IO was a perspective-altering experience for me. I suddenly saw every collection of similar entities as an industry. Then I began thinking that way about the countries in a hemisphere. There was USA Inc., Mexico Inc., and Canada Inc. The idea of interdependency was clear to me. What resonated about IO was that it affirmed that companies and industries are a lot more complex than the simple production function that traditional microeconomics makes them out to be. Competition is not deterministic, and companies do have some control over their destiny. The savvier (which is more about "street smarts" than I.Q.) the people running them, the more control they have.

At about the same time, I was introduced to Nelson and Winter's classic book, *An Evolutionary Theory of Economic Change*.[2] They challenged the basic precepts of microeconomics head-on. Finally, I thought as I read it, someone other than the IO economists gets it. They really get it. I did not understand all the calculus in the book, but I did not have to. You do not, either. The text is straightforward, well-written English. They knew they were iconoclasts about mainstream economics, but they went about it with civility.

Soon after I finished Nelson and Winter, Birger Wernerfelt's discipline-changing paper, "A Resourced-Based View of the Firm," sailed into print. It was short—ten pages—but it upended the perch of Michael Porter, who had held sway since the late 1970s with his IO-based "positioning school" of strategy. Wernerfelt came at the subject of company analysis not from

---

[2] Nelson and Winter, *An Evolutionary Theory.*

the product side of the microeconomists but from the resource side—the supply side, if you will. A new perspective, the resource-based view (RBV), emerged.

A recent article[3] provided some fascinating background color to what gave rise to Wernerfelt, a trained mathematical economist, writing this seminal paper. In 1983, he took a job at the University of Michigan, which assigned him to teach a graduate course in strategic management. It was not a course he knew much about. Someone gave him a recent syllabus that included the first chapter of Porter's *Competitive Strategy*. Said Wernerfelt:

> I couldn't see how this was compatible with equilibrium [the traditional approach to economics—WDM], in the sense that I was thinking, "so we are educating 50,000 MBAs a year and now they all learn that such and such is an attractive industry and therefore they all enter that industry." And now it's going to stop being attractive real quick.[4]

He went on:

> It just struck me that unless you put something in, that could generate some heterogeneity in the strategies, the five forces offers just a recipe for disaster . . . so I wrote this thing down (as a teaching note) and it was not something that took me any time. I mean, it was just like "Oh, this is obviously the way to look at it." I often mention the example of analysts on sports television that apply these arguments all the time (i.e., that this is a tall team, so we're going to try to play a lot of high balls in the box).[5]

The essential points of Wernerfelt's paper were:

- Heterogeneity among competitors shifts the analytical focus from the domain, whether industry or strategic group, to the company.
- A company's strategy should be underpinned by its strengths.
- Future strengths will evolve from today's strengths.
- Managers need to seek out not-level playing fields where their firms' resources give them a leg up.

---

[3] Lockett, et al. "Resource-based View." Abstract is available at: http://papers.ssrn.com/sol3/papers.cfm?abstract_id=957031.
[4] Ibid., 1127.
[5] Ibid.

- Therefore, before it ever chooses where or how to compete, a company should understand its unique resources.
- Porter's idea that a firm can thrive on the incompetence, mistakes, and ineptitude of its competitors was erroneous because market mechanisms would either run such competitors out of business or teach them the errors of their ways.

Like Nelson and Winter before him, Wernerfelt paid homage to "the seminal work" of Edith Penrose.[6] As noted in Chapter 1, her primary argument was that a firm's ability to grow profitably was constrained by the abilities of its senior managers. I had seen the problem she described up close when growth exploded at United Video Inc. (UVI) where I was its CFO before getting crossways with the COO and getting fired. For a while, we compensated for what we did not know by working 100-hour weeks.

A few years after I left, most of the top cadre had turned over, except for my successor, whom I had plucked from my corporate alma mater, Union Pacific Corporation. He was the CFO when the company, then renamed United Video Satellite Group (UVSG), went public. It bought *TV Guide* and put its content into the UVSG satellite programming guide. Top management turned over again. UVSG later merged with Gemstar. It took a while, but Gemstar hit the rocks and was taken private in an LBO.

It had come full circle: United Video was a new LBO when I joined it in 1979. Satellite communications pioneer Larry Flinn had bought it for $4.75 million ($4.5 million in debt, and $250,000 cash). The deal later made him a billionaire.

My points here are twofold: (1) the lack of management skills constrains profitable growth, and (2) companies change, whether they want to or not. These ideas bring us to evolutionary economics. The phrase itself tells the story—economic phenomena evolve. Some might call it "economics from the biological perspective." I think that is stretching it a bit, but if it helps you get your arms around it, be my guest.

Perspective

Unlike mainstream microeconomics with its cornerstones of rational people, welfare (in an economic sense) maximization, and production functions, evolutionary economics comes at economics from pillars of resource endowments, competitive heterogeneity, and interdependencies. Its perspective is the *process of change*, how and why it happens, and what the implications are

---

[6] Penrose, "Growth of the Firm." The third edition of this wonderful book came out in paperback in 1995, the year before Penrose died. Her tome is the easiest-to-understand book on economics that I've ever read.

for companies, institutions, domains, and growth. Though Nelson and Winter (and Wernerfelt and Penrose, too) were trained first as traditional neoclassical economists, they themselves evolved, and in quite different directions.

In our work at the nexus of valuation, strategy, and economics, we use the tools of evolutionary economics to help us better understand our client companies. Central to that understanding is a key question: "Why do customers do business with *this* company rather than its competitors?" Most middle-market companies think they know, if only anecdotally, why their customers do business with them. Few actually measure the "why." But as the old saying goes, "If you're not measuring it, you can't manage it."

Our perspective using evolutionary economics differs somewhat from the perspective of the discipline itself. We are interested, first, in the company's routines: *how* it does what it does. That is why we ask for a soup-to-nuts narrative of the client company's operating cycle. We want to know the sequence and the time frame of each step in that cycle. More often than some might expect, what the top dog tells us turns out not to be true. We do not get concerned about that, unless the leader wants to argue about it. At that point, she is arguing her *beliefs* against our *facts*. It is never much of a contest, and it invariably enhances our credibility with the owner or CEO.

Tenets

The underlying tenets of evolutionary economics are simple and easy to understand. First and foremost, it makes room for both entrepreneurship and innovation. Traditional economics ignores the change that these two forces impose on a free society because there is no role for either entrepreneurs or innovation in the neoclassical model.

Evolutionary economics also embraces the notion of heterogeneity among competitors. This heterogeneity has an implication for valuation professionals: Forces inside the firm account for far more variation in rates of return than do forces outside it. It also removes the valuation of private equity from the list of cookie-cutter services on which some professional-service sectors thrive. In addition, it means that we must understand *why* this company performs at the level it performs because that *why* is going to be different from the whys of its competitors. This is weighty, weighty stuff.

Tools

Evolutionary economics offers a number of tools to help valuation professionals unlock business wealth. As in prior chapters, I discourage readers from inferring the relative importance I attach to these tools from the sequence in which they are presented. I have tried to array them in an order that makes logical sense to me. I hope it does likewise for you.

Competitive heterogeneity

Resourced-based view of the firm

Routines

Capabilities

Path dependence

Innovation

The implications of growth

Competitive Heterogeneity

As noted, the idea that competitors are more different than they are alike is a key tenet of evolutionary economics. Like nearly everything else in this discipline, it is at sharp odds with the teachings of traditional microeconomics. However, evolutionary economics has one thing going for it that the neoclassicists do not have: data. Exhibit 5.1 makes that case.

Date	Citation[1] (pub/vol/pp)	Title of Paper (Author[s])	Cohort	Sources of Variation in Rates of Return (ROR)^2								
				Domain (DOM)					Company (CO)			
				IND	SG	Year	IND x Year	Total	Corporate	Firm	Firm x Year	Total
1991	*SMJ*, 12, 167-185.	How Much Does Industry Matter? (*Rumelt*)	A	8.3%	NI	0.0%	7.8%	16.1%	0.8%	46.4%	36.7%	83.9%
			B	4.0%	NI	0.0%	NI	4.0%	1.6%	44.2%	NI	45.8%
1996	*SMJ*, 17, 653-664.	Markets vs. Management: What Drives Profitability? (*Roquebert, et al.*)		10.1%	NI	0.4%	2.3%	12.8%	17.9%	37.1%	NI	55.0%
1997	*SMJ*, 18 (Summer Spec. Issue), 15-30.	How Much Does Industry Matter, Really? (*McGahan & Porter*)		8.1%	NI	NI	NI	8.1%	10.5%	35.0%	NI	45.5%
				18.7%	NI	NI	NI	18.7%	4.3%	31.7%	NI	36.0%
1999	*JIE*, 47, 373-398.	The Performance of U.S. Corporations: 1981-1994 (*McGahan*)		27.9%	NI	NI	NI	27.9%	-0.1%	37.1%	NI	37.0%
				10.7%	NI	NI	NI	10.7%	-0.2%	23.7%	NI	23.5%
				14.0%	NI	NI	NI	14.0%	-0.2%	27.0%	NI	26.8%
2000	*SMJ*, 21, 739-752.	Corporate and Industry Effects on Business Unit Competitive Position (*Chang & Singh*)	A	19.4%	NI	0.9%	0.9%	21.2%	4.3%	52.7%	NI	57.0%
			B	25.4%	NI	0.3%	1.8%	27.5%	8.5%	46.8%	NI	55.3%
2002	*MS*, 48, 834-851.	What Do We Know About Variance in Acct'g Prof.? (*McGahan & Porter*)	Hi	16.3%	NI	1.1%	NI	17.4%	23.7%	59.1%	NI	82.8%
			Lo	6.9%	NI	0.2%	NI	7.1%	8.8%	32.5%	NI	41.3%
2003	*SMJ*, 24, 1-16.	Is Performance Driven by Industry- or Firm-Specific Factors? (*Hawawini, et al.*)		6.5%	NI	1.9%	4.2%	12.6%	NI	27.1%	NI	27.1%
				11.4%	NI	1.3%	2.9%	15.6%	NI	32.5%	NI	32.5%
				8.1%	NI	1.0%	3.1%	12.2%	NI	35.8%	NI	35.8%
2003	*SO*, 1, 79-108.	The Emergence and Sustainability of Abnormal Profits (*McGahan & Porter*)		29.6%	NI	1.7%	NI	31.3%	30.0%	38.7%	NI	68.7%
				22.5%	NI	0.4%	NI	22.9%	22.8%	54.3%	NI	77.1%
2007	*SMJ*, 28, 147-167.	Firm, Strategic Group, and Industry Influences on Performance (*Short, et al.*)		14.7%	6.4%	NI	NI	21.0%	NI	79.0%	NI	79.0%
				19.2%	15.0%	NI	NI	34.2%	NI	65.8%	NI	65.8%

							DOM			CO	
JIE = Journal of Industrial Economics							17.7%		MEANS	51.4%	
MS = Management Science											
SMJ = Strategic Management Journal				standard deviation			8.3%			20.0%	
SO = Strategic Organization											

average R^2 if in a narrow range; presented separately if range isn't narrow

NI =   Not Included in research

Mean R^2 of Company effects	51.4%	© 2009
Mean R^2 of Domain effects	17.7%	BECKMILL RESEARCH
Company R^2 ÷ Domain R^2 =	**2.9**	www.beckmill.com

Exhibit 5.1   Selected Papers (1991-2007): Sources of Variation in Rate of Return

The exhibit summarizes nine papers published in top-tier academic journals over a 16-year period. They come from different scholars using different data sets, different methodologies, and different time frames. Overall, company-level sources account for 2.9 times as much variation in rate of return as do domain sources. But each paper sends the same message: Companies within an industry (read "domain") are more different from one another than are industries themselves. That notion, above all, is at loggerheads with traditional microeconomics.

Now, in my valuation work, I am about what is, not what might be. Therefore, I go where this research points me: I spend the lion's share of my time on the *company* level of unsystematic risk. Domain analysis matters, to be sure. We must analyze it. But the company itself matters much more. That might seem logical to readers, but it is nice to have data backing us up. These data will give us serious ammunition for what follows later in this chapter and in this book.

For now, though, know that these published papers affirm and reinforce the data from Morningstar/Ibbotson and from Duff & Phelps: In the valuation of SMEs, unsystematic risk is a big deal. In our view, it is the heart and soul of what we who value middle-market companies do.

Resource-Based View of the Firm

Now we know that companies are not homogeneous any more than the people who comprise them are. So what? Here's what: Resources. The word that subsumes those differences is *resources*. Resources are all of the strengths and weaknesses of a company. This, in turn, leads us to what is arguably the most important concept in the strategy literature in the last 25 years:[7] the resource-based view of the firm.

The RBV has two premises:

1. Every company has a unique endowment of resources.
2. That endowment is immobile and nonportable.

These tenets make for great diversity among firms. That notion of differences among firms also resonates with what biology teaches about survival: Diversity matters.

Evolutionary economics theorizes that firms are different. The published research affirms that. Differences are rooted in resources *and in how*

---

[7] That literature, incidentally, is nothing if not multidisciplinary, just as the general manager's job is itself multidisciplinary.

managers configure, combine, and modify those resources. That makes assessing top management a key aspect of business valuation.

I hasten to add that in the United States in 2010, judging people is anything but de rigueur. In fact, if anything, being called "judgmental" is almost tantamount to being labeled a racist. But professional judgment, up close and personal, is a key aspect of our responsibilities to our clients, to the courts, to regulators, and to the public. We are just jiving all of them, not to mention ourselves, if our reports fail to present a clear-eyed view of the reality we see. We must not be mean-spirited about it, but we certainly have to spell out that reality.

Routines

First introduced in 1963,[8] routines came to the fore in 1982.[9] They are the lifeblood—the DNA, if you will—of how things get done in any organization. Here are two definitions of routines.

> Our general term for all regular and predictable behavioral patterns of firms is "routine." We use this term to include characteristics of firms that range from well-specified technical routines for producing things, through procedures for hiring and firing, ordering new inventory, or stepping up production of items in high demand to policies regarding investment, R&D, or advertising and business strategies about product diversification and overseas investment. In our evolutionary theory, these routines play the role that genes play in biological evolutionary theory. They are a persistent feature of the organism and determine its possible behavior (though *actual* behavior is determined also by the environment); they are heritable in the sense that tomorrow's organisms generated from today's (for example, by building a new plant) have many of the same characteristics, and they are selectable in the sense that organisms with certain routines may do better than others, and, if so, their relative importance in the population (industry) is augmented over time . . . [M]ost of what is *regular and predictable* about business behavior is plausibly subsumed under the heading "routine," especially if we understand that term to include the relatively constant dispositions and strategic heuristics that shape the approach of a firm to the nonroutine problems it faces.[10]

---

[8] Cyert and March, *An Behavioral Theory.*
[9] Nelson and Winter, *Evolutionary Theory*, 14–15.
[10] Ibid.

And:

> [They] include all of the processes, policies, and procedures, official and
> unofficial, formal and informal, that shape how information is gathered
> and transmitted, decisions made, resources, allocated, performance moni-
> tored, and activities controlled and rewarded. The allocation of decision
> authority within the firm—what decisions are made by which people at
> what levels, with what oversight or review—is a key element here. The pro-
> cesses also include the routines through which work is done and the mech-
> anisms through which these are altered. These features may involve
> explicit contractual elements as well as "implicit contracts," more or less
> formal, shared understandings about how things are to be done.[11]

Routines involve activities in which people engage so often that they
do them intuitively, unconsciously, and automatically. As such, they tend
to become embedded in companies' cultures. To the extent that a firm's
routines are clearly conceived and well executed, they tell a lot about how
the organization will deal with the *nonroutine* issues that arise from time to
time. Routines also guide learning and offer a path to improving efficiency.

The downside—and this is a significant exposure in most organizations—
is that they can also promote inertia, rigidity, and tunnel vision. Changing
bedrock routines is disruptive. It rattles people's comfort zones. It forces them
to think about things that either they might not want to think about or they
have never questioned. Any way one slices it, changing long-standing routines
can ruffle feathers and create conflict.

Low-value-added routines should be documented. A few days ago, I sat in
a café listening to the owner train a new employee about how to run the cash
register, select certain buttons for certain food categories, ring them up,
make change, and so on. It was the end of the day. The owner had gotten
there before dawn, so she was tired. She repeated the different routines
quickly and just once, doing it from memory. The new guy, however, was
semi–glassy-eyed, which she did not notice because she was in a hurry to
leave. I could only imagine the additional commitment of time to resolving
conflicting sources of information that she had set herself up for—with no
awareness that she had done so.

Having run a few cash registers myself and having been responsible for
others running them, I know that operating a cash register is not an activity
where creativity is welcome. It is low value but essential. Therefore, the key is
zero variation in how the task is performed. Absolutely zero. Variation means
volatility, which costs money. Memory is no substitute for documenting
routines.

---

[11] Roberts, *The Modern Firm*, 17–18.

Without that documentation, the inevitable result is chaos on either a small scale or a bigger one. The place where I have most often seen chaos in my career is in accounting departments. Having talked with many owners and operations-oriented CEOs over the years, I know that most believe that what is done in accounting has no connection—zero linkage—to a company's operations. That is demonstrably false, of course, but it is a common view. The operations of an accounting department are merely a mirror of how the business itself functions more broadly.

In January 1978, just 32 months out of undergraduate school, I was hired as the controller of a $3 million family-owned (not my family!) retailer and wholesaler of art and engineering supplies. The company had been in business since 1919 . . . and had never had a controller. My predecessor was called the office manager. The company's outside accountant had insisted on calling the next person in the job the controller. The CEO later told me that he had "no idea why" but that he went along with it anyway.

I did not spend much time inquiring as to how the accounting department was run because, at that point in my career, I had worked for two megacorporations—Union Pacific and Borg-Warner. It never occurred to me that the accounting at the small company would be any less professional than it was at my previous employers. I was in for a big surprise.

The company had two locations: one in Tulsa and the other in Arkansas. I worked at the headquarters location in downtown Tulsa. The company's flagship retail store was six or seven miles away, in southeast Tulsa. My first morning on the job, I received the handwritten "Daily Cash Report" from the big store. It had certain sales categories on it with a total. The total was then tied to the credit card transactions, checks, and cash in the register, less cash that was there to start the day. (Beginning Cash varied each day!) As I looked at the breakdown of currencies and coins, I saw 20s, 10s, 5s, 1s, 50-cent pieces (the U.S. money supply had a lot of those in those days), quarters, dimes, nickels, and pennies.

And IOUs.[12]

I gasped. IOUs?

I got on the phone, called the executive vice president overseeing the store, and gently inquired about the IOUs. The conversation went about like this:

"Oh," he said, "we make advances to our sales guys out of the cash drawer."

"No, you do not, Everett," I said. "Not anymore."

---

[12] They certainly didn't have investor-owned utilities in mind.

"But, Warren," he said, "that's the way we've done it for the last 30 years."

"Everett," I said, "if we were going to do things here the way we'd always done them, Bill would have never hired me. Please collect the cash advances by the end of the business today tomorrow. Tell me how much you want each guy's cash advance to be, and I'll get the checks cut and delivered to you this afternoon. All I ask is that your people settle up their advance in full before year-end so we don't have to risk having the IRS perceive the advances as noninterest-bearing loans. We'll have brand-new checks on your desk first thing in the morning on the first business day next year. No fuss, no muss, no bother."

"OK, Warren," he said. "But I don't understand."

"Everett," I said, "I want to make your life easier and my life easier. If we do that, we'll both live longer, and we'll have a lot more fun on our jobs. One of the keys to that is simplifying and separating some routines around here that have become commingled and convoluted over a long period of time. A cash register exists to store incoming money and make change. It has no other purpose. It's not a bank. It doesn't make loans or cash advances.

"Oh, and did you know that your cash register operations were over $10,000 short in 1977? Cash advances are one of the reasons. It's not the only one, but it's symptomatic."

He went for it.

The next morning I got my second "Daily Cash Report." I quickly skimmed it. "IOUs" wasn't there. "Petty Cash" was.

Again, I picked up the phone. "Everett," I said, "what's this petty cash stuff on this report?"

"We handle petty cash out of the cash drawers here, Warren."

"The heck you do. Stop it right now, please."

"But, Warren, you don't understand."

"And what is it that I'm missing here, Everett?"

"That's the way we've always done it."

I thought I might need a recording for the poor guy. Instead, I took a deep breath and softly repeated my script from the day before about doing things the way we had always done them. I asked him to designate someone to be responsible for petty cash. He did. We agreed that $100 would do the job.

I went next door to our downtown building and bought a small container with a lock and slots that would hold coins. I called a printer and had several pads of prenumbered petty cash receipts printed up in duplicate.

I sent the cash box, the receipts, and $100 in cash and coins to poor Everett via our delivery van. I also sent him some simple written instructions, including at what level he should ask for petty cash to be reimbursed.

From these two changes, the company's cash register operations went from over $10,000 short in 1977 to $7.18 long in 1978. The first day that the big retail store's cash drawers "balanced," I sent them a case of champagne out of my own pocket. They were flabbergasted.

Now, 31 years later, I would eat my hat if that company was still handling its cash register operations the same way. But I would bet the same principles are still in effect. Sometimes employees have lived their work lives in chaos for so long that they think it is normal. Show them a different and better way, and they quickly realize all the other things they could have been doing that would add value. So, consistent with the notion of "evolutionary," routines evolve and change. They have to. Capitalism does not allow companies to stand still.

Here is the takeaway: Show me chaos in any department in a company, and I will show you a department whose recurring, low-value-added routines are not documented. It is as sure as the sun coming up in the morning. Point this out to your clients, and you will be adding value to their companies. And to yours.

Capabilities (Dynamic and Otherwise)

Those who run the company are responsible for configuring a company's operations. That means, among other things, that they must combine a company's resources and its routines into *capabilities*.[13] As nearly as we can determine, the term "capabilities" was first used in an economic context by George B. Richardson in his classic 1972 article, "The Organization of Industry."[14] He wrote that "organizations will tend to specialize in activities for which their capabilities offer some comparative advantage."[15] It follows that companies will seek activities that permit them to draw on the same capabilities in different market segments. That, in turn, leads to what Rumelt called "related diversification,"[16] which means acquiring or starting businesses that are closely related to a firm's primary wealth-creating activities.

But just what is a capability? The Wharton School's Sid Winter (of "Nelson and Winter" fame) has probably written more on the subject than anyone else. Here is his definition:

---

[13] Whether a capability creates distinctive advantage—and, if so, the durability of that advantage—requires qualitative analysis. We covered a great tool for conducting such analysis with Jay Barney's "VRIO framework" in Chapter 3.

[14] Richardson, "The Organization of Industry."

[15] Ibid., 888.

[16] Rumelt, *Strategy, Structure.*

An organizational capability is a high-level routine (or collection of routines) that, together with its implementing input flows, confers upon an organization's management a set of decision options for producing significant outputs of a particular type.[17]

We think of capabilities as the value-creating (revenue-enhancing and/or cost-minimizing and/or rivals-disrupting) activities that a company does better than its competitors. Obviously "capabilities" and "routines" are not synonymous. Winter lists three differences:

1. Capabilities are large in terms of their scale and their significance to the firm's prospects for survival and prosperity
2. Unlike routines, which are often tacit, invisible, and automatic, capabilities are visible and known to senior managers. Capabilities are choice mechanisms that come with "decision options"; routines are not and do not.
3. "Finally, the reference to 'implementing input inflows' is a reminder that is as relevant for routines in general as for capabilities, but perhaps more significant in the context of capabilities. It is a reminder that the coordinating information flows and information processes of a capability are only its nervous system; producing output requires actual input services from its bones and muscles."[18]

Capabilities cannot be bought on a stand-alone onesie-twosie basis, of course. In fact, unless one buys an entire firm or division to get possession of desired capabilities—which, even then, is unlikely to be successful due to the "path dependence" we cover in the next section—they must be built. The building process has four key components: (1) aspiring, (2) coordinating, (3) learning, and (4) reconfiguring.[19] Because of their vital importance of capabilities in unlocking business wealth, we discuss these briefly.

Aspiring. Before it can build a capability, a firm must first aspire to do so. That sounds like a tautology, but it is not. The aspiration—which is not like the kind found in constructing a capability that other firms can emulate (think operating a new machine)—comes from someone's or several someone-ones' imagination. The aspiration might recognize external opportunities heretofore either not present or unrecognized.

---

[17] Winter, "The Satisficing Principle."
[18] Ibid., 277–278.
[19] Teece, et al., "Dynamic Capabilities."

Coordinating.   The coordination of routines within companies tends to be firm-specific. Research shows that, within an industry, variability in coordinating and integrating mechanisms is considerable.[20] This is further evidence of the viability of evolutionary perspectives of organizations. So, it follows that, since routines are the building blocks of value-creating capabilities, such capabilities themselves are also likely to be firm-specific. That subjects them to causal ambiguity (factors that cannot be observed, such as teamwork, personal relationships, etc.) and, again, to path dependence.

Learning.   When it comes to creating capabilities, the importance of an organization's capacity to learn and adapt cannot be overstated. Learning invariably involves experimenting, trying something, failing, trying again, and finally doing it better/faster/more accurately. If the learning is not done inside the firm, it will be done outside by its competitors, and then it will be a game of catch-up played by the lead dog's rules. Learning is a social undertaking that involves sharing knowledge and ideas. Silo-type organizations (e.g., General Motors) encounter huge challenges in the internal-learning arena.

Reconfiguring.   The nature of capitalism is change. Therefore, even the most value-enhancing capabilities will need to change. If they do not, either a competitor's sudden innovation will make them obsolete or the natural evolution that is the essence of capitalism will do so. Being able to reconfigure capabilities means that a firm must be flexible and also on the lookout externally for developments that call for reconfiguring its key capabilities. This is not something that comes to most market leaders naturally or easily.

My favorite examples of reconfiguring unique capabilities come from the world of professional golf. At the top of their games, Phil Mickelson and Tiger Woods[21] made major changes in their golf swings. They recognized that, if they did not, their success would not last. The agony that both went through to effect the changes was painful for their fans to watch. Neither won much for a while. But both finally mastered their new swings, and both stormed back to the top. These are truly unusual individuals because it is contrary to human nature to make big changes when avalanches of cash are landing in one's bank account.

Let me say a few words about *dynamic capabilities*. Those are capabilities that allow a firm quickly to adjust its capabilities to market changes and

---

[20] Clark and Fujimoto, *Product Development Performance*. See also a study of 18 window-air-conditioning plants in Garvin, "Organization and Management."

[21] Notwithstanding his indefensible personal lapses.

innovation. They are most often seen in technology-based industries. The classic paper on this kind of capability is the one by Teece, Pisano, and Shuen discussed in an earlier footnote.[22] I commend this seminal paper to your reading and reflection.

Aspiring, coordinating, learning, reconfiguring—these are the key stages of building new capabilities, dynamic or not, and rebuilding old ones. It sounds a lot easier on paper than it is in practice. A primary reason for the difficulty is the subject of our next section.

Path Dependence

The essence of path dependence is that history matters. What happens today is significantly affected by what happened yesterday. That is true in organizations, too, where path dependence is frequently equated with "the genes of the founder." That is not exactly true, but it is close enough. Path dependence constrains an organization's ability to search for solutions and to change. Path-dependent behavior builds on itself, which limits motivation to look elsewhere for solutions to problems. Rather, path dependence encourages minor tweaks to the same-old same-old, even if the results are monumentally inferior or inefficient. A story conveys the lesson.

It involves the typewriter, which Christopher Latham Sholes patented in 1868. However, he received many complaints that the keys jammed. He tried different keyboard configurations, which, some cynics said, were intended to slow down typists, the reasoning being that, if they could not type fast, the keys could not jam. Rearranging the keys into what is today the QWERTY keyboard eliminated the jamming problem.

At a kind of "world series of typing" held in 1888, a contestant using touch-typing on a QWERTY keyboard demolished his opponent, a break-neck hunt-and-peck artist using a different keyboard configuration. His hunting-and-pecking fingers were a blur, but he still finished far behind the "inefficient" QWERTY user, despite the fact that QWERTY required smaller, weaker fingers to hit keys that were used more frequently ("a" for the pinky finger, "o" for the fourth finger, and "e" and "* #" for the third finger). The only vowel the index fingers strike is "u."[23] QWERTY today, like the Windows operating system, is widely derided and castigated. But its presence is dominant, so it is unlikely to be dethroned anytime soon, no matter how unintuitive and illogical it is. This is a good example of why the first-mover advantage is alive, well, and real.

Path dependence bears on business valuation because of its power to help us understand why things are the way they are. It imparts sense-making

---

[22] Teece, et al., "Dynamic Capabilities."

[23] Purists will rightly argue that "y" is also an index-finger strike as in *my* and *by*.

to inefficient practices. Path dependence makes change difficult. Thus it is no accident that new ideas in industries tend to come from new players bringing different views of how things work to the competitive milieu. Because of the obstacle it poses to making drastic changes, path dependence is a key contributor to the demise of many organizations.

Innovation

Innovation is the flip side of path dependence. We remind readers that traditional approaches to economics have no role for innovation, perhaps because it is inherently disequilibrium-causing. Innovation is also not conducive to mathematical modeling, which is another strike against it in traditional microeconomics.

And when we talk about innovation in business, we do not mean the gadgets and gizmos that seem to be the typical innovations. No, the major source of business innovation is at the management level. That is the source of new practices, new processes, and new perspectives. These innovations cannot be patented. Even if they could be, it would not happen because the required disclosures would tip competitors to the details of feats shrouded in causal ambiguity and secrecy.

No, the real innovations are in routines—how things get done—and in management analysis—new ways to frame and understand the business. These are below-the-radar innovations that do not get much publicity. For instance, a longtime client of ours has fancied itself for over 60 years as a power line construction company. For decades, the lion's share of its revenues came from the "distribution" phase of delivering electricity services to businesses, government, and consumers. Power line work is dangerous. Employees in that sector do get killed because of lax safety practices. In the wake of tornados, hurricanes, and ice storms, the business can be extremely lucrative.

A new CEO took over at our client company in 1997. He had no background in either construction or electric utilities. He set about asking the kinds of dumb questions that most of us valuing a business in a domain we have never worked in before tend to ask: lots of "why" and "how" questions. It was not long before this power line construction company starting doing work on traffic signals for municipalities. With the move in some locales toward burying electrical lines underground, horizontal drilling and tunneling capabilities similar to those used in oil exploration, though not nearly as far below the surface, came into play. The problem with subterranean work is that it is not dangerous, has low barriers to entry, and is highly competitive. The new CEO determined that, to be a serious player, he had to grow the business. Grow it he did, from about 400 employees in 1997 to more than 1,700 now, and without any acquisitions. Along the way, the company began doing home electrical inspections and recommending ways to reduce fire hazards and utility bills. It also got into lucrative transmission work from which its small size had previously excluded it.

That power line construction company no longer calls itself that. It is now a "company committed to great infrastructure." That is management innovation. It is a money-maker and a wealth-creator.

The Implications of Growth

From evolutionary economics, we also get a new perspective on growth. The neoclassical view of growth did not emerge until the late 1950s. That was when economists were having a difficult time trying to explain increases in work productivity by increasing capital investments. The statistics were producing residuals (error terms) larger than the variation explained by changes in factors of production. Then economist Robert Solow wrote a paper[24] that labeled the residual "technical advance," à la Joseph Schumpeter. The idea immediately took root and sprouted among Keynesian researchers. No one ever reported to the public that neoclassical growth theory did not explain much about growth.

Here is how Nelson and Winter put it:

> The amended neoclassical formulation represses the uncertainty associated with attempts to innovate, the publicness of knowledge associated with the outcomes of these attempts, and the diversity of firm behavior and fortune that is inherent in a world in which innovation is important. Thus, it is unable to come to grips with what is known about technological advance at the level of the individual firm or individual invention, where virtually all studies have shown these aspects to be central. This has caused a curious disjunction in the economic literature on technological advance, with analysis of economic growth at the level of the economy or the sector proceeding with one set of intellectual ideas, and analysis of technological advance at a more micro level proceeding with another. . . . The tail now wags the dog. And the dog does not fit the tail very well. The neoclassical approach to growth theory has taken us down a smooth road to a dead end.[25]

So we see a direct tie between growth and innovation, neither of which the traditional approach to economics handles at all well. Luckily, heterodox economists have a different take on this. Our guiding light here is Edith Penrose.

---

[24] Solow, "Technical Change."
[25] Nelson and Winter, *Evolutionary Theory*, 202, 205.

In her classic *The Theory of the Growth of the Firm*, she saw the enterprise as a "bundle of resources," primarily human ones, which she viewed both as the key to profitable growth and as the constraint thereon. The thesis of her book is that the ability of a firm to grow profitably is constrained by its resources *and* by the skills of its managers. What she did not say was that rapid growth has impoverished far more shareholders than it has ever enriched because managers either are not prepared for the growth or do not have the skills to manage it, or both. And hiring new managers from outside in high-growth situations is the riskiest of hiring decisions.

Penrose took the average cost curve of traditional microeconomics and turned it on its head. She argued that its U-shape was a function not of the scale of output but of the rate of growth in output. Changing the rate of output affects average cost much more than steady output at a lower or higher level.

She argued that it was the *change* in rate of output that caused the sharp upward trajectory of the average cost curve. That is particularly true for many employees, who tend to function best when routines are repetitive. The repetition facilitates learning, which raises productivity. Growth creates new jobs for existing employees, who have to start all over in another new job. That jacks up per-unit labor costs.

Growth also demands new employees. Their integration into the existing labor force raises costs and stretches managers, who already have plenty to do just trying to ride the bucking bronco of growth. Faster growth also stresses existing plant capacity and wears out equipment, which requires replacement sooner, not later. This reduces cash flow and further strains resources.

Penrose's findings resonate with our experience. A $200 million company has different problems and requires different skill sets from one that takes in only $20 or $30 million, which itself is hugely different from one generating $2 or $3 million. Few managers can grow their own skills to the extent that such a revenue increase demands. The result, which in our shop we call the "Nightmare Scenario," is that the top line goes north while the bottom line heads south. Everyone is working harder, but not smarter, than before.

Rapid growth is more likely to make a company, rather than break it, if the enterprise does two things: (1) invest in infrastructure (especially IT) and (2) grow the people.[26] Without the former, the equivalent of constructing a 30-story building on a 3-story foundation is the result. It will fall down. If the people do not grow, either the bottom line sinks or new managers

---

[26] See Warren Miller, "The Grim Reapers."

have to be brought in. The latter is especially risky because, in this situation, a bad hire is worse than no hire at all.

The key is for companies to plan for growth, not react to it. No plan is perfect, of course, but any plan trumps no plan. And any plan should include the requisite investments in people and infrastructure. We have a lot more to say about the people side of those investments in several places later in this book.

Unlocking Business Wealth

Evolutionary economics offers the value-enhancing–oriented professional a panoply of wonderful tools. Where the enhancement instruments from organization theory in Chapter 4 were diagnostic, not firm-changing, these combine diagnostics and firm-changing mechanisms. Evolutionary economics is rooted in heterogeneity and differences among firms. We know from strategic management that there are two ways to compete and two spheres in which to do it: cost leadership and differentiation, respectively, and industry-wide or focus, respectively. The heterogeneity that is at the root of evolutionary economics offers a way for the firm to draw on its own unique resource endowments to create unique capabilities that are valuable, rare, imperfectly imitable, and organizationally aligned with its strategy, people, architecture, routines, and culture.

Edith Penrose's work gives us ways to help clients temper and manage rapid growth. Path dependence helps us understand why organizations do not make sea changes. That helps us be realistic in both our expectations and recommendations. The RBV reinforces all of this in its broad view of companies and how they are unique: resource portfolios.

This matters because a key value driver of value maps is pointing a way to value creation that is realistic, builds on existing capabilities and skill sets, and broadens the firm's scope while reducing its risk. The tools from evolutionary economics help keep our feet and our map firmly connected to the company's reality. That is what makes value maps so powerful yet so challenging. They are not the consultant's typical one-size-fits-all solution in search of a problem. The problem comes first.

Summary

This chapter has offered seven tools from evolutionary economics. It has described some history of the discipline, along with its perspective and basic tenets. It is a perspective that seeks to understand and explain companies not as homogeneous production functions with predefined choice sets and deterministic outcomes but as heterogeneous organisms that must evolve and change in order to avoid the creative destruction that is the essence of capitalism and free markets. There is no standing still, and there is no going back. This perspective embraces the innovation, change, and growth that traditional microeconomics glosses over. It is descriptive, not normative. Above all, it is powerful and relevant. Use it. We do.

Additional Reading

Barney, Jay B., and Delwyn N. Clark. *Resource-Based Theory: Creating and Sustaining Competitive Advantage*. New York: Oxford University Press, 2007.

Becker, Markus C. (ed.). *Handbook of Organizational Routines*. Northampton, MA: Edward Elgar, 2008.

Dosi, Giovanni, Richard R. Nelson, and Sidney G. Winter. *The Nature and Dynamics of Organizational Capabilities*. New York: Oxford University Press, 2002.

Foss, Nicolai J. (ed.). *Resources, Firms, and Strategies: A Reader in the Resource-Based Perspective*. New York: Oxford University Press, 1998.

Helfat, Constance E., Sydney Finkelstein, Will Mitchell, Margaret Peteraf, Harbir Singh, David Teece, and Sidney G. Winter. *Dynamic Capabilities: Understanding Strategic Change in Organizations*. Malden, MA: Blackwell, 2007.

Magnusson, Lars, and Jan Ottosson. *Evolutionary Economics and Path Dependence*. Northampton, MA: Edward Elgar, 1997.

Metcalfe, J. Stanley. *Evolutionary Economics and Creative Destruction* (The Graz Schumpeter Lectures). New York: Routledge, 1998.

von Hippel, Eric. *The Sources of Innovation*. New York: Oxford University Press, 1994.

Tools from Austrian Economics

The focus of the last of the conceptual chapters in our journey toward helping clients unlock the value of their businesses is on Austrian economics (AE). Unlike the evolutionary and industrial-organization subdisciplines, Austrian economics is not a school within economics but a distinct way of looking at economic phenomena. By embracing real-world analysis, it rejects the false precision of the elegant mathematics of static equilibrium analysis. Austrians believe that economies are too complicated ever to be in equilibrium; they might tend in that direction, but complexity, dynamism, time, and ignorance make achieving it tantamount to an intellectual snipe hunt.

Before getting into an overview of the history of this unique school of economics, I want to explain how I came upon it. It is relevant to the theme of this book. Like many who have sat through traditional classes in micro- and macroeconomics, I came away thoroughly dissatisfied with the subject matter, underlying theory, and enabling assumptions. But departments of economics, at least back when I was at their mercy, were closed intellectual hubs. That has not much changed today, despite compelling evidence that the Keynesianism and highfalutin mathematics to which many of today's economists steadfastly cling have almost nothing to teach us about how to think about the economic challenges of 2009. So I lived with a void. I read a paper on strategy and AE when it was first published,[1] but it did not really register with me until, totally frustrated by the inability of traditional microeconomics to shed any substantive light on my work in business valuation, I dug it out and reread it in 2005.

(continued)

---

[1] Jacobson, " 'Austrian' School of Strategy."

(*continued*)

The light bulb came on and stayed on. I have spent much of the last five years drinking from an intellectual fire hydrant that can finally quench a thirst that parched my throat for over 30 years. My AE library now exceeds 40 volumes, and I presented papers at the annual Austrian Scholars Conference in 2008, 2009, and 2010. I commend this remarkable set of ideas to you.

Hitler's march through Europe denied the postwar world the chance to avoid decades of the expensive failure of Keynesian economics. It is possible that the United States and other countries embracing free markets might have followed Hayekian economics.[2] The economists at the University of Vienna, which was Ground Zero for the Austrian movement, were mostly Jewish. They fled to different and distant refuges, and the collegial synergy that is essential in intellectual uprisings was lost.

The roots of what became Austrian economics began at the University of Salamanca in Spain in the sixteenth century. There, the Late Scholastics, a group that followed the philosophy of St. Thomas Aquinas, studied and wrote about private property, supply and demand, trade and foreign exchange rates, the subjective nature of value, the information-conveying importance of price, the state, and even inflation. Nearly 500 years later, Joseph Schumpeter called them "the first economists."

Economic historians embrace Richard Cantillon as the first great economic theorist. Not much is known about Cantillon, except that he was an ecumenical guy: an Irishman with a Spanish surname who lived in France for years. In 1732, he wrote an essay entitled *Essai Sur la Nature du Commerce en General* (*Essay on the Nature of Commerce*). In it, he defined "long-run equilibrium" as the balance of flows of income. He conceived a two-part system in which he developed a theory of price, based on costs of production, and a theory of economic output, which he based on factor inputs and technology. He thus laid the foundation for classical economics. He was also the first academic to use the word "entrepreneur." He defined it as one who had "the willingness to bear the personal financial risk of a business venture."[3]

---

[2] Indeed, Friedrich von Hayek shared the 1974 Nobel Memorial Prize in economics with Gunnar Myrdal, who later said he would never have accepted the Nobel had he known he would have to share it with Hayek. Myrdal's arrogance epitomized the view of the collectivists who held sway at the time.

[3] Sobel, "Entrepreneurship."

In 1803 economist Jean-Baptiste Say published *A Treatise on Political Economy*. In it, he proposed Say's Law (supply creates its own demand). He was among the first to observe that the value of something depends on its utility to the user, not on its costs of production; this was a radical idea at the time because of the perceived value of labor itself more than the marginal productivity of labor, which is a very different thing. Say also noted the important role of entrepreneurs in creating value by shifting resources to their highest and best uses.

Over four decades later in his 1848 book, *Principles of Political Economy*, John Stuart Mill fine-tuned the definition of "entrepreneur" first offered by Cantillon by saying that it refers to someone who assumes both the risk *and* the management of a new venture. Mill thus separated the entrepreneur from passive investors.

Less than a quarter century after Mill's seminal work, Carl Menger founded what has become known as Austrian economics.[4] Working by day as an economic journalist, he took four years to write his first book.[5] It formulated a new theory of price—value, if you will—by linking the "objectivity" of market prices set by businesses to consumers' subjective judgment of value in the choices they made. Classical economists, including Smith, Ricardo, and Hume, had ignored the role of consumer preferences in determining price. They thus explained only the supply side of supply and demand; they ignored the demand side. Menger provided a rationale for it. His book got little attention at the time, so he continued to toil alone in his intellectual vineyard.

After tutoring Hapsburg Crown Prince Rudolph for three years, Menger was appointed a full professor on the University of Vienna's law faculty by Rudolph's father, Emperor Franz Joseph, in 1879. No longer dependent for his sustenance on satisfying the daily demands of an individual employer, Menger was freed up to go after the Historical School of economics, which was then dominant in Germany and elsewhere. This school held that no general economic laws could outweigh the description of time and place and that, therefore, economic theory did not and could not exist. What mattered was merely examining and understanding history. This made for a politically convenient framework in which no government could violate economic laws because such laws did not exist. Led by Gustav Schmoller, the German historicists were dismissive of Menger's type of "abstract

---

[4] Along with Frenchman Lèon Walras and Englishman William Stanley Jevons, Menger was a founder of the "marginal revolution." The three men worked independently and used different methods to develop the theory of marginal utility, which is on of the cornerstones of modern economics.

[5] Menger, *Principles of Economics*.

theorizing." In fact, in an attempt to isolate Menger from respectable economists, the Germans had labeled his approach "the Austrian School."

Menger was not deterred. In 1883 he wrote a book that launched an
intellectual frontal assault on the Historical School.[6] The Germans
responded with fury, and what became known as the *Methodenstreit* (methodological debate) between the Austrian School and the German Historical School was joined. Eventually, with the help of Menger protégés Eugen
von Böhm-Bawerk, Friedrich von Wieser, and, later, Ludwig von Mises, the
Historical School faded away. Unfortunately, it was replaced not by the
Austrian School but by Keynesian macroeconomics and mathematical
microeconomics.[7]

In that regard, it is useful to note one name that we intentionally omit
from our list of Austrian economists: Joseph Schumpeter. Schumpeter was a
brilliant economist (e.g., he cofounded the econometrics movement in the
United States) but one whose views "evolved" seemingly as a result of what
was in political vogue at any given time. A disciple of Walrasian equilibrium
theory, Schumpeter was in no way a member of the Austrian movement,
despite the fact that he was a native of Austria who studied alongside Mises.
He was also colorful: In his later years, he was fond of saying that he aspired
to be the world's greatest economist, its greatest horseman, and its greatest
lover. "Unfortunately," he would say, "the horses are not cooperating."

Hayek (1899–1992) studied under Mises, as did Israel Kirzner and
Thomas Sowell. Kirzner, now retired from New York University (NYU), men-
tored and inspired a cadre of other economists in New York. They have now
banded together under the banner of the NYU Colloquium on Market
Institutions and Economic Processes. Others prominent in the Austrian
School were Ludwig Lachmann, Murray Rothbard, and Fritz Machlup. The
mantle of Austrian economics today is also alive and well within the
Economics Department at George Mason University, where Nobel laureates
James Buchanan and Vernon Smith hold appointments, as do Peter Boettke,
Russell Roberts, Peter Leeson, and emeritus economic historian Karen
Vaughn. It thrives, too, at the Ludwig von Mises Institute in Auburn,
Alabama, which sponsors an annual Austrian Scholars Conference and con-
ducts ongoing educational activities under the guidance of senior faculty
members such as Peter G. Klein (University of Missouri), Nicolai J. Foss
(Copenhagen Business School), and Joseph G. Salerno (Pace University).

After the Vienna core of the Austrian School fled from Hitler, the
school toiled in obscurity for over 40 years. Mises taught at NYU (his

---

[6] Menger, *Investigations.*

[7] The economic slide that began late in 2007 and helped bring the Obama Administration to
power has given a second wind to the Keynesians.

position funded by a private foundation), Machlup at Princeton, and Hayek at the University of Chicago (though at the Committee on Social Thought, *not* in the Economics Department). Realizing that Austrian scholars had almost no one to talk to who shared their views, Hayek founded the Mont Pèlerin Society in 1947; although its membership has certainly changed over the last 62 years, it remains vibrant—and almost Austrian to the core.[8]

Three events and one economic phenomenon helped resuscitate the Austrian School. All occurred in the 1970s. The phenomenon was "stagflation," an economic state in which growth is slow and inflation is high. According to Keynesian economics, such a state was impossible. The fact that it came—and stayed—for several years called the basic precepts of Keynesianism into question. Along with stagflation came the first of three events: the death of Ludwig von Mises in 1973. Mises was the reigning *éminence grise*, the guru without peer, of the Austrian School. His dominance discouraged the debates that are necessary in any intellectual movement. Even with stagflation raging, the second event would never have occurred without the death of Mises. That event was the now-famous gathering of classical liberals, as the Austrians had come to be called, in South Royalton, Vermont, in June 1974. About 40 of them converged on a crumbling old motel that had one bathroom per floor, which made for a kind of dormitory ambience in the mornings. They came to hear Israel Kirzner, Ludwig Lachmann, and Murray Rothbard hold forth on a variety of issues of the day, including Austrian capital theory (Lachmann), equilibrium versus the market process (Kirzner), and the Austrian theory of money (Rothbard). Also presenting a paper ("Inflation, Recession, and Stagflation") were Gerald O'Driscoll and Sudha Shenoy. The weeklong conference, which was organized and substantially funded by the Institute for Humane Studies, was memorialized in a book, now out of print, entitled *The Foundations of Modern Austrian Economics*.[9]

The final event, which everyone at South Royalton hoped for but no one anticipated, was the awarding of the Nobel Prize in economics to Hayek in December 1974. That, along with increasing dissatisfaction on the part of policy makers with the tools of Keynesianism, made

---

[8] A prominent exception is Richard Posner, founder of the "law and economics" movement in jurisprudence and senior judge on the Seventh Circuit Court of Appeals in Chicago. The title of his recent book, *A Failure of Capitalism: The Crisis of '08 and the Descent into Depression* (Cambridge, MA: Harvard University Press, 2009), is over the top. In it he discloses that he recently read Keynes's *The General Theory of Employment, Interest, and Money* and succumbed to its blandishments. Will the by-laws of the Mont Pelerin Society allow him to remain a member? I, for one, hope not.

[9] Dolan, *Modern Austrian Economics*.

economists more open to different ideas. The failed presidency of Jimmy Carter watered the seeds that bloomed into the rise of Reagan and of Margaret Thatcher in the United Kingdom—both devotees of Hayek's and ardent quoters of his *The Road to Serfdom.* The Austrian School was back on the scene, its star ascending once again.

Perspective

Austrian economics eschews econometrics and static analysis. Rather than a utopian end state of perfectly competitive equilibrium, AE is concerned with the *market process.* Kirzner puts it this way:

> We see the market as made up, during any period of time, of the interacting decisions of consumers, entrepreneur-producers, and resource owners. Not all the decisions in a given period can be carried out, since many of them may erroneously anticipate and depend upon other decisions which are in fact not being made. Again, many of the decisions which are successfully carried out in a given period may not turn out to have been the best possible courses of action. Had the decision-makers been aware of the choices others were making during the same period, they would have perceived opportunities for more attractive courses of market action than those actually adopted. In short, ignorance of the decisions which others are in fact about to make may cause decision-makers to make unfortunate plans—either plans that are doomed to disappointment or plans which fail to exploit existing market opportunities.
>
> During the given period of time, exposure to the decisions of others communicates some of the information these decision-makers originally lacked. If they find that their plans cannot be carried out, this teaches them that their anticipations concerning the decisions of others were overly optimistic. Or they may learn that their undue pessimism has caused them to pass up attractive market opportunities. This newly acquired information concerning the plans of others can be expected to generate, for the succeeding period of time, *a revised set of decisions.* The overambitious plans of one period will be replaced by more realistic ones; market opportunities overlooked in one period will be exploited in the next. In other words, even without changes in the basic data of the market (i.e., in consumer tastes, technological possibilities, and resource availabilities), the decisions made in one period of time generate systematic alterations in the corresponding decisions for the succeeding period. Taken over time, this series of systematic changes in the interconnected network of market decisions constitutes the market process.

The market process, then, is set in motion by the results of the initial market-ignorance of the participants. The process itself consists of the systematic plan changes generated by the flow of market information released by market participation—that is, by the testing of plans in the market. As a matter of considerable theoretical interest we may investigate the possibility of a state of affairs in which *no* market ignorance is present. We would then have a pattern of perfectly dovetailing decisions. No decision made will fail to be carried out, and no opportunity will fail to be exploited. Each market participant will have correctly forecast all the relevant decisions of others; he will have laid his plans fully cognizant of what he will be unable to do in the market, but at the same time fully awake to what he *is* able to do in the market. Clearly, with such a state of affairs the market *process* must immediately cease. Without autonomous change in tastes, or in technological possibilities, or in the availability of resources, no one can have any interest in altering his plans for the succeeding periods. The market is in equilibrium; the pattern of market activity will continue without change period after period.[10]

But the perspective of AE is not just external. It is internal, too. "Central to this perspective on market process are the twin notions of ignorance and discovery."[11] Roberts and Eisenhardt continue:

Strategy is fundamentally concerned with a firm being unique in some competitively advantaged way. Moving past this broad observation, strategy scholars have relied on variants of economics to develop the logic by which firms achieve the competitive advantages that lead to superior performance. Theories of strategic positioning (such as [Porter's] five-forces framework) rely on industrial organization economics to argue that superior performance is derived from a unique configuration of tightly linked activities that create a defensible position. Resource-based theories rely on the several schools of microeconomics to argue a strategic logic that competitive advantage derives from valuable, rare, inimitable, and non-substitutable resources that may be leveraged across different products and markets. Similarly, Austrian economics can also be used to draw out implications for firms' strategy.[12]

---

[10] Kirzner, *Competition and Entrepreneurship*, 9–11.
[11] Roberts and Eisenhardt, "Austrian Insights."
[12] Ibid., 347.

Roberts and Eisenhardt then go on to offer six insights from AE to firm-level issues:

1. **Logic of opportunity.** Because wealth creation results from entrepreneurial discovery, managers should seek out uncertainty that they know how to manage rather than building defensible positions from which to repel rivals' attacks.
2. **Routines versus simple rules.** In turbulent markets, the Austrian view suggests developing a few simple rules to guide decision making about which opportunities will be considered and which will not. Routines work fine in stable markets, but simple rules trump them in volatile ones.
3. **Role of time.** The Austrian perspective suggests the fork in the road between exploitation (pursuing today's opportunities) and exploration (ignoring today and gearing up for tomorrow) is real indeed. Therefore, "We're gonna dance with who brung us" isn't necessarily the right view. Austrians believe managers must choose between path-*dependent* and path-*breaking* actions.
4. **Real-time learning.** As with other insights on this list, the Austrian view is not on perfection but on iterative improvement. Successful companies encourage learning-by-doing, trial and error, and trial again. They do not automatically penalize failure because they know the seeds of success are often embedded in the learning that comes from failing.
5. **Modularity.** Using the concept of "loose coupling," managers can arrange resources in modular fashion. This allows them to invoke whole sets of resources rather than picking and choosing among a veritable grab bag of them. Modularity allows for configuring in new and different ways.
6. **Internal processes.** Effective processes help organizations get beyond experiential learning to different bases for getting, reconfiguring, and discarding existing resources.

In short, the Austrian perspective is both external *and* internal. Among the five nontraditional disciplines forming our perspective, that dual outlook makes it unique.

Tenets

The five central tenets of Austrian economics are straightforward.

1. Human action is central. It is not accidental. It is purposeful.
2. Competition is an iterative process that takes time and reduces ignorance.

3. Value is subjective. It really *is* in the eye of the beholder.
4. The entrepreneur is central to growth and economic progress.
5. Institutions—the rules of the game—have a major impact on economic outcomes. Ever-changing institutions destabilize markets because they obscure what the rules are as well as what they might become. Therefore, the bases for managerial decision-making seize up until institutions calm down. During the first quarter of 2009, we saw markets' reaction to the uncertainty of institutional change. They did not know what change to believe in.

Tools

The tools of AE are distinct. They are simple and clear-eyed, but they are *not* easy. Some of them do not comport with the politically correct fashion of a society that increasingly seeks to reward failure and stupidity while avoiding placing responsibility on individuals.

Purposeful human action

Disequilibrium

Subjectivity of value

Incentives

Institutions

Entrepreneurship

Qualitative analysis

Knightian uncertainty

Once again, I implore readers to infer nothing in terms of relative importance from the sequence in which the tools are presented here. As before, I have aimed to array them in an order that makes sense to me. I hope it does likewise for you. If not, read them in whatever order works best for you.

Purposeful Human Action

"Purposeful human action" describes a deliberate choice made by an individual "in a conscious effort to substitute more satisfactory conditions for less satisfactory ones."[13] This is an action rooted in basic economic scarcity. It matters in valuation because so much of what passes for acceptable behavior in organizations has little to do with making things better, other than

---

[13] Mises, *Social and Economic Evolution*, 224.

the political position of "the behaver."[14] To the extent that the valuation professional can see this, she can ask the penetrating questions necessary to get to the explanation of *why* such behaviors are allowed to persist when their outcomes are so transparently toxic.

Again, we are back to the business of making judgments here. Again, in America in 2010, this is not only unfashionable; it is quasi-unacceptable. To more tender and pampered sensibilities, it is also unacceptable. Someone's feelings might be hurt. We are not in the business of hurting people's feelings, but we are in the business of seeing reality for what it is, explaining it clearly and tactfully, and then letting the chips fall where they may. If that makes the client happy, terrific. If it does not, terrific. If it does not, it should not, and it must not, change what we do. If it does, then we have become the worst kind of "pander bears."

Disequilibrium

The notion of disequilibrium is vital because it strikes at the heart of much of what the discipline of finance stands for today. With disequilibrium, we have no capital asset pricing model. We have no betas. We have no normal distributions, except by chance. I have nothing personal against the field of finance. I just wish it insisted on a greater level of intellectual integrity in its underlying theory.

Let me take this a step further. The idea of a stock's beta suggests that, if we take more risk to achieve an upside, we are taking the same level of risk on the downside. For decades this has been one of the pillars of modern portfolio theory (MPT). A related facet of MPT is the efficient frontier, which represents the trade-off between risk and return, again premised on the dubious notion of equilibrium.

To be sure, organizations that should know better, including the Chartered Financial Analyst (CFA) Institute and its CFA curriculum, have inhaled the idea of equilibrium in capital markets hook, line, and sinker. Yet it is *not* true. It is not only the outsize returns that legendary investors such as Warren Buffett have produced—there are outliers in any distribution— that give the lie to equilibrium. But it is also the investment methodology devised by E. James Breech, founder of Cougar Global Investments, L.P. (CGI), a Toronto-based money management firm. Breech's quantitative methodology marries "downside risk management" (i.e., "Thou shalt not lose thy clients' money") with "rational beliefs systems" to limit downside risk while preserving the upside. CGI has done this consistently for over a

---

[14] Think of it as you would "the decider."

decade, thus proving it is no accident. In fact, Breech's model compelled him to pull his clients out of 95% of their equity holdings in January *2008.* We should all have had the good fortune of his insights.

Subjectivity of Value

We have all heard the old saying: "Value is what you get, price is what you pay." Few of us have ever really thought about what that statement really means. The two measures—value and price—are distinctly different. Price is an objective measure. Value is subjective. Yet neoclassical economists, which means most economists on the scene today, equate price and value. I wonder what they do when they decide to buy a car. Or take a vacation. Or buy a stock. Presumably there is a little potential for "alpha" built into their decisions.

The subjectivity of value gives rise to a crucial aspect of competitive strategy, one we have mentioned previously: differentiation and its industry-segment cousin, focus differentiation.[15] The basic idea behind these strategies is, quoting Michael Porter, *perceived uniqueness. PERCEIVED.* I do not know about you, but if that does not mean "subjective," I do not know what does. And that is the central thrust of differentiation in both forms: creating perceptions, usually through such marketing-related decisions as the choice of price points, distribution channel, and promotional strategy. As management guru Tom Peters says, "Perception is all there is."

Incentives

Few ideas in AE are as important as incentives. Yet few ideas among SMEs are as widely misunderstood and misapplied. Earlier in this book, we mentioned the Palo Alto Research Center (PARC), Xerox Corporation's storied incubation laboratory for new ideas, and how misaligned the "O" in "VRIO" was in Xerox's incentives. That is why it never realized the tremendous potential of the many innovations PARC produced.

Let us start with this: If you want to change the behavior in an organization, you will save yourself a lot of time and lost credibility with clients if you start with changing the incentives. People respond to incentives . . . if they value them over the alternatives. That is another way of saying they will go for the incentive if its opportunity cost is not too high. Let's explore that.

---

[15] Not to be confused with the *differentiation* used by Lawrence and Lorsch in *Organization and Environment.*

The classic article on incentives was published in 1975. "On the Folly of Rewarding A, While Hoping for B,"[16] used a series of real-world examples to explain behavior in dysfunctional incentive systems. Two examples will suffice.

In World War II, U.S. troops could not come home until the war was over. Incentive: Win the war.[17] In Vietnam, in contrast, troops could come home after 12 months. Incentive: Do not worry about winning, just survive for a year. It is no wonder that some troops experienced the phenomenon known as fragging: A too-eager-to-win officer or senior non-commissioned officer would find himself the target of a live grenade rolled into his tent while he was sleeping. Because of the incentive to survive, troops went after those on their own side who were threats to their survival.

The second example comes from the nonprofit sector: orphanages. Ever wonder why it takes so long and is so expensive to "adopt" a child?[18] Well, appoint yourself executive director of an adoption agency and ask yourself: How can I increase my pay in my current job and my prestige with my peers around the country? Answer: more staff, bigger budget, longer operating cycle. After all, the only place I can go from my current job is to a bigger one somewhere else within the "industry." How better to demonstrate my qualifications for more responsibility and higher pay than to show how I increased the resource base in my current job? If that means lobbying the state legislature to make adoption more complicated—the better to identify "better parents," of course—then, of course, that is what I will do. If it means supporting my national trade association in its efforts to get federal tax credits for adopting a child, well, I can increase my staff's pay *and* also the cost of adoption by something approximating the amount of the subsidy.

This is not cynicism—it is Human Nature 101. If you say you reward performance, but do not measure it, and then sanction those who take a few extra minutes on their lunch break—perhaps to tend to a sick child or look in on an aging parent—employees *do* get the message: Kiss off performance, but make damned sure you get back from lunch on time.

This is why incentives are so important. But take it one step further: Conduct a customer loyalty survey for your client looking to sell her business in a few years. Make sure you test it on a focus group first.

---

[16] Kerr, "On the Folly."

[17] About which Ross Perot, when he became a member of the General Motors (GM) Board of Directors after GM bought his company, Electronic Data Systems, said, "It takes General Motors five years to design and build a new car. We won World War II in four-and-a-half." And we wonder why that auto maker is in trouble?

[18] I put "adopt" in quotation marks because anyone who thinks it is illegal to sell a child in the United States has not tried to adopt one.

Also make sure the survey instrument has a dependent variable (e.g., "Overall, how satisfied are you with your most recent experience with our company?"), key independent variables that are largely uncorrelated with one another (i.e., multicolinearity is not present), and a big enough level of expected responses to support however many independent variables there are. Analyze the results using multiple regression or factor analysis, and then present a set of recommendations to the client about new incentives that will align employees' behaviors with what customers say they value most. Now *that is* what adding value is all about. Aligning internal behaviors with external expectations is another phase of the value map to unlock business wealth.

Institutions

Some of us may scratch our heads when we ponder the role of institutions in value creation. Yet they play a vital role. Institutions are nothing more than the rules of the game. Put more formally, they are the constraints—legal, social, economic, or cultural—on behavior in human exchange. By defining and limiting individuals' choice sets—as an economist would put it—institutions provide structure to everyday life.

Institutions can be formal or informal. On the formal side, we have agreements and written rules governing contracts, corporations, and individuals. We also have laws (statute and common) and constitutions. Informal institutions include beliefs, norms of behavior, and unwritten codes of conduct.

Institutions are *not* synonymous with organizations. If they were, the rules would be indistinguishable from the players. Institutions frame the rules, and organizations aim to win within that set of rules. One prominent scholar puts it this way:

> Institutional constraints include both what individuals are prohibited from doing and, sometimes, under what conditions some individuals are permitted to undertake certain activities. As defined here, they therefore are the framework within which human interaction takes place. They are perfectly analogous to the rules of the game in a competitive team sport. That is, they consist of formal written rules as well as typically unwritten codes of conduct that underlie and supplement formal rules, such as not deliberately injuring a key player on the opposing team. And as this analogy would imply, the rules and informal codes are sometimes violated and punishment is enacted. Therefore, an essential part of the functioning of institutions is the costliness of ascertaining violations and the severity of punishments.

Continuing the sports analogy, taken together, the formal and informal rules and the type and effectiveness of enforcement shape the whole character of the game. Some teams are successful as a consequence of (and have therefore the reputation for) constantly violating rules and thereby intimidating the opposing team. Whether that strategy pays off obviously depends on the effectiveness of monitoring and the severity of punishment. Sometimes codes of conduct—good sportsmanship— constrain players, even though they could get away with successful violations.[19]

Institutions serve the useful purpose of reducing uncertainty, though they sometimes do not do it very efficiently. Institutions also change, but only incrementally. Discontinuous change in institutions is the rarest of rare birds. It is not that it cannot happen. It is just that it almost never does. The Patient Protection and Affordable Care Act of 2010 is, at this writing, the most recent example of sweeping change. In the United States, other broad proposals for radical change have failed consistently: privatizing a portion of Social Security during the Bush administration, nationalized healthcare during the Clinton administration, and "synfuels" during the Carter administration.

We see informal rules in certain economic structures, most notably oligopolies. For instance, recall the first five rules of behavior of the oligopolist in good standing: (1) Never, (2) _never_, (3) _never_, (4) _never_, (5) NEVER compete on the basis of price. Recall, too, that "tacit collusion" is legal, but "overt collusion" is not. Similarly, some industries have formal rules concerning safety, security, and confidentiality of information; the professions also have formal rules, which is one thing that sets them apart from lines of work that are not considered to be professions.

Even some domains have informal rules. In Charlottesville, Virginia, for instance, it is not acceptable for one land-surveying firm to hire, or try to hire, the employees of another. "It's just not done," the CEO of one client company told us. "We wouldn't do it to them, and they wouldn't do it to us." So far, at least, he is right. Engage in blood-letting price competition? No problem in that niche. Just do not go poaching someone else's employees.

It is crucial, therefore, to ask each client if there are informal norms of behavior—unwritten "rules of engagement," if you will—that apply in their domains. Knowing these will help you construct the appropriate value map later.

---

[19] North, _Institutions, Institutional Change,_ 4.

Entrepreneurship

The Austrian take on entrepreneurship is bimodal. One school, generally associated with Ludwig Lachmann, believes that economies not only are never in equilibrium but also do not trend toward it. The other view, popularized by Israel Kirzner, is that entrepreneurs see opportunities in disequilibrium and, through their actions, move an economy toward equilibrium. Whether it gets there is not important to us.

For valuation professionals, the important thing to keep in mind about entrepreneurship is that companies, even smaller ones, need the entrepreneurial *spirit*: that is, a willingness to take risks, try it, fail at it, learn from failing, and try again. That spirit applies to both the existing line(s) of business and new ones. This spirit, which is especially helpful when it is embedded in the company's culture, is essential to keeping the firm from locking up on success.

Success lockup occurs when a company is succeeding beyond its wildest dreams. Revenues are gushing, margins are expanding, and bank accounts are fat. As I have written elsewhere in this book, it is this scenario that is *the* hardest one in which to effect any change whatsoever. More than one business owner in this situation has looked at me as if I were a man from Mars and asked, "Miller, if you're so smart, why aren't you rich like me?" So I take them through my in-free-markets-success-is-a-moving-target soliloquy, reassure them that I am not trying to undermine their success, and state unequivocally that my aim is to make their success more durable, less easy to imitate, and less susceptible to sudden disruption by an entrepreneur who sees the world working differently from the way the successful client company sees it.

It never ceases to amaze me how quickly companies become intoxicated with their success. Some managers—and owners—get the big head and start believing that all that money they are accumulating arises because they are smarter than everyone else.

They then surround themselves with toadies and yes-people, the better to avoid disagreement. They fail to realize the value of the squeaky wheel— the guy who invariably raises questions that have uncomfortable, maybe even threatening answers. He and those like him are an established firm's entrepreneurs. Every company needs them, but few successful ones have them. That is a major reason why only 5% of family businesses make it to the third generation.

Qualitative Analysis

Many of us in the valuation community are more comfortable with the "objectivity" of quantitative analysis than we are with making qualitative judgments. It never ceases to amaze me how some of our colleagues complain that the guideline public company method of valuation is "too subjective" while they take refuge in the objectivity of discounted cash flow. Forecasts are "objective"? Growth assumptions are "objective"? It's even worse when someone wants to "capitalize earnings," thus failing to grasp that (1) capitalization is just a unique form of discounted cash flow and (2) "earnings" in growing businesses typically exceed free cash flow. Cash is what matters, yet these folks think it is synonymous with net income. Well, net income is an opinion. Cash flow is a fact.

The Austrian school eschews quantitative analysis because it believes that people and economics are too complicated to model. Instead, it proceeds logically—Socratically, if you will—with cause-and-effect analysis. True Austrians are value-neutral in their analyses. They see it as their job to describe the effects of an action, without regard to whether those outcomes are desirable or not.

We are not so clinical. Once our financial analysis is near completion, we, too, proceed in Socratic fashion. We are about *why*. To get to why requires asking a question related to an effect—a ratio, for instance—and then listening to the response. That response typically leads to another question, if for no other reason than the effect we are trying to get to the basis of is an indicator of low or high performance somewhere in the organization.

So, in our on-site interviews, we do everything we can to take the edge off what is inherently stressful, sometimes uncomfortable, and always intense. We make it a point to dress like the typical employee at that client company. We do not want to be perceived as one of "the suits."

We also sit on the same side of the table as the person we are interviewing. For one thing, we do not want an obstacle obstructing our view of what is going on on the other side of the table. For another, we avoid artificial barriers that might inhibit communication.

We do some other things to reduce the level of tension. We are informal. We start off by asking the individual if he knows the purpose of the interview. Invariably, everyone does. We tell them that nothing they say to us will be attributed to them, either directly or by implication. We say that we seek only the truth as we try to understand certain aspects of the company. Then we ask if the individual is willing to help us do that. That is a hard question to say no to.

We speak softly. We use lots of "weasel words." Adverbs detract from good writing, but they are essential in our interview process.

Our approach in these interviews is qualitative, Socratic . . . and rigorous. Anyone who thinks Socratic-style interviewing is not rigorous and demanding has not tried it. We know of no other way to unearth causes. We do not begin with any preconceived notions. We depend on intuition, the ability to make nuanced observations, and a willingness to ask tough questions in a nonthreatening way. After all, if we cannot see the reality of a company clearly, how can we value it correctly?

Knightian Uncertainty

Frank H. Knight was the dean, as it were, of the Chicago School of Economics. As readers know, more than a few Nobel laureates were (and are) on the faculty at the University of Chicago.[20] Knight's classic book, *Risk, Uncertainty, and Profit*, was first published in 1921.[21] In it, he drew a bright line between "uncertainty" and "risk." He defined risk as having a discernible probability distribution. Uncertainty, however, has no such distribution, according to Knight, thus, the phrase "Knightian uncertainty."

This matters to Austrians because only under uncertainty do true entrepreneurs exist. Real entrepreneurs attack problems because, to borrow a phrase, they don't know that they don't know. That is, they believe there *is* risk, but not uncertainty. Whether driven by passion (most of us) or a refusal to accept a certain status quo, entrepreneurs see the world differently. Let me share a story that readers might find helpful.

Early on—my third valuation engagement, it was—I saw that the issue of unsystematic risk was the heart of valuing private equity. It just jumped off the page at me. I had kind of pogo-sticked my way through the valuation minefield in my first two gigs, doing things in a by-the-book way, not paying much attention to human factors, relying on financial analysis, and so on. Both were pretty mechanical (and lousy) pieces of work.

My third engagement was a tobacconist in a city in the Midwest. This was in the heyday of cigars. The owner and her late husband had had their store for over 35 years. Demand for cigars had spiked to the point that there was almost no available supply for new entrants. We estimated that our client had something over 60% of the local market. New players came to her to buy their cigars—at retail.

She was also a marketing wizard. Her store was located in the most upscale shopping area of that city. She teamed up with restaurants in that complex to have "Cigar Nights," which packed the restaurants and sold hundreds of high-priced cigars. She sponsored local sports events, provided boxes of cigars to charities to raffle off, and made herself a fixture on the local speakers' circuit. Her store even had a walk-in humidor.

---

[20] A noninclusive list: Gary Becker, Ronald Coase, Robert Fogel, Milton Friedman, James J. Heckman, Robert Lucas, Merton Miller, Roger Myerson, and George Stigler. As this is written, Becker, Fogel, Heckman, Lucas, and Myerson are still at Chicago.

[21] Knight, *Risk, Uncertainty, and Profit*.

Well, the tools I had at my disposal were just not up to the task of risk assessment. No way. So I went back to my days as a Ph.D. student and quickly constructed a three-level framework to help me keep the risk factors straight—macroenvironment, industry, company. I did not know how the levels related to one another. All I knew was that unsystematic risk was far too complicated to be covered with a checklist. It still is.

What I needed was a framework that helped me ask the right questions. In the valuation business as in no other, with the exception of medicine, if you are not asking the right questions, the answers do not matter. Given that every company is different from every other company, there is simply no comprehensive list of questions that tick-and-tie types can use to do what needs to be done. Like every other case of one-size-fits-all, it does not. It cannot. Every company is different, and those differences are far more than marginal.

At the time I devised the first cut of the framework, I drew the macroenvironment as a square (that is how General Electric did it in the 1950s) and put Porter's five-forces framework inside it. I then made a big red dot to represent the company in the center of his framework in the "Rivalry" section. It was primitive, but it helped me keep things straight.

I then looked in vain for data. More troubling, in my view, was the fact that the valuation bible of that time—from our esteemed colleague Shannon Pratt—devoted all of a couple of paragraphs in a 900-page book to the issue of unsystematic risk. Truth be told, the clients he worked with did not have much unsystematic risk (i.e., they were pretty big). Those that did have it could not have afforded his services.

As additional books came out—from Gary Trugman, Chris Mercer, George Hawkins, Jim Hitchner—they, too, treated the subject with alarming brevity. Again, all I could conclude was that these guys' billing rates took them out of the realm of smaller companies—not mom-and-pops, but firms in the $2 million to $5 million revenue range—where they just did not have to grapple with the kinds of risk issues that most of us in this business have to contend with.

Most important, at least from my standpoint, was that none of these books dealt explicitly with the cause-and-effect relationships which, in my view, are the heart and soul of valuation. They seemed to think that identifying the symptoms—ratio exemplars—was all there was to it. I think it is a lot more complicated than that. I also believe that without getting at the causes, one is unlikely to understand what he is valuing and, thereby, is unlikely to get it right.

I have pounded my spoon on my highchair about unsystematic risk for a long time, and I will continue to do so, even as I continue to improve my understanding of it and the cause-and-effect relationships that make it the issue that it is. But our work in this area is a great example of uncertainty: I had no idea whether I could be successful in getting my arms around the problem, but I knew I had to try. It was either that, or, out of basic respect for clients who would otherwise pay me for work that neither they nor I understood, quit business valuation altogether. I chose to bang away at this problem because it is the most riveting intellectual issue of my career.

Unlocking Business Wealth

Austrian economics offers a different way of looking at economic phenomena. Unlike traditional microeconomics, it not only makes room for the entrepreneur. It insists on the entrepreneur being present. It also emphasizes the subjectivity of value, thus giving the lie to the neoclassical idea that price and value are somehow equal. It sees competition as a *process* with no natural end state. Again, this puts it in diametric opposition to traditional approaches, which start with a utopian end state but have nothing to say about the journey toward it.

Make no mistake about it: Unlocking business wealth *is* a journey. And, because there is no stopping point in free markets, it is a never-ending one. However, the value-mapping process will help you understand the cause-and-effect relationships that obstruct wealth creation. Once you get your arms around those, the rest, while not easy, is doable at a level that will delight both your clients and your bank account.

Austrians hold the notion of proper incentives in high regard. If you look at many of the public policy issues that seem to vex our body politic today—from schools that run like war zones, to the highest healthcare costs on the planet, to a dichotomy of shrill politics on Capitol Hill—the solutions lie in restructuring the incentives. Teachers, healthcare providers, healthcare consumers, and politicians behave the way they do because theirs are the behaviors that the current incentive systems reward. If we want to begin to solve these or any other problems, including those in the typical SME, we have to understand whether any current incentives reward goofy behavior. Then, and only then, can we design new ones that encourage the behavior businesses—and societies—need.

Regardless of what you might have thought about the applicability of economics to valuation heretofore, I cannot recommend the study of Austrian economics highly enough. It will help you see and understand economic issues in ways you might never have thought possible.

Summary

This chapter on conceptual underpinnings of nontraditional disciplines has dealt with Austrian economics. Unfortunately, space does not permit me to plumb this particular subject at the depths I would prefer. AE offers tools that give us significant insights into causal relationships. It points up the importance of diversity in organizational thinking by highlighting the importance of entrepreneurs. Even well-run businesses need squeaky wheels asking questions whose answers everyone else stopped thinking about years ago.

Austrian economics also offers us a different way to think about the subject of uncertainty and, especially, how it is different from risk. That alone is worth the price of admission, we believe. Let us know if you agree or not.

Recommended Reading

Alston, Lee J., Thráinn Eggertsson, and Douglass C. North. *Empirical Studies in Institutional Change.* Cambridge, UK: Cambridge University Press, 1996.

Chafuen, Alejandro A. *Faith and Liberty: The Economic Thought of the Late Scholastics,* 2nd ed. Boston: Lexington Books, 2003.

Hayek, Friedrich von. *Individualism and Economic Order.* Chicago: University of Chicago Press, 1948.

Hayek, Friedrich von. *Prices and Production,* 2nd rev. ed. London: Routledge, 1935.

Hayek, Friedrich von. *The Pure Theory of Capital.* Chicago: University of Chicago Press, 1941.

Kresge, Stephen, and Leif Wennar. (eds.). *Hayek on Hayek: An Autobiographical Dialogue.* Chicago: University of Chicago Press, 1994.

Hazlitt, Henry. *Economics in One Lesson.* New York: Crown, 1979.

Hazlitt, Henry. *The Failure of the New Economics: An Analysis of the Keynesian Fallacies.* Princeton, NJ: D. van Nostrand, 1959.

Holcombe, Randall H. (ed.). *15 Great Austrian Economists.* Auburn, AL: Ludwig von Mises Institute, 1999.

Kirzner, Israel M. *The Driving Force of the Market: Essays in Austrian Economics.* New York: Routledge, 2000.

Kirzner, Israel M. *Essays on Capital and Interest: An Austrian Perspective.* Northampton, MA: Edward Elgar, 1996.

Kirzner, Israel M. *How Markets Work: Disequilibrium, Entrepreneurship and Discovery.* London: Institute of Economic Affairs, 1997.

Lachmann, Ludwig M. *Capital and Its Structure.* London: G. Bell & Sons, 1956.

Lachmann, Ludwig M. *The Market as an Economic Process.* Oxford: Basil Blackwell, 1986.

Langlois, Richard N., and Paul L. Robertson. *Firms, Markets, and Economic Change.* New York: Routledge, 1995.

March, James G., Martin Schulz, and Zhou Xueguang. *The Dynamics of Rules: Change in Written Organizational Codes.* Stanford, CA: Stanford University Press, 2000.

Ménard, Claude, and Mary M. Shirley. *Handbook of New Institutional Economics,* Dordrecht, The Netherlands: Springer, 2005.

Mises, Ludwig von. *Human Action,* Auburn, AL: Ludwig von Mises Institute, 1998.

O'Driscoll, Gerald P., Jr., and Mario J. Rizzo. *The Economics of Time and Ignorance,* 2nd ed. New York: Routledge, 1996.

Popper, Karl R. *The Logic of Scientific Discovery.* New York: Harper & Row, 1965.

Vaughn, Karen I. *Austrian Economics in America.* New York: Cambridge University Press, 1994.

Blogs Worth Looking in On

- **Organizations and Markets** (http://organizationsand markets.com). As a strategy and valuation guy, I believe that this blog is the best there is. Nicolai Foss (Copenhagen Business School), Peter Klein (U. of Missouri), Dick Langlois (U. of Conn.), and Lasse Lien (Norwegian School of Economics and Business Administration), along with temporary guest bloggers, do an incredible job. Klein is the most prolific blogger. I do not know how he has the time to do anything else, but he obviously does because he is well published and in A journals, no less.
- **ThinkMarkets** (http://thinkmarkets.wordpress.com). This blog bills itself as "a blog of the NYU Colloquium on Market Institutions and Economic Processes." The colloquium is chaired by Mario Rizzo (*The Economics of Time and Ignorance*) and includes William Butos (Trinity College), Gene Callahan (Cardiff University), Young Back Choi (St. John's U. [N.Y.]), David Harper (NYU), Sandy Ikeda (SUNY–Purchase), Roger Koppl (Fairleigh Dickinson U.), Chidem Kurtas (www.mutualfundsmarts.com), and Joe Salerno (Pace U.). It is a top-flight blog.
- **The Coordination Problem** (www.coordinationproblem.org). Until New Year's Day 2010, this site was called The Austrian economists. The protagonists here are mostly from the George Mason U. branch of AE. They include Pete Boettke, Peter Leeson, and Frederic Sautet (all of GMU), Chris Coyne (West Va. U.), Steve Horwitz (St. Lawrence U.), and David Prytchitko (No. Michigan U.). They say that their goal is to "clarify the confusions and demonstrate the continuing relevance" to economics today of the insights of Menger, Bohm-Bawerk, Mises, Hayek, Lachmann, Rothbard, and Kirzner.
- **Café Hayek** (www.cafehayek.com). A great blog, again from GMU. Lead guys are Russ Roberts and Don Boudreaux.
- **EconTalk** (www.econtalk.org). Russ Roberts interviews contemporary giants of economics. Downloads are free.
- **Free Advice** (http://consultingbyrpm.com/blog/). This is the blog of prominent Austrian economist Bob Murphy of Nashville. It's quirky, unpredictable, and invariably interesting.
- **Mises Economics Blog** (http://blog.mises.org/blog/). Pretty predictable libertarian-leaning posts here. I don't believe in mixing economics and politics, so I am not a big fan of this one.
- **Orgtheory.net** (http://orgtheory.wordpress.com/). This is not an AE blog by any means. However, there is a fun rivalry between its bloggers and those who post at Organizations and Markets.
- **The Liberty & Power Group Blog** (http://hnn.us/blogs/4.html). At this writing, 24 contributors comprise the blogging group here. Robert Higgs's insights are, in my view, the primary reason to look in on this one. He is a wonderful student of the Great Depression and gives the lie to the traditional causes of the Depression, the contributions (especially the lack thereof) of the New Deal to getting us out of it, and what really got us out of it (hint: It was not World War II).

PART

II

POURING THE FOUNDATION

CHAPTER 7

The Straight Scoop on Value Drivers

The legendary "Sage of Omaha," Warren Buffett, has a track record for spotting value that the rest of us can only covet. But we can feast on some of the methodological crumbs under his table if we can identify whether a company has sources of distinctive advantage and, if so, whether they have staying power. Our subject is a topic about which more misleading ideas exist than the bad information that ten-year-olds spout off about how to make a marriage work: value drivers.

Definition

Before saying what a value driver is, let us say what it is not. First and most important, despite what many financial professionals say, it is *not* a financial ratio or other financial-statement metric. It is not days' sales outstanding (DSO), return on investment, return on invested capital, marginal tax rates, or gross margin.[1] Such metrics and ratios result *from* value drivers; they are not a synonym *for* them. Ratios are the effects of underlying causes. Moreover, except in sports franchises, research universities, the recording industry, and professional services firms, a value driver is not a person. So, for now, we use the term "value drivers" as a placeholder for those causes. However, in addition to being the cause of a ratio effect, just what *is* a value driver? Some creative Internet searching uncovered these definitions:

> [A value driver is] an activity or organizational focus which enhances the perceived value of a product or service in the perception of the consumer and which therefore creates value for the producer. Advanced technology, reliability, or reputation for customer relations can all be value drivers.[2]

---

[1] www.deloitte.com/dtt/article/0,1002,sid%253D94592%2526cid%253D118560,00.html; see "The five pillars of value creation."
[2] http://dictionary.bnet.com/definition/Value+Driver.html?tag=col1;trackDictionary

Value drivers vary by type of business. While reputation and cost control are always important, other factors can matter. For example:

Restaurants—are known by reputation for good food and a positive dining experience. Value (profit) drivers for a successful restaurant include: location, concept, menu, quality of cooking and wait staff, and cost control.

Technology Companies—must have a core product/technology or "know how" that solves a customer problem. Key value (profitability) drivers include: highly skilled workers, quality and cost control, and R&D (research and development).

Professional Services Firms—are known by reputation. Key value (profitability) drivers include personal relationships, highly skilled staff, and cost-effective service delivery.

Retail—brand/merchandise mix and location are critical. Key value (profitability) drivers include inventory management and cost control.

Frequently, value drivers are "intangibles" and employees. Intangibles (intellectual property) and human resources (who go home at night) can be protected and leveraged through a combination of business strategies and legal protections. Business strategies include incentive compensation plans to recognize, reward, and retain high-performing employees. Legal protections include requiring key employees to sign non-solicitation/non-disclosure agreements, registering trademarks and copyrights, and taking steps to protect proprietary information/trade secrets such as recipes and formulas. Contracts with key players, including partners, customers, and suppliers, are also important.[3]

Value drivers are the characteristics likely to either reduce the risk associated with owning the business or enhance the prospect that the business will grow significantly in the future. Familiar value drivers include proprietary technologies, market position, brand names, diverse product lines and patented products. Some less obvious value drivers you may not have considered are routines capable of improving or sustaining cash flows, well-maintained facilities, effective financial controls, and fraud-prevention initiatives.[4]

---

[3] http://www.smartfast.com/pages/bus-value.html
[4] www.evancarmichael.com/Buying-A-Business/2777/Uncover-your-companys-key-value-drivers.html

Value drivers are embedded in valua*tion.* If a wholesaler or retailer has unusually high inventory turns for its line of business, we must assume either that (a) it has special insights into purchasing relative to its peers, and/or (b) it is doing a lot of drop shipping (i.e., straight from manufacturer to customer). It is then incumbent upon us to learn, during our on-site interviews, *why* it is (a) or (b) or both.

Similarly, if a firm has low DSO relative both to its peers and to its own payment terms, then it might know how to get invoices into customers' hands faster than its competitors. Or it might use personal relationships to get checks cut faster. Or it might have online technology that accepts credit cards in payment of invoices. Or it might have worked out deals with its customers to remit via bank wire. It might also use technology to gather data— from the pick tickets, from the shipping dock, and from the common carrier—that triggers the issuance of an invoice in PDF that is automatically e-mailed to customers' accounts payable personnel. Again, the time to find out *why* is during the on-site visit.

With those examples in mind, consider the three basic parameters of valuation: (1) profitability (measured by free cash flow), (2) expected growth in profitability, and (3) risk. Valuation varies directly with the first two and inversely with the third. Therefore, let us derive a definition of value drivers we can all use and understand:

> Value drivers are those capabilities, activities, or routines, which (1) reduce risk, (2) increase free cash flow, or (3) raise expected growth in free cash flow, or any combination of the three preceding characteristics.

Value Drivers versus Balanced Scorecards

Few business consultants are deep or original thinkers, so they tend to drift from fad to fad. They love gadgets, especially those that have the potential to put buckets of money in their pockets. If it is Tuesday, it must be total quality management.

One such gadget is the balanced scorecard (BSC). For small and medium enterprises, we think it is the worst idea since managers believed that e-business was a separate line of business. That latter mistake cost companies billions and arguably created to the air rushing out of the dot-bomb balloon. The BSC arrived on the scene in 1992 with "The Balanced Scorecard: Measures That Drive Performance."[5] The BSC's gadgetry has been supported by a steady stream of books, articles, workshops,

---

[5] Kaplan and Norton, "The Balanced Scorecard."

Web sites, and even an organization called the Balanced Scorecard Collaborative (www.the palladiumgroup.com).

Four "perspectives" comprise the BSC: financial, customer, internal process, and innovation and learning. Companies adopting the BSC develop a series of measures for each of these four perspectives. In the BSC's first incarnation, the question "Of all the measures you could have chosen, why did you choose these?" was hard to answer, and the BSC quickly fell on hard times. In the mid-1990s, Kaplan and Norton finessed this problem with the development of "strategy maps." In a later *Harvard Business Review* article, they even advocated the creation of a slot called the Chief Strategy Officer, whose job probably depends on the continuing use of the BSC. I inquired into the BSC early on, even attending a three-day Kaplan-Norton seminar in Florida in 1997. I came away persuaded that it was feasible only in big companies with lots of money and, likely, gobs of underemployed staff. Palladium's list of "Hall of Fame" organizations[6] tends to confirm that. Note the presence of Chrysler and of the U.S. Postal Service. In fact, at least one-quarter of the 100 firms on the list as of this writing are nonprofits and government agencies. If you want to have some fun, click on the link for the Texas State Auditor's Office;[7] you'll get the spiel for the Tennessee Valley Authority.[8] In my view, the BSC is just a glitzy and expensive version of management-by-objectives.

Why Value Drivers Matter

Our view is we get value right, in part, by getting value *drivers* right. That means understanding how the business works and its economics. Absent that, we cannot know how or *why* the firm creates value—for shareholders *and* for customers—if indeed it does. Only when the return on invested capital exceeds the weighted-average cost of capital is value created.

The fact that a firm is in business and reports accounting profits is a necessary, but not sufficient, condition for value creation. To address the "sufficient" requirement, economic value added (EVA) uses "accounting anomalies" to normalize generally accepted accounting principles deficiencies in order to transition from an accounting picture of performance to an economic one.[9] A recent book on EVA asserted there are more than 160 such anomalies.

---

[6] See www.thepalladiumgroup.com/about/hof/Pages/HofViewer.aspx.

[7] www.thepalladiumgroup.com/about/hof/Pages/HofViewer.aspx?MID=75

[8] www.thepalladiumgroup.com/about/hof/Pages/HofViewer.aspx?MID=74

[9] See Ehrbar, *EVA*; Stern, Shiely, and Ross, *The EVA Challenge*; and Stewart, *The Quest for Value*. Beware of that last tome: Besides being 800 pages long, it has no index.

Even when economic value is created, though, the question remains: *How* was it created? What are the company's value-creating capabilities—its value drivers? How durable are they? These are complex and difficult questions that require nontraditional valuation tools to answer.

Value drivers are not—repeat, *not*—financial ratios. DSO that is low relative to industry figures does not, in and of itself, create value. It might be a symptom of value creation, however. By the same line of reasoning, inventory turnover is not a value driver. Neither is gross margin. Or operating margin. These are ratios, and useful ones, to be sure. But saying they are value drivers is like saying that it is dark at night. Good ratios are tautologies, *ex post* indicators of the possibility of value creation.

We all know that valuation is prospective. Therefore, we need *ex ante* ways of gauging value. How else can we estimate the present value of future benefits?

Understanding value drivers offers another tool for us to use in getting valuation right. Value drivers are rooted in *behaviors*—organizational routines,[10] activity patterns,[11] and capabilities comprising combinations of resources.[12] Moreover, since companies within competitive domains are heterogeneous, not homogeneous, behaviors differ among companies. It is the job of the analyst to understand these behaviors and their relationship, if any, to value creation.

Value drivers differ from critical success factors (CSFs). CSFs arise in the context of being successful in an industry. Certain of them must be present in a given domain in order for a company to be successful in that arena. These may relate to minimum efficient scale, capital structure, economies of scope, and so on. Because CSFs are shared across companies, they are not unique. Seen another way, CSFs are just another cost of doing business for successful players in a given domain.

Not so with value drivers. Unlike CSFs, value drivers *are* unique. If they're not, then they won't be value drivers for long. They result from causal relationships inside a company. Not only *can* analysts identify, measure, and empirically test them; we *must*. It is one thing to *believe* that a

---

[10] Nelson and Winter, *Evolutionary Theory*, 14.

[11] Grant, *Contemporary Strategy Analysis*. This superb book is used in strategic management courses in a number of top-tier MBA courses. Trained as an economist, Grant brings rigor and erudition to the conversation. He is also a first-rate writer who explains esoteric notions in everyday terms.

[12] Barney's *Competitive Advantage* comes from an easy-to-understand scholar who has written about value creation and value drivers for almost two decades. One of his many contributions to our understanding of wealth creation is the VRIO framework. For those who would rather wade than dive into strategic management, I recommend Barney's book.

capability or a routine is a value driver. It is quite another to *know*. We need to believe it when we know it, not vice versa.

The only way to know for sure is to test the hypothesis that a particular capability does not contribute to value creation.[13] Luckily, such testing is not complicated. Well-designed customer satisfaction surveys analyzed using factor analysis or multiple regression are a good way to test the existence and the efficacy of value drivers. Then, using the VRIO framework, which we discussed in Chapter 2, we can assess their staying power.

The rest of this chapter touches briefly on capitalism's unique feature of self-renewal. It also describes types of value drivers, gives an example of how to unearth one, and offers a simple way to test their staying power.

The Regenerative Power of Capitalism

Here is how Schumpeter put it:

> The opening up of new markets, foreign or domestic, and the organizational development of the craft shop and factory to such concerns as U.S. Steel illustrate the same process of mutation that incessantly revolutionizes the economic structure *from within*, incessantly destroying the old one, incessantly creating a new one. This process of Creative Destruction is the essential fact about capitalism.[14]

My favorite analogy to success in free markets is looking through a telescope at Saturn. It is a fascinating planet with those bright rings around it. But if you walk away from the telescope for a few minutes and then come back to look again, you'll find that Saturn is not there. It has moved on, as it were.

It is not there because two things moved: Earth and Saturn. Earth moved in two ways.[15] Spinning at something over 1,000 miles an hour—that's a mile every 3.6 seconds—a place on Earth where even a powerful telescope was mounted would quickly be out of telescopic sync with Saturn. Also, Earth goes around the Sun every 365¼ days with an average orbiting radius of nearly 93 million miles. That makes the orbit's annual path—its circumference, if you will: ∏d (pi × diameter)[16]—about 584 million miles. That's about 1.6 million miles every day, or 18½ miles each second. And what about Saturn, which is the sixth-closest planet to the Sun (Earth is

---

[13] This is the *null* hypothesis. If the hypothesis is "rejected" (has a big F-statistic), the capability *does* contribute to value creation.

[14] Schumpeter, *Capitalism, Socialism, and Democracy.*

[15] http://sse.jpl.nasa.gov/planets/profile.cfm?Object=Earth&Display=Facts&System=Metric; accessed on April 26, 2009.

[16] Even though the orbit is not a circle, it will serve for our purposes here.

number 3)?[17] It makes a full trip every 10,756 days, or 29.4 Earth years. With an orbiting radius averaging 885.9 million miles, Saturn moves at about 6 miles per second. So, if you're away for five minutes, Earth rotated 83 miles and moved about 5,550 miles in its orbit, while Saturn went about 1,800 miles in its. No wonder you cannot see it.

Success in capitalism is much the same way. It is a perpetually moving target. Unlike astronomy, where changes in position are easy to predict and a telescope can be calibrated to keep Saturn in view, at least until the Sun comes up, free markets are neither linear nor predictable. A competitive domain that has not changed much in several decades might change radically in the space of just a few years; ask independent booksellers about Amazon or land-line telephone companies about cellular technology. A domain that has changed rapidly for a quarter century might slow down for a while—personal computers come to mind.

Capitalism has brought more freedom and a higher standard of living to a greater number of people than any other system known to humankind. Yet it is an unforgiving taskmaster. It demands change at the worst conceivable time: when the heavens have opened up and are raining money on managers, shareholders, and employees who have struggled for years to make a company successful . . . "overnight." That is when change is most important and most difficult. But competitors, whether on the gridiron or in the workplace, keep going 24/7. Teams and companies that pause to bask in the warm sunlight of success find themselves suddenly in the dark being trampled by hungrier, leaner, faster-moving rivals.

Soon after we moved to Virginia in 1997, a large, local accounting firm in another city contacted us to inquire if we could do a valuation for one of its audit clients. We said we would like to explore the possibility. One thing led to another, and we ended up with the engagement.

The client was an industrial-supply company. It sold janitorial, cleaning, and safety supplies to a broad corporate clientele of end users. The company was doing about $12 million in annual revenue. It was a first-generation family business run by someone who, it turned out, held computers in low regard. In distribution, that is comparable to cordless bungee-jumping.

(continued)

---

[17] http://sse.jpl.nasa.gov/planets/profile.cfm?Object=Saturn&Display=Facts&System= Metric; accessed on April 26, 2009.

(continued)

The company had over 30,000 stock-keeping units (SKUs). Its warehouse was unlabeled and unmapped. When I asked how they knew where things were, they said, "We remember."

The primary shareholder was a control freak. That is not uncommon in entrepreneurs, of course, but this guy was not much interested in controlling people. He wanted to control inventory. With a turn that was below 20% of the industry's average, he obviously was not doing a very good job of it. The company was having to borrow more and more money to finance inventory levels that rose at about three times the rate of sales increases. What made the problem a real head-scratcher was that the firm had a top-flight IT system that could spit out purchase orders based on the parameters of purchasing: safety stock, lead time, volume discounts, economic order quantities (EOQs), and SKU-level sales trends.

Ironically, the firm also had a well-paid, competent purchasing guy a couple of years from retirement. He had been brought in from a major retailer a few years before when the audit firm told the company it had to get a handle on inventory; he drew a decent salary (about $120,000). He also held a prestigious credential—the CPM (Certified Purchasing Manager)—that is hard to come by. The guy had a glittering resume. He knew purchasing. When I asked him about inventory, though, he smiled and said, "You need to talk to Ron about that." "Ron" was the CEO.

I had accumulated quite a few things to talk to Ron about, especially inventory and matters related thereto (unlabeled warehouse bins, manual order picking, not arranging orders to be delivered on a last-in, first-out basis on delivery trucks, etc.). It was one of those situations where, in the words of legendary Marine General "Chesty" Puller, you could "Shoot in any direction and hit something that needs to be hit."

Ron was reputed to work very long hours. One night I was driving back from Reagan Airport in Washington, D.C., and decided to take a spin past the company. It was past midnight. Ron's car was there, and his office light was on. I did a similar thing a couple of weeks later on my way to Richmond late one night to catch an early flight the next morning, and he was still there.

I had been warned ahead of time that he was hypersensitive to anything he perceived as criticism. Even forewarned, I still stepped on a few land mines and saw his volcanic temperament at full strength. The louder he got, the softer my voice got. My wife taught me that one. "They have a hard time yelling if they have to strain to hear what you're saying, dear," she said. She must have had Ron in mind.

Figuring this was going to be a tougher interview than most I have had with owners and CEOs, I opted to tread lightly. I thought. So I used all of the usual "weasel words"—"kinda," "maybe," "I'm confused," and so on—

that I deploy when I am trying to elicit sensitive information. I chose what I thought was a softball topic: the warehouse. I asked about the lack of barcode labels—"or any labels at all, for that matter"—and he went off like a Roman candle. He started pounding his desk and wagging his index finger at me. However, I was determined to finish, even if he threw a fit after every question I asked.

As those on defense often do, the first thing he said was, "You don't understand. Our business is DIFFERENT!" As we noted in Chapter 4, that little four-word phrase is one that we have heard so often over the years that we made it an acronym: OBID. It bears repeating.

"How's that?" I said, not telling him that I had been the controller (with oversight responsibility for purchasing) in a wholesale and retail business that had 50,000 SKUs.

"This is an INDUSTRIAL SUPPLY business!" he thundered.

"And?" I said softly.

"What do you mean, AND?!!" he bellowed.

"Well, it was the only word I could think of," I said, smiling. That seemed only to make him madder. By the time he got done taking *my* inventory, he seemed to feel better. Running me down lifted him up. That was fine with me.

He finally conceded that the warehouse needed to be labeled, that the auditors commented on it every year, but that he just had not gotten around to it. I asked him why he did not let the purchasing guy and the warehouse manager worry about it, and he said that both of them "rely too much on the d***ed computer. I don't. I KNOW what's going on, and I don't need a computer to tell me."

"I see," I said.

"Are you being a wise a**?" he snapped.

"No, sir, Ron. Wouldn't dream of it."

When we got to the issue of inventory itself, Ron allowed as how he did not trust "that computer stuff." I asked him about "EOQs."

"What are those?" he said.

"Economic order quantities," I said.

"What kind of textbook theory did that come from?" he asked.

"Wal-Mart," I said quietly.

I don't think he could decide whether to scream, laugh, or cry. I sat there, waiting to see what would happen next.

He put his head in his hands and told me how tired he was, how hard he worked, and how much his wife worried about his health. I grunted at all the right times. Finally, he 'fessed up: "I don't trust the computer printouts for purchase orders, so I manually override every one of 'em."

Bingo. There it was.

(*continued*)

(continued)

The company ended up with a very low value, principally because of Ron. And where were most of its biggest deficiencies? In routines, of course. That is a common repository of causes for companies whose revenues have outstripped the ability of those in charge to manage.

Ron's wife turned out to be right. He landed in the hospital for ten days due to exhaustion. He still refused to delegate purchasing, though. The purchasing guy retired on time and rode off into the sunset. The warehouse never did get labeled, as far as I know.

Ron's company was liquidated in a Chapter 7 bankruptcy in 2007. It was an unnecessary end to a company that had such great potential. Dorothy and I drove past his house recently. It had a "For Sale by Owner" sign in the front yard. Distrust needs a 12-step program.

Assessing Durability

Client companies often assert they have a "competitive advantage," a much-used and abused phrase these days. As noted earlier, we prefer to call it "distinctive advantage" because "distinctive" also implies uniqueness, and we find that notion resonates with focus differentiators. If the firm has no data that we can use to confirm the existence of such advantage(s), we try to observe them ourselves. We also ask for permission to talk to a few customers to gather some anecdotal evidence. The advantages often exist.

The challenge then becomes, à la Buffett, to gauge the durability of each advantage. The VRIO framework that was introduced in Chapter 2 will jump-start that assessment.[18] The combination of high free cash flow *and* "Yes" replies to the four VRIO questions suggests a degree of durability. The extent of it depends on your judgment and your analysis. As we also pointed out in Chapter 2, even with a patent supporting an advantage, recall the three-legged stool about sustainable competitive advantage: Rumelt's take, the 22nd Amendment to the U.S. Constitution, and "Stale in the Saddle."

The most successful companies seek to craft "causal ambiguity." It creates confusion when rivals try to understand why a company is successful. Such ambiguity muddies up the cause-and-effect relationships a competitor seeks to identify as part of its grasp of its rivals' behaviors. Not surprisingly, one of the best ways to craft such confusion is through intangible capabilities.

---

[18] Barney, *Competitive Advantage*, 138–162.

For example, a middle and senior management group that has been together for years knows, as only longtime teammates can, what each team member is thinking. They speak in code—short words and phrases, abbreviations that have meaning formed over years of working closely. A nod, a glance, a single word—each seemingly insignificant to the untrained eye—can compel fast and far-reaching action. But the observer will not know because he will not be able to connect the effect to the cause. Low executive turnover is a good measure for detecting the likelihood that such teamwork is present; measures of trust are, too. If turnover is low and trust is high relative to competitors' measures, chances are that this intangible—which is nowhere on the balance sheet—is a real asset.

Put another way, to the extent that competitors can understand the cause-and-effect relationship(s) underlying a company's success in a given arena, they might be able to imitate or substitute their own capabilities, thus neutralizing a rival's advantage. That is almost impossible with intangible drivers such as management teams with low turnover and high trust. That is why we not only ask about turnover in our valuation engagements but also request short resumes of key people. Those documents, along with what we hear from employees throughout the organization—but *especially* with rank-and-file employees—tell us a great deal about whether the management team functions intuitively and effectively . . . and does so with the trust of the rank and file.

Intuitive behavior is virtually impossible for others to replicate. As unusual as it sounds, it is likely that not even those who are conducting themselves automatically and intuitively can explain it. They "just do it." The causal ambiguity thus created is a powerful competitive weapon—and a value driver.

More tangible capabilities might be able to be imitated, replicated, or substituted against. Those that are widely held are not rare and thus offer no lasting distinctive advantage. But they *can* afford holders competitive parity. That is not all bad. Parity might, after all, buy a company the time it needs to come up with mechanisms that result in sustainable advantage.

Summary

Value creation requires value drivers. Metrics are not value drivers; they are symptoms. Capabilities and activities drive value. Creation of one or more of a company's value drivers typically occurs either when a company is born or as a result of customer loyalty surveys. Knowing what drives value helps the firm align the behaviors and activities inside it with the expectations and value perceptions outside. It sounds simple, and it is. But Simple ≠ Easy.

Additional Reading

Akalu, Mehari Mekonnen. "Measuring and Ranking Value Drivers," 2002. Tinbergen Institute Discussion Paper No. TI 2002-043/2. Accessed from http://ssrn.com/abstract= 310999, on April 24, 2009.

Esty, Benjamin C. *Note on Value Drivers*. Boston: Harvard Business School Publishing, 1997.

Ganchev, Oggie. "Applying Value Drivers to Hotel Valuation." *Cornell Hotel & Restaurant Administration Quarterly* 41, No. 5 (2000): 78–89

Laitinen, Erkki K. "Value Drivers in Finnish Family-Owned Firms." *International Journal of Accounting and Finance* 1, No. 1 (2008): 1–41

Marr, Bernard. *Strategic Performance Measurement: Leveraging and Measuring Your Intangible Value Drivers*. London: Butterworth-Heinemann, 2006.

Parmenter, David. *Key Performance Indicators: Developing, Implementing, and Using Winning KPIs*. Hoboken, NJ: John Wiley & Sons, 2007.

Scott, Mark C. *Value Drivers: The Manager's Guide to Driving Corporate Value Creation*. Hoboken, NJ: John Wiley & Sons, 2000.

CHAPTER

The "OT" in SWOT Analysis:
The Macroenvironment

In Chapter 1 we introduced the trilevel unsystematic risk framework. It was created because, as a practical matter, the number of factors comprising unsystematic risk is huge. There are far too many to put into a questionnaire, unless we want an 18-wheeler to carry it around in. Such a document would miss the mark because of what it must exclude due to constraints of time and ignorance, not to mention paper. Therefore, we concluded that we needed a simple and straightforward tool that would give us a limited number of essential external parameters on which to base our initial research and analysis. That is the process that gives rise to the questions that we later include in a set of custom-tailored questionnaires to be used during our on-site interviews. However, I am getting ahead of myself.

From the literatures of organization theory (the macroenvironment) and industrial organization (domain), we derived the first two levels of the trilevel framework. In this chapter, our focus in on the outermost set of risk factors, the macroenvironment.

Defining the Domain

As noted briefly in Chapter 3, the first step in external risk assessment is to define the domain (industry or segment) in which the client company competes. This arises because the unit of analysis in such assessment is *not* the company but the domain. The fact that few smaller companies compete industry-wide has given rise to the analysis of industry subgroups. As also discussed in Chapter 3, these segments are called "strategic groups." Here is an excerpt from one of our reports:

> In this engagement, we define the domain as a strategic group. Such a group is a subset of competitors that do not compete industry-wide. The

seven retail pharmacies in and around Rockbridge County, Virginia, comprise the relevant strategic group in this engagement.

Beginning with such an explicit definition, our research is precise and productive, especially with the help of articles from such archives as Factiva or LexisNexis. Even if a given article is not about, say, pharmacies in Rockbridge County, Virginia, it can still discuss economic conditions in Rockbridge County, the unemployment rate and economic trends in Rockbridge County, natural disasters in Rockbridge County, the demographics of Rockbridge County, lifestyles and values in Rockbridge County, and so on. Demographic trends, in particular—population growth and age cohorts—will have a major impact on future demand for pharmaceutical goods and services. So will political activity at the federal level.

More on Strategic Groups

Within an industry, the underlying economic structures of many groups differ from that of industry-wide competitors. For example, the oligopoly that dominates the market for auditing services for publicly held companies vaporizes when audit firms target closely held concerns. In fact, as noted in Chapter 3, the FTC has found major differences in the structures of these groups. Local and regional domains tend to be more concentrated than the national one. In particular, the FTC says the incidence of oligopoly is higher locally and regionally than nationally.

The primary parameter for a strategic group is its target market. Therefore, if a particular company aims at customers that are only local or only regional, then its "industry" becomes a strategic group defined, in part, by that particular geographical constraint. Because a strategic group is nothing more than a mini-industry, its structure is analyzed the same way an industry's is.

A group's members compete head to head with one another and not with firms in other groups. In Chapter 3, we gave examples of three such domains: accounting firms, lodging, and new cars.

Concentration within Industries

Structure derives, in part, from the degree of concentration. Below is a summary of concentration in major industry groups:[1]

- Agriculture/forestry/fishing (SICs 01-08): not concentrated
- Mining (SICs 10-14): "loose oligopolies"

---

[1] Adapted from Scherer and Ross, *Industrial Market Structure*, 79–81.

- ♦ Limestone/sand/gravel: low nationally, high locally and regionally
- ♦ Copper/iron ore/uranium/lead, and so on: moderate to high nationally
- ♦ Chromium/molybdenum/nickel/diamonds: high
- ♦ Crude oil refining: moderate-to-high nationally
- ♦ Construction (SICs 15–17): low nationally, some concentration locally
- Manufacturing (SICs 20–39): varies greatly[2]
- Transportation (SICs 40–47): fragmented, except locally
- Communications (SIC 48): generally high except in radio broadcasting
- Public utilities (SIC 49): generally high, but with pockets of local competition
- Wholesale/retail trade (SICs 50–59): generally low concentration nationally and in larger local markets
  - ♦ Exceptions: smaller (<100,000 population) markets are concentrated; food retailing, which has tended to be locally concentrated, is becoming less so
- Financial services (SICs 60–67): varies
  - ♦ Banking: high locally, increasing nationally
  - ♦ Health/life insurance: concentrated at state level (because of regulation)
  - ♦ Other insurance: low
  - ♦ Securities brokerage: high but changing due to policy
  - ♦ Real estate brokerage: low except in very small towns
- Service industries (SICs 70–89): varies
  - ♦ Hotels/motels: low
  - ♦ Laundry/dry cleaning/barber-beauty shops: low
  - ♦ Accounting: low except in very small towns
  - ♦ Law: low except in very small towns
  - ♦ Medicine: moderate; regulation/entry barriers combine to keep prices high
  - ♦ Repair services: low
  - ♦ Amusement/recreation services: high except in large cities

In general, the incidence of national oligopoly is low. However, in local and regional markets, it occurs often. That has implications for

---

[2] Ibid., 82–85. The table on p. 83 shows that 199 of 448 four-digit manufacturing SIC codes have CR4s (four-firm concentration ratios) equal ≥ 40, which policy-makers, economists, and academics tend to use as a threshold at which to be mindful of the presence of a potential oligopoly.

valuation professionals because well-functioning oligopolies can reduce risk by tacitly colluding. In essence, all the players know "the rules of competition," but no one talks about them (that would be price-rigging)—among competitors.

Unit of Analysis

Once we have defined the domain, we are ready to begin the analysis. The macroenvironment is a set of six remote forces over which the typical company has little control. Because of that remoteness, they generally have the potential for lesser impact on the individual firm. That holds even during an economic meltdown like the 2007 to 2009 experience. The very remoteness of the macroenvironment gives it a range of risk premiums that is narrow compared to those of the domain and of the firm itself.

At the outset of the process of external risk assessment, it is important to point out again that all firms within a given competitive domain face the same set of external factors. To repeat what we first pointed out in Chapter 3, that means that all rivals in that domain have the same two external risk premiums. Therefore, and repeating again, the *unit of analysis* in *all* external risk assessments is the domain, *not* the client company.

If you have just raised a skeptical eyebrow, let me ask: How can they *not* be? The external factors are the same magnitude for all players in a given domain. *It is how each competitor responds to those factors that matters.* Therefore, do not confuse the domain with the company. Different companies respond in different ways, so we should not be surprised to find significant differences among them. This is why there is such heterogeneity within industries.

We also know that the domain will be either the strategic group of which a company (or division) is a part or, if it competes industry-wide, the industry itself. Few SMEs do, so the strategic group is the domain in most engagements.

To repeat: The very first task of the analyst, therefore, is to *define the domain by determining the one or two parameters that define the strategic group.* In our shop we do that before we ever draft an engagement letter. That helps us focus our attention early on and not waste time having to restart our analysis because we never defined the scope of what we are supposed to analyze. Having made about every mistake one can make in the research phase of the valuation process, I have come away with two ironclad rules:

1. Define the domain first.
2. Do the research top down. That is, start at the most remote level, the macroenvironment. Work your way through that, and then analyze

the domain. Then, and only then, are you ready to analyze the client company itself. By then you should have a lot of clues about what to look for in your analysis of the subject company. If you start at the bottom—the firm—and work your way up toward the macroenvironment, you will get your research head handed to you because you will have to start over at least once, and probably many times.

Trilevel Unsystematic Risk Framework

Recall from Chapter 1 that we constructed a trilevel framework to help us analyze unsystematic risk. Our framework began in the early 1990s with four macroenvironmental forces, five industry ones, and a bright red "X" for the company. It has evolved to six macroenvironmental forces, six more in the domain, and who-knows-how-many in the company itself. These three levels comprise the foundation of so-called SWOT (**s**trengths, **w**eaknesses, **o**pportunities, **t**hreats) analysis. The "OT" is external (macroenvironment and domain), and the "SW" is internal (the company). (See Exhibit 8.1.)

So where are we going with this?

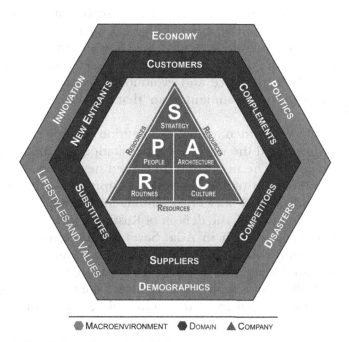

Exhibit 8.1 Trilevel Unsystematic Risk Framework 1

Answer: toward better alignment. Aligning a company's internal strengths and weaknesses with the external opportunities and threats it faces in such a way that it has a distinctive advantage enables it to outperform its peers. That is because few companies in the SME space understand the notion of alignment. The challenge for the analyst is to apply the trilevel framework to the analysis and then ask Socratic questions during the on-site interviews.

Let us take another step: We know from Schumpeter and also McGahan that firms and industries are constantly evolving. That is why the assumptions of traditional microeconomics and its insistence on equilibrium, homogeneity, and static analysis are not helpful in valuation. The most successful firms are the toughest to value because they are the ones that have had to change to keep hitting the moving target that is capitalism's trademark. Lest anyone has any doubt: Management matters!

Because each of the three levels of risk has a different proximity to the company, each should have a different range for its potential impact on risk and on, thereby, the equity discount rate. The macroenvironment should have the narrowest range, while the company itself should have the widest because it can most affect, for better or for worse, its own performance.

History and Background

The macroenvironment graphic began life as a square at General Electric in the 1950s. Labeled economic, technological, social, and political, this four-force framework survived intact for over four decades. Even today we still see it in the form of P.E.S.T. Analysis (political, economic, sociocultural, and technological). Experience and evolution have taught us that there is more to the macroenvironment than that. Luckily, we are in good company.[3]

After the Cold War ended, global competition became a reality. Trade barriers came down, and the world got more competitive than many of us ever thought it could. The new world unleashed new forces. We saw, first, the 1997 self-immolation of the Long-Term Capital Management hedge fund, which included two Nobel Prize winners in economics as principals. That was followed quickly by the default of Russia on its international debt and then by a credit crunch in Asia. Several years later, 9/11 hit the United States. That provided us with the "Disasters" dimension.

About the same time, the social dimension, previously defined as encompassing both demography and lifestyles, came to be regarded as overly broad. This resulted from technological advances that enhanced

---

[3] Hitt, Ireland, and Hoskisson, *Strategic Management.*

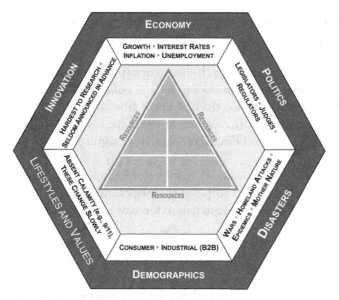

Exhibit 8.2   The Six Forces of the Macroenvironment

sellers' abilities to segment markets with great precision. It also came from more trade giving more choices to more consumers. That led to their increasing unwillingness to buy something that was not *exactly* what they wanted. The latter phenomenon, which some call "mass customization," was egged on by the pick-your-own-features approach of Dell Computer.

Thus two new factors replace the social factor: demographics (consumer and industrial) and lifestyles and values. With some detail added, the resulting hexagon[4] is shown in Exhibit 8.2.

Why Does the Macroenvironment Matter?

From one perspective, the macroenvironment—which is *not* synonymous with the *macroeconomy*[5]—matters because it affects risk. Even though it is logical to believe that risk rises as we move through risk factors from the size premium to the company itself, macroenvironmental factors might *decrease* risk in a domain. Here is an example: High interest rates are the bane

---

[4] Adapted from ibid., 50–60, and from Fahey and Narayaman, *Macroenvironmental Analysis.*

[5] Sometimes called the macro economy, the word refers to macroeconomic forces only— gross domestic product (GDP), monetary and fiscal policy, business cycles, unemployment (which in strategic groups is a local or regional measure), and growth. From the term "macroeconomy," we get "macroeconomics," which studies whole economies.

of most economic activities, but are precursors of higher profits in the pawn-shop and outplacement sectors. In those domains, a lousy economy might reduce the cost of capital.

Beyond risk, understanding the macroenvironment helps the analyst *understand the business of the firm she purports to value.* A client assumes that we understand its business. If we do not know how and why it works the way it does, how can we defend the value we estimate for it? A book in the study regimen for the Chartered Financial Analyst designation puts it this way:

> [Understanding the business] involves evaluating industry prospects, competitive position, and corporate strategies. Analysts use this informa-tion together with financial analysis to forecast performance.[6]

It is worth noting that "understanding the business" is the first of five steps "that an analyst undertakes" in a valuation.[7] Additional aspects of understanding the business include understanding the structure of its do-main, "overall supply and demand balance," competitive analysis, and strat-egy, especially the ability of the company's people to *execute* its strategy successfully.

The Forces

We move now to a discussion of the analysis and interpretation of invest-ment-specific risk at the macroenvironmental level. This is unsystematic risk at its most remote. The six forces in the macroenvironment circumscribe the valuation entity's domain, which, in turn, circumscribes the valuation entity itself.

As previously illustrated, the six dimensions of the macroenvironment are economy, innovation, lifestyles and values, demographics, disasters, and politics. To their detriment, managements in many smaller companies fail to think through how they might respond to changes in these forces. Small-business owners seem to believe that they cannot do anything about them, so why bother? One example: Many do not even join industry trade associations.

In contrast, we in the valuation community must analyze, interpret, and quantify the effect of macroenvironmental forces. Their impact will vary across domains because no single one is the same as any other. Moreover, the effect of free markets guarantees that our macroenvironmental analysis, like our valuation, is a snapshot at a particular point in time: the valuation date. Like free markets generally, macroenvironmental forces also change.

---

[6] Stowe, et al. *Equity Asset Valuation*, 29.
[7] Ibid, 9.

Economy

In most domains, this is the most important factor in the macroenvironment. For business owners and CEOs, it is usually the most frustrating, and with good reason: It involves interest rates, inflation, unemployment, gross domestic product (GDP), and fiscal and monetary policy—all factors beyond their control. Except for unemployment, each is measured nationally. It is important for the valuation professional to understand how changes in these forces affect the risk profile of the domain.

A cautionary note: Even experienced analysts sometimes cut and paste into their reports economic summaries from well-regarded vendors. It shows up under a heading of "Economic Outlook" (or similar wording). Besides failing to include attribution for these summaries, analysts are apt not to make the connection between economic factors and their impact the domain(s) in which the valuation entity competes.

It is as if readers are supposed to figure it out for themselves. Many readers know by heart the eight "factors to consider" in Section 4 of Revenue Ruling 59-60. Recall Factor 2: "The economic outlook in general and the condition and outlook of the specific industry in particular." Substitute "domain" for "industry" and then connect the dots. We recommend writing your own outlook and keeping the domain squarely in mind. You will automatically connect the dots.

Innovation

As pointed out earlier in Chapter 5, most innovation is in the form of new methods in *management*—that is, new perspectives, new understanding, new measurements, new reports, and new ways to bundle resources. In contrast to patents, copyrights, and breakthrough products and services, management innovation operates below the radar screen, unless the CEO (e.g., Jack Welch) is high profile. Management innovation is also a major contributor to the heterogeneity across competitors in a given domain.

However, R&D activities can also result in innovation. R&D tends to occur in larger companies, especially those in industries where products and services have short shelf lives. Less volatile domains, especially those in so-called low-tech industries, might not invest in much R&D, though venture-funded enterprises are often a conspicuous exception. For analysts, the problem with R&D-related innovation is that it is seldom announced in advance. Besides making it harder to research and harder to forecast, announcing the likelihood of a breakthrough, like the announcement of an engagement to be married, might create expectations for a seminal event that does not happen. Such announcements can also cannibalize sales of existing technology. And sometimes, despite a ton of hype, an innovation might not be an innovation at all. Microsoft's 2007 introduction of its long-overdue Vista operating system is a case in point. That is why, for longer-term perspectives, we are partial to *Technology Review* (www.mittech nologyreview .com) and the World Future Society (www.wfs.org).

Appraisers should also contact the relevant trade association(s).[8] We always ask to speak to the librarian. In visiting with librarians over the years, we have noticed their pent-up desire to talk. We infer that few people talk to librarians. They can be incredible and invaluable resources.

In the absence of such a librarian or of the trade association itself, the valuation professional must use his imagination. For instance, if one is valuing a trash hauler, he learns that commercial hauling rates are based on volume of trash, frequency of pickup, and tip fees (fees paid to operators of refuse dumps). One need not know about an Oklahoma City–based firm called Liftpak, L.C. (which holds patents on industrial trash-compacting technology that can reduce the volume of trash by as much as 90%) to be able to envision the potential impact of such an innovation on the fortunes of a trash hauler whose revenues depend heavily on commercial customers. Think about it: 90% compacted trash = far fewer pickups = fewer trucks, fewer employees, and, eventually, far fewer trash haulers. Even without knowing about Liftpak, the savvy appraiser should include in her analysis a caveat about what could happen if a black-box contraption came to market.

More important to the valuation, that caveat would not be the last word on the subject. Later, at the company level of risk assessment, one would need to write about what the firm was doing to protect itself from such an eventuality. Does it even recognize the possibility? What is the company's mix of commercial and residential customers? Has it incentivized its salespeople to try to increase the number of residential customers because they have less incentive to make the investment in a Liftpak-like gizmo? Has it tried to make pricing more attractive to such customers? Has it attempted to create switching costs for residential customers?

Lifestyles and Values

Trends in values and lifestyles can affect demand for a company's product or service. Divorce rates can matter. So can trends in food, clothing, housing, education, and entertainment. That is true even in a B2B industry such as wholesale appliance distribution. On the surface, a distributor selling to appliance stores or directly to home builders might seem impervious to divorce rates and single parents. But a mother and father living apart will need two refrigerators, even if they are smaller than the single unit they

---

[8] See www.asaecenter.org/directories/associationsearch.cfm for a searchable database of over 51,000 associations.

would have if they shared the same household. The inventories of savvy distributors reflect that.

Perhaps because they are inculcated at an early age, values change more slowly than lifestyles. For instance, mothers who never marry is good news for education and the daycare industry, even as children growing up without dads in the home are often bad news for society as a whole.

Demographics

Both industrial and consumer demography subsume the characteristics of a population. On the consumer side, for instance, age, education, family size, rate of household formation, disposable income, and birth and mortality rates affect not only demand but also the design and delivery of products and services. (Think about those single-adult appliances.) Data on the consumer side are easy to come by through the U.S. Department of Commerce and its Bureau of Economic Analysis.

At a minimum, we want to know about domain demographics—how many firms, how fast they are growing, the mortality rate among firms, the rate of new entrants, and how growth in demand for the industry's output compares with growth in GDP. If the target market is businesses, we want to know the same things about that market, too.

Business demographics data, in contrast, are harder to come by and, thus, might not be free. Our first choice is always one or two relevant trade associations; however, the quality and depth of these vary widely. Wall Street research reports that focus on a given industry, rather than a particular company, can be extraordinarily helpful, as can the various business censuses taken every five years by the Bureau of the Census. ZapData (www.zap data. com) offers a searchable database of 14 million businesses; price varies according to the number of companies and of data elements to be downloaded.

Disasters

Originally this dimension was labeled "International." Global competition has obviated the need for that. We relabeled it "Disasters" in the wake of 9/11. As the world faced the potential of a swine flu pandemic in the spring of 2009, we were glad we did. The media drew parallels between that outbreak and the mislabeled Spanish flu pandemic of 1918, which killed an estimated 50 million people worldwide.[9]

Disasters come in many forms, some not as visible as others. In Europe, for instance, low birth rates are causing shrinkage in most countries'

---

[9] www.cdc.gov/ncidod/eid/vol12no01/05-0979.htm.

populations, even considering increasing immigration. That is a problem because pensions in Europe tend to be wholly funded by governments, unlike the 401(k) scenario in the United States. American readers can imagine what the situation here would be like if there were no 401(k)'s. The combination of falling birth rates and no 401(k)'s means that Europeans will hit the entitlement wall long before Americans do. We're seeing it in Greece.

Politics

Our work must consider four essential political facets: legislative initiatives, regulatory policy, judicial decisions, and future electoral results. The latter matters because elections matter. As we see in the Obama administration in Washington, winning politicians are apt to push legislative, regulatory, and judicial changes. Regardless of one's politics, we could predict with a high level of confidence in the summer of 2008 that a President Obama's legislative agenda, regulatory policies, and judicial nominees would differ significantly from those of a President McCain. A sea change in the midterm 2010 elections could mean "change we can believe in" in the opposite direction. Those differences affect the performance of domains, and we must be about the business of anticipating and explaining potential changes based on different electoral outcomes.

Consider, for instance, the minimum wage. In an industry with low barriers to entry, it is a critical economic factor. Moreover, minimum wage is no longer just a federal issue. States, and even some cities, set their own minimums, sometimes as a result of pressure from unions that cannot prevail in the nation's capital. In Florida, for instance, there have been two hikes in the minimum wage in recent years. The impact on the hospitality sector that is the backbone of Florida's economy could hardly be greater.

Another example: If the Obama administration follows through on its stated goal of having Congress raise taxes on high-income individuals, the increase in tax rates will increase the cost of equity capital for all enterprises. That is because hikes in marginal rates for individuals hit those who own or have stakes in S corporations the hardest.

Good sources of political data include trade associations, legislative and congressional Web sites, and articles in either local or national newspapers, all of which usually have searchable databases. Unlike some research archives, these are usually free.

Local politics are more susceptible to pressure from business groups and companies. That influence is seen in the contributions of political action committees and in lobbying activities of trade associations. If a corporate officer is a major supporter of an influential political figure, that support can mean a more benign (or less malign) political environment for the industry and maybe for the firm. Of course, if the political horse that supporter backs turns out to be "President Dewey,"[10] then the effect is apt to be the opposite, particularly if a hot issue during the campaign affects the domain.

Summary

The configuration of external risk factors can help or hurt a domain. The effect depends on the facts and circumstances of the situation at hand. Recall here the wisdom of Revenue Ruling 59-60: "No formula can be devised that will be generally applicable to the multitude of different valuation issues arising in estate and gift cases"[11]—or any other cases, either.

Remember, however, that it is essential to *define the domain* before one does any analysis. More than any other single action, defining the domain improves efficiency, increases realization, and reduces the incidence of mistakes. We consider it the *sine qua non*[12] of business valuation. If we do not get that right, we are unlikely to get anything else right, either.

Many of the data involved in analyzing macroenvironmental risk are "soft." In fact, in four of the six dimensions, that is all we have; only Economy and Demographics have hard data consistently. Whatever the data, though, our analyses must be comprehensive, thorough, and rigorous. They must also be based on "the elements of common sense, informed judgment, and reasonableness."[13] Even if an analyst believes that the aggregate impact of the macroenvironment in a given scenario is neutral, macroenvironmental analysis is essential because it enhances both one's understanding of how the business works and one's credibility with readers.

We always end the presentation of our macroenvironmental assessment with a paragraph summarizing our analysis. We focus on the two or three most important findings and explain why they matter. Whatever approach one deploys—cost, market, or income—a sound, done-from-scratch macroenvironmental analysis will help the analyst to understand better the domain of which the valuation entity is a member and the external risk factors it faces. That understanding plays out in a better and more accurate estimate of value. It remains the job of the analyst to quantify qualitative information. We defer the explanation of how we do that until after we have finished presenting all three levels of unsystematic risk.[14]

---

[10] http://en.wikipedia.org/w12iki/File:Deweytruman12.jpg.

[11] Revenue Ruling 59-60, Sec. 3.01.

[12] Latin for "Without which, (there is) nothing."

[13] Sec. 3.01.

[14] See Appendix A at the end of Chapter 11.

Additional Reading

Miller, Warren D. "Three Peas in the Business Valuation Pod: The Resource-Based View of the Firm, Value Creation, and Strategy." Chapter 12, 305–327, in Robert F. Reilly and Robert P. Schweihs (eds.), *The Handbook of Business Valuation and Intellectual Property Analysis.* New York: McGraw-Hill, 2004.

The "OT" in SWOT Analysis: The Domain

In this chapter we discuss how to apply the middle level of the trilevel framework of unsystematic risk. Like our discussion in Chapter 8 on the macroenvironment, this level of analysis is not difficult . . . once one has developed a precise definition of the competitive domain.

The Roots of Domain Analysis

Industry analysis came to the fore in the late 1970s through the influence of Michael Porter; his 1974 Ph.D. was in a then-obscure branch of economics called "industrial organization." IO focuses on two areas: (1) antitrust and regulatory issues and (2) the structure, conduct, and performance of industries. Note the presence of that word "conduct"; think "behavior" or, even better, "strategy." IO is real-world economics. You can see it around you almost every day.

In Chapter 3 we presented the S-C-P paradigm that is the basis of the study of industries. We pointed out the feedback loops from Performance to both Conduct and Structure and from Conduct to Structure. We noted that domains are in a constant state of evolution and change.

Our definition of the S-C-P branch of IO is "the study of market structures and the behavior of firms within markets." As we wrote in Chapter 3, "This is the economics of *imperfect competition*, which is where the real money is made."

As its name implies, the *unit of analysis* in traditional industrial organization is the *domain*. Therefore, in our industry (or strategic group) analysis, we focus the discussion on the forces of that domain, not on individual firms.

Oligopolies Large and Small

The combination of deregulation, new technology, and rivalry between the antitrust people at the FTC and those at the U.S. Department of Justice (DOJ) has eliminated many of the oligopolies that existed in the United

States 30 years ago. Americans over 40 can remember when ABC, CBS, and NBC had over 90% of the viewing public. We can remember when the Big 3 Detroit automakers ruled not only the United States but the global automobile industry. Some oligopolies remain—we cited the ready-to-eat breakfast cereal industry in Chapter 3. But most have gone by the wayside.

For its part, deregulation got its start in 1975 during the Ford administration when brokerage houses' rates were deregulated by the Securities and Exchange Commission (SEC). As part of a term paper I wrote for an undergraduate finance class back then, I interviewed several brokerage managers in Oklahoma City. I remember the Merrill Lynch manager telling me that he thought brokerage rates should be fixed because firms in his industry were "like public utilities." He wished. Deregulated rates made for a massive consolidation in what was then a fragmented industry. Venerable names—Bache & Co., Goodbody, E.F. Hutton, and dozens of others—fell by the wayside.

The pace of deregulation picked up during the Carter administration. The chairman of what was then the Civil Aeronautics Board (CAB), Cornell economist Alfred Kahn, convinced his colleagues to let the market, not the federal government, set prices for airline tickets. When the CAB announced its intentions, the outcry was deafening . . . from the airlines themselves. Those nonplaying captains of industry much preferred competing in Washington to competing against their rivals. Airline fares plunged, new entrants got in, and old and storied names (Pan American, Braniff, Eastern, etc.) went by the wayside. So did the CAB itself.

Recall from Chapter 3 that one of the Porter's original five forces was Substitutes (a product or service which uses a different technology to meet the same need as the product or service being substituted against). In the wake of airline deregulation, the effect of substitutes torched the intercity bus industry, which was then a cozy duopoly between Greyhound and Continental Trailways.

Deregulation then went into overdrive with the administrations of Reagan and the first Bush. The breakup of the venerable Bell Telephone Co. monopoly by a lone federal judge, Harold Greene, opened the door to consumer choice in long-distance telephone. New companies, led by Bill McGowan's MCI, entered what had been a lucrative cash cow for AT&T. The competition and the growth in long-distance usage encouraged innovation, and then cellular technology came on the scene. Today so-called land lines—POTS (plain old telephone service)—are a declining business. Many Americans do not even have them, relying on their cell phones instead. In recent years, the old telecoms have entered the cable business, giving new headaches to a formerly capital-intensive industry that was already beset with competition from satellite providers of television programming.

Other industries that had long slumbered in a stress-free environment of regulation suddenly had to awaken. Competition came to cable television, electric utilities, and even public accounting, when a federal court ruled that the industry's long-standing prohibition against advertising denied vital information to clients.

Segue: When I talked my way into the University of Oklahoma in 1973 with a 1.6 cumulative GPA, I decided to major in finance. That lasted all of one semester because the first embargo by the Organization of Petroleum Exporting Countries hit the United States in October 1973. The U.S. economy quickly turned down, but I noticed that the demand for accounting majors held up. So I became a double major in finance and accounting. My late start in my accounting concentration, combined with an ice-cold economy (the Dow Jones Industrials hit 580 in the spring of 1974), imposed a last-semester burden of 12 hours of accounting courses on me. I would not wish that on anyone.

Before I graduated in 1975, though, a close friend and I crashed a Beta Alpha Psi chapter meeting at the University of Oklahoma. A partner from one of the then–Big 8 accounting firms was the featured speaker. During the Q&A, I asked, "Who does your firm's marketing?" The accounting majors turned and looked at me as if I had called Mother Teresa a hooker. The partner stammered and stuttered and tried to duck the question. I stayed after him. He finally conceded that, yes, his firm did have something called "business development." A rose by any other name . . . .

Of course, the introduction of price-based competition to public accounting, in concert with a generally benevolent view of mergers on the part of regulators, led to the Big 8 shrinking to the Big 6 and then the Big 5. After Arthur Andersen was taken out by the courts, we were left with four global firms. Talk to any CFO of a substantial public company about today's market for audit services, and she will yowl about the dearth of choice. The oligopoly in audit services for large public companies is nearly airtight: Big 4 firms have a 98% market share of the 1,500 companies whose revenues exceed $1 billion. At the other end of the market, non–Big 4 firms have nearly 80% of the audit-services market for public companies with revenues below $100 million.[1]

Like anything else in business valuation, though, the question of oligopoly "depends." In most cases, it depends on how we define the domain. The FTC-DOJ wrecking ball has knocked down many national oligopolies. Regionally and locally, however, the structure is alive and well. When oligopolists abide by the primary rule of competition in their domain— "Thou shalt NEVER compete on price"—well, the life of a business

---

[1] www.webcpa.com/prc_issues/2008_3/26820-1.html

executive in a functioning oligopoly beats working for a living. Later in this book I'll tell the story of our experience with a key player in niche oligopoly of the national industrial supply sector. It happened early in the life of Beck-mill Research, and it was an eye-opener.

Since then, we have always tried to get a handle on the structure of the domain in which a prospective new client competes before we send out an engagement letter. That is because, when we see pre-engagement indications of an oligopoly, we always ask the CEO, "On what basis do y'all compete?" If she says, "We kill 'em on price," well, unsystematic risk at the company level just went up! We know the engagement is likely to be a tough slog, and we price accordingly. We will have a lot more to say about our approach to pricing in Chapter 18.

Price Competition in an Oligopoly

As noted in Chapter 3, implicit in the concept of oligopoly is the notion of interdependence among the players. Their fortunes are intertwined, so they sink or swim together. That is especially true when one competitor decides to compete on price. It can be a domain-wrecker if the errant competitor cannot be quickly and severely punished. Rivals try to accomplish that by further dropping their prices faster than the black-sheep player. Word travels fast in an oligopoly.

Price competition descended on the "suite software" oligopoly in 1993 when Philippe Kahn, CEO of Borland International, slashed the price of his firm's Quattro Pro spreadsheet from $495 to $49 in a desperate attempt to buy share. It did not work. He had to sell Quattro Pro to Novell a year later at the same time that Novell bought WordPerfect Corporation (WPC). WPC's fortunes spiraled downward because it was not efficient enough to compete in the sub-$500 market; WPC's deteriorating condition was exacerbated by its slowness in converting from the MS-DOS platform to Windows. Kahn's aggressive approach to pricing also hurt Lotus Development Corp., which IBM took over in a surprise hostile move in 1995.

But Kahn succeeded grandly on one dimension: He drove down the price of applications software for individual consumers across the board. Prices were not the only thing that went down. So did the number of "bootleg" copies of software that people would make for their friends who had not paid for it.

Published Industry Risk Premiums

Beginning in its 2000 edition, Ibbotson Associates (now owned by Morningstar) began publishing Industry Risk Premiums (IRPs), presumably in response to requests from the valuation community. In the Valuation Edition of its 2010 *Yearbook,* Morningstar arrayed its industry-level risk premiums (IRPS) for 479 two-, three-, and four-digit SIC codes.[2]

Because of the importance of business diversification as a way to both reduce risk and ramp up growth, few public companies compete in just one SIC code. For multi-business enterprises, Morningstar assumes that risk occurs ratably across business segments according to their revenues. By excluding privately held firms, most of which are SMEs, and by prorating risk according to segment revenue, Morningstar's IRPs are biased downward (i.e., the sample is biased in favor of bigger companies and bigger divisions). Therefore, IRPs are apt to be understated.

Moreover, these premiums are drawn from public companies. Because of their size, many more of them compete industry-wide rather than in strategic groups. That size factor also enables them to reduce risk by diversifying into different lines of business, another indication that using IRPs as proxies for private companies will likely result in overestimates of value due to underestimates of risk. As seen in Chapter 8, the underlying structure of strategic groups often differs significantly from their industry-wide structure. That alone should whistle prudent appraisers off IRPs for most, if not all, work involving SMEs.

Nonetheless, we must devise a way to quantify the upper and lower bounds of each of the ranges for macroenvironmental, domain, and company risk. To begin that process, we used aggregate IRPs data in the 2009 edition of *SBBI.*[3] Recall that the year of the yearbook covers economic activity in the year before.

Upper Bound

- At the three- and four-digit SIC level, eight SICs comprising 150 business segments meeting Morningstar's criteria had IRPs $\geq$ 10%. Their weighted-average IRP = 11.98%.
- Using the same method with SBBI IRPs data in the 2008 *Yearbook,* the upper limit for *total external* risk was 12%.
- Risk premiums usually fall in bear markets, which 2008 certainly was.
- They rise in a rising market, which, after an early nosedive, 2009 turned out to be.
- Since 1926, market averages have risen in more years (60) than they have fallen (24).[4]
- Therefore, we conclude that a *robust upper limit for total external unsystematic risk at year-end 2009 is +12%.*

---

[2] Ibbotson, *2010 SBBI Yearbook,* 32–41.

[3] We update these ranges annually in the spring of the year.

[4] Ibbotson, *2010 SBBI Yearbook,* Table B-1 (Large Company Stocks: Total Returns), 164–165.

Lower Bound

- Similarly, three SIC codes had IRPs $\leq -5\%$. For these 39 segments, the weighted-average IRP was -5.71%.
- Rounding up, we get a total lower limit for external unsystematic risk of -6%.

It should surprise no one that we do not use Morningstar's IRPs in our own reports. We do, however, use them against other experts in litigation. In a high-dollar divorce case on the East Coast, I easily prevailed over a well-known opposing expert who had applied an Ibbotson IRP in his build-up method estimate of the equity discount rate. For a temp/permanent placement firm focused solely on financial services, he used a -3.58% IRP in the wake of the stock market contraction in 2000. That is right—a negative IRP for a company for which conditions on Wall Street were make-or-break. To come up with his indicator of value, he used capitalization, a nothing-if-not-dubious practice to use on volatile cash flows, which the client company certainly had. His third major innovation was that he had included in his capitalization calculation a $400,000 decline in receivables (to $900,000) in 2000; in other words by Year 3 of his capitalization period, accounts receivable would be negative.

Working for the nonpropertied spouse, he estimated a value of $3.3 million; I came in at $900,000. The case settled for $1 million.

Now, if you are still tempted to use a published IRP, ask yourself:

- **How long after the IRP computation date is the valuation date?** Remember, IRPs are a function of betas, which change over time and tend to revert toward the mean (1.0).
- **How many firms are included in the computation for the IRP?** Fewer are worse from a statistical standpoint. We like to see at least 15 companies (it is one-half of the statisticians' rule of thumb for randomness), but we will take 10. Note: Of the 479 IRPs, 179 (37%) are based on fewer than 10 companies.
- **Do you understand how the underlying beta is calculated?** Betas vary according to the underlying market index one uses, the frequency with which they are calculated, the number of months over which they are computed, and the type of beta used (full-information beta versus sum beta versus beta calculated using ordinary least squares). For these reasons, we calculate our own betas. That way we know how we got what we have.

Morningstar uses a "full information beta" methodology for its IRPs.[5] This approach to calculating beta relies on a sales-based

---

[5] See ibid., 28, 84–85.

weighting scheme that includes data from firms that are not "pure plays" in a given industry. Those tend to be larger companies because they are diversified. That reduces risk, which means lower betas. Not surprisingly, "full information betas" are notably lower than their pure-play counterparts. Lower betas make for lower IRPs.

- **Does the industry risk premium make logical sense?** For example, −0.65% is the IRP for restaurants (SIC 5812);[6] it was −0.94%, 1.72%, and 0.58% in 2007, 2008 and 2009, respectively. Yet any banker will attest that lending to restaurants is perilously close to self-destructive activity. Research shows that about 60% of restaurants go out of business during their first three years in existence.

- **If you do not believe in using the capital asset pricing model (CAPM) to estimate the cost of capital for an SME, why would you use an IRP based on the CAPM?** One expert has a pithy characterization: "IRPs are just CAPM in a build-up wrapper."

The Domain

The next set of forces is the one over which a company may exert more control, though the extent will vary according to both the individual firm and the domain's structure. There are six factors in the domain (see Exhibit 9.1).

New Entrants

The threat of new entrants creates risk for incumbents. The extent of that risk depends on a myriad of factors, the most important of which are growth and profitability in the domain. The likelihood of new entrants is correlated positively with both. A new player typically faces one or more barriers to entry. These are hurdles, if you will, that the new entrant must clear in order to compete.

Whether in the form of entry or mobility barriers, the analysis is the same. These fall into five categories that are shown in Exhibit 9.2.

Competitors

How intense is margin pressure among players in a given domain? How is market share distributed among them?[7] Price cuts induced by slackening demand in high-fixed-cost arenas (e.g., airline transportation), by frequent innovation, by quick actions/reactions, by protracted advertising

---

[6] Ibid., 38.
[7] See Appendix 9A.

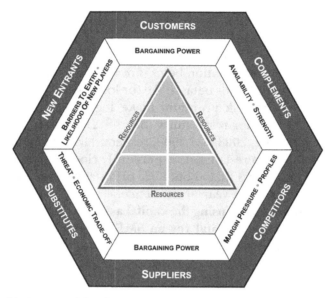

Exhibit 9.1   Six Forces of the Competitive Domain

Source: Adapted from Michael E. Porter, *Competitive Strategy: Techniques for Analyzing Industries and Competitors* (New York: Free Press, 1980).

campaigns—all reduce margins. Structural factors that *increase* competitive intensity are:

- **Numerous players that are about the same size** (no advantages).
- **Slow growth in demand** (says Warren Buffett: "It's not until the tide goes out that you can tell who's been swimming naked").
- **Undifferentiated output** (audit firms have this problem).
- **High fixed costs/perishability** (produce; airlines; hotels/motels).
- **Capacity must be added in large increments** (there are scale economies in both the manufacture and the purchase of new planes).
- **Exit barriers** (which keep players that should exit from doing so).
- **Diverse competitive strategies** (in this situation, no firm can be all things to all comers, even though cost of capital will rise as some less savvy firms try to have more than one strategy anyway).

Customers' Bargaining Power

Certain aspects of customer groups can reduce or increase a domain's risk by increasing/reducing its revenues and margins. Factors that *increase* customers' bargaining power and thus increase domain risk include:

Exhibit 9.2   Entry and Mobility Barriers

<table>
<tr><td rowspan="1">

Natural

Barriers

to

Entry

</td><td>

- ■ **Economies of scale.** Falling cost per unit of output within a given timeframe. Traditionally scale economies are thought of in terms of manufacturing. But larger companies can reap scale economies in advertising, purchasing, and training, too, to name just a few. Market leaders typically enjoy these economies.
- ■ **Differentiation.** Buyers' perceived uniqueness of either a product or service. Differentiation is the source of so-called brand awareness. It is why such companies as Lexus, Chanel, Budweiser, Ralph Lauren, Bose, and Ritz-Carlton advertise in carefully-chosen venues.
- ■ **Cost disadvantages independent of scale.** Inefficiencies caused by uncontrollable factors. Examples include proprietary technology, favorable access to raw materials, know-how, favorable geographic locations, and the learning curve.
- ■ **Contrived deterrence.** These are investments that firms make to deter entry. Such investments have three characteristics: (1) they *force* a firm to fight if a new player enters; (2) they are highly specific; and (3) they are made loudly and publicly. The most common example is highly specialized production or warehouse facilities.
- ■ **Government policy.** Less common today than several decades ago, but still a factor. Examples include sanctioned monopolies (electric utilities, cable TV companies); prohibited entry (foreign airlines flying point to point inside the United States); tariffs/import quotas (sugar); non-tariff trade barriers (slot-machine manufacturing in Japan).

</td></tr>
</table>

- **Undifferentiated domain output.** It makes customers' decision-making easier by focusing their attention on price.
- **Domain output is a significant portion of customers' cost structure.** It induces customers to bargain hard and shop for alternatives.
- **Customers' bottom lines are negative.** This increases their sensitivity to price and encourages them to push back in cases where, if they were highly profitable, they wouldn't.
- **Threat of backward integration.** It depends on entry/mobility barriers.
- **Access to full information.** Buying airline tickets on the Internet has put downward pressure on ticket prices after the industry decided to stop paying commissions to travel agents. They accounted for "only" 80% of the airlines' ticket revenues!
- **Domain's product or service is unimportant to the quality of the customer group's output.** This creates pricing sensitivity.

- **Customers incur no switching costs.** When the airlines ditched their primary distribution channel—travel agents (not airports!)—they made travelers savvier buyers. Then they eliminated the Saturday–night stay with which they had gouged business travelers. That took out switching costs. Then they treated the customers like dirt. And finally, of course, they wondered why their customers were not loyal.

Suppliers' Bargaining Power

Like customers, supplier groups may increase or decrease a domain's costs. Conditions that *increase* suppliers' power and the domain's cost of capital include:

- **Supplier group is highly concentrated** (few suppliers, many buyers).
- **No substitutes exist for suppliers' output** (and so no price ceiling).
- **Domain is *not* a significant purchaser of suppliers' output.**
- **Suppliers' output is highly differentiated.**
- **Suppliers could forward-integrate.**

Substitutes

A substitute uses a different technology to satisfy the same need that customers have. Thus it tends to put a ceiling on the price that can be charged for the product or service being substituted against. Our favorite example of a substitute is TurboTax, a product that encourages otherwise sensible people[8] to do their own tax returns. When demand for a substitute goes *up*, demand for the product being substituted against goes *down*. Some examples of substitutes include:

- Driving vs. flying.
- Cell phones vs. land lines
- Cell phones vs. cameras
- Smartphones vs. laptops
- Beer vs. wine vs. distilled spirits
- Oil vs. coal vs. electricity vs. natural gas vs. nuclear power vs. "green" technologies
- Dining out vs. carry-out vs. grilling steaks at home
- Movie tickets vs. movies-on-demand (from cable/satellite TV) vs. DVD rentals
- Sporting-event tickets vs. Pay-Per-View

---

[8] Which is how the current Secretary of the Treasury got his nickname, "TurboTax Tim."

- Compact discs vs. MP3 downloads vs. long-playing records
- Timeshares vs. resorts
- Mediation/arbitration vs. going to court
- TV news vs. online sources of information vs. newspapers
- Snuff vs. cigarettes vs. pipes vs. cigars
- E-mail vs. snail mail

Complements

First popularized by a 1996 book,[9] this sixth force has come to the fore in our advanced industrial economy. Complements are sometimes called "complementors"; they are *not* the same as competitors. A complement can be a product or a service. When demand for a complement goes *up*, demand for the product/service being complemented also goes *up*. Companies today are on the lookout for complements for their products and services. Besides contributing to the rise of networking and strategic alliances, complements are now a force in the domain framework. Their popularity has also increased the frequency with which strategic alliances are formed. A few examples of complements are:

- Golf clubs, golf balls, golf tees, golf lessons, rounds of golf.
- Airline transportation, lodging, car rentals.
- Computers, software, IT support services.
- TV programming, TV networks/cable TV.
- Baseball games, hot dogs, popcorn, peanuts, beer.
- Razors, razor blades, shaving cream, after-shave lotion.
- Cell phones, cellular minutes, bluetooth devices.
- Men's suits, dress shirts, neckties.
- Swimming pools, diving boards, bathing suits, sunscreen, beach towels.
- Automobiles, gasoline, car insurance, tires.

Summary

When we have completed our analysis of the domain, we summarize the positive and negative influences in one paragraph, just as we did with the macroenvironment. This is the lead-in to the major challenge in analyzing unsystematic risk: quantifying it. Published research tells us that the range of the domain's risk premium will be bigger than that of the macroenvironment,

---

[9] Brandenburger and Nalebuff, *Co-Opetition.*

but not so wide as the company's; we deal with all of this in detail in Appendix 11A. For now, keep these key points about domain analysis in mind:

- Define the domain precisely.
- Strategic groups are common in domain analysis for SMEs.
- Always have S-C-P in mind.
- Avoid boilerplate, except in the first paragraph or two.
- Except in the context of the distribution of market share when discussing the rivalry force, do not cite individual companies.
- Explain, do not assert.
- Oligopoly is alive and well in many regional and local domains.
- Individual forces in the six-force framework are unlikely to exert equal influence on domain risk.
- Government regulation often reduces risk. (Check the rates of return that "regulated" electric utilities enjoy.)
- An oligopolist cutting price is the economic equivalent of cheating on one's spouse.

In Appendix 9A we discuss competitive analysis. Pay particular attention to how to estimate market share because of its implications for inferring domain structure and, thereby, domain conduct, and, by implication, something about domain performance.

Additional Reading

Brock, James. *The Structure of American Industry*, 12th ed. Upper Saddle River, NJ: Prentice Hall, 2008.

Cabral, Luís M.B. *Introduction to Industrial Organization*. Cambridge, MA: MIT Press, 2000.

Carlton, Dennis W., and Jeffrey M. Perloff. *Modern Industrial Organization*, 4th ed. Boston: Addison-Wesley, 2004.

Carroll, Glenn R., and Michael T. Hannan. *Organizations in Industry*. New York: Oxford University Press, 1995.

Child, John, David Faulkner, and Stephen Tallman. *Cooperative Strategy: Managing Alliances, Networks, and Joint Ventures*, 2nd ed. New York: Oxford University Press, 2005.

Ferguson, Paul R., and Glenys J. Ferguson. *Industrial Economics: Issues and Perspectives*, 2nd ed. New York: New York University Press, 1994.

McGahan, Anita M. *How Industries Evolve*. Boston: Harvard University Press, 2004.

Oster, Sharon M. *Modern Competitive Analysis*, 3rd ed. New York: Oxford University Press, 1999.

Porter, Michael E. *Competitive Strategy: How to Analyze Industries and Competitors*, updated ed. New York: Free Press, 1998.

Shepherd, William G., and Joanna M. Shepherd. *The Economics of Industrial Organization*, 5th ed. Long Grove, IL: Waveland Press, 2004.

Tirole, Jean. *The Theory of Industrial Organization*. Cambridge, MA: MIT Press, 1988.

von Clausewitz, Carl. *On War*, Michael Howard and Peter Paret (eds. and trans.). Princeton, NJ: Princeton University Press, 1976.

Appendix 9A
Competitive Analysis and Estimating Market Share

It is a source of never-ending amazement to us that competitors are seldom mentioned, much less explicitly analyzed, in valuation reports. It is as if the client company competes in a vacuum. Competitive analysis is an essential component. Among other reasons, market share (part of the S in S-C-P) has implications for the C and the P in S-C-P. Such analysis is a crucial aspect of strategy-making more generally. It is an important aspect of conventional business valuation and one that is usually overlooked.

Competitive analysis is also a key consideration in devising exit strategies for business owners. That makes it a critical aspect of value enhancement. A company's closest rival often can (and will) pay the highest buyout price in the shortest time frame with the least hassle. Competitor profiles offer the client company choices with which to position itself for sale later on. For instance, it might choose to buy and install a software system that one or more desirable purchasers are already using. That reduces risk, makes due diligence much easier, and eliminates conversion expense for the buyer, all of which increases the price for the seller. We are working with a company right now that is doing exactly that. A firm can also make itself attractive down the road by, say, opening a new office in the same city where its first choice of a buyer already has operations because the buyer would realize an instant pop on its bottom line by combining the two offices. The client firm can accomplish similar overlaps in customer bases, distribution channels, and advertising. Those overlaps can increase the purchase price because a buyer can see ways to immediately increase revenues/reduce expenses.

Analyzing Competitors

We keep our analysis simple. We want to help the client anticipate what a rival is likely to do if the client makes a major move. Porter's book has a nice chapter on analyzing rivals.[10] We like his breakdown of a competitor profile into four components under two broad headings:

1. What Drives the Competitor
   - Future Goals—where it wants to go
   - Assumptions—about itself and how the domain works
2. What the Competitor Is Doing and Can Do
   - Current Strategy—how it competes (e.g., focus/differentiation)
   - Strengths and Weaknesses—key aspects of each

---

[10] Porter, *Competitive Strategy*, 1998, 47–74.

Future Goals.   We summarize each rival's financial goals, unusual aspects of its culture, its risk tolerance, organizational structure, key managers—their backgrounds, experience, and extent of consensus among them—known incentives, and contracts that may inhibit their ability to act. We find that most owners carry much of this information around in their heads. Getting them to talk about it is easy. However, if you get a blank look when you ask about it, the company level of unsystematic risk goes up (again).

Assumptions.   These are crucial because they tell us a lot about how a rival is likely to move toward its future goals. Assumptions also give us insight into how well other companies see reality, at least compared to how our client sees it. Does a rival buy into the conventional industry wisdom? Newer entrants often view themselves and the domain differently from how long-time players see them. An unusual organizational culture can cause a rival to do strange things. For instance, Sears ran into intense employee opposition when it wanted to sell its catalog business. In 1887, Sears had launched its Chicago office by providing mail-order products to farmers, and longtime personnel wanted to hold on to that traditional part of the business. The catalog operation was finally sold, but only over the objections and angst of insiders. Their angst resulted from their realization that if Sears would ditch what started the company, the company had little commitment to anything or anyone . . . including *them*. They read it right.

Savvy growing companies also move up the advisory food chain where outside expertise is concerned. Bigger advisory firms bring new perspective, new questions, more referral potential, and bench strength that the entry-level group cannot touch. On occasion, there may be a lone advisor who can be the catalyst to major organizational changes because she brings insights, ideas, and experience to which the growing enterprise has never been exposed. We play, and have played, that role for a number of client companies.

Current Strategy.   We covered the four options—cost leadership and differentiation for companies competing industry-wide and focus/cost leadership and focus/differentiation for those competing in strategic groups. We cannot overemphasize our belief that, for most SMEs, focus/differentiation is the strategy of choice.

Capabilities.   Here is where it all comes together. Goals, assumptions, and strategy give us insights about:

> the *likelihood, timing, nature,* and *intensity* of a competitor's reactions. Its strengths and weaknesses will determine its *ability* to initiate or react to

strategic moves and to deal with environmental or [domain] events that occur.[11]

We want our client to have a handle on the alignment in the businesses of key rivals. Well-aligned companies are more profitable and can grow faster than their rivals. They are also much more of a menace to their competitors. The client should have a reasonable grasp of key rivals' abilities to respond quickly to a major move, to embrace change, and to persevere in stressful and difficult circumstances. Some clients take the profiling further and try to assess what major (and possibly disruptive) actions its main rivals might take, whether they are apt to make "head fakes" (i.e., appear to make moves that they do not, in fact, make), what it takes to provoke an archrival to action, and how effective that player is likely to be in any attempt to retaliate.

Having these kinds of insights into its rivals gives a client company a better sense of when to choose to fight and in what context. The idea, of course, is to make strategic thrusts to which rivals either cannot respond (because they do not have the resources) or can respond only at great expense or disruption to their existing ways of doing business. That means a key aspect of this type of analysis is to try, like any good military general, to get enough into the heads of rivals to know what they will and will not do. Remember the words of George C. Scott in the classic movie *Patton* after his troops defeated Rommel's in the African campaign of World War II. He shook his fist in the air and bellowed:

Rommel, you son of a bitch. I read your book![12]

Estimating Market Share

If we stop a business owner and ask, "What were your company's revenues last year?" we are apt to hear, "None of your business." However, if we ask that same owner, "How many jobs has your company created for this community?" well, that is a number the owner loves to blurt out. We know from the Duff & Phelps data set that headcount is a good, if not the most statistically significant, measure of size. It is also a number that is easily obtained.

We use number of full-time equivalent employees as a proxy for a company's sales. The correlation between FTEs and revenues varies from firm to firm in a domain, depending on efficiency, management savvy, technology, culture, and each company's view of how things work,. However, because a

---

[11] Ibid., 63. Italics in original.
[12] http://rogerebert.suntimes.com/apps/pbcs.dll/article?AID=/20020317/REVIEWS08/203170301/1023

domain's economic underpinnings pose the same magnitude of risk to all players, the relationship between sales and number of people on the payroll must hold at some level. It is not perfect, of course, but little in the valuation arena is.

We ask the people running the subject company to estimate share for their company and for each of its closest competitors. In our experience, most owners have remarkable insights about share, both their own and their competitors'. Later in the valuation process, we access www.zapdata.com to estimate total employment in the domain. We could also call the companies themselves or chambers of commerce to get headcount data—companies are *proud* of the number of jobs they have created for their communities! We estimate a company's market share based on its FTE employees as a percentage of total employment in the strategic group. The headcount equivalent of the four-firm concentration ratio (discussed in Chapter 3), then, is the sum of the proxy market shares of the four biggest competitors.

If we wanted to, we could also compute a Herfindahl-Hirschman Index (discussed in Chapter 3). We would do that in a situation where market share was heavily skewed toward one dominant company.

CHAPTER

10

Getting to "Why": Analyses, Composites, and On-Site Interviews

Getting value maps right requires sound financial and operational analysis. The resulting metrics are the "whats" of the client. They are the symptoms of performance. We cannot get to the causes until we have a clear picture of what is being caused. In other words, we cannot explain *why* until we know *what*.

An essential part of knowing what is having a handle on the type of economic activities that are at the core of what the client company does. Certain financial ratios—current ratio, DSO, inventory turn, return on assets, and so forth—cut across domains. But there is more to the whats than just ratios from balance sheets and income statements. Different sectors have industry-specific metrics. In retail, for instance, revenue per square foot is key. In construction, it is the EMR (experience modification ratio). In banking, it is the operating ratio. In wholesaling, it is how many SKUs.[1] In make-to-order manufacturing, the months of backlog and trends therein are early-warning signs of expansions or downturns. In semiconductors, it is the book-to-bill ratio. In pharmacies, it is the percentage of revenues from compounding. In professional services, it is the "utilization rate" (billable hours/year ÷ 2,000 hours) and the "realization rate" (hours billed ÷ hours worked). In the cell-phone space, 1 minus the "churn" (percentage of customers lost in a year) is a predictor of revenue stability—a higher percentage indicates lower revenue volatility.

Financial Ratios

Income statement and balance sheet analyses give analysts snapshots of different relationships. The analysis uncovers what we call "aberrant ratios."

---

[1] A #13 green widget is one SKU. A #13 polka-dot widget is another. A #12 polka-dot widget is yet another.

Those are key because they point us toward the explanation of why this business performs as it does and how it is likely to perform in the near-term future.

Most readers of this book know that ratios come in four flavors. They comprise the acronym PALL:

1. **P**rofitability (margins and returns)
2. **A**ctivity (turnover)
3. **L**iquidity (ability to meet short-term obligations)
4. **L**everage (the extent of interest-bearing debt used to finance assets).

These are basic.

Another category of metrics is growth. Too many analysts measure it in terms of the compound annual growth rate (CAGR) over a period of years. We are not keen on CAGR because it connects only the first and last points in the time period; it ignores interim performance. We prefer trended growth, which is the slope of a least-squares regression line among the data points. This measure is a better predictor of short-term growth and also a better indicator of the stability of the business. Of course, a constant rate of annual growth over any period means that CAGR and the trended growth measure will be equal. The greater the difference between them, however, the less stable and less predictable is the performance of the company.

A Key Metric

An important measure, and one that we seldom see, is the cash-conversion cycle; it is also called the "net operating cycle." This is how long it takes the company to convert the activities that require cash into cash itself. The longer the cycle, the more cash is needed. A shortening cycle is positive because cash will be freed up to invest in new equipment or pay dividends. A lengthening one is just the opposite. Here is the formula:

$$
\begin{aligned}
&\text{days of inventory on hand } (365 \div \text{inventory turnover}) \\
&+\text{DSO } (365 \div \text{accounts receivable turnover}) \\
&\underline{-\text{average payables period } (365 \div \text{A/P turnover})} \\
&= \text{Cash Conversion Cycle}
\end{aligned}
$$

Obviously, the longer the cycle, the greater the amount of cash required. In our experience around SMEs, we have found that most have too much inventory, are too slow in collecting receivables, and pay their vendors too quickly. As a result, they tend to require far more cash than the economic activity of the business really justifies. In particular, we have observed that managing inventory is especially challenging for many smaller enterprises. They seem obsessed with not having back orders, even if accepting an occasional stock-out would boost their cash flow.

The cash conversion cycle is sector-specific. Trying to compare such cycles across industries is a waste of time, except out of sheer curiosity. The cycle also depends on policy choices made by owners and managers. For instance, tough payment terms and riding customers to pay promptly is apt to put a damper on sales growth. That will reduce both DSO and days of inventory on hand.

Finding Sector-Specific Metrics

Where are these "other metrics" found? We first ask the client company. We also look at in the 10-K filings of guideline public companies. We often find such metrics in the first section (business) and in the MD&A (management discussion and analysis). If we come up empty there, then we search analysts' reports. On occasion, we will call an analyst and talk about a specific industry. Be forewarned, though: Analysts can be tough to get on the telephone. Other resources for identifying unusual metrics include trade associations (don't forget that librarian) and Standard & Poor's Industry Reports (they can be pricey). One time we hired a University of Virginia graduate economics student. He turned out to be an absolute encyclopedia and a bargain at 50 bucks an hour. Such a deal.

The Analysis

Once we have our ratio and metrics ducks in a row, we are ready to do the quantitative analysis. We do that inside our GPC template. It is complex and sophisticated with lots of moving parts. It populates automatically from FetchXL. It also size-adjusts valuation multiples automatically (we choose from Morningstar/Ibbotson or one of the eight Duff & Phelps measures) and calculates coefficients of variation (CVs). It has a separate sheet for our client company's information, and that feeds into what we call "The Comps Sheet."

But its main virtue is that, by size-adjusting the multiples, we typically end up with at least 12 GPCs and sometimes 20 or more. It was not long ago that the leading reference books in the valuation field said that from 4 to 7 GPCs were sufficient. In tight oligopolies—pharmacies, for instance—that might be all we can get these days. But in most analyses, we end up with far more than that.

The additional companies, or "records," as statisticians label them, increase the "degrees of freedom" (another statistical term). In plain English, it means that the greater the number of companies in the analysis, the lower is the likelihood of material error. We review the profile of each company, usually in Yahoo! Finance. We exclude pink-sheet companies, most firms whose stock is selling for under $5/share, and companies which are not current in their SEC filings. If the client company operates under generally accepted accounting principles, we drop non-U.S. companies, too. If our client is routinely profitable, we drop unprofitable GPCs from further consideration. We also look closely at growth expectations in the GPCs versus those of the client firm.

If we have to, we can growth-adjust the multiples, too, though this is much less common than the size adjustments, which we do routinely. Growth adjustments require obtaining analysts' growth expectations for each GPC. That can be a problem with smaller companies that have little or no following from analysts.

As with everything else we do in valuation, we go where the facts and the data take us. We focus on the multiples with the lowest CVs as these are the best correlates of enterprise value. We want to understand more than just the fact that certain ones have low CVs. As always, we want to understand the *why*. If we cannot explain why, then we do not use the multiple. GPC analysis *must* be more than a monkey-see/monkey-do mechanical exercise. If it is not, it is brain-dead.

The Fundamental Adjustment (NOT!)

Our template has an algorithm in it that enables us to avoid the fundamental adjustment. We also avoid lots of potential grief with the Internal Revenue Service or opposing counsel. We select a percentile within the array of public companies where the client's performance on the metrics we deem to be the most important ones is split 50-50 (i.e., it outperforms the percentile on half the metrics and underperforms on the other half). As a practical matter, we usually work with six ratios. We have found that eight are too many. Only infrequently do we work with just four. To emphasize our choices, we use bigger fonts on the ones we choose. We also create upward-pointing arrows on a light green fill on those where the company performs better than the percentile of public companies and downward-pointing arrows on a pink fill for those where it performs worse.

Explanations

In our report or calculations memorandum, we are careful to explain the metrics we chose and why they are important. We also discuss the multiple(s) we selected and why they matter. With a typical array of, say, 15 GPCs, our CVs are usually in the 30% to 50% range, though we have had them as low as 7%. If we use two or more multiples, we have to decide how to weight them because we have to explain that process, too.

How to Construct a Composite

When our GPC analysis is complete, creating a composite is a no-brainer. We add up each of the line items—all the revenues, all the Cost of Goods Sold figures, all the accounts receivable, and so forth—of the GPCs. We then reduce them to common-size balance sheets and income statements. We also calculate composite ratios and metrics. We put the client company's common-size financials and its performance metrics alongside those of the composite.

We know many analysts who use data from the Risk Management Association (RMA). We do not. For one thing, RMA's samples are biased: Figures depend to a large extent on data in applications for bank loans. Not exactly random, is it? Worse, we do not know who those companies are. As strong believers in disclosure and transparency, we would rather construct our own composite from the final cut of GPCs. That way, we know where it came from. It is also a logical extension of our GPC analysis. Why otherwise sensible analysts go outside for composites is beyond us. Get it set up in a spreadsheet one time, and you are good to go until the Financial Accounting Standards Board turns the traditional format for financial statements into something different.

Prepping for the On-Site Interviews

At this point, we are ready to begin our preparation for the interviews that are the underlying purpose of the on-site visit. Our small shop usually turns a valuation assignment around in about 90 days. The interviews tend to happen around Day 70 in that cycle. This is where the rubber truly meets the road in our perspective on the valuation process, because it is where we get at the underlying causes of the metric/ratios "effects." Getting to *why*—what causes what—is, for us, the heart of the matter.

We believe these interviews are the most underrated, underappreciated, and underused aspect of the valuation process. Too many analysts make them into a social event. Others visit the client just to talk to the top people. Still others serve up puff-ball questions that anyone with an IQ bigger than their hat size can knock out of the park. One litigation-support guy I have known for years never did any site visits until I asked him how he could have any credibility testifying without having seen the premises and talked to the people. He said he had never thought of it.

Our Interview Questions

We have a basic set of questions that we ask everyone. Some are scaled; others are not. We also have additional questions custom-tailored to each individual. We gear these to the particular metrics with which that individual will be familiar. Unlike some of our colleagues, we do not send these questions out in advance. We think that invites collusion on the part of those whom we would least want colluding.

Once we ask a basic question, though, the process becomes Socratic. We ask a question and get an answer. The answer creates another question and another answer. The second answer triggers another question and another answer. And so on. Where these conversations go cannot be scripted. There is no audit or valuation program that can possibly anticipate every question. So we start with a basic set of questions, depend on our good listening skills, and pose additional questions based on the answers we get. It is intense.

Whom to Interview

We want to talk to the key people, of course. But we also want to talk to those whose jobs put them in a position to be able to shed light on the aberrant metrics that our analysis uncovers. We *never* limit our conversations in a function responsible for an aberrant ratio to the person running it. We want to talk with some underlings, too. Sometimes they see the world far more clearly than those in charge. And, but for the luck of the gene pool, they would be running the company and those who at the top would be driving trucks or working on the shop floor.

By the time we are ready to choose whom we want to interview, we are also conversant with the key operating and staff functions that matter in whatever line of economic activity the client company is engaged in. In *any* distribution business, wholesale or retail, the twin focuses must be on purchasing and on sales and marketing; do not overlook the deployment of technology in such businesses, either—the Internet continues to exert serious margin pressure on retailers and wholesalers.

In manufacturing businesses, we look in the chart of accounts for re-work-related expenses. If those are not there, we ask how they know what their "yield" is. In business services and professional services firms (PSFs), it is about realization, client retention, and incentives for landing new clients. But it is also about measuring profitability by client in PSFs. If the largest client has the lowest realization, maybe that client belongs with our subject company's closest competitor.

If inventory turn is lousy (or great), we want to talk to the folks in purchasing or procurement or whatever name it goes by in a particular company. If DSO is too high (or too low), we talk to the controller and the person overseeing accounts receivable. If that person is also the controller, then we talk to an accounting clerk or two. If the firm is overstaffed, as most closely helds are, then we schedule whoever oversees human resources for an interview. We also talk with department heads about what routines they use in deciding that they do or do not need to create a new position. How they measure productivity, especially in staff positions, also comes up in those conversations.

Before we ever arrive on-site, we ask the owner or the CEO to send out an e-mail to those we have selected. In fact, we volunteer to provide the verbiage for the top dog to send out. A typical e-mail reads like this:

> As you know, we have retained Beckmill Research, LLC, to provide us with some strategic advice and counsel. As part of our work with Beckmill, its founder, Warren Miller, will be here with his wife, Dorothy, for individual interviews with certain employees. Those will run from 30 minutes to about an hour.
>
> I respectfully request that you be completely candid and open with him. Express what you believe, and don't hesitate to do it strongly, if that is how you feel. I will not try to find out later who said what to him. Even if I did, though, he wouldn't tell me, which is one of the many reasons that we chose Beckmill and not some other firm. Thank you in advance for your candor and your cooperation with Warren.

Conducting the On-Site Interviews

Once we are prepared, the interviews themselves are pretty straightforward. However—and I cannot emphasize this too strongly—we never cease to be amazed by what we find out during these interviews. We have uncovered porn addicts, had druggies 'fess up, and provided handkerchiefs for several dozen sniffling employees.

Interview Process

We expect to spend 30 to 60 minutes with each employee we select. If we have a large number of folks to interview, these talks might carry over to a second day. It happens. If we expect the interviews to be contentious or delicate, Dorothy (my wife and partner) sits in. She takes notes, but her primary reason for being there is to be a witness if one is needed later. Her very presence has, I believe, kept that from ever happening.

We are careful about how we dress for these interviews. Being lumped in with the "suits" crowd is a tough obstacle to overcome. I cannot recall the last time I wore a necktie for the on-site visit. I wear "business casual," of course, but, more often than not, I'll be in jeans. That seems to put most employees at ease.

As noted in Chapter 6, if we are in a conference room, I make it a point to sit on the same side of the table as the employee. If there is a window into the room where we meet, even the employee's office, I insist that we sit with our backs to it. No distractions.

I begin by handing each interviewee my business card and asking each to tell me their understanding of why we are talking. That gives me a chance to hear, in their own words, what they have been told. I was copied on the CEO's e-mail to them, of course, but that does not guarantee that the recipient's understanding is the same as mine. I also reinforce the idea of airtight confidentiality. Even then, though, some employees will not trust me. I believe it is not personal, and I don't take it that way. As a result of their life or work experience, some folks do not trust anyone.

Consistent with our commitment to each employee, we do *not* attribute anything someone says to us to that individual. We also do not characterize what they say in such a way that a given employee could be identified from our characterization. I believe in protecting sources. I also want employees to speak freely and candidly. The best way to encourage that is to promise that they will not be identified, either directly or indirectly, later in any conversations or written reports.

That said, we do encounter those who want to politicize the process. We refuse to play. Others do not trust the process, and they refuse to buy in. That is their right, of course, and we tell them that. We also tell them that we never confuse having rights with being right. Those of you who know me will not be surprised to hear that I have said the same thing to more than one business owner, too.

We start out with casual, nonthreatening questions. These questions generally put the employee at ease. We are not there to dish dirt or cast aspersions on anyone. We are there simply to get at the truth.

I make it a point to speak softly and use lots of "weasel words"—tons of adverbs. Those are effective in this venue, even though we disparage their use in reports. Adverbs dilute the impact of what we're trying to say, and, if the employee is guarded or afraid, we can usually put the person at ease with these "aw-shucks," "kinda-do-you-maybe-think" types of questions.

If all of this seems like overkill, it is not. Trust me on that. We are there to get our arms around what causes the metrics to be what they are. As I have said repeatedly in these pages, if we cannot explain why, then, as far as I'm concerned, we failed miserably in the assignment.

Interview Sequence

We talk to the owner or CEO last. For one thing, we do not want to appear to be checking out with underlings whatever she might have told us had we talked to her first. For another, the lead person is always interested in our assessment of those to whom we spoke.

We are careful about what we say here. However, if we encountered employees whom we believed to be either truly outstanding or truly not-outstanding, we say so, and we explain why. We then ask the owner or CEO why that person's performance is what it is. As a result, we often learn important information about the individuals in question.

I was lucky enough to have learned a lot about interviewing during my tenure at Union Pacific in the mid-1970s. Because most of our audits were operational, we would not learn much if we thought all of the action was in the accounting department. At one point, we audited the purchasing function at Union Pacific Railroad (UPRR), then one of four UP subsidiaries.[2] As part of our work, we compared commodity prices with prices on purchase orders from UPRR's purchasing group. We were told early on to be on the lookout for any purchasing employee who was supporting a $300,000-a-year lifestyle on a $30,000 salary.

We found one such individual in the Los Angeles purchasing office. As a result, I became the audit staff expert in greyhound racing. Not buses—pooches. The story is too long to detail here, but part of the consideration the high-living employee was alleged to have received from a vendor was greyhounds. A not-pleasant kennel owner in southwestern Oklahoma pulled a gun on me when I knocked on his front door and wanted to talk to him about it. I eventually persuaded the guy to put his gun down and talk to me, but, when I got back in my car, my hands shook for quite a while.

Railroads use lots of steel in their maintenance-of-way operations. Track wears out and has to be replaced. One of our guys noticed that all steel purchases came from U.S. companies. This was back when the Japanese were making strong inroads into the U.S. market because they had more efficient production processes and newer plants; the United States had destroyed many of their steel facilities during World War II.[3]

A $950/month junior auditor on our staff asked the director of purchasing why the railroad did not buy steel from non-U.S. companies. The director had never noticed. It seems that the budgets prepared by the maintenance-of-way people used prices gathered from U.S. companies because "that's the way [they'd] always done it." We finally learned that the guy who bought steel had been a P.O.W. in a Japanese camp during WWII and vowed he would never forget or forgive what they did to him and

---

[2] It has since sold or spun off the other three: Champlin Petroleum Company (which became Union Pacific Resources and was later acquired by Anadarko Petroleum Corp.), Rocky Mountain Energy Company (which had vast mineral reserves in Wyoming, Utah, and Colorado), and Union Pacific Land Co. (aka Upland Co.), which held a lot of commercial real estate in Las Vegas, Los Angeles, Nebraska, and several other states.

[3] This was long before the creation of the World Trade Organization to monitor "dumping" and other activities that artificially reduce prices in international markets.

his buddies. His view was certainly understandable, but it was also costing UP's shareholders millions of dollars in excess costs. One thing led to another: The man took early retirement, and the railroad began buying steel from the Japanese.

I tell this story about how we got to "the why" about steel purchasing at UP to reinforce the idea that causes are not found in financial statements. Only effects are. Whether we can explain the causes or not is how we define the difference between success and failure. Not only does our discussion of cause-and-effect relationships enhance our credibility on the valuation side. It also tells about things that need fixing. We embed those in the value map we later create.

Summary

We covered a lot of territory in this chapter. Financial analysis is seldom complicated. The important thing is to find out about industry-specific metrics and incorporate those into our analysis using guideline public companies. Size-adjusting valuation multiples enables us to include many more firms in our analysis than we would otherwise have. More firms = more degrees of freedom, which means less likelihood of material error. With your GPC analysis, you have the elements of your industry composite looking straight at you. It is a simple matter of combining income statements and balance sheets. Our template also avoids the fundamental adjustment, which is another real plus.

Then, however, it is time to prepare for the on-site interviews. These occur late in the process because we do not know enough to merit asking for people's time until then. We choose our interviewees based on the business functions toward which aberrant metrics and ratios point us. Our engagement letter requires the CEO or business owner to send out an e-mail to those whom we want to interview. We provide the verbiage for that e-mail, and we are copied on it. In it, the CEO tells how important it is for the employees to be candid and straightforward in their responses to my questions. He tells them that their conversations with us are strictly confidential and that no one will be identified later, either directly or indirectly.

We talk to underlings before we visit with managers, and we talk to them before we talk to the owner or CEO. Starting at the top and working our way down is a prescription for bad interview results, not to mention the possibility that the higher-ups might think we are checking out what they told us with their subordinates.

We have a series of "standard" questions that we ask everyone. We also develop specific questions for those working in particular functional areas whose aberrant ratios and metrics have landed on our radar screens. Our written questions are only the beginning, however. They get the ball rolling. It is a Socratic process: We ask a question, hear an answer, ask another question related to the answer, get another answer, ask another answer-related question, and so on. These interviews run 30 to 60 minutes, and sometimes longer. It is an exhausting process that cannot be scripted. As with everything else we do, having preconceived notions is dangerous. We go where the facts and the data lead us. Whether it makes the owner or CEO happy has no impact on what we do.

We dress like the people we are talking to. We sit on the same side of the table as they do. We give them our business cards at the beginning and confirm that they understand the ground rules and why we are talking. We speak softly, maintain eye contact, and use lots of weasel words when asking questions that might make them uncomfortable. We do *not* tape-record interviews.

If we do these interviews the way we should, we will come away from them with an understanding of the client company that we never would have gotten any other way. We will be able to explain "the whys" that cause "the whats." Our credibility with any reader of our report or calculations memorandum will be sky high because of our ability to tell a story in an interesting and objective way.

But we cannot do that until we summarize our interview findings in the context of the SPARC framework. That is the subject of the next chapter.

11

The "SW" in SWOT Analysis: The Company and SPARC

To repeat and reemphasize what we have said before: We conduct our analysis top down. That is, we begin with the macroenvironment, then move to the domain, and then to the subject company. We have tried it bottom up. It does not work. We found ourselves having to start over and over and over again. This is a process. Trust the process, and you will be rewarded.

We know from the published research that the potential for good or bad things to happen is greatest at the company level. Some companies are their own worst enemies. The market process of selection weeds them out. Sometimes that takes time. Others survive but never grow to be what they could be.

Our favorite real-world example of such an enterprise is a company that we will call Military Gizmos Corporation (MGC). I have changed its name to protect the guilty. Its founder is a man with intuitive product ideas. He thinks it up, and the target market—the U.S. armed forces—goes for it. I have never met anyone quite like him. He has a gift. He is squandering it. And he has no idea that he is.

He is a former military officer who reached the rank of captain and got out during the "peace dividend" years in the early 1990s when the Defense budget plummeted. He started making "little elastic gizmos" in his garage at night before he mustered out. His family helped, and so did his neighbors. After his discharge, he moved his wife, kids, and business to the mid-Atlantic region. He and his wife decided they did not want to raise their children in an urban war zone, so they moved to a rural area. They set up their business in

(continued)

(*continued*)

an old plant that once housed a textile manufacturer that employed several hundred people. That company went under in the late 1980s, and the building had remained empty until MGC moved in.

The wife was the majority owner of the business so it would qualify for preferences for woman-owned enterprises. He ran it, and she kept the books. Revenues took off. MGC was soon generating $3 million annually. Unfortunately, they both got a bad case of the Big Head. She didn't know what she didn't know; he thought he was God's gift to business. When he was named "Businessman of the Year" by the local chamber of commerce, it only got worse.

MGC continued to add to its product line. Revenues continued to grow briskly. The bottom line didn't. In fact, as sales went north, profits went south. That phenomenon, which Dorothy calls "the Nightmare Scenario," tends to be empirical confirmation that current management is in over its head. It fails to invest in infrastructure, and it fails to develop its people. Growth overwhelms the abilities of the incumbents to manage, so they overstaff. That one shows up in comparing annual revenues per full-time employee with public company comps. MGC was no exception.

It had a talent for finding and hiring beaten-down people in key management slots. They were tired. Their skills were obsolete. But the husband was TSMOTP (the Smartest Man on the Planet). If anyone had any doubt about that, he would tell you. If you looked as if you didn't hear, he'd tell you again in a louder voice.

The financial arm, meanwhile, was running a make-for-stock manufacturing firm on Microsoft Money software. It would have been hilarious were it not so pathetic. The company was marginally profitable. The couple bought the building, put it in their own limited liability company, and paid themselves rent. Having both grown up in families that lived on the wrong side of the tracks in small towns, they were already succeeding far beyond their own wildest dreams and far more than anyone on either side of their family ever had.

They finally hired a top-flight marketing guy. The man was good. He and his wife had founded, grown, and cashed out of a $20 million company in a big city. They wanted the pace of small-town living, so they moved to the countryside. They did not have to work, but TSMOTP convinced the husband that the two of them could do great things. Against his wife's advice, the husband signed on with MGC.

It was a train wreck. The CEO vetoed every good idea the marketing guy had. After all, the top guy was TSMOTP. Ask him. The marketing guy finally quit in frustration. The financial arm of MGC spiraled out of control. Revenues were over $6 million, but the fees for tax preparation were well over $20,000 a year. Its accounting firm was not gouging its client. The outside accountants had to make many major adjusting entries to the general ledger just to get to a decent set of numbers from which it could prepare the tax returns. The accounting firm finally suggested to the CEO that he get a "real CFO." He fired the firm.

Over the next few years, he hired and fired several more. As revenues neared $10 million, profits remained marginal, and tax-preparation fees continued to escalate, it fired that individual and, over the next four years, hired and fired several more CFOs. Today MGC is still in business. It makes a little money, but not much. The CEO and his wife have paid off their house. They own a rustic weekend vacation home. They employ nearly 100 people. Marketing, finance, and IT remain in states of continual upheaval and chaos.

The couple will never know how much they could have made because they never gave their business a chance. Yes, they worked hard. Heck, they had to. They could never sustain any relationship with knowledgeable advisors or capable managers. They would now have a net worth well into eight figures, and they wouldn't have to work as hard, if only they would let go. They cannot. Or will not.

They are the smartest people on the planet. Just ask them. Fifty years ago, the character Pogo in the comic strip of the same name said it best: "We have met the enemy, and he is us."

This chapter deals with the "SW" of SWOT analysis: strengths and weaknesses. These attributes, which are called resources, are internal to the company. Those running it are responsible for organizing the enterprise in such a way that it minimizes the potential damage that internal weaknesses and external threats can inflict, uses its strengths to take advantage of external opportunities, and aligns itself to keep pace with the rate of change outside its boundaries. It aims to accomplish those objectives by configuring resources to render productive services to the firm and its stakeholders. This is a dynamic, iterative, and ongoing process that determines a company's ability to grow profitably. It sounds a whole lot simpler than it is.

In our discussion of the "SW," we cover three key subjects:

1. Finding cause-and-effect relationships
2. Identifying value drivers and value destroyers
3. Testing for the durability of value-creating capabilities

We end with an appendix that ties the recent chapters together by demonstrating how to quantify unsystematic risk.

Cause-and-Effect Relationships

The purpose of on-site interviews is to discover the underlying causes of the effects identified during the analysis leading up to the site visit. Those causes fall within five possible categories: strategy, people, architecture, routines, and culture. Thus we have the SPARC acronym (see Exhibit 11.1).

We now want to plumb the outermost band, resources—a company's strengths and weaknesses. The most important of these, according to Edith Penrose, is the experience of those running the company. That affects all the other productive services that can be derived from the resource portfolio. Therefore, we focus not on the resources themselves but on the productive services they deliver.

Resources

Few resources are on the balance sheet or the profit and loss statement; in fact, the most important ones (teamwork, reputation, transparency, etc.) are not there. In Exhibit 11.2, we Jay Barney's approach to types of capital—financial, physical, human, and organizational from chapter 2 because it is so important[1].

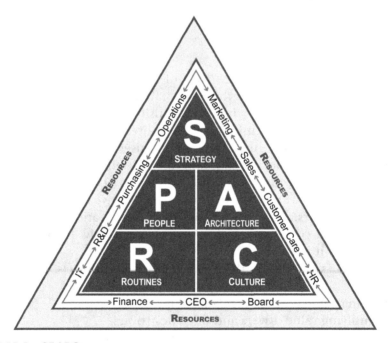

Exhibit 11.1   SPARC

---

[1] Barney, *Sustaining Competitive Advantage*, 134.

Exhibit 11.2 Types of Capital

❏ **financial capital** = funds from investors and lenders

Financial Capital

Examples of Resources	Measures
Borrowing capacity	1. Debt ratio versus industry average. 2. Debt-equity ratio versus industry average. 3. Net cash flow to Total Invested Capital
Liquidity	1. Quick ratio 2. Current ratio 3. DSO versus industry average. 4. Inventory turnover versus industry average. 5. Credit rating 6. Gross cash flow ÷ net cash flow to equity
Ability to raise equity capital	1. ROE versus industry average 2. Net profit margin versus industry average.
Sustainable growth rate	1. ROE × (1 – dividend payout ratio)

❏ **physical capital** = the physical endowments a firm requires

Physical Capital

Examples of Resources	Measures
Productive capacity	1. Annual revenues ÷ FTE employees 2. Annual revenues ÷ production square feet 3. "Line" square feet ÷ as a % of total square feet
Investment service	1. CapEx versus depreciation expense 2. Accumulated depreciation ÷ gross fixed assets
Dedication to maintenance	1. Maintenance expense/revenues versus industry average
Flexibility of fixed assets	1. Market value of equipment ÷ book value
Technological commitment	1. Average RAM per computer 2. Average age of PCs 3. Average age of software applications 4. Number of computers ÷ FTE *employees*
Access to suppliers	1. Weighted average distance from which goods are received

(continued)

Exhibit 11.2 (Continued)

❑ **human capital** = resources of **the individuals** who comprise the firm (knowledge, education, training, insights, intelligence, etc.)

Human Capital

Examples of Resources	Measures
Education	1. Σ years of education ÷ FTE employees
Training	1. training hours/year ÷ FTE employees
Knowledge	1. Σ educational reimbursement ÷ FTE employees
Employee commitment	1. % of absentee days versus industry average 2. Σ sick leave taken ÷ Σ sick leave available
Leadership ability	1. Weighted average manager rating by FTEs
Trust	1. Annual number of workplace thefts 2. Number of complaints to HR (or ombudsman)
Experience	1. Σ years **with Company** ÷ FTE employees

❑ **organizational capital** = attributes of the people comprising **the firm** (teamwork, reputation, speed, etc.)

Organizational Capital

Examples of Resources	Measures
Loyalty	1. Employee turnover versus industry average
Teamwork	1. $ cost of rework ÷ FTE employees 2. Σ years with company ÷ number of managers 3. Performance of company's sports teams
Reputation	1. Overall customer satisfaction 2. % of revenue from repeat customers 3. Average length of customer relationship
Product innovation	1. Σ # of patents 2. Revenues from patents and copyrights 3. R&D $ ÷ revenues versus industry average
Process innovation	1. % of employees making suggestions/year
Speed	1. Number of organizational levels

Source: Jay B. Barney, *Gaining and Sustaining Competitive Advantage*, 3rd ed. (Upper Saddle River, N.J.: Pearson/Prentice-Hall, 2007).

That is why we look hard at nonfinancial resources:

- **Physical capital.** Productivity (annual revenues ÷ full-time employees); investment service; technological commitment
- **Human capital.** Training; knowledge; commitment; experience
- **Organizational capital.** Loyalty; teamwork; reputation; speed

To be sure, many SMEs don't monitor these measures. They should, though, and that's the point. Financial statements are an essential starting place. But there is more to measurement than the numbers on those statements.

Productivity

We zero in on this one. Most closely held firms are overstaffed; that shows up in a company's average revenues per FTE versus that of the composite we constructed from the GPCs. Because most domains are increasingly competitive, we also want to know how many dollars and how much time a company invests in training and developing its employees.

Tenure

We also compute what we call "employee duration"—the total tenure of employees divided by the number of them. It is hard for a team to perform well if its membership changes frequently. A count of the number of W-2s a company issued last year versus the number of its full-time employees provides a snapshot of turnover.

Adjustments

During our analysis, we examine whether any "normalizing adjustments" to financial statements are necessary. These occur to comport with the essential objectives of presenting assets and liabilities at their fair market value and presenting revenues and expenses as if they were recurring. The former is required under the asset-based approach, and the latter under the market and income approaches.

From this exhaustive analysis, we identify key ratios and relationships that account for the major differences between the company's relative performance (its income statement) and financial condition (its balance sheet). We now have the key "nucleotides," if you will, of the company's DNA. If that DNA can be thought of as a disease, then nucleotides are only "symptoms." As valuation professionals, it is our job to explain *why* those symptoms are what they are. That is the primary purpose of the on-site visit.

Interviews

The greater the number of matters requiring follow-up from our analysis, the longer the on-site visit will take and the more people we ask to talk to.[2] At a minimum, one full 10-hour day is required. We don't confine our interviews just to the top cadre. If we spot what we believe is a problem area, we will want to talk with several people who, we hope, can shed light on the problem. If a company's inventory turnover is low, for instance, we look first to the purchasing function. If its average collection period seems long, we want to talk to those performing billing, invoicing, and collections functions as well as to the company's controller.

While we are on the subject of billing/invoicing/collections, let me say this: Billing, which is *not* a synonym for *invoicing*, is a *line* function. Show me a slow invoicing process, and I'll show you lax billing routines . . . or a slumbering controller. I will also show you a company that doesn't have nearly as much cash as it could have.

We noted in Chapter 10 that a subset of the questions in each interview is the same. Human resources professionals call this a "structured interview"; it allows us to compare responses to the same questions by different people. It is not a test of veracity but of perspective. The same action or policy is interpreted different ways by different people. That is often illuminating.

Value Drivers and Value Destroyers

The answers to "Why?" reside in value drivers *and* value destroyers. As noted in Chapter 7, these are *activities*. They are *not* financial ratios, despite the misconceptions of many of our brethren. The five elements of SPARC are the key determinants of value creation and value destruction. The twin essences of analysis at the company level involve (1) identifying a firm's value drivers (if any) and assessing their durability, and (2) finding its value destroyers (if any) and determining whether they can be either eliminated or lessened. To repeat: Value drivers are *not*—repeat NOT—financial ratios or other metrics.

In our experience, value drivers and value destroyers reside most often in routines. In declining order of their connection to causes are architecture, culture, people, and strategy. That is the sequence in which we discuss them here.

We lead with routines because they are such a powerful source of underlying causes. We are going to spend a lot of time and space on them here,

---

[2] We refer readers to our paper, "Using SPARC to Enhance Value for Clients," *Value Examiner* (March-April 2008): 22–32, 39. It is available for download free from our Web site, too, after a brief registration process.

and we do so in the context of the 11 functions circumscribing the five SPARC elements.

Routines

Routines are most often the culprit of value destruction because the limited attention span of most entrepreneurs and owners of SMEs compels them to dismiss routines. That is a huge mistake. The way a $2 billion company conducts its daily activities is very different from how a $20 million firm does. And the routines in the $20 million enterprise are very different from those in a $2 million small company. What worked at $2 million probably won't work at $20 million.

The routines that create the most chaos are those that are least valuable and not documented. These get short shrift because they are deemed not to be important. New hires are trained in routines by employees drawing on their memories. That guarantees chaos at some level because few people can remember everything, either on the teaching or the learning side. That is why documentation, especially of low-value-added tasks, is vital.

There are seven key places to look to gauge the adequacy of routines: (1) billing and invoicing; (2) payroll; (3) monthly closing; (4) purchasing; (5) the "customer master"; (6) how hiring decisions are made; and (7) the annual budget process. The fact that the majority of these are of a financial nature is not because that is my comfort zone. It is because chaos on the accounting side of a business reflects chaos on the operating side. The accounting function is a downstream function. It reacts.

Now, to the extent that *any* of these processes are done *outside the accounting software*, routines have a problem. In particular, inquire about the frequency with which account analyses are done. Notice if financial statements are prepared in Excel. These two issues point to an inadequate chart of accounts and to failure to use the report-writer function found in most accounting software packages, respectively. An accounting system is an information system. It serves three masters: (1) the generally accepted accounting principles master, (2) the Internal Revenue Service/tax master, and (3) the management-information master. The last of those masters gets short shrift because most SMEs' charts of accounts come from either external accountants or the accounting software vendors themselves (who are advised by the external accountants). The result is a chart of accounts with insufficient detail and inadequate use of subaccounts to create the information that management needs to run the business. There are lots of data, but little information. That, in turn, gives rise to the proliferation of Excel spreadsheets. If your client has Excelitis, it needs a transplant, usually of routines, but sometimes of people, too.

Information Technology. The first indicator of inadequate routines in IT is a system that is down often and unexpectedly. Most SMEs should outsource the management of their IT to companies that do IT for a living. They would see operations at significantly lower cost and almost no stress. Another indicator of poor IT routines is programs written in-house for which there is no documentation. If the program crashes, either the person who wrote it originally has to resuscitate it or, if that person is no longer around, the company has to try to document the program after the fact or get a new one written. No software should be written in-house without full documentation. And security should be such that programs and applications cannot be changed without updating the documentation. Companies that run IT departments for a living do this far better than most SMEs. Is there a Help Desk? If not, where do people go for IT support? Is there a disaster recovery plan? Is *everyone* computer-literate? Is there any custom software? If so, is the documentation written and current? Where are backups kept? Who maintains the company's Web site? Are complaints to the webmaster forwarded up the food chain? Is the copyright on the Web site current? Is the Web site "brochureware"? Is there a reason for people to register on the Web site? Are registration data collected? What does the lead IT person think of "the cloud"?[3]

Research and Development. The first question should be "What kind of research and development efforts do you folks have around here?" If you get the thousand-mile stare in the four-foot room, you might be on to something. We are strong believers that even small companies should do some R&D every now and then. They may not get the tax credit for it—that credit is available only to product-related R&D—but that does not obviate the need for R&D in services offerings; in how simple everyday tasks can be done faster, better, less expensively, and more accurately; or in better ways to gather, process, and disseminate information. There probably will not be an R&D department, but there should be people, probably managers, spending a chunk of their time every month on these kinds of issues.

Purchasing. The subject company's inventory turnover versus the industry average is the first metric to look at. Then ask about cycle counting in the warehouse or on the shop floor. Cycle counting is a great way to keep inventory records accurate and current. It sure beats the chaos of a year-end inventory. In distribution, inquire as to what percentage of sales the 50% slowest-moving SKUs account for. Ask how the decision to purchase is

---

[3] See "Sky's the Limit," *Barron's,* January 4, 2010, and "Security in the Ether," *Technology Review* (January-February 2010).

made. If it is manual, and the company is anything other than a mom-and-pop operation, you can be sure that it needs fixing. Ask whether anyone with a crucial role in purchasing is a member of the Institute for Supply Management (www.ism.ws, formerly the National Association of Purchasing Management) and is a CPM (Certified Purchasing Manager). The CPM is a demanding and rigorous designation. Do the purchase people understand "EOQs"[4] and "safety stock"? What percentage of orders requires a back order?

Operations. Begin with a walk through the warehouse or manufacturing facility. Pay particular attention to where inventory is stored and how bins or containers are labeled. If they are not labeled at all, low inventory turn relative to the industry composite is a cinch. Are orders picked in reverse order to the sequence in which they will be delivered or shipped? Do employees wear hard hats and adhere to good safety practices? Is the operations area clean and well organized, or is junk all around? Do the walkways have clear boundaries with colored tape? Is rework tracked? Are statistics for mispulled merchandise kept and tracked? Are there any Environmental Protection Agency exposures for disposal of scrap, solvents, lubricants, and so forth? Are the company's drivers' records checked annually? If a manufacturing facility, how is production scheduled? Are key people members of the Association for Operations Management (APICS)? Are key people APICS-certified? How are bottlenecks on the shop floor handled? Has anyone read *The Goal*?[5] What percentage of incoming orders has to be expedited? What is the turnaround time on a new order?

Marketing. Does the company have a logo? A tagline? Does it appear to understand branding? Is its logo crisp and simple? Is the tagline easily remembered? Does it reflect the values or skills or something unique about the company that will resonate with customers? Check the Web site. Does it have a blog? Is it posted to at least weekly? Does the company have any advertising specialties (e.g., pens, golf balls, "sticky pads," etc.) to give to customers and visitors? Does it have an ad agency? Are its business cards printed on both sides (why waste 50% of the real estate on a card)?

---

[4] Economic order quantities.

[5] Eliyahu M. Goldratt, *The Goal* (Barrington, MA: North River Press, 2004). I have yet to meet a top-flight manufacturing professional who has *not* read this book.

Sales.   What processes does the company use for CRM (customer relation-ship management)?[6] How much does the company use technology for record-keeping, electronic "ticklers," submitting orders, and so on? Are the commissions sufficient both to motivate and to keep the company sufficiently profitable? How is the sales force organized—by geography, distribution channel, customer's industry, company size? Are there incentives to develop new customers? Is there a target number of new customers each year? Is there a target level of revenues from new customers each year? What is the churn in customers? Are appointments drop-in, or are they scheduled? If the latter, by whom? Do the salespeople have trouble seeing whom they need to see at the customer's work site? Is the catalog online or on CD? Is there video online or on DVD?[7] Are training materials available online? Are FAQs for more compli-cated machinery and equipment online? What is the incidence of warranty claims? Does it own its salespeople's vehicles, or do they? Will the documenta-tion for using the vehicle pass muster with the IRS?

Customer Care.   What is the rate of customer complaints per 1,000 orders delivered? How much does it cost to resolve a customer complaint and how long does it take, on average? How far up the company's food chain do peo-ple get involved? Does the president personally conduct *all* exit interviews with customers? Is customer care outsourced? If so, to whom, and what have been the results? Are customers assigned to particular customer care repre-sentatives? If so, how is the decision made as to which representative gets which customer? What are the incentives in customer care that motivate employees to resolve problems? Are those calling or e-mailing customer care solicited to rate their experience afterward? Does customer care track and aggregate complaints as to type of complaint and/or the line of business of its customers?

Human Resources.   Does the lead human resources (HR) person know the different headcounts at which various pieces of regulation kick in? How does the company fill new positions? (If the firm is unionized yet fills its positions from internal referrals, it is on thin ice with regulators.) What is the firm's EMR (experience modification ratio)? How often are perform-ance reviews given? Do employees have the right to disagree with perform-ance reviews? How closely is pay tied to performance? Can employees access their own records online? Is the company's personnel manual available

---

[6] Each call should have three main sections: call summary (who, what, when, key information, duration of the call), analysis (decision-makers, issues, competitors, probability of closing the sale, guesstimate of long-term value of this particular customer), and what's next.
[7] The CD-ROM is a declining technology.

online? How often is the manual reviewed and updated? Is the current version *accurate*? Does the company use personal development programs (PDPs) to prepare its people for higher levels of responsibility? What percentage of base pay are the average employee's fringe benefits? Does it have an effective disciplinary program in place? Could the company survive without the services of its lowest 10% of performers? If so, why are they still there? Does the firm have any program for communicating with the families of employees? Does the firm have an employee wellness program aimed at reducing healthcare claims and insurance premiums?

Finance. How long does it take for monthly financial statements to be published? Are there standard closing entries, including payroll accrual? Does the company remit payroll taxes electronically through the Electronic Federal Tax Payment System? What is the process for opening an account for a new vendor? For a new customer? What about the usefulness of the chart of accounts? Is spreadsheetitis running amok in the finance function? Does the company have a lockbox? Does it send its invoices electronically? How often? Does it send monthly statements in addition to invoices (shudder)? What does it do if it receives statements from a vendor? How does it record vendor invoices that offer a discount for prompt payment, at gross or at net? Does the company run credit checks before it extends credit? At what point after an invoice is sent, but remains unpaid, is a collection effort launched? Are notes kept for collection efforts? Does the company accept credit cards? Does it have permission to run credit and records checks on its key employees annually?

CEO. How visible is the CEO to employees? How does she spend her time? Does she know when to delegate and when not to? Does the CEO use technology to make her life easier? If relatives are on the payroll, do they get treated differently from nonfamily employees? Does the CEO publish her own PDP so that all employees can see it? Does the CEO "understand the numbers"? How does the CEO hear criticism of her performance? Does she get an annual physical? Is the CEO developing at least two internal successors? At what age does the CEO expect to retire? Does the CEO have a blog? How does he communicate with customers? With employees?

Board. Because of the cost of directors and officers (D&O) insurance, savvy SMEs rely on a council of advisors rather than a formal board mechanism. Councils are highly effective and deliver an impressive benefit-to-cost ratio if they are used properly. How often does the board/council meet? Does it get meeting materials in advance? Does it get a chance to contribute to the Agenda? Does it review budgets? Capital expenditures?

Succession issues? Litigation? How were members of the governing body chosen? For how long do they serve? Are term limits in place? How much are they paid?

Architecture

We have found that four aspects of architecture have the most causal explanatory power. They are: (1) incentives, (2) boundaries, (3) structure, and (4) alignment.

Incentives.   We cannot overemphasize the impact of incentives on people's performance. There is a multifaceted and delicate balance to strike in designing incentives, however. That balance is between short term and long term, between the individual and the group, and between the division and the company. Overemphasize any one of these three dyads, and the incentives will morph into disincentives. In general, the higher the position in the company, the more long term, the greater the focus on the group, and the greater the emphasis on the company that the incentives should create.

We are strong believers in deferred compensation for senior people. For one thing, it lengthens their decision-making horizon. For another, it acts as a kind of "golden handcuff" to tether them to the company. A competitor might succeed in hiring them away, but the cost to the competitor will be considerably higher than it would otherwise be.

What about PDPs? If companies are lucky and are not acquired, those without PDPs find themselves facing a dilemma: They have people in key jobs who are in over their heads, yet they have trusting cultures where replacing a longtime employee with a stranger from outside would be viewed as heresy, if not treason. PDPs should be a key aspect of the incentive program at all levels of high-growth companies.

Boundaries.   Too many SMEs try to do everything themselves in the mistaken belief that they can "save money." There are good ways to save money, and there are expensive ways. Some examples of the latter for a company: creating its own Web site; administering the HR function inside; designing its own business cards, logo, and tagline; doing IT inside; outsourcing janitorial services (why cannot people clean up after themselves?); trying to create its own "buzz"; and not forming informal alliances with firms in related industries to cross-sell products and services.

Structure.   Most SMEs pay little heed to their organization structures. That leads them to have far too many layers, structures that do not comport with how the business should work, and reporting relationships that are convoluted. These create a variety of problems. Too many layers mean that the company is likely to decide slowly, be too centralized, and take too long to process information. Structures that remained in place even as the business itself changed will create such inefficiencies as longer operating cycles, lower cash flows, and higher borrowing costs. As for convoluted reporting relationships, well, I've seen IT guys running shipping and receiving, receptionists with no supervisors, and CFOs overseeing parts of operations. I'm not arguing for bureaucratic specialization here, just for some common sense. The problem is that, as organizations grow, evolve, and change, many of them fail to revisit and reconsider issues of structure. That oversight can be expensive.

Alignment.   Good alignment means good fit between a company and its external environment. Good fit is defined by the match between internal management processes and structure, on one hand, with the characteristics of the external environment, on the other. The mediating mechanism between a firm and its environment is its strategy. The key point here is to match structure and processes with the external environment. Firms without such matches are known in the strategy literature as misfits.[8]

For instance, a volatile environment calls for an internal organization that is flexible, fast on its feet, and good at processing information quickly. A company facing such an environment is apt to have considerable informality, fluctuating teams formed to address ad hoc challenges, and incentives that are based less on explicit goals than on innovation and teamwork. So, while the structure is fluid, internal integration is necessarily tight.

In contrast, a public utility in most states is going to face an external environment that is dominated by regulatory and political questions. It is likely to have low employee turnover, rigid structures, and by-the-book procedures. Such organizations tend to attract employees who want stability, predictability, and minimal risk in their working lives. The trade-off for such security should be lower pay.

Culture

A firm's culture is an expression of its shared values, beliefs, and acceptable behaviors. We subscribe to the notion of T^3: Truth + Transparency = Trust. Honest and transparent founders tend to beget honest and transparent organizations. It is easy to get preachy about these traits, but I am not aware

---

[8] See Miles and Snow, "Hall of Fame."

of research that shows that such companies are any more or less successful than their neurotic and dysfunctional counterparts.[9]

In our experience one of the most problematic cultures for SMEs is one where the founder was or the successor is a conflict-avoider. Don't misunderstand: Conflict-avoiders are interesting clients. But the cultures of firms headed or founded by such individuals are, well, challenging, to say the least. For one thing, the inmates are often running the asylum; that is, subordinates often seem to be in charge because the conflict-avoider is only as good as his (we've never had a client with a conflict-avoiding woman at the top) most recent conversation. The result is that no one trusts anyone, and everyone walks on eggshells. The conflict-avoider never understands that he creates infinitely more conflict by ducking conflict than he ever would by bellying up to the bar and taking them on, one by one.

Segue

A few years ago we had a client company run by a charming man who was also one of the world's preeminent conflict-avoiders. I mean, this guy had zero tolerance for conflict. His company, then generating about $40 million in annual revenues, was a zoo, a study in distrust. One day the CEO, the CFO, the lead HR guy, and I were going to go to lunch. The CEO got clotheslined by an unexpected phone call, so I took the CFO and HR guy aside and stipulated these conditions:

- The CEO would order first.
- The guy placing ordering next would order something different from what the CEO had chosen.
- The other two of us would follow suit and order what our colleague had ordered.

"I have a twenty-dollar bill for each of you," I said, "if David [not his real name] doesn't change his mind and get what we get." The other two guys couldn't say "You're on!" fast enough.

We did, and he did. After lunch, I tucked two crisp new twenties into my money clip and grinned like a Cheshire cat. Truth be told, I wish I had lost. But I knew I wouldn't. This fellow just couldn't stand the level of conflict

---

[9] For a riveting book devoted to the subjective of dysfunction, see Manfred F.R. Kets de Vries and Danny Miller, *The Neurotic Organization: Diagnosing and Changing Counterproductive Styles of Management* (San Francisco: Jossey-Bass, 1984). It helps that Kets de Vries, now at INSEAD in The Netherlands after a long stint at the Harvard Business School, is also a trained psychoanalyst.

implied by ordering something different from his three dining companions. You can imagine what his companys ambience was like.

People

A company's longtime employees tend to self-select. They are often similar in belief, temperament, upbringing, and values. They are attracted to the company by the same incentives. So there is an overlap between people and architecture. Such overlaps are not uncommon in the SPARC framework.

From a causal perspective, for instance, the question about people is often one that arises from culture: What is "the deal" between the firm and its employees? That is, what implicit contract is there? For instance, the firm says, often without saying so explicitly, that "If you do this, this, this, and this, we will do our best to keep you employed." Bill Hewlett and Dave Packard built Hewlett-Packard (HP) on a foundation of "no layoffs." As long as they ran the place, there were none. There were occasional pay reductions to avoid layoffs, but there never was a reduction in force. When a layoff finally occurred under a successor, it traumatized the workforce. Now I hear that HP is installing sensors in work areas to determine how much time people spend at their desks. In departments where the at-the-desk component is judged to be inadequate, HP will send the employees home, have them telecommute, and gradually shrink the space it pays for. That is about as far from the original "HP Way" that Hewlett and Packard instituted as a heart attack is from heartburn.

Companies run by conflict-avoiders often have longtime employees in jobs that are beyond their capabilities to perform well. It is not their fault. They were never asked to develop the skill sets. (That would be conflict!) We believe that such occurrences are the fault of management, not of the individual in the job.

In 1979, I was brought in as the CFO/treasurer/controller in the turnaround at United Video, Inc. Its capital structure was 94½% debt (most of it at prime + 250 basis points), and Jimmy Carter was president. Interest rates were stratospheric and moving higher. My predecessor was fired on a Friday, and I showed up the following Monday morning. The company had poor internal controls. Its IT was run by what in those days was called a "service bureau," and it was attempting a cultural transformation from a sleepy point-to-point, tariff-driven microwave relay system across several states in the Midwest and Southwest to a bells-and-whistles coast-to-coast satellite communications firm. I spent most of my first day on the job in conversations with the people in the accounting department, learning about them, what went wrong with my predecessor, and what they aspired to be.

My top assistant carried the title of assistant controller. She was a recycled executive secretary with six hours of college accounting courses. I saw very quickly that I needed a lot more horsepower in that job than she had. But I also knew that I needed her institutional knowledge, or else I'd be forever stepping on political and cultural land mines. She was also a hard worker who never complained about long hours or weekend work.

I started looking for a stronger number two. Eventually I concluded that I could not afford the risk of hiring someone whose work habits I didn't know. So I reached back to my professional alma mater, Union Pacific Corporation, and hired away one of the top guys on the audit staff there. I did so with the permission of the general auditor, who was sure I could not entice one of his rising stars to leave. During the hiring process, we flew him to Tulsa for an interview. He resonated with all of the right people. But I was not going to make him an offer until I had resolved the problem of what to do with the current number-two person.

The day after his visit, I called her in for a chat. I sat on the same side of my desk as she did, thus making it more a conversation between peers. I asked her what she thought of our visitor the preceding day. She said she thought that he was terrific and that we ought to hire him. I said, "Linda, what job title would we give him?"

"Assistant controller," she said.

"But that's your job," I said.

"I don't care what you call me as long as you pay me," she said. That was the opening I was looking for. I suggested that we give her a different title, one with less cachet but more cash. She loved that idea. So I demoted her, gave her a nice pay bump, and hired the guy from Union Pacific. It was one of the best things I ever did for that company and for myself.

My point is this: Companies that keep promoting long-term employees without giving them the tools to be successful do their people no favors. Such employees are well respected for their work ethic, loyalty, and company cheerleading. But they are often in over their heads, and that is easy to spot.

Strategy

A few paragraphs ago, strategy was referred to as the "mediating mechanism between a firm and its environment." A company's choice of strategy represents its choice of how it will achieve fit between its inside (SW) and its outside (OT). The determination of strategy arises from answers to two short questions embodied in Exhibit 11.3.

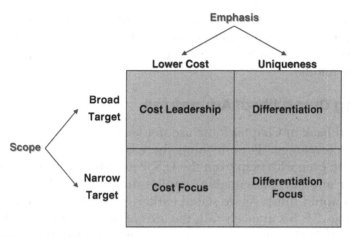

Exhibit 11.3   Competitive Strategies

Scope.   Will it compete industry-wide or in a strategic group? Few SMEs compete industry-wide. They lack the resources, management talent, and infrastructure. Competing industry-wide requires reach, and that is expensive. So they compete in a subsection of the industry, a mini-industry, as you know, called a "strategic group."

Emphasis.   Will it compete on price or on differentiation? To repeat what I said earlier, there can be but one cost leader in a domain. Everyone else that competes on that basis is playing a game of catch-up, and playing it by someone else's rules. That is a bad idea, unless your company is the cost leader. The beauty of a strategy of differentiation is that the sources of differences are limited only by the imaginations of the people running the company. If Starbucks can differentiate coffee, surely there is hope for the rest of us.

Competing on price is a brain-dead way to try to make a buck. If your firm competes on price but is not the big dog in the market, it is consigned to earning a rate of return below its weighted average cost of capital (WACC). So its WACC is really out of whack. If it's not the market leader but is competing on price, the question is "Why?" For the overwhelming majority of SMEs, focus/differentiation is the best strategy. It keeps the firm out of the way of market leaders with big footprints, boatloads of resources, and take-no-prisoners managers.

Before we close this section, let us return to the ugly specter of a firm trying to be all things to all people. This is what Porter calls "stuck in the middle." Some companies mistakenly see "being flexible" in their choice of strategy as being sensible. One well-selling textbook even *encourages* "stuck in the middle," heaven forbid.[10] Its authors seem to believe that the rare case where a single company—Hewlett-Packard laser printers come to mind—can be both cost leader and differentiator is an argument favoring stuck in the middle.

Assessing Durability of Advantage

As we noted back in Chapter 2, we are not keen on the phrase "sustainable competitive advantage." For one thing, there is no such thing. Capitalism will not permit it, even with help from the U.S. Patent Office or government regulators. For another, "sustainable" implies durability far longer than most companies would think. As we stated earlier, we prefer the phrase "distinctive advantage." It fits in nicely with the idea of differentiation. If differentiation is "perceived uniqueness," then it seems to us that the resulting advantage(s) should be "distinctive," at least. Besides "sustainable competitive advantage" has become an overwrought, hackneyed phrase. When I hear people who know nothing about strategy use it—as I have, many times—then I know it's a phrase that thoughtful professionals should toss into the dumpster.

Back to VRIO

As noted earlier in this book, we ask every employee we interview a set of common questions. The question "Why do customers do business with this company rather than with its competitors?" is intended to isolate insiders' perceptions of the subject company's unique capabilities. If we hear the same one(s) several times, as we often do, then we turn to the VRIO framework[11] to draw a bead on the potential durability of the capabilities. Let's go there now.

The maximum number of questions is just four—about V, R, I, and O. Let's reiterate them anyway, just to make sure we understand the process of assessing the durability of a capability. They should be asked in sequence, but the "R," "I," and "O" questions should be posed only if the answers to the one(s) preceding are yes:

V = Is the capability valuable (as evidenced by customer satisfaction surveys), or does it increase revenues or reduce costs?

R = Is it rare (how many competitors have it)?

I = Is it inimitable (can rivals replicate/substitute against it)?

---

[10] Thompson, Strickland, and Gamble, *Crafting and Executing Strategy*.
[11] Barney, *Gaining and Sustaining Competitive Advantage*, 138–162.

O = Are the company's architecture and incentives aligned so as to re-inforce and encourage replication of the capability?

The VRIO graphic can be seen in Exhibit 11.4.

If a capability is not valuable, it's a disadvantage that raises the client company's cost of capital. If it's valuable but not rare, it offers competitive parity, which buys the firm some time. That's not necessarily bad. If the capability is valuable and rare but not inimitable, then it confers a temporary advantage with (temporary) above-normal performance attributable to that capability in the offing. But it is temporary because the competition can imitate it or substitute against it. But if the answer to all four questions for a given capability is yes, then distinctive advantage of some unknown duration and above-average performance should be the case.

It is the responsibility of those who run the company to draw from resources to create unique capabilities that pass the VRIO test. In most SMEs, the capabilities form a strategy of focus/differentiation. That strategy is the linchpin of alignment among the four elements of SWOT. Strategy-making is a continual process of iteration and recalibration because change and evolution are the only sure things in free markets. Capitalism is a demanding and unforgiving system, but it is also the only one that has endured, however imperfectly and in whatever versions around the world.

Let us return to our friend, Ron, whom we met in Chapter 7. Where did his approach to purchasing fall in SPARC? One could argue that it was part of routines—the tasks the firm did on a regular basis. Someone else might assert that it fell under architecture—how the company was designed. My own view is that routines is a better call, but architecture can work, too.

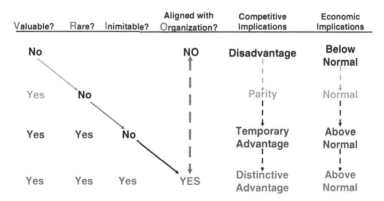

Exhibit 11.4   VRIO Assessment Tool

Source: "Beyond that *What*: Using SPARC to Determine the *Why* and Add Value for Clients," at NACVA's 2008 15th Annual Consultants' Conference, June 11, 2008, in Las Vegas. Used with permission.

The more important question, it seems to me, is where Ron's capability stacks up under VRIO analysis. To the first question—Is it valuable?—the answer is clearly no. So it is not a distinctive advantage but a distinctive *dis*advantage. To reinforce that, ask if it reduces risk, increases cash flow, or raises expected growth in free cash flow. If it does none of those, it undermines all three.

Summary

This chapter has presented and discussed how to uncover the causes that underlie a company's aberrant metrics (i.e., effects). The causes are value drivers or value destroyers. Many are rooted in routines; SMEs often fail to give routines their due. Causes can also arise from the other four elements of SPARC, but routines are the most common source.

In most cases involving SMEs, strategy should take the form of focus/differentiation. The capabilities that underpin the strategy must be tested empirically on a regular basis for value, rarity, inimitability, and organizational alignment to establish some level of advantage. Ideally that advantage is distinctive advantage. The strategy must be revisited, reiterated, and recalibrated continually. That is the nature of the capitalism beast.

Appendix 11A

Bringing It All Together: Quantifying Unsystematic Risk

The software related to this book is in Excel. Registration on our Web site is required before you can gain access to the Wiley Web site to use the software. Read the instructions before attempting to use it. We have done our best to keep it simple, even though we acknowledge the high complexity of the task of quantifying, in a logical and defensible way, the unsystematic risk of any client company. Send your questions, comments, and constructive criticisms to SPARC@beckmill.com.

Remember, we know that the potential for risk increases with proximity to the firm. From the −9% maximum bound at the low end, we made two simplifying assumptions:

1. The low-end constraint for each of the three levels is −3%. It might vary slightly, but, in our view, that is not important because negative risk premiums seldom occur in valuing SMEs.
2. The upper end for the macroenvironment is +3%. Again, it might be a little higher or a little lower, but that is not, in the scheme of things, important because we have much bigger fish to fry, especially at the company level.

We should also desire a set of risk ranges that is robust enough to be used by everyone, including venture capitalists. In Exhibit 11.5 we combine our two simplifying assumptions with the data from Morningstar/Ibbotson and from the published research.

As we said earlier, remember to conduct your analysis top-down. That is, begin with the macroenvironment, then move to the domain, and then to the subject company. Bottom up does not work.

We have designed the software so that it gives the analyst limited discretion at each of the three levels of unsystematic risk. Unlike other models in circulation, our ranges are based on empirical research. Therefore, we do not allow changes to the three ranges. We do, however, allow the

Exhibit 11.5   Ranges of Risk Premiums for Unsystematic Risk

Macroenvironment (MAC):	$-3\% \leq RP_{MAC} \leq +3\%$
Domain (DOM):	$-3\% \leq RP_{DOM} \leq +9\%$
Total range for external risk (EXT):	**$-6\% \leq RP_{EXT} \leq +12\%$**
Multiply EXT by 2.9 (in 2009) and . . .	
Company CO:	$-3\% \leq RP_{CO} \leq +35\%$
Total RP Range for Nonsize Unsystematic Risk (UR)	$-9\% \leq RP_{UR} \leq +47\%$

analyst to weight the major factors within each level of risk. Weight in each case must total 100%. If it does not, the software will automatically increase or decrease the weight of the largest factor in order for the total to equal 100%.

We also allow the analyst to add her own questions beneath each factor, but only at the company level. That reflects our belief, which is based on the literatures of organization theory and industrial organization, that the macroenvironment and domain levels of risk can be analyzed and quantified quickly and easily. The questions need not vary much across engagements.

That changes at the company level, however. Functions will vary across companies. Circumstances will be unique because of the heterogeneity among firms. That is why the software allows—and we encourage—the insertion of additional questions that reflect the facts and circumstances of your client company.

We do not believe that *every* question you ask during an on-site interview merits insertion in the software. We certainly do not do it that way in our shop. But we do add questions that reflect the aberrant metrics whose causes we are seeking to identify.

Here is an estimated equity discount rate that assumes all relevant factors are maximally negative at year-end 2008:

risk-free rate		3%
(normal) equity risk premium		6%
size premium		4%
macroenvironment	3%	
domain	9%	
company	<u>35%</u>	<u>47%</u>
	Total	**60%**

Yes, early-stage venture capital (VC) seekers might have more risk. But the 60% figure certainly puts us in the VC ballpark. We believe that any framework must be robust enough to play in the VC space.

Of course, this range assumes a going-concern premise of value. If the premise were liquidation, either forced or orderly, an additional risk premium could apply. There might also be extreme situation-specific circumstances that justify one or more additional risk increments. But we believe these seldom apply in the universe of 99% of the companies that the business valuation community appraises.

12

SPARC Archetypes among Small and Medium-Sized Enterprises

This chapter is one of the shortest in the book. It discusses five archetypes of SMEs. These archetypes are drawn from SMEs we have encountered in over 400 engagements spanning 17 years. They arise from a variety of domains; among the few two-digit SIC/NAICs codes not represented are biotech/pharma and high technology. We decline engagements in those arenas because of the vast industry-specific knowledge required to be competent valuing such firms. One of the many things we love about the work we do is the diversity of businesses with which we are privileged to work. To be any good at valuing biotech or pharma or tech firms, we believe one must specialize and do it full time. That level of specialization, while lucrative, is too confining for us.

To develop these archetypes, I reviewed deliverables from every engagement in our firm's history. I read old reports, calculations memoranda, and advisory documents, making notes of SPARC components as I went along. Five consistent and repeating types of companies emerged. Then, with encouragement and suggestions from two guys named Russ—Russ Hudson of StrategeMetrix, LLC and Professor Russ Coff of the Goizueta School of Business at Emory University—we christened the five archetypes. They comport with Porter's generic competitive strategies (see Chapter 2), plus another for "stuck in the middle."

We call these "enterprise archetypes" because each has its own pattern of characteristics that tend to repeat themselves in firms across domains. These are easy to remember because each starts with the letter *e*—as in "enterprise."[1]

---

[1] This connection originated with my good friend, colleague, frequent collaborator, and sometime partner in intellectual crime, Russ Hudson, DBA, CPM. His approach to valuation is also rooted in the strategy discipline.

We began with the key ideas from a classic paper about exploitation and exploration.[2]

Whether industry-wide or not, a company that exploits does more of what it already does in hopes of driving down its costs, reducing its price, and imposing misery on its rivals. We chose "Exploiter" and "Extender" for this archetype's industry-wide and focus versions, respectively. We followed the same process for companies that engage in processes of exploration (i.e., is seeking new and different products or ways of delivering services). We paired the "Explorer" with the "Experimenter" for industry-wide and strategic-group scopes, respectively. For Porter's hapless stuck-in-the-middle competitor, we chose "Equivocator." The term conveys the chronic confusion, contradictions, and inconsistencies in how it does business and why it chooses as it does.

This "gang of five," so to speak, resulted from my effort to create a set of labels that were more intuitive than Miles and Snow's (M&S) classic typology composed of Defender, Prospector, Analyzer, and Reactor.[3] More recently, I was inspired by the work of Rich Burton and Børge Obel[4] who also embraced M&S. Finally, though, feedback from scholars convinced me not to channel M&S but to go with something new and easy to remember.

In the next section, we pair the archetypes for cost leadership: Exploiter and Extender. The section after that profiles the industry-level and focus archetypes for differentiation Explorer and Experimenter, respectively. The final section deals with the Equivocator.

In each section, we discuss the characteristics and features of each twosome's **S**trategy, **P**eople, **A**rchitecture, **R**outines, and **C**ulture. The only difference between the two archetypes constituting each pair is whether it competes industry-wide or not. Most SMEs do not, of course, but even if one does—and we have a current client that does—the SPARC profile does not change.

Exploiter and Extender

The Exploiter is our name for Porter's industry-wide competitor embracing cost leadership. Its focus counterpart is the Extender. We chose the

---

[2] March, "Exploration and Exploitation."

[3] Miles and Snow, *Strategy, Structure*. They based their typology on Child, "Organizational Structure."

[4] Burton and Obel, *Organizational Diagnosis and Design*.

latter because it connotes doing more of the same rather than something different. These players are usually the market leaders in their respective domains. The cost leader is concerned with change and innovation only to the extent that it helps reduce its costs, the better to cut its price and inflict pain on its cost-cutting imitators and its do-it-different rivals.

Strategy

Exploiter and Extenders have narrow fields of vision. They are driven to be the best they can be at what each does, which is what it has always done, only now it does it faster, better, and less expensively. Each is confident that lower price will protect it from the bells-and-whistles features of its differentiating rivals.

People

Exploiters and Extenders are usually led by a scientist or an engineer, often one from the industrial-engineering side, oriented, as they are, toward efficiency in plant layouts. One might think a flinty-eyed accountant could do well as the CEO of a cost leader. We have seen that just once. Every other cost leader CEO has been a scientist, an engineer, or a nondegreed founder who would have graduated in engineering or one of the hard sciences had he not run out of either money or patience.

The exemplar CEO of an Exploiter is former Intel CEO Andy Grove. He escaped to America from his native Hungary during the 1956 uprising in that country. He received his Ph.D. in chemical engineering in 1963. His motto, which was also the title of his best-selling book, was "Only the paranoid survive."[5]

Architecture

Exploiters and Extenders centralize decision-making. Within divisions, the organization structure is functional with rigid reporting silos reporting upward. There are seldom any liaisons across functions, except for the division general manager or, farther up the food chain, the CEO/owner herself. Information is not shared across functions, and employees are seldom cross-trained. The emphasis is on low-cost, error-free output that delivers a simple product or service at a market-leading price. "New" is welcome only if it reduces cost or increases quality.

---

[5] Grove, *Only the Paranoid Survive.*

Routines

Exploiters and Extenders seek routines that are easily replicated. They are by-the-book companies that document everything. They tolerate zero variation in everyday work. To the extent that routines are changed or new ones emerge, the change is almost never bottom up. Ideas are solicited from throughout the firm. The watchword of the Exploiter is "simplicity." Not ease but simplicity.

Culture

The culture of Exploiter and Extenders is engineering- and math-oriented. Those are the backgrounds they seek to attract. "You can't manage it if you don't measure it" is their mantra. Their cultures extol creativity only in the context of cost-reduction or price-reducing innovation. Except in domains where products have short half-lives, R&D expenditures, which are low as a percentage of sales, are predominantly process-oriented. Exploiters and Extenders are not big on marketing, except to the extent that it can help increase share.

Explorer and Experimenter

The Explorer and its limited-scope sibling, the Experimenter, are as different from the Exploiter and the Extender as Lexus is from a cash-for-clunkers vehicle. In fact, the watchword for both Explorer and Experimenter is "different." More than other types of competitors, these players understand that distinctive advantage is built on being different and on not following the crowd.

The differences arise from their views of how things should work in their domain and of what capabilities are required to make that vision a reality. So differentiation is rooted in unique capabilities that customers see as valuable, that are rare in the domain, that rivals cannot replicate or substitute against without extreme disruption to their existing ways of doing business, and that are organizationally aligned within the differentiator's architectures to reward the behaviors that bring customers back again and again.

Strategy

Differentiation, either industry-wide or focus. Differentiators, recall, charge a higher price than do cost leaders such as Exploiters and Extenders. For Explorers and Experimenters, cost matters, but margin from a higher price point for an innovative product or service that competitors cannot replicate anytime soon matters much more. The challenge for differentiators is to keep their eye on the moving target that is distinctive advantage.

People

More often than not, one finds people with marketing backgrounds leading Explorers and Experimenters. However, an occasional scientist or engineer can be found in the CEO's chair—George Buckley of 3M and Bill Hewlett of HP come to mind—if the nature of the firm's business requires hefty R&D. Our exemplar Explorer CEO is Procter & Gamble's Bob McDonald. He succeeded the legendary A.G. Lafley in 2009. Both Lafley and McDonald are P&G "lifers," and both took the marketing route to general management.

Founded in 1837, P&G is the quintessential "brand management" company. At P&G, "the brand" is everything. P&G creates brands, acquires brands, and sheds brands. The key training ground for any employee is as a brand manager. Those who excel in that job are earmarked for future stardom, unless they leave or do something dumb. When P&G can, it creates or acquires complementary products for its existing brands, as when it bought high-end specialty retailer The Art of Shaving in 2009 to extend the Gillette brand it bought in 2005.

One of the products that P&G got with the Gillette deal was the Oral-B toothbrush, which promptly took its place with Crest toothpaste, Scope, Fixodent, and Braun in the P&G Oral Care Division. P&G jettisoned Gillette's toothpaste brand, Rembrandt. In 2008, 23 of its brands each generated more than $1 billion in revenues. Another 20 brands each accounted for at least $500 million. These 43 brands produced 85% of revenues and 90% of profits.[6]

Architecture

The differentiator's decision-making mechanisms are the converse of the cost leader's: Most decisions are decentralized. Rather than steep organizational structures, Explorers' structures are flat with wide spans of control enabled by technology. This enables Explorers to react quickly, to make quick decisions, and to communicate faster. Silos are few, and liaisons (integrators[7]) often bridge gaps between functions to facilitate the sharing of information. On the product side, Explorers and Experimenters have major R&D commitments. Their products often use technology to increase

---

[6] 2009 P&G Fact Sheet, www.pg.com, November 29, 2009.
[7] Lawrence and Lorsch, *Organization and Environment.*

the productivity and margins of services and further differentiate their services offerings.

At the SME level, most Explorers and Experimenters reinvest major portions of their free cash flow in further innovating. As this is written late in 2009, we have a small (12 employees) client company in the services space that has ponied up $80,000 for new robotics and $70,000 for leading-edge enterprise software. As its rivals in a small strategic group have dropped like flies during the downturn, this company has put its capital-spending pedal to the metal and never flinched, even though it had to write off over $100,000 in bad receivables that it let accumulate during the 2003–2007 boom. Its next investment will be in special laptops so that its field employees can communicate directly with the new software from offsite locations.

Routines

Whereas cost leaders aim to minimize variation in virtually every Routine, Explorers and Experimenters aim at minimizing it in low-to-no-value-added routines. They have a high tolerance for variation aimed at adding value, even when it falls flat. (Recall how Post-its became a leading product at 3M.) Unfortunately, differentiators sometimes put so much stock in the creative process that they forget there needs to be an outcome.

Culture

Differentiators build their cultures around what makes them different. These are belief systems that say, in essence, "We *are* different." They celebrate that. They screen prospective employees to ensure that they will fit into such a high-spirited environment. They cultivate diversity, of course, but not for reasons of political correctness. They seek it out because they know that from diversity come new products and new services. So long as the basic values of the organization are present, the rest, they believe, will take care of itself.

Unfortunately, both Explorers and Experimenters at the top of their games can overlook what competitors are doing. They can forget about the evolution of domains. They can discount the impact of new players whose different views can change domains.

A great example of the latter is the United States' record companies when, first, Napster and then the iPod came to market. What did those companies do? They hunkered down, secure in the mistaken belief that the only way to sell music was on CDs that customers had to buy, even if they did not like half the songs that were on the CD. Napster and iPod empowered the customer with choices at an à la carte price that generated more revenues from a lower price point than the record companies ever dreamed of. Those companies just continued to sit on their duffs, wallowing in denial. By the time they figured it out, it was too late.

Equivocator

Finally there is the confused and self-contradictory Equivocator. It refuses to choose. It wants to be all things to all people. One day it is inveighing its managers to reduce costs. The next it tells them to innovate and be different. It has no idea what it wants to be when it grows up, which it never will. Reward systems and incentives change constantly. So do routines. Organizational restructurings are frequent. A favorite trick of the Equivocator is merging with another Equivocator. Somehow they believe that combining two failing competitors will produce a world- class company. The merger of Delta and Northwest Airlines is a textbook case of that kind of thinking.

We in the valuation community see it playing out right now as the American Society of Appraisers (ASA) thrashes about wildly, undecided about whether it wants to continue to be a "multidisciplinary" organization—all things to all people, in other words—and merge with, say, the Royal Institute of Chartered Surveyors. A proposed combination of ASA with the Appraisal Institute went south when the AI turned thumbs down. The problem for ASA is that the real estate appraisers who controlled the organization for so long are now in decline, largely because state licensing has supplanted the need for the rigor of the ASA credential. That is not necessarily good for clients, but regulators do not care. They want to solve a problem that a balkanized profession of real estate appraisers refused to solve on its own. (Are the membership organizations in the valuation community listening?)

Strategy

The Equivocator has no consistent strategy. Economic Darwinism eliminates most Equivocators before they become public companies, but we have seen many Equivocators in the SME space. Sometimes we are surprised by their willingness to limp along producing lousy returns and disrupting their otherwise prosperous rivals because sentiment creates an exit barrier that keeps them from folding so long as they can draw breath.

People

Equivocators are run most often by people with financial backgrounds. Their risk aversion plays out in their discomfort with making a commitment to a given way of competing and then staying with it, even if times get tough.

They tend to be numbers-obsessed and not people-oriented enough. They disdain marketing and can believe that customers use price as their only buying criterion.

Being an Equivocator saps resources because so much is wasted. Small companies can afford such inefficiencies least of all. However, we have heard young people say that they want to start a company, but they do not want to limit their options. Starting a company and making it successful require passion. Those who refuse to limit their options are advertising to one and all that they have no passion because passion tends to be single-minded.

Architecture

The Equivocator has no overarching approach to organization design. It is one way this month and a new way next month. If decentralization is not working, it will centralize, and vice versa. I have seen 50-person companies with more organizational layers than Toyota. I have seen project-type companies whose people participate in multiple projects at the same time never embrace a matrix structure. When I suggested it to a consulting firm once, they told me I was crazy. Too often the people running such companies are linear thinkers in a multitasking world.

Routines

The routines within Equivocators are notable for their absence. That is because organizational life within the Equivocator is sheer chaos. The best place to see the chaos is in the accounting arena. That is the first place we look because it mirrors the rest of the company. Yet some owners of Equivocators continue to believe that the financial function is independent from what goes on elsewhere in the company. Show me a firm that is in chaos on payday, and I will show you an Equivocator.

Culture

Politics govern the cultures of Equivocators. That is because there is no consistent belief system, no group of values that people hold near and dear, and nothing that recurs often enough to convey the idea of "That's how we do things around here." Thus Equivocators' cultures tend to be political minefields governed by fear and disinformation. Most of them last longer than they should simply because the owner refuses to give up.

Summary

Each of these archetypes has normative implications, just as an oligopoly does. Like the oligopolist who, when asked how his company competes, says, "We kill 'em on price!" the would-be differentiator that gets upset by not squeezing every last nickel out of its operations or the alleged cost leader that wants to pour tons of money into R&D for new products are Equivocators that do not yet know it.

Within SMEs, the Experimenter should be the most common archetype we encounter. That is because (1) it offers more ways of succeeding—the potential sources of differentiation are limited only by the imagination of those running the company, and (2) competitors are often unsophisticated so they mistakenly compete on price, even though they do not have the scale to be successful. But we do not see committed Experimenters often. We think that is because they are uncomfortable with marketing, not sure about the value of well-done customer loyalty surveys, and not altogether certain that customers are willing to pay a higher price, even though the woman in charge drives a Mercedes and uses custom-made Pings to get around the links.

Competing on price makes decisions too easy for customers. As said earlier in this book, that type of competition is tantamount to a race to the bottom of the ocean . . . and the divers are wearing cement wet suits. Differentiation is the strategy that offers an SME the highest probability of succeeding.

PART

III

TALES FROM THE FIRING LINE

CHAPTER 13

Construction and Manufacturing

We turn now to a series of vignettes taken from actual valuation and consulting engagements. These are mini–case studies that highlight certain aspects of the approach taken in this book. We are going from theory to practice. Good theory leads to sound practice, and that is why we began with the theory of Chapters 2 through 6 and followed it with six chapters in Part Two, Pouring the Foundation.

These are not comprehensive examples. They are snapshots and snippets from engagements. They highlight successful problem-solving and successful companies. They also show how to get at underlying causes and then to design solutions to them. Although quotation marks are used to re-create conversations, those exchanges are paraphrases of what was actually said. I don't use a tape recorder, so I have to rely on notes and memory. But I think that the quotations lend an aura of reality and immediacy to the stories. I hope you agree.

Rather than just tell each story separately, I have created a simple structure for the vignettes; "V-M" means "Value Map." Everything in the "Findings" section was learned during our on-site interviews. That is why I cannot overemphasize the importance of the site visit and thorough and thoughtful preparation for it. It is a world-beater of a valuation tool if you put it to work correctly.

After each "Findings" section, I use bold for the element in SPARC that was the cause. I think that makes them easier to read and, more important, easier to refer back to later on. As always, I welcome your comments, observations, and constructive criticism. Let me hear from you via SPARC@ beckmill.com.

Construction

Overview.   EConCo is a 50-year-old niche contractor operating from three locations and employing about 300. The work is dangerous. It is done in searing heat and bone-rattling cold. The second-generation owner, a CPA, took over in the late 1970s. At the suggestion of his senior managers, he approved what turned out to be a successful effort to toss out the labor union in a "decert" election.

Metrics

1. December bottom-line hemorrhage every year.
2. High experience modification ratio (EMR) due to on-the-job fatalities.
3. Annual Disposable Tools Expense was about 3% (> $1 million) of gross revenues.
4. Company prepared payroll in-house weekly, which meant that the accounting function was overstaffed. Controller was a graduate of a two-year "business college"; the CFO came from EConCo's audit firm.
5. Internal successor recommended our firm to the CEO as the outside advisor in the succession process.

Interviewees.   Crew chiefs (2); division general managers (GMs) (3); long-time employees (5); controller; chief operating officer (COO); CFO; vice president of human resources; CEO.

V-M Findings

1. Company paid bonuses based on performance from January through November. Employees gamed the system by manipulating the job-by-job percentage-of-completion figure on November 30 every year. The result was overstated profits for the 11-month period and a twelfth-month sea of red every year. Neither the auditors nor the CFO (who came from the audit firm) ever asked about it. (SPARC)
2. EMR = the ratio of a company's actual workers' compensation losses to the losses expected of a company in that line of work. EConCo's EMR was above 1.0, and customers were demanding a reduction to 0.8 in 24 months. It had a safety manual that had not been updated in years. It also had a $500,000 deductible on its workers' compensation policy. Customers did not want contractors with high EMRs because they thought such companies reflected poorly on their choices

as representatives of their communities. Regulated monopolies carry high stakeholder responsibilities.

ECorCo's culture was big-time macho. "Real men don't need safety" was the way one interviewee put it. Even when "the word comes down from on high," said another, "we ignore it." He added: "Except for the guy that gets hurt, there is no penalty for bad safety and no reward for good safety. We get our bonuses anyway." (SPARC)

3. There were no controls on Disposable Tools. Any crew chief could buy them and charge them to EConCo. No purchase order was required. (SPARC)

4. Weekly pay was a holdover from days when the workforce was unionized. For employees in remote locations, paychecks were overnighted and then handed out by supervisors. (SPARC)

5. I had known the successor candidate for over 35 years. I was tipped off that he had had his residential electrical service turned off several times, once when he was playing golf with the CEO of a customer company. The CFO, who opposed the would-be successor's ascension to CEO, said the guy was always late turning in the receipts for his company credit card. (SPARC)

SPARC Elements

Architecture
Routines
Culture

V-M Solutions

1. Pay bonuses after audit is completed each year; defer major portions of bonus for higher-ups in the company. They had to be on the payroll to collect, except in case of death, disability, or retirement.

2. Institute 30-minute safety-training session with every crew at the start of each workday. Crew chief and three subordinates to discuss safety practices in the context of work to be done that day. Crew chief documents the presence of each attendee. No bonuses to be paid in any division with a fatality during the year; deferred portions cannot be paid until the division has gone at least 24 consecutive months without a fatality. If it fails to make the 24 months in the 36 months following a fatality, bonus portions accrued and deferred are forfeited.

3. Disposable Tools Expense to be budgeted and tracked at the crew level. Every crew begins with the same inventory of Disposable Tools. Crew chief is responsible for the inventory and for documenting the need for replacement. Result: This expense declined by > 90% the first year it was handled this way.

4. EConCo announced that it was going to require every employee to get paid via direct deposit. The third highest-paid employee in the company with a base pay of $165,000/year led a protest meeting at corporate headquarters. His face was red with rage as he began by exclaiming "I don't want anyone else to know my bank account number!" The CFO informed him that the account number was on every check he wrote. The angry employee's eyebrows went almost to his hairline as he thundered, "Are you jivin' me?"

5. The successor's handling of the company's expenses as well as his failure to control his own spending was a problem. I could imagine creditors hounding him at corporate headquarters. But the man was also my friend. I told my wife that I just needed to withdraw from the engagement and refund the client's money. She disagreed: "If you do that, George will get the job and run the company into the ground because *you* quit. You are going to cost 300 people their jobs because of a friendship? Are you kidding? How would you feel explaining this to *60 Minutes*?"

   She is tough. That is just one of the many reasons that we are a team.

   The following week in my hotel room, I made a list entitled "What We Know"; it was a single page of bulleted facts about the successor. I printed it on my portable printer, marched into the CEO's office the next morning, and sailed it across his desk. He read it and said, "What do you want me to do?"

   "Call it off," I said.

   "I can't do that," he replied. "George and his wife were in town last weekend house-hunting. We had them over to our place for supper."

   "OK," I said, "put it off." This was in March.

   "I can do that," he said. "Until when?"

   "New Year's."

   "How about October 1?"

   "Deal," I said. "When are you going to tell him?"

   "Well, I need to call him," said the CEO.

   "There's the phone," I said. "It's not going anywhere."

   He looked at it and then at me.

   "It's still there," I said, pointing at his phone.

He sighed, picked up the receiver, called George in a city several hundred miles away, and said, "George, this is Jack. Warren has something he wants to tell you," and handed me the phone.

I kid you not. That's how it came down.

I quickly slid out of the phone call, shifted gears, and suggested that we put a majority of outsiders on the board and buck the question to them. The CEO loved that idea. I worked with him to determine the skill sets the company needed. I then located the people, screened them discreetly, and contacted each one to see if he might be interested. Each was. The CEO talked with each one and was enthralled. I then drew up a lengthy "Company Profile" memorandum for the CEO's review. He circulated it to the full board ten days in advance. The board met for the first time in July and made the decision to turn down the successor in October. The successor quit the company, went to work for a direct competitor, and died of a single massive heart attack 14 months later; it turned out that an aunt and an uncle had died the same way and at his age (53). By then, I had helped the CEO negotiate a deal with one of the outside board members to become the CEO. It was an awful end to the most searing professional experience of my career.

Postscript. The new CEO worked miracles. He spent his first six months on the job asking questions and gathering information. Over the next 12 years, the company's workforce more than tripled, and its revenues almost quintupled. Its value skyrocketed, its cost of capital plummeted, and it is now in a multistage employee stock ownership plan process that provides an exit for the majority shareholder and job continuity for employees. But I still shudder every time I think about it. I believe I did the right thing, but I am still sad about it.

Specialty Publishing I

Overview. PubCorp is a venerable midwestern trade publisher. When we got involved, it was a third-generation family-owned company; its shareholders had made a policy choice, documented in board minutes, not to be involved in the company's day-to-day management. Its business model combines industry- and profession-specific magazines with trade shows targeting those same industries and professions. It is successful and **well respected**. Revenues were $150 million when we began working with it on acquisitions in the proprietary database space. One thing then led to another.

Metrics

1. At least one senior executive had quit the company for five years running—the day after receiving their annual bonuses. No one could understand why.
2. The CFO was a controller. Worse, his communication skills were lousy, he didn't delegate, and his people spent three weeks every month closing.
3. PubCorp wanted to get into the database business because it saw fat margins and high growth there, two things it didn't have in its existing lines of business.

Interviewees.   CFO; CEO; senior vice presidents (2); non–executive chairman of the board; administrative assistants (2); division GMs (3); advertising sales reps (4); accounting supervisors (2).

V-M Findings

1. The first thing to understand about *any* publishing company is its roots in one of the oldest industries on earth—the Gutenberg Bible was printed over 550 years ago. Old industries at a glacial pace change.

   The client company adopted a bonus plan that incorporated publishing-industry standards. These "standards," which we confirmed were just that, had two features that should be on any list of How-Not-Tos: (a) no portion was deferred, and (b) the performance metrics on which bonuses were based were "after allocations"; this ensured a political brawl during the budget cycle every year over what the allocation method would be. Savvy companies keep allocations off the table and out of the bonus discussion. (SPARC)
2. The CEO thought that closing for three weeks a month was normal. He had also never heard the phrase "management accounting." Don't misunderstand: He was in most other respects a top-flight CEO, but he simply did not know much about finance and accounting. He was nearing retirement and said that he knew he had "to fix the CFO problem." He decided to retain us to find a new CFO. (SPARC)
3. Proprietary databases are a different domain from PubCo's existing ones of publishing and trade shows. In the late 1990s, firms in the new space sold at sky-high multiples that seemed to have no connection to the actual performance or growth prospects of the target company. At least as bad, the buyer (our client) used *only* discounted cash flow in its valuation of prospective targets. It

also used a one-size-fits-all 10% weighted average cost of capital (WACC). (**SPARC**)

SPARC Elements

Strategy
Architecture
Routines
Culture

V-M Solutions

1. We batted .500 on the bonus issue. We were not able to convince the client to ditch allocations, but we were successful in persuading the board to defer major portions of bonuses for the senior management cadre. Besides acting as a kind of golden handcuff—they had to be on the payroll for the deferred portions to be paid—they raised the cost to a competitor of hiring away a senior manager because PubCo's employee would be leaving a chunk of money on the table. At least as important, the deferrals also lengthened the decision-making horizon of the people running the company.
2. We were paid over $75,000 to conduct an exhaustive nationwide search for a new CFO. We do an occasional executive search, but only for existing clients because (a) we do not want to be full-time head-hunters, and (b) we want to have to live with the results of our work. Over the years, we have developed a rigorous method for conducting such searches. It includes visiting the semifinalists in their homes with their spouses or significant others. We conduct some basic non-invasive testing, give candidates a heads-up that we will need their per-mission to run a credit check (and that they cannot be hired without one), and confirm credentials, including education. We produce three finalists whose only substantive differences are style and employ-ment history. We write lengthy profiles on each of the finalists and provide the CEO with a list of basic questions to ask each of them. No matter whom the CEO chooses, a bad hiring decision is impossible. In fact, we are so confident of our process that we guarantee the client that the successful candidate will be there for at least a year, or we will conduct a second search at no charge.

   In the case at hand, one finalist had spent almost two decades with General Electric—if you're looking for expertise in manage-ment accounting, GE wrote the book. A second finalist was a respected veteran of the publishing industry. The third came from a company whose financial arm was run by ex-GE financial managers. With considerable negotiating help from us, the client hired candidate 3, who was extraordinarily successful in his new job. He also pulled down a $450,000 bonus one year, thanks to allocations.

3. We introduced the client to guideline public company analysis and size-adjusted multiples. We also taught them how to estimate a WACC based on the risk profile of the target company. We showed them how to estimate working-capital needs and also convinced them to use tax-effected net income, even though the company was an S corporation. Someone has to pay the taxes, we said, and the client bought that.

   We also conducted discreet competitive intelligence on prospective targets. Our work included surveys that asked their customers to force-rank the target company and its competitors on a variety of issues. That precluded customers from identifying who our client might be. A few refused to participate because we would not disclose the client's identity. The result was fewer acquisitions for PubCo but higher-performing ones whose cultures were a better fit.

   The downside to the acquisition program was that our client could not make the transition from a print mentality to an information services mind-set. The cultural change required was overwhelming. The retiring CEO might have gotten it done had he delayed his retirement for, say, a decade, but he wanted out. So, the old "print heads" won, and the company suffers big time in economic downturns. As a result of an antitrust enforcement action, it later received a license to a lucrative database business. But it had to exit from that business because of its inability to dislodge the print-head approach to business.

Postscript.   After the turn of the new century, the CEO retired, and a family member (by marriage) decided that he could run the company. He is a smart man—just ask him—but he does not have the temperament for the job. However, even with deferrals, the bonuses are still over the top, so his direct reports remain with the company.

Specialty Publishing II

Overview.   MiniPubCo, a publisher of location-specific entertainment guides, was not far from going under when we arrived on the scene. It was run by a general manager with megalomaniacal tendencies who saw himself as a business genius. We were brought in to analyze the situation, assess the salability of the firm, and make recommendations to the board.

Metrics

1. The company was consistently in the red.
2. It was often sued for libel; the GM was always named as a codefendant who was alleged to have slandered the plaintiff(s).
3. It had 14 owners, each of whom was on its board.
4. The monthly financial statements were a joke.

Interviewees. Board members (5); the GM; the art director; the photographer/administrative person; sales representatives (2).

V-M Findings

1. Unbeknownst to the board, every day the company bought lunch for the GM and his second in command, an administrative person whose capacity for ingratiating behavior was truly stunning to behold. (SPARC)
2. The GM had a hair-trigger temper and believed he was always right. Truth being the definitive response to both libel and slander, he invariably believed that he was bulletproof, despite the legal expense. (SPARC)
3. There was no agenda for the monthly board meetings. Every meeting was a free-for-all where nothing was accomplished. Out of disgust, some members just quit attending. (SPARC)
4. This company was Exhibit A in the pantheon of "Companies Running QuickBooks Running Amok." The accounting records were upside down. (SPARC)

SPARC Elements

People
Architecture
Routines

V-M Solutions

1. The company reclaimed its credit cards. Employees used their own plastic and submitted expense reports monthly. The outside accounting firm reviewed the expenses of the GM and his assistant. He was allowed one business lunch weekly, but only with sponsors or prospective ones. He had to document the purpose of the lunch, what was discussed, and so forth. This is IRS Compliance

101, we know, but it was revealed truth to the client company and to its directors.

2. The board told the GM that if he lost or settled one more lawsuit, they would fire him. He did, and they did. His replacement, the art director, lacked self-confidence, but she was not an egomaniac. As a successful mother, she brought humility and people skills to a company that needed both. Over time, she developed an ample reservoir of self-confidence that played well with everyone.

3. Four people owned about 75% of the shares. We recommended that the board be reduced to five people—the four bigger shareholders, plus another member chosen by the remaining ten smaller holders. The latter position was for a one-year term, the better to give each smaller owner, over time, a voice in governance.

4. At our urging, MiniPubCo hired a part-time degreed accountant. She was a stay-at-home mom who sought part-time work. Over time, she straightened out the books, and the company began getting reliable financials.

Postscript.   Unfortunately, the collapsing economy of 2008–2009 dried up the demand for entertainment on which the company's fortunes depended. When entertainment demand went away, advertising did, too. MiniPubCo tried to survive with discounted ads and a bare-bones staff. It limped along for a while, but the owners had to keep ponying up cash, even for a thrifty GM. They finally shut it down.

Specialty Manufacturing

Overview.   SpecManCo was a $20 million manufacturing company. It was founded by one of the great inventors in the U.S. petroleum industry. He was also the worst operating manager I have ever seen. He had an ugly habit of screaming at shop employees for no reason and with no warning. He was a creative genius and a control freak. His son, who had been a successful tax lawyer outside his father's company, had joined it, ostensibly as the successor. The founder was 78 years old and ran the company with an iron hand. There was a potential successor on the payroll, but he needed seasoning and development.

Metrics

1. Marginal profitability and heavy debt.
2. Low productivity (measured by annual revenues ÷ average number of full-time employees).

3. High incidence of rework on the shop floor.
4. A continuing stream of new patents—for "tools"—from the founder and one of his engineering protégés (who was also the likely successor).
5. Glacial decision-making slowed down production and sales of customized products.
6. There was no succession plan in place, primarily because, in our view, there was no active board.

Interviewees.   CEO; executive vice president; vice president–engineering; controller; more than a dozen shop-floor employees and supervisors.

V-M Findings

1. The firm had low profitability for several reasons: low productivity, significant rework, and an unnecessarily long operating cycle due to inefficiency. Division operating people ignored the budgets prepared by the accounting department at corporate headquarters. (SPARC)
2. High turnover contributed to low productivity. But lack of training, no documented routines, and nepotism in the extreme were important factors, too. The founder's son, daughter, and son-in-law were all on the payroll, the latter two at salaries far above what they could command in the open market. Most important, the founder regularly "went off on employees" and showered them with verbal abuse that was nothing if not personal. (SPARC)
3. The cost of rework was not tracked, causes of rework were not recorded and analyzed, and individuals whose efforts caused rework were not coached about how to improve their performance. (SPARC)
4. The only person at SpecManCo with whom the founder had a good relationship was the vice president of engineering. That was because he, too, was creative. He also had extraordinary intelligence. Most important, he would tolerate no abusive language or treatment from the founder. When the founder saw his protégé walk out one day and stay away for a week incommunicado, his behavior toward the protégé changed markedly and for the better. (SPARC)
5. The founder controlled everything. He second-guessed everyone, including his son. Nearing 50, the son craved the approval he had never received from his father. The old man was no fool—he knew that the way to control his son was to continue to withhold approval. So he did.

But there's more to this story. I worked closely with the son before convincing him to seek help from a family-systems therapist to deal with his father's refusal to affirm anything the son had ever done. He and I would have supper together and map out our work schedule for the next day. By the time he got to work the following morning, our schedule had flip-flopped. I thought it was because the old man was on the phone every night. He wasn't. His wife was, cracking the whip on her children and grandchildren in the business. In most substantive respects, she ran the business without ever setting foot on the premises. To this day, I have never met her. (SPARC)

6. Over time and with help from his protégé, we convinced the founder to put a succession plan in place *and* have it reviewed by a board with a majority of outsiders. He didn't like the idea, but he went along with it. One of the first actions of the new board was to ask him to take a physical. That resulted in a quintuple bypass operation, after which it suddenly dawned on everyone that the company had no "key-man insurance." For a 78-year-old man who had just had bypass surgery, the insurance premiums were stratospheric. But the company bit the bullet anyway. Within two years, the protégé became CEO, and the insurance policy was allowed to lapse. (SPARC)

SPARC Elements

People
Architecture
Routines
Culture

V-M Solutions

1. We began by convincing the founder to let the operating divisions prepare their own budgets. That gave them ownership that the current practice, wherein the accounting department prepared all budgets, did not permit. We persuaded him that his job was to set long-term goals and review the short-term plans to ensure that they were moving in the right direction. We had two things going for us: (1) his age and (2) by his own admission, he was "sick and tired of being sick and tired."

2. The founder/CEO was serious about his religion. I managed to persuade him that his actions toward employees, however well intended, were not merely counterproductive but also not in keeping with the

religious beliefs he expressed. Those actions were also expensive. He agreed to refrain from the personal attacks. But old habits die hard, and he broke the agreement the second day it was in force. I then sat him down and convinced him to give me three sizable checks, each one made out to politically left-of-center organizations he could not abide. I told him that if I ever heard of him degrading another employee, I'd mail one of the checks. "The problem here is that you're not feeling any pain for behavior that is costing you buckets of money. It's not the size of the check that'll hurt you, sir," I said. "It's all the mailing lists you're going to land on and all the phone call solicitations you're going to get from organizations you can't stand." It worked out fine. As long as I was involved with the company, I never heard that he had engaged in the abusive behavior again. I later heard that he lived in terror that one of the checks would be mailed. It never happened.

I also persuaded him to let his protégé, the engineering VP, take over operations for a two-year period. That would be good training for him as the founder's successor. Founder and protégé agreed.

They also agreed that one of the protégé's first orders of business was to get a company-wide employee manual in place and also commission write-ups of recurring procedures for each department in operations. This was soon after the confirmation hearings for Judge Clarence Thomas to become a justice on the U.S. Supreme Court, and there had been a rush in corporate America to get written policies on sexual harassment into employee handbooks.

We were asked to solicit employees about what they thought they needed to do their jobs better. (We convinced the company that employees were unlikely to respond candidly if they thought the founder might see their responses.) Several dozen substantive suggestions came back. The new lead operating guy approved most of them, and productivity quickly shot up. Within six months, it exceeded the industry average.

3. A set of accounts related to rework was added to the chart of accounts. Rework was tracked, and individuals responsible for it were coached constructively. Employees prepared detailed documentation for low-value-added routines. Within 90 days, rework had plummeted, though it was still nowhere near six sigma.

4. We urged the founder to do something similar to what some other founders had done: Step out of the CEO's role and focus on what he was good at, which was inventing products. He would still be the chairman, so he would remain in control. But someone with a better temperament would sit in the CEO's chair. He agreed. Inventing new

products was all he wanted to do in the first place. He was in his element and even learned to have fun with the other engineers. New products multiplied like rabbits.

5. At our recommendation, the founder began to decentralize the organization structure. With our help and board approval, he initiated a program of incentives for GMs, gave them certain spending authority, and, by insisting that divisions prepare their own budgets, imposed budgetary ownership on them. The pace of everything at the company picked up. People were no longer second-guessed, except during the budget cycle, which was appropriate. (Needless to say, there were no allocations that affected bonuses.)

6. With active involvement by and encouragement from the board, the protégé succeeded his mentor two years later.

Postscript.   Six years later, the firm was sold for to a Big Board company for $46 million in a stock deal. The acquirer's stock tripled in 15 months.

Packaging

Overview.   When we were introduced to it, FoamCo was a small family-owned manufacturing business that employed 14 people and generated $1.9 million in annual revenue. Though it wasn't a start-up, it resembled one in many ways. The patriarch had sold his interest in a packaging firm in another state and retired with an eight-figure net worth. He and his wife had lost their oldest son to a drunk driver eight years before. Their middle son was successful as a traveling salesperson selling building products, but they had persuaded him to quit that job to work with his father and younger brother in the year-old packaging firm. They had no business plan, just a familial backer with a big checkbook. We were asked to value the company and also look at the possibility of an exit for the father.

Metrics

1. Declining revenues in a strong economy.
2. Low productivity (annual revenues ÷ number of full-time-equivalent employees.
3. Low advertising outlays (< 0.2% of sales).
4. Bare-bones Web site.
5. Disorganized shop floor.

Interviewees.   Patriarch; both sons; six employees.

V-M Findings

1. Packaging is a cyclical business. If the U.S. economy is booming, packaging is usually strong. However, FoamCo's revenues were falling and had been for six months. It had no marketing plan; its approach was scattershot and inconsistent. All three principals were sure that the only way to compete was on cost. The problem was, however, that FoamCo had insufficient scale to be even remotely competitive and still generate a return commensurate with the risk the patriarch was taking.

   The irony is that the older of the two surviving sons was a topflight sales guy. Unfortunately, his socialite wife refused to forsake her social position in a major metropolitan area to move to a small city with no Junior League. So her husband commuted more than 100 miles each way three days a week because she insisted that he not be away overnight. Whenever he was at the manufacturing facility or was making sales calls, she called his cell phone incessantly. At one point, he wondered if she was checking up on him. She had no reason to, but that would have made no difference to her.

   The older son called on companies his father knew from his days in a similar business. These were older, mature companies that bought almost solely on the basis of price. The son proposed promotions, even a golf tournament, to his father, but the old man said that was a waste of time and money.

   The younger son was, well, strange. He brought his dog to work with him. Other employees asked if they, too, could bring their pets, but they were told no. The younger son spent at least two hours a day "walking" his dog, which resembled a small horse. He had never worked in any business besides this one. He was a new and undistinguished graduate of the college in his hometown. When he told me his major was economics, I asked him if he thought opportunity cost was a nifty idea. He stared at me wide-eyed and said, "What's that?" His entry-level title was executive vice president. (**SPARC**)

2. Like many small companies, this one was overstaffed. The two sons and their father made all the decisions, even though a knowledgeable manufacturing professional was in charge of operations. He had no authority, though. FoamCo had no budgets, no performance standards, no production scheduling, no job costing, no hiring process, no quality control, and no knowledge among the three principals of how to organize a shop floor to minimize bottlenecks and maximize throughput. Except for the lead manufacturing guy, no one had read Eliyahu Goldratt's *The Goal* (Barrington, MA: North River Press, 2004), either. The top-flight manufacturing people I know think that

book is about the most important one they've ever read; one guy told me he rereads it every year, "just to keep me focused on what matters." FoamCo's manufacturing person told me he hadn't had any luck persuading either son or their father to read it. "They don't understand manufacturing," he said. (**SPARC**)

3. As noted earlier in this book, most smaller companies should pursue a focus/differentiation strategy. Again, *anything can be differentiated*. Anything at all. Instead of targeting a couple of nearby market segments of particular types of businesses, FoamCo was relying on the *Thomas Register*[1] for information about prospective customers. It was using a shotgun when it should have used a .3006. (**SPARC**)

4. Even in the summer of 1999, Web sites were common. In an old industry like packaging, FoamCo could have gotten the jump on most of its competitors, but especially the ones in its region, by putting money into a good Web site. It didn't do that because the patriarch still believed in doing business "the old-fashioned way." In some things, that's great. In technology, it seldom is. (**SPARC**)

5. FoamCo's EMR was almost 1.5. That alone would have yelled at most business owners. But the patriarch/check-writer was a salesman, not an operating guy, so it meant nothing to him. He did say to me at one point that FoamCo's workers' compensation premiums seemed to be "pretty stiff." Part of the problem with the EMR was that the company had no safety program and didn't enforce hard-hat rules. Another part of it was that the patriarch and his sons, especially the younger one, refused to let the manufacturing guy do what he knew how to do—run the manufacturing side of the house, including the safety aspects. (**SPARC**)

SPARC Elements

Strategy

People

Architecture

Routines

Culture

---

[1] This venerable publication ceased hard-copy production in 2006. It holds itself out as "the most comprehensive resource for finding information on suppliers of industrial products and services in North America." It is now online at www.thomasnet.com.

V-M Solutions

1. As we got into the valuation, we quickly saw that there were bigger fish to fry. The client agreed that we should take on an advisory role. We helped FoamCo formulate a quick-and-dirty marketing plan based on industrial demography within 100 miles of the manufacturing facility. The older son made the calls and pitched the company as a "local, Virginia-owned" firm. New customers piled on board, and sales reversed their downward slide. The younger son continued to bring his dog to work because neither his dad nor his brother would set him straight.

2. Based on our research into guideline public companies, we worked with the company to set a benchmark ratio of revenues to FTEs. Anytime someone could be hired without the projected ratio falling below the benchmark, FoamCo's hiring light was green. Increasing sales raised productivity, but there were still too many people on the payroll. FoamCo's principals refused to lay off anyone. Productivity never reached the benchmark, either, so the patriarch continued writing checks.

3. and **4.** We convinced the dad that investing in a good Web site was money well-spent. We helped the three principals find a web developer who would do more than just brochureware, though, that was about all most businesses had in the late 1990s. The Web site aimed at three SIC segments that were well represented within a 100-mile radius. The older son began writing articles for trade publications in those three segments, too.

5. At our suggestion, FoamCo brought in a manufacturing consultant. He recommended, among things, that the patriarch stay away from the business, except for one day a week. To his credit, the older son delivered that message to his father. To the latter's credit, he went along with it. The younger son disagreed with the recommendation.

Postscript. The value of the company went up, but not for long. The patriarch was the older brother of Ron, the hapless control freak we first met in Chapter 7 (of this book, not bankruptcy). The older man's wife was pounding on him pretty hard to retire and spend more time with her. So he and his sons merged their company with Ron's. They went into (the real) Chapter 7 together. The older son went back to selling, and the younger son went to work for yet another uncle's company in a related business. I saw his job history online recently. In chronological order, his job titles were executive vice president, vice president, and analyst. That pretty much tells his story and FoamCo's.

Business to Business

Businesses that sell to other businesses—so-called B2B companies—get short shrift in marketing books. It seems that these B2B enterprises are not seen as very sexy or interesting. I have found them riveting since I began my career in valuation in 1993. Many of the enterprises remain low tech, even in the age of iPhones. Scholars pay them little heed. Even when a B2B enterprise is written about in the popular business press, the night-and-day differences between it and companies that make or sell stuff for the consumer market are seldom mentioned.

The domains covered in this chapter of real-world vignettes cover an interesting waterfront. It includes safety equipment, construction materials, and antique building materials reclamation. Calling that collection eclectic does not do it justice. My experiences with these companies make for some of my favorite stories. Storytelling is how I approach the writing of a valuation report: A client company has a story, and I'm the one who tells it. My job is to make it interesting but objective; informative but not boring; and thorough but not superfluous. I've never begun a report with "Once upon a time," but I have thought about it.

The format of Chapter 13 continues in this one. After each "V-M Findings" section, I use bold for the element in SPARC that was the cause. I think that makes them easier to read and, more important, easier to refer back to later on. As always, I welcome your comments, observations, and constructive criticism. Let me hear from you via SPARC@beckmill.com.

Safety Equipment/Supplies

Overview. FirstAidCo was a $2.2 million wholesaler when it picked our name out of the Yellow Pages and called. It had a loan coming up for renewal, and it was concerned about that. It thought that it needed a financial advisor and maybe a valuation, too. It was family-owned—Mom, Dad, sons-in-law (2), and daughters (2).

Metrics

1. Glacial inventory turnover (1.2x versus 5.0x in an industry composite based on guideline public companies (GPCs).
2. Overpaid family members.
3. Low liquidity (0.6x versus 1.1x in GPCs), which led to a heavy (4:1) debt-equity ratio

Interviewees.   President and CEO (Mom); chairman (Dad); two daughters; two sons-in-law (one commuted to Houston from home in Oklahoma City); outside accountant; bank president; warehouse manager; inventory/purchasing manager.

V-M Findings

1. The first-aid supplies sector falls under the heading of "industrial supply." Even though our initial contact was in 1996, most of the industry was computerized. FirstAidCo had just installed an IBM AS400 minicomputer but had rejected installation of the inventory-control/purchasing module. It seems that the chairman didn't trust computers. As he said to me, "I know what we sell and what we need, and I can write out a purchase order faster and better than any computer system can." This was a company with over 18,000 SKUs, including leftovers from the U.S. bicentennial in 1976. Its warehouse was not labeled, bar-coded, or mapped. When I asked the warehouse manager what his troops did when an inventory bin was filled up, he said, "Put the stuff somewhere else." "How will everyone know where?" I asked. "That's a great question," he said. "Neither Rob [chairman] nor Margaret [CEO] thinks that labeling the warehouse is necessary. I've told them that it's one of the reasons our inventory turn is so low and our debt is so high, but they don't believe it. In fact, the last time I told them, they said they'd fire me if I ever brought it up again."

   The warehouse manager was right: An unlabeled 18,000-SKU warehouse has T-R-O-U-B-L-E written all over it. But there was far more to it than that. Not getting the inventory/purchasing module in the new minicomputer was a colossal error. It turned out that the chairman hated computers. He didn't trust them, he didn't understand them, and, according to him, "Our business has done just fine for 18 years without computers. We don't need 'em now." When I told him that if FirstAidCo's inventory turn was just 3x, his company would have no interest-bearing debt, he said, "I don't believe you." I offered to prove it to him, but he shrugged and said he didn't have time. (**SPARC**)

2. Five of the six family members on the payroll were overpaid. One son-in-law was honest, hardworking, and in over his head—but he knew it. He was starved for someone who could and would teach him. (He told me that he learned more in our short time together in Houston than he had absorbed in six years on the FirstAidCo payroll. Sometimes such talk is shameless sucking up, but, having spent two days with the guy, I believed him. He was a sponge for knowledge and assimilated it on the fly.

   One daughter rode herd on receivables and the other on payables and payroll. Both were hardworking, if unspectacular, performers. The other son-in-law played a lot of golf, supposedly with customers, though he never documented how he spent his time. It was rumored that he spent most of it just driving around, and gasoline records appeared to affirm that.

   The father was the high-energy guy in the company. He was a salesman from the Willy Loman old school—kind, considerate, low pressure. He knew how to sell, but he couldn't teach anyone else to do it. He appeared to resent the fact that he was supporting his "local" son-in-law by keeping him on the payroll when, in his heart of hearts, he knew the young man should be encouraged to find work elsewhere.

   The mother became CEO to take advantage of government set-asides (quotas) for woman-owned businesses. Unfortunately, she didn't know what she needed to know to perform acceptably as CEO. She thought the family should come ahead of the business. When I told her that every company I'd ever seen do that no longer existed, she accused me of lying to her. She insisted that all family members on the payroll were paid what they were worth and that no adjustments needed to be made. I responded that the combination of slow-moving inventory and excess family compensation was slowly bleeding the company into insolvency. (**SPARC**)

3. That FirstAidCo's liquidity was low and its debt-equity ratio was high was predictable. How could such outcomes be a surprise for a firm where (a) the family in the business was seen as being more important than the business itself, (b) inventory turn was a fraction of the industry average, (c) the purchasing guy was clueless about modern purchasing techniques, (d) the chairman was a Luddite, and (e) family members were overpaid and, in most cases, underperforming?

   Again, though, metrics and financial ratios are the symptoms, not the disease. They are the "what," not the "why." For this company to borrow more money and expect to get healthy was like an alcoholic expecting to sober up with a case of whiskey. (Cop-out: **SPARC**)

SPARC Elements

Strategy
People
Architecture
Routines
Culture

V-M Solutions.   Short of turning over the company to a knowledgeable professional to run, these problems had no solutions. The changes required were massive, especially those related to culture. The family offered me the chance to run it. I said that I would, but only under these four conditions:

1. FirstAidCo would form a council of advisors with two family members and three outsiders, but each independent councilor required my approval.
2. No family member except the son-in-law in Houston could be on First-AidCo property during regular business hours.
3. No family member, except for the Houston son-in-law, could draw a paycheck if Mom and Dad would gift some of their stock to the children going off the payroll, the kids could then, if FirstAidCo could afford it (unlikely in the short term), receive distributions that might replace some of the salaries they had lost.
4. I would draw no salary but would, instead, be paid 20% of the increase in the company's value on my watch, value to be determined by a full-time business appraiser independent of both them and me.

Postscript.   They refused. I resigned the engagement. FirstAidCo limped along for several years on retirement funds lent to it by Mom and Dad, but it finally went into Chapter 7. Mom and Dad are now old . . . and poor. Their fate was avoidable, but I doubt they would ever concede that, concede that.

Industrial Supply

Overview.   In 1992–1993, IndSupCo was a $50 million business in the apparel niche of the industrial supply space. The company is well known to those who work in the heavy manufacturing, construction, and transportation sectors. Although employees of its customer companies were the ultimate users of its products, those firms typically subsidized the purchase of apparel because not doing so had implications for employee safety and, thereby, for workers' compensation costs. Its new CEO was an old friend of ours who thought a valuation would be a good idea. He wanted to consider getting a value-based management system up and going.

Metrics

1. Company growth lagged industry growth.
2. No by-market-segment revenue data.
3. In a sector driven by marketing and logistics, the company had a top-flight marketing professional (its newly hired CEO) but no one with an in-depth grasp of logistics (i.e., mathematical modeling, optimization, etc.).
4. Gross margin trailed industry gross margin.

Interviewees. CEO, vice president—operations, purchasing manager, controller, lead product designer, various branch managers.

V-M Findings

1. and **2.** Despite an earnings before interest and taxes (EBIT) margin > 12%, the company had a "legacy" (mainframe) computer system. Every request for data required a new COBOL program. Even though client-server technology had arrived, IndSupCo had seen no need to upgrade its information technology. Its IT staffers were old-school and IBM-bred. When I saw the monitors with green fonts on black backgrounds, I wondered if I was in a time warp. It turned out that the firm was in an airtight, decades-old oligopoly (CR4 > 90!) where the other three major players had highly differentiated product offerings and carefully targeted marketing efforts. (**SPARC**)
3. IndSupCo leased branch warehouses around the nation but had no disciplined approach to analyzing whether a given warehouse was situated in an optimal location. Warehouse employees were not highly skilled, so the question of location didn't depend on access to a knowledgeable labor pool or to optimal delivery routes. Logistics had come into its own with the advent of supply chain management as a result of quantum improvements in IT, yet, as noted, IndSupCo's IT system was barely out of the Stone Age.

The oligopoly removed any sense of urgency from both officers and employees because the company luxuriated in margins that most industrial-supply firms would kill for. But that wasn't because of its approach to its business; but in spite of it. (**SPARC**)

4. We traced the lower-than-average gross margin to the firm's remarkable lack of knowledge about its customers in anything other than an anecdotal context. Not to beat a dead horse here, but part of that resulted from its legacy IT. But even that could be finessed, at least in part, had anyone at the firm thought to put SIC codes into the customer master. No one had, so the firm really didn't know to whom it was selling. That prevented it from figuring out why its customers bought from it rather than from one of its three big rivals.

When I first used the word "oligopoly" at a meeting of its senior managers, the CEO scoffed and said, "Speak English, Warren." I wrote O-L-I-G-O-P-O-L-Y on a whiteboard and then drew a simple diagram that illustrated the interdependency among players in a well-functioning oligopoly, as this one was, despite the client company's ignorance about the structure of its own industry. When I repeated my "First Five Rules of the Oligopolist in Good Standing," the seven others in the room nodded. But when I asked, "So, since you don't compete on price, how *do* you compete?" The sales vice president replied, "Differentiation." I asked what the source(s) of its differentiation were. He said, "Our name." "Simple as that?" I asked. He nodded. I said, " Well, we'll see about that." (**SPARC**)

SPARC Elements

Strategy

People

Architecture

Routines

V-M Solutions

1. and **2.** We couldn't do anything about the IT system except comment on it, which we did in our report. However, we recommended that the firm commission us to do a study of its 1,500 largest customers to find out (a) which market segments were the bigger contributors to its annual revenues, (b) the size (in terms of headcount) of its typical customer company, and (c) whether a

company's method of subsidy appeared to affect the annual apparel purchases of its employees.

3. We recommended that IndSupCo become a visible player in what was then the Council of Logistics Management (CLM), now the Council of Supply Chain Management Professionals (www.cscmp.org). In those days, the CLM had a top-flight education program with a wide range of course offerings and books for its members. It also had a well-attended annual conference. We suggested that IndSupCo become a sponsor and get a large booth.

4. We said that we thought the results of the customer study would contain inferences about how to increase differentiation. (That turned out to be the case.)

Postscript. In the process of conducting the study, we created a multiple regression data set that contained 1,476 customers and 77 independent variables. We then used stepwise regression analysis to tease out the statistically insignificant variables—they were responsible for a lot of noise but little else.

We found that six two-digit SIC codes were statistically significant ($p < .05$) in terms of annual purchases relative to employee headcount. We also found that companies that subsidized a specific dollar-level of purchases by their employees bought far more per employee than did companies that subsidized percentage-of-dollars purchases. That was an unexpected finding. We speculated that employees might not understand the concept of percentage and how to apply it to the purchasing decisions they made. We recommended that IndSupCo initiate a contest among its regional sales representatives to convert "percentage subsidizers" to "dollar-subsidizers."

The CEO went for it. The following year, companies that converted from "percentage" to "dollars" generated $3.5 million of additional revenue at a 45% gross margin. That 7% sales increase alone was more than twice as much as any increase IndSupCo had had in the preceding 25 years. By targeting the six two-digit SIC codes as the primary sources for new customers, IndSupCo got another $3 million in revenues the next year. It also increased its overall gross margin by 225 basis points (bp) and its EBIT margin by more than 300 bp. Its overall revenues went up by 13%. Not bad for a somnambulating company in a mature sector facing a weak economy.

We also accessed proprietary databases, wrote elaborate spreadsheet macros to debug data. We then used the "clean" data to construct customized calling lists for the firm's inside telemarketer to use. He sang our praises, even as this brought us over $60,000 more in revenue.

In the process, the firm also reduced its cost of capital, and it did so in 1994, a year of rising interest rates and a slow-growth economy. Its contribution to the profitability of its U.K.-based conglomerate parent helped increase the parent's market multiple . . . and the bonuses of those at IndSupCo. And the company installed a client-server system.

Construction Materials

Overview.   The founders of ConMat Corp. launched it in 2000. They had worked together at a previous company in a similar line of business. When that firm was sold, they decided they didn't like the new environment, so they went out on their own. ConMat's 2004 revenues were $3.5 million, up from $2.7 million in 2003; it forecast 2005 sales to exceed $4 million. When we were retained early in 2005, it was thinking about putting itself up for sale. All the owners worked in the business, and they were tiring, both of working hard and of one another.

Metrics

1. Low productivity.
2. Low-quality accounting practices.
3. Key performance measures (DSO, return on assets, inventory turnover, etc.) exceeded those of its two potential likely buyers.
4. Ill-prepared to undergo due diligence by a prospective.
5. Tension in the workplace.

Interviewees.   The four principals, an inside salesman, outside accountant.

V-M Findings

1. In a low-margin sector, its annual gross profit per FTE was $87,000 versus $112,000 at its preferred buyer. We attributed this to unrealized economies of scale that would kick in only when the company's revenues exceeded about $6 million. Insufficient funded debt (debt-equity ratio was less than one-quarter that of its targeted buyer) constrained its ability to grow. (**SPARC**)
2. The outside accountant was not a CPA. We thought ConMat needed a CPA firm because it needed to have its financial statements reviewed (at least), and maybe audited, before it put itself on the market. Any buyer's perception of risk, and the cost of its due diligence effort, would increase significantly without reviewed or audited financials. (**SPARC**)
3. The company was managed conservatively in most respects. On one hand, that was good: It didn't have too many SKUs (only

900), and it shipped directly via LTL (less than truckload) from suppliers' factories to fill nearly half of its orders. Its cash position was strong, and the owners' paychecks were modest and reasonable. On the other hand, much of its approach to managing was seat-of-the-pants, a fact that had the potential to hurt it later if its revenues were much larger. Our concern was that ConMatCo might be putting itself up for sale a few years earlier than it should. Still, we were directed to contact two potential buyers, both Big Board companies. (SPARC)

4. The company was not ready for buy-side due diligence, primarily because, in our view, the four principals were too focused internally. None had gone to college—that's not a sin in and of itself, of course—but none understood the need to look outside more and more as it grew. Its warehouse setup was poorly conceived. Despite the excellent inventory turn, its 900+ SKUs were not bar-coded. As important as anything, its behind-the-curve computer system did not enable it to generate pick tickets in reverse sequence from the order in which deliveries would be made. That inefficiency made for excessive warehouse staffing. (SPARC)

5. When we first visited with the four owners, before we drafted an engagement letter, the atmosphere did not feel right. It was one of those things that savvy analysts pick up on as soon as they come on the premises of such a place. People didn't smile much, the lighting was poor, and the aura of the place was quasi-funereal.

   When we drove away from our initial shake-and-howdy meeting with them, I said to Dorothy, "Whatcha think?" "Something's not right," she said. "Agree," I replied. "Where or who do you think the problem is?" "The sales guy," she said. I said, "Bingo. We gotta find out what's going on." (Toss-up: SPARC or SPARC)

SPARC Elements

People
Architecture
Routines
Culture

V-M Solutions

1. We introduced the four principals to a commercial lender at a community-based bank with a reputation for targeting SMEs. She clicked

with the CFO and was able to explain how the company would benefit from taking on a little more debt.

2. We introduced the four principals to three local CPA firms whose partners we knew, respected, and trusted.

3. We reached out to the in-house merger and acquisitions (M&A) people the two would-be buyers, both listed on the Big Board. Based on how we profiled our client, both were eager to talk some more. We said we would be back in touch with them "at the appropriate time"— we continued to hope that we could persuade the principals not to sell just yet.

4. We recommended that ConMatCo get new software that fit its high-SKU warehouse situations. There were several affordable off-the-shelf solutions that, with a little tweaking, would mesh well with its business and pay big dividends in profitability and free cash flow.

5. We continued to perceive pervasive unease in the company. Dorothy and I decided to schedule the on-site interviews for a Saturday, when things were quiet. Due to other demands on their schedules, we talked to the sales guy first, then the warehouse manager, then the general manager, and finally the CFO. It wasn't until we got to the CFO that we uncovered the problem.

She was an absolutely straight-up and conscientious owner. As I sat across the desk from her in her office, I sensed that she was more on edge than usual. So I began with easy questions intended to put her at ease. I served up puff-balls, and her responses knocked each one out of the park. She seemed to relax a little.

By prior agreement with Dorothy, I leaned forward, reached out and put my hand on the CFO's, and gently said, "You know, we believe that something is just not right here. No one has said anything to us, but both Dorothy and I just have strong gut hunches that something's wrong. We've felt it from the first moment we set foot in here. What on earth are we sensing that we can't put our fingers on?"

The CFO looked at me like a deer looking into headlights. Her eyes welled up, and she began to cry. I quickly pulled out a handkerchief and handed it to her. (I had long ago made it a point to carry a couple of clean handkerchiefs with me during the on-site interview process. I didn't need them often, but they sure came in handy when I do.)

"It's, it's, it's—" she stammered.

"It's what?" I asked softly.

"It's, it's, it's . . . George!" She finally spit out the word (not his real name) of the sales guy out.

"And?" I said.

"He, he, he, he's, he's . . . into pornography!" And then she began sobbing.

Dorothy jumped up, went around the desk, and put her arms around the CFO's quaking shoulders. I sat there, dumbstruck. I'd seen and heard a lot of things in my then-12-year valuation career, but never porn. It rocked me for a minute or two. The CFO calmed down, and Dorothy sat down again. Then I leaned forward yet again and said, "Do you mind telling me a little more about this?"

She told us the whole story—how one day she had gone to visit with George in his office when, unbeknownst to her, he was out in the warehouse. She went around to his side of the desk to leave a note in his chair, and that's when she saw what was on his computer screen. She said she gasped and almost fainted. She went ahead, left the note, and said nothing. She wanted to discuss it with her husband that night.

With his encouragement, she approached her other two partners, neither of whom had any idea about the problem . . . but both of whom doubted her, even though, she said, they didn't come right out and say so.

She was savvy with personal computers and knew how to reconstruct the path of a browser. So, one evening after George had headed for home, she showed the other two exactly what he spent several hours a day doing.

The three of them talked briefly about various courses of action but reached no conclusions. They agreed to say nothing to George but to think about it for 48 hours and then reconvene off-site. They met at her house for several hours but had no idea what to do. Their major concern was that George was their only salesman and that, if he left, ConMatCo's sales would tank. They thought that, a year or two out, the inside sales guy would have enough product knowledge to begin selling outside to prospective new customers, but he wasn't ready yet. They were also afraid of a legal battle with George, and they didn't want the humiliation in their community of being known as people who had a porn addict for a business partner.

They kept the problem to themselves and talked to no one outside the firm about what their options might be. They finally agreed to confront George and demand that he stop. They did. He laughed at them and told them they couldn't do a thing about it because, if they did, he would blab their names all over town and to the media and then, he said, "I'll sue the hell out of all three of you for slander." The best defense is a good offense, even in the most unlikely of contexts.

They backed off. George continued to do as he pleased. He continued to provide no accounting of his time. His partners didn't know what a call report is, until I brought up the subject. He spent three or four hours a day in his office with the door closed. Sales continued to grow, and, on the surface, everything looked fine. That's how it stood when we arrived on the scene.

Postscript.   With the three partners' permission, I set up a meeting for them with the senior partner in the local office of a large law firm; we attended, too. He is an M&A guy with whom I have occasionally worked. I knew him to be experienced, no-nonsense, fearless, and savvy. Most important, Dorothy thinks he is top-drawer. She has a sense about people that I can only dream about. It's a remarkable asset, one that I do not and will never get.

By prior agreement with the three principals, I led off with a short history of ConMatCo and brief backgrounds of each of the principals. I then said that our firm had been retained to do a valuation to see if selling the firm would provide enough money for the four partners to live comfortably for the rest of their lives. I briefly described the problem with the sales guy and was careful to mention the younger inside salesman and what I saw as his potential.

Our lawyer colleague didn't flinch. He spoke softly as he stared a hole in each of the three partners.

"I don't sell lawsuits," he began. "I never have and, after 35 years, I'm not about to start now. You have no choice but to run him out of your company, and the sooner, the better. You don't need to worry that he will do anything in response. When I get done talking to him, he'll be damned glad just to get out of town quietly.

"Look," he continued. "George doesn't have a leg to stand on. You folks strike me as good and decent people. But you're behaving like battered spouses. You think you can't live without this abuser. Let me tell you: You can, and you must. I'll tell him in no uncertain terms that if he thinks he's going to try to hurt this business, I'll have his ass in a sling before he gets out of the batter's box. I'll convince him that he'll never work in this town or in this state again. Not ever. He'll settle quietly and fairly and steal quietly off into the night. You'll never hear from him again.

"My only concern is whether your inside sales guy can rise to the occasion. Based on what you've told me, I'm betting that he can. People have a way of doing that when the chips are down. It's kind of like being in combat: You're a nervous wreck until the first shot is fired. Then you do what you have to do. It's pretty automatic. I found that out in 'Nam.

"Warren, what do you think?"

"I agree with every word you said, Richard, except that you said it better than I ever could. Certainly I don't know employment law in our state well enough to know what to do, and even if I thought I did, getting you involved was still the best option. I don't practice law without a license.

"I'm certainly onboard to fill George's job with the inside sales guy."

I looked at the partners. They looked as if they'd been socked in the stomach. "Do you think George might be encouraged to introduce Mitch to the company's biggest and best customers, maybe under the premise of training him to support George so that the company will have two outside sales guys instead of just one?"

The partners weren't sure. Each looked scared to death. They said they wanted to talk things over privately. My immediate hunch was that they didn't have the spine to do what Richard had suggested. Somehow, they just didn't believe him. Dorothy and I did.

Well, our hunch was right. George is still a 25% owner. I valued the firm at a significant discount to what it would have brought without George. Con-MatCo is still in business, and I'd wager that George's three partners are now even more battered than they were in the spring of 2005.

One other thing: The bigger of the two NYSE firms acquired the smaller one. Then the big one, which is one of the Dow Jones 30 Industrials, hit the skids and had to fire its CEO in an ugly, public, and expensive incident. Then it decided to sell the division that included the NYSE company that it had bought. Private equity buyers kicked the tires, and one overpaid big-time. In today's economy, it can't be doing well.

I estimate what I call the OCOP (opportunity cost of pornography) in this case at about $6.3 million. That's the difference between what I think the firm would have brought late in 2006 or early in 2007 and what I valued it at as of the end of 2004, porn addict included.

Antique Building Materials Reclamation

Overview. OldCo was a rapidly growing $6.7 million company that reclaimed materials from old structures, piers, mills, factories, and so on, that were scheduled for demolition. It was founded several decades before we arrived on the scene late in 2005. The owner was a serial monogamist who preferred marriage over courtship, and he was, as he approached retirement age, feeling the financial burden of his marital history. He wanted to grow the company to $20 million in five years and sell it. He even thought he had a buyer. But he also had a 20% minority holder—an internationally prominent businessman—with whom he wanted to work a deal to take out. His minority partner had bailed him out of a tough situation 12 years before and was now providing out of his personal funds a multimillion-dollar line of credit for OldCo. We were retained to estimate two values for the firm: (1) under the fair market value standard and (2) under fair value, the standard for shareholder oppression in the state in which OldCo was chartered and operated.

Metrics

1. Overpaid senior managers.
2. Key ratios—asset turnover, quick ratio, inventory turn, return on assets, EBIT margin—below the 25th percentile in a 12-public-company array.
3. Steadily growing debt ratio (71% in 2005, up from 51% in 2001).
4. Three-week monthly close.
5. C-corporation status with appreciated real estate inside the corporation.
6. "A culture of chaos" (direct quote).

Interviewees.   CEO, COO, CFO, IT director, CEO's administrative assistant, two shop-floor managers, various lower-level employees.

V-M Findings

1. The majority shareholder had a volcanic and incendiary temperament. The youngest of many children in his family, he was an "oops kid"—an unplanned arrival who arrived relatively late in his parents' lives. According to people who had known him in his childhood, he was, in late middle age, as he was growing up: If he didn't get his way, he'd yell first and sulk later. When he berated employees, which was often, loudly, and publicly, his comments were personal, loud, and insulting. Some employees ended up in tears. The sum of these behaviors was that he had to overpay his senior people in order to retain them. (SPARC)
2. There were *no* documented ways to do anything anywhere in OldCo. Some managers were in jobs for which they were demonstrably not qualified. Others had come to work for the company straight out of high school decades earlier, were still there, and had learned little, except how *not* to manage, since arriving. In its 2005 fiscal year, the "Training Expense" account in its general ledger had a balance of -0-. Predictably, OldCo had far too many people on its payroll, and not one of them had any idea or understanding of the series of supply-and-demand systems that comprise the typical shop floor in manufacturing. (SPARC)

3. The debt ratio was climbing steeply because OldCo had little focus. It also had Cost of Goods Sold and expense structures that its revenues were insufficient to support. The founder spent a lot of time in China trying to "do deals" with the Chinese that would bring in a lot of money with little expense. It hadn't worked yet, but he was still spending over 70 grand a year shuttling back and forth. He invariably had expensive reservations because he kept changing them right up until the last minute. (SPARC)

4. The three-week monthly close resulted from the fact that the controller kept the books open until OldCo had "made its revenue number" for a given month, even if it took until the twentieth of the next month to do it. He did that in concert with the operating people because they knew that if they didn't meet the revenue forecast, there would be hell to pay with the majority owner. (SPARC)

5. We were stunned to find out early on that OldCo was still a C corporation. It had lucrative real estate and commercial buildings locked up inside that C-corp. structure. Its tax returns were prepared by a law firm whose managing partner is one of the most pompous people I've ever met. I mean, this guy was off the charts. Several years before this engagement began, I had the misfortune to find myself seated at the same table with him at a professional meeting one night. He held forth pontificating and finally turned to me and said, "So what do you think about that?" I smiled big and said, "Not much. Can you say any of that in simple English?" He thought I was joking. Little did he know.

   Anyway, this guy and his firm had been the majority owner's tax advisor ever since OldCo was founded. The law firm clearly slumbered right through the 1986 Tax Reform Act . . . and I'm not even a tax guy! (SPARC)

6. I got my first look at one aspect of the chaos when I happened to be on the premises on payday. The last (corrected) paycheck wasn't issued until, I later heard, after 8 p.m. that night. During the day, a steady stream of people queued up to complain to the controller about their checks. I was informed a few days later that such nuttiness "happens every payday."

   The controller didn't trust the accounting software, nor did he know how to make it do what he wanted it to do, so he rekeyed every transaction into Excel. With 48 FTEs working out of three locations, it doesn't take a rocket scientist to figure out just how inefficient his approach was. I mean, the guy worked 18 hours a day, 7 days a week. But that was his choice. He was a decent enough guy but with serious professional shortcomings. (**SPARC**)

SPARC Elements

> **P**eople
> **A**rchitecture
> **R**outines
> **C**ulture

V-M Solutions.   Before getting into what we did with this company, let me say at the outset that there wasn't much we could do to make things worse. I was reminded of the comment of the legendary Marine, Lewis B. "Chesty" Puller, when he discovered that the First Marine Division he then commanded was surrounded by 50,000 Communist Chinese troops in Korea.

A young war correspondent asked him, "General Puller, what are we going to do?"

"Do, hell!" snapped the crusty old general (who was the holder of five Navy Crosses, the nation's second-highest military honor). "We've got those b**tards right where we want 'em: We can shoot in any direction and hit one!" That's how it was at OldCo. Almost any change we suggested would be an improvement.

1. We persuaded the majority shareholder to form a council of advisors. This body, which I've written about at length over the years, would be a group that (a) didn't work for him, (b) he didn't know, (c) he couldn't control, so that (d) they were not afraid of him and didn't have jobs and kids' college educations depending on his volatile temperament. Since we prepared the list of people for him to choose from for the council, we knew going in that he would hear things that he did not want to hear. We thought this was essential.

    We also recommended that he reduce the base salaries of senior managers and, instead, motivate them through bonuses based on both corporate and individual performance. He went for that.
2. We told him that he needed a manufacturing expert to come in and bring order to the operating side of the business. He said he'd been in manufacturing for years and didn't need any help.
3. Unfortunately, his refusal to bring order to operations caused us to tell him his firm's debt ratio would continue to rise. It did.
4. When we told him that the reason he wasn't getting his monthly financials until at least the twenty-fifth day of the following month was that his people refused to set themselves up for his verbal abuse by missing sales targets, he called me a liar. I gave him an earful of Marine-style

commentary and ended with "Don't you ever call me a liar again, dude. You got that?" He looked at me wide-eyed but was never rude to me again.

5. His tax lawyer successfully resisted the council's unanimous recommendation to elect S status, and the majority owner did nothing about it.

6. We got our work done, got paid, and got out after forming the council of advisors. Four months later, the majority shareholder decided that he didn't like hearing what the council had to say, so, one afternoon about two hours before a scheduled council meeting, he pulled the plug on it.

Postscript.   The 20% shareholder sold out at the fair-value estimate we made. The housing market on which OldCo depended for resale collapsed in 2007. The majority shareholder ran out of money but managed to sell OldCo the following year to a multibillion-dollar, closely held conglomerate based in Scandinavia. Last we heard, he hated where he worked and was chafing under corporate control of any kind. But he had also put a few million bucks in his pocket. The conglomerate did him the favor of buying stock and not assets. It was chump change to them, but it saved him a bundle in taxes. However, the conglomerate did dump the local legal pontificator.

CHAPTER

15

Transportation

In this chapter, the vignettes are from the transportation sector. I think you will find them offbeat, at least. Then again, we all know that valuing closely held companies is an offbeat line of work. But, for those of us who bore easily, I don't think there's a better one, offbeat or not.

We cover three unrelated domains in this chapter: transportation collection services, LTL trucking, and freight forwarding. As with every company, each of these has its own tale. My job is to tell it. The format from Chapters 13 and 14 continues. As before, your comments, observations, and constructive criticism are solicited and most welcome. E-mail me at SPARC@beckmill.com.

Transportation Collection Services

Overview. In 1997 MedColServ Inc. (MCSI) was formed to hold the spin-off business of a corporation that began as a specialist in processing medical reimbursements for physicians. At the time of our valuation for year-end 2001, MCSI was an S corporation. It was the dominant player in a very small niche, the disclosure of which would out the company. The shares were divided 51/49% between two owners who didn't get along. We were engaged by the 51% holder to value the 49% slice. MSCI was based in a state that required a "super majority" (i.e., 2/3) of shares for major corporate actions).

Metrics

1. Revenues doubled to $2.2 million in 2001; 68% of revenues came from five customers.
2. Headcount more than doubled in 2001 to 49.
3. The CFO was the 51% owner's spouse, who was not a trained financial professional.
4. MCSI had two small branch offices besides its primary location.
5. Days' Sales Outstanding (DSO) = 69 days.

6. No budget for 2002.
7. CEO was an ex-college football player who thought nothing of renting jets to ferry his friends to weekend games at company expense

Interviewees.   The 51% owner/CEO, CFO, operations manager, HR director, two nonmanagement employees.

V-M Findings

1. and **2.** It is no exaggeration to say that growth at the company was out of control. Annual revenue per FTE of $45,000 tells that story. It could afford to do that only because it was well capitalized and because of its location in an economically deprived region where wages were rock-bottom.

    At least as important, in 2000, 45% of revenue came from a company owned by the 49% holder. In 2001, less than 5% did, and still, sales more than doubled. The conflict between the owners was beating up the company they owned together. The tales about the CEO's spending that the 49% owner heard about put severe stress on what once was a close friendship—the minority holder was the best man at the CEO's fifth marriage. (**SPARC**)

    The HR guy, who was hired late in 2001, brought needed management experience and perspective to the young company. He was in the process of persuading the CEO, a man who would rather do something (anything?) than not do it, that the question of whether to create a new job could be analyzed before someone was hired. The CEO was resisting, but we were guardedly optimistic that the HR man could bring him around. (**SPARC**)

3. The CEO's spouse was trying hard but freely admitted that MCSI would benefit from having a financial professional onboard. Her husband, in contrast, said, "Look, how tough can putting numbers into a computer be?" (**SPARC**)

4. The performances of the three "outlying employees," whose jobs were to smooth relations with insurance companies, were not measured. The money they spent on expense accounts, though, exceeded $20,000 each, or nearly 3% of annual revenue. The farther branch was about 1,500 miles from the home office. (**SPARC**)

5. As bad as it might look, that DSO was actually pretty good, given that MCSI had created a new industry with its business model. Customers were still getting used to having an effective collections agent. The bigger problem was that five companies accounted for 68% of 2001 revenues. (**SPARC**)

6. At our behest, the CEO did prepare a sales forecast for 2002 and 2003. When I asked him to do it by customer—bottom up, in other words— he said, "That's impossible." I told him how to do it, but he ignored me. (SPARC)
7. I warned the CEO via e-mail that he faced big problems, not just with his 49% holder but potentially with the IRS, if he didn't connect the chartered jet trips with MCSI's basic business. (SPARC)

SPARC Elements

People
Architecture
Routines
Culture

V-M Solutions

1. We strongly recommended the creation of an MCSI council of advisors. The CEO liked the idea but said that he would schedule each meeting so that it would run into a weekend of golf . . . by chartered jet, of course. He even mentioned St. Andrews and Carnoustie. I was aghast. Short of hog-tying him, I couldn't see any way to get this guy under even a modicum of control.
2. At my suggestion, the HR guy convinced the CEO to institute a hiring freeze until a performance review system was in place *and* the performance of every employee had been reviewed.
3. I came away from my interview with the CFO/spouse unpersuaded that she could (or would) stand up to her husband, unless she thought it threatened her cushy lifestyle. She did allude to that, so I worked that angle pretty hard, saying "Unless you folks are made of money, it's only a matter of time." I also convinced her to bring in the CPA firm that had recommended my retention to help install a budget. At my behest, she also told her husband that he, she, the HR guy, and the operations manager needed to meet every Monday morning and include a representative from the outside CPA firm once a month. Her guy went for it.
4. The outside accountant was also a golfing buddy of the CEO. Over time, the accountant managed to convince the majority holder to eliminate the company credit cards and, instead: (a) make significant cash advances to affected employees (which they were required to settle up before the end of each year, or the IRS could construe

them as interest-free loans) and (b) promptly reimburse employees when they turned in their expense accounts, but with the stipulation that the company reserved the right to disapprove egregious expense items. Meals and entertainment spending fell by over 80%.

5. Alarmed by the revenue concentration among a few customers, we also encouraged the CEO to instigate a bonus program rewarding representatives who got their "five-firm revenue-concentration ratio," as we called it, below 25% *without* a decline in their territories' year-over-year revenue. The CEO's wife and outside accountant convinced him of the risk of sales concentration, and he went for our suggestion.

6. The CEO refused to "waste time" with a full-blown 2002 budget. He did, however, agree to the preparation of a bottom-up sales forecast. When he saw its benefits, he promised he would direct the preparation of a comprehensive budget, including capital outlays, for 2003.

7. The CEO also committed to "getting with the program" where airline charters were concerned. Of course, we were there in the spring, and football season didn't begin for another five months.

Postscript.   As the old saw goes, there is good news, and there is bad news. The bad news is that, despite the careful and non–finger-pointing tone of what in those days was called a draft of our report, the CEO still went into a rage when he read it. Our firm's policy is that, on fixed-price engagements, we get paid *before* we send out what today is called "Incomplete Work Product—for Discussion Purposes Only." In the case of MCSI, we got paid, including expense reimbursement, before we released the draft. We never heard from the guy again, and he wouldn't take or return our phone calls. The CPA said not to worry about it, so we're not.

Something—I'd like to think it was our work, at least in part—eventually had an impact. In the summer of 2009, more than seven years later, headcount only recently hit 75. We hear that revenues have multiplied sixfold.

LTL Trucking

Overview.   TransCo is an LTL trucking company based in the Midwest. Revenues are well into nine figures. It began when it was sold for a pittance to a cadre of freight-agency owners by its corporate owner when the parent company got into severe financial trouble. When we were introduced to the company, the U.S. economy was robust. The financial ringer in the transaction— to which we were not advisors—was that the new owners had to pay the old parent several million dollars a year in monthly installments for five years to support a legacy IT system. The overhead and inefficiency of that system were staggering, but the new firm had not provided for a new IT system in its business plan. As important as that oversight was, it was not the biggest problem. It was only the symptom. (This was a calculations engagement.)

Metrics

1. Slackening sales and falling gross margin in a booming economy.
2. Heavy leverage, including an 18% note to a board member.
3. Unhedged exposure to rising gasoline prices.
4. A shareholders' agreement that looked to have been written by a first-year law student.
5. Board minutes that might have come straight out of *Lord of the Flies* (for those unfamiliar with it: http://en.wikipedia.org/wiki/Lord_of_the_Flies)

Interviewees. CEO, CFO, two other direct reports to the CEO, six board members, middle manager who introduced me to the company.

V-M Findings

1. The CEO, whom the board thought was top drawer in every respect, wasn't. He was a very nice guy who had never been a CEO before. Before ascending to the top job, he had spent 25 years as a sales guy. As CEO, he spent most of his time buffering his senior managers from inquiries by intrusive board members, all of whom (a) were shareholders in TransCo and (b) owned companies that were upstream intermediaries in TransCo's supply chain. The CEO was on his fourth marriage to a woman younger than his 20-something daughter; his last three spouses had worked at companies where he had worked before coming to TransCo.

   I should also mention that I learned that the CEO had also survived three bouts of cancer. There was no succession plan because, as a board member told me, "No one wants to sound morbid by insisting on talking about succession." I said that the CEO didn't have to have cancer in his health history for a company to have succession plans in place, not just for the top dog but for each of his direct reports. The board member, who was a third-generation owner of his family's business, said, "Well, we sure don't do that at our company." He had never worked anywhere else except at his family's firm.

   The gross margin problem resulted from price competition. TransCo said that it was a differentiator and that its six sigma program—most senior managers were "black belts"—was its primary basis for differentiation. (**SPARC**)

2. The board members had ponied up over $10 million of equity. Among other things, the CEO asked me if I could find "two private equity firms" that were willing to inject equity capital into TransCo if its lead bank decided to bail out. Stunned, I explained to him that private equity firms did not wait around checkbook in hand, to play second fiddle to banks that got cold feet. I also said that if private equity got involved—which I thought was a good idea—then it would do so *only* (a) with convertible preferred paying a hefty dividend and (b) with full control of the board. The CEO said he didn't think the board would go for that. (**SPARC**)

3. The CFO, who had his job *only* because he was a close friend of the CEO, had never thought of hedging. As gasoline approached $3 a gallon, he said he didn't think it would go any higher. I told him that savvy companies handled big risks by embracing those they knew how to manage and hedging the rest, although not necessarily through the use of futures markets. Outsourcing was a form of hedging, I pointed out, and offered up the IT function as a prime candidate. (**SPARC**)

4. TransCo's law firm was a one-office firm based in the city where TransCo was headquartered. I'll say it again: I don't practice law without a license . . . but missing from the shareholders' agreement were two key features: (a) a "tag-and-drag" section and (b) a provision detailing a valuation process if one was needed. I introduced TransCo's board chairman to the senior partner in a 500-lawyer, multicity firm with a substantial client base in LTL transportation. The chairman said he thought the company didn't "need any law firm that is that high powered." Then he began talking about the day when TransCo would do an initial public offering. (**SPARC**)

5. Each Board member *knew the LTL business*, but not one *knew business*. In fact, the biggest problem this company had early in 2006 was its Board. (**SPARC**)

SPARC Elements

People
Architecture
Culture

V-M Solutions. In conjunction with our initial calculations engagement, we prepared a document using the SPARC framework as the basis for value-enhancing recommendations. Here are the major ones:

- Conduct statistically valid customer satisfaction surveys and link the results to incentives for employees, agents, and owner-operators.
- Add outsiders to the TransCo board.
- Defer portions of executive bonuses (to lengthen recipients' decision-making horizons and to slip a golden handcuff on them).
- Upgrade audit and law firms.
- Initiate personal development programs (PDPs) with all employees.
- Distinctive advantage comes from doing things that other firms cannot do or doing them in ways that rivals cannot imitate, except at high cost and/or extreme disruption to their existing business model. TransCo's six-sigma program is laudable, but it is *not* and must not be the basis for differentiation. Any LTL firm can do six sigma and load up with black belts. Instead, formulate strategy by combining the feedback from customer satisfaction surveys with TransCo's unique organizational capabilities. Then develop metrics for the key capabilities comprising the strategy.

Postscript.   A year after my initial calculations project, I was brought back for a follow-on that included a presentation to the board of a range estimate of value along with a detailed rationale of the firm's valuation. As readers know, this request hit the "sweet spot" of our portfolio of valuation-related services.

As I made my presentation, which was nothing if not crystal clear and well documented, I developed a keen empathy for General Custer. You might have heard his last words: "Where on earth did all of those angry Indians come from?" To mix the metaphor a little, it reminded me of my days as a CFO on the receiving end of shoot-the-messenger. The questions I got were, well, naive, at best. A small sample:

- "Why do you say we need outside directors? They don't know anything about our business."

  My response: "Well, for starters, I hear you questioning why the Big Board's rules require its listed companies to have a majority of outside directors on each board. You also say you want to cash out, either through an initial public offering or through sale to a big company. Having outside directors will reduce risk—and, thereby, increase value—in both cases."
- "What's so bad about spending $7.5 million a year on IT? That's only about 3% of revenue."

  My response: "Well-conceived IT systems have scale economies. TransCo's has *dis*economies."

- "Why do you say that we need to 'reconcile disparate investment goals of shareholders into a coherent exit strategy'?"

  My response: "One of the virtues of having outside directors is that they can take a disinterested view of this company. Each of you guys owns a company that siphons off revenues before TransCo gets its slice of the sales pie. A casual observer might question whether the goal of any TransCo director is to do right by his company or right by TransCo. Directors have a legal duty of loyalty to the firm on whose board they serve. If there is a conflict, then they should quit the board."

- "Why do we need a new CPA firm? The one we have is doing just fine by us."

  My response: "The Sarbanes-Oxley Act of 2002 created the Public Company Accounting Oversight Board (PCAOB). Among other accountabilities, the PCAOB (a) writes auditing standards for public firms (thus relieving the American Institute of CPAs of that mantel), (b) registers CPA firms that are approved to audit publicly-held companies, and (c) monitors the quality of work done by those firms. I believe TransCo needs an audit firm that is on the PCAOB registry. I don't guarantee that audit quality will improve; I do guarantee that audit fees will go up. But the virtue of having such a firm is that, like having outside directors already on the board, when you guys go to cash out, you'll do so with lower risk—and, as a result, a higher price—whether you do an initial public offering or sell to a bigger company. If TransCo wants to present itself as a sophisticated company, we can't look as a closed society of good ol' boys."

- "We've had this law firm from the beginning, and you say we need a new one. Why? These guys are the best in town and probably in the state."

  My response: "I hate to sound like a broken record, but we are thinking and talking in parochial terms. There's not a man in this room whose company generates even half as much revenue as TransCo. There's not a guy here who's not here by virtue of a beneficient gene pool. Common failings of small companies that are protected by a corporate parent and that are suddenly on their own are that they often think small, hire small, and do small. As with outside directors, as with a PCAOB-registered audit firm, so it is with a law firm. We don't need a silk-stocking New York firm, but we do need one that (a) has done initial public offerings and (b) advises publicly held companies. The current firm does neither of those. That increases risk, which reduces the value of you guys' equity in TransCo."

- "Why do we need a succession plan for the CEO? He's high energy, in great shape, and is doing a great job."

    My response: (The CEO was at the table.) "My recommendation for a succession plan has nothing to do with the CEO we have. I like him. He's a good guy. But—here we go again, guys—do you want to reduce risk or do you want to make political statements that make you feel good, but, in the longer term, reduce value?

    "We need a succession plan, *not* just for the CEO but for the CFO and every one of the others reporting directly to the CEO. I have never seen a company where, if the CEO didn't have a successor, anyone else had one. It just doesn't happen. Underlings take their cues from the guy in front. If he doesn't think having a successor or two in place and ready to go is a good idea, no one else will, either.

    "And, in fairness to the CEO here, this is not a matter of morbidity or fear of a medical recurrence. This is simply a matter of reducing risk, protecting shareholders—you guys—and increasing the value of this company. Almost everything you guys are questioning is, in one way or another, about reducing risk.

    "If you don't want to increase the value of TransCo, don't change a thing. That's the best advice I can give you if, in fact, that's what you want to do. But you can't have it both ways. You can't say you want a higher value for your shares but continue to make a series of risky and suboptimal choices. It's just that simple, guys. From the end of 2005 to the end of 2006, we estimate that the value of this company has fallen from a range of $19 million to $23 million to a range of $13 million to $15 million. Take the midpoint, and that's a decline of 30%. During that same period, the S&P 500 rose by 13.6% and the Dow Jones Transportation Index by 8.7%. Markets are sending us a message. It's up to us to decide whether we're going to listen or not. I hope we choose to listen up."

Postscript.   The CEO died of cancer a couple of years after my presentation. The Board went outside for his successor and hired an interim CEO. His first day on the job, he said he would "make no decisions" other than those related to operations until his permanent replacement arrived; there was no timetable for that. The Board dithered, squabbled, and did not begin a search. Five months later, his wife lost her job, so he needed health insurance and asked if he could be the permanent CEO. By then, he was receiving substantial negative reviews. The Board hired him anyway.

Freight Forwarding

Overview. Global Freight Forwarders, LLC (GFF), was a high-growth third-party logistics (3PL) company that did business worldwide but had particular expertise in China and India. It was owned by three co-equal principals. Revenues were north of $10 million, which isn't bad for 12 employees in a company launched from a standing start in 2002. However, in the 3PL space, there are major reimbursable expenses—the industry calls them "pass-throughs." These are reported as revenue and are then offset in Cost of Services Sold (COSS). That is why the gross margins of publicly held 3PL companies such as C.H. Robinson Worldwide Inc., Pacer International Inc., and Hub Group Inc. are well below 20%. Yahoo's "Air Delivery & Freight Services" industry group shows a domain-wide gross margin of 16.1% as of August 2009. This was a value-added calculations engagement, the purpose of which was to estimate a range of value for the purpose of two partners buying out the third, who wanted to retire.

Metrics

1. High revenue growth; declining earnings before interest, taxes, depreciation, and amortization (EBITDA).
2. Stratospheric meals-and-entertainment (M&E) expenses.
3. Above-average productivity (revenues ÷ FTEs).
4. Zero "Training and Development" expense.
5. Tax returns were done by a "tax service."
6. Unfunded buy-sell agreement.

Interviewees. The three principals, office manager, operations manager, sales manager, three account representatives.

V-M Findings

1. GFF's niches in China and India were driving growth. It helped that one of the principals was born in Asia. (SPARC)
2. 2007 M&E expense was more than $1 million. During our on-site visit, three employees alleged that GFF buried the procurement of sexual partners in its M&E expense. If true, it would be violating the Foreign Corrupt Practices Act of 1977 (FCPA). The two going-forward shareholders said that they wanted to grow GFF to $100 million and then bail out. (SPARC)
3. GFF had made an early investment in high-quality IT infrastructure. It then outsourced almost 100% of the mountains of data entry work

to India. That left stateside employees to focus on taking care of customers, something truly unique that set this company far apart from its closest competitors. (SPARC)

4. There was a "bright line" between the three principals and GFF's employees. One principal thought that investing in training and developing employees was crucial, a second thought it was a waste of money, and the retiring partner was an older conflict-avoider who had no stake in fighting that battle—he just wanted out.

5. GFF's accounting firm had prepared its tax returns until 2004. GFF then changed to a "tax service" because, the president told us, "The CPA firm was charging us too much." With GFF's permission, we talked with the managing partner of the small local accounting firm; he told us that he and his partners "were relieved" when GFF took its tax business elsewhere. "We didn't want the exposure," he said. We didn't ask, but we inferred he was referring to the FCPA. (SPARC)

6. The principals told us that no one had ever advised them to fund the buy-sell agreement. We noted that the lawyer the firm used at its inception, when the buy-sell was executed, was one thing, but that, given its current size and aspirations, it needed to move up-market with its law firm and, eventually, with its tax advisor, who, GFF's president argued vociferously, was a CPA. I finally told him that I had never seen a CPA whose firm was named a "tax service." I also said that, while there probably were such firms, they were few and far between and that I'd be willing to bet him a thousand bucks that the incumbent "tax service" was not owned by a CPA. He almost took the bet but then thought better of it. He would have lost because I'd perused on the state board of accountancy's Web site: The name of the owner of the "tax service" wasn't there. (SPARC)

SPARC Elements

People
Architecture
Routines
Culture

V-M Solutions

1. We didn't recommend any change in what GFF was doing on the revenue side. Clearly it was hitting on eight cylinders, and maybe more.

2. While stipulating "We don't know for sure," we expressed concern to the principals about possible FCPA exposure. With the permission of the outside CPA firm, we also noted that it said it was "relieved" when GFF decided to go elsewhere for tax services, "and that's not a good thing, guys."

3. We had nothing but praise for the insightful investment in IT and subsequent outsourcing of data entry to India. It gave the company a huge leg up over its competitors.

    However, by not requiring each employee (including owners) to sign an NSNDA as a condition of employment, it failed to protect these truly stunning achievements. Unlike noncompetes, NSNDAs are easily enforced and are an inexpensive way to protect intellectual property, including proprietary knowledge and relationships with customers and suppliers.

4. The "bright line" was an explicit indicator of centralized decision-making, which GFF had in spades. We told the principals that they should not expect to grow to $100 million without erasing the bright line. There is no way to run a multi-office $200 million enterprise with global reach and frequent person-to-person interactions with customers by having decision-making reside in two individuals.

    Sidebar: To demonstrate to the two staying principals that they had really not thought through the implications of the bright line they had drawn, I asked them if they ever flew together or rode in the same car together. They said, "Of course we do." I then asked how much GFF would be worth if both were ever wiped out or disabled in a freak mishap. The president glared at me (he did a lot of that!), but his partner stared at me and then said, "George, he's right. We have to fix this."

    Not wanting to be the arbiter of a public disagreement between principals, I quickly pointed out the desirability of PDPs as a way of finding out who had the desire to learn by stepping up and investing some of their off-hours time in increasing their learning, skills, and knowledge. I also suggested that GFF form a council of advisors, even though I knew the company had a little (!) cleaning up to do first. I noted that, in the event of unforeseen disaster, a council could also be a save-the-company feature if it were chosen properly (i.e., not stacked with cronies), were treated with respect by the principals, and met every quarter with an agenda into which councilors had input.

5. We met over supper with the two principals who would own the company after the buy-out of their partner. I minced no words about the

M&E expenses (which did *not* include some that were reimbursed through COSS). I asked them how on earth they could "spend over $1 million" on M&E in a firm like theirs. "What are you doing?" I asked. "Drugs? Women? What?"

The president grinned sheepishly and said, "Definitely not drugs."

I pounced. "Then women, huh?"

"Ummmm, yeah, you might say that."

I said, "Well, the problem is that, if I can figure that out, anyone can. And if anyone can, your backside is sticking out about like Bill Clinton's wagging finger when he said, 'I did not have sexual relations with that woman.' When he made that ill-considered remark in 1998, there were no legal implications in his choice of behavior the legal stuff came later. There are in yours. The FCPA is real. It has teeth that were sharpened by the enactment of the International Anti-Bribery Act of 1998. You're on thin ice, guys."

By this time, the president appeared to have developed a healthy respect for my willingness to butt heads with him over serious issues. He asked, "So how can we stop this in midstream?"

"Well, the obvious solution is to blame someone else."

"I like that," he said. "What do you mean?"

"Seat a serious, carefully selected council of advisors and make them the fall guys. We helped a two-owner company smaller than yours do that. At our suggestion, they blamed the council for having its foot on their neck to collect $150,000 in over-90-days receivables from one longtime customer that they were (then) not willing to lose. That single customer was threatening the liquidity of their firm.

I then said that when their M&E act was cleaned up and a council was seated, they should go back to their CPA firm, explain the steps they'd taken, and ask if the CPAs would take them back if they didn't have to worry about the FCPA. They said they would.

I also warned them, however, that about the time their revenues hit $50 million, they should be thinking about moving up the advisory food chain, not to one of the global accounting firms but certainly to one that was in the "Second Eight," as I call firms 5 through 12. "That will give comfort to buyers because they will not have to extend as great, as long, and as expensive a due diligence effort as they otherwise would." The owners nodded.

6. "Along the same lines," I said, "you need a bigger law firm. Any lawyer who would fail to tell you that a buy-sell ain't worth much if it's not funded is doing you no favors. You guys are big enough and

profitable enough that you don't have to have cheap advisors. TAN-STAAFL, you know (There Ain't No Such Thing as a Free Lunch). You get what you pay for. You need the help. Besides, the outsiders on your council will feel much better." The two guys agreed and said they would follow up.

Postscript. We thought we would get the gig to help them seat the council. We didn't. They didn't follow through. Somehow, they managed to take out their partner for the low end of seven figures. I just hope the two principals don't fly or drive together and aren't carrying much debt on their personal financial statements.

16

Specialty Retailing

The focus of this chapter is specialty retailing, a sector hard hit by both the internet and the current economic downturn. Still, as in most matters of strategy for SMEs, focus/differentiation remains the order of the day. But shortening the supply chain also dumps dollars into owners' bank accounts.

We cover two jewelry stores (one pretty ordinary, at least on the surface, and the other catering exclusively to military personnel), a struggling building materials retailer dealing with the forthcoming entry of a Home Depot in rural Virginia, and a small-town pharmacy fattening its margins by "compounding." We think that each of these has lessons for valuation professionals (and business owners), and we hope you agree.

Jewelry I

Overview. Olde Time Jewelry Inc. (OTJI) was born in the Detroit suburbs during the Great Depression. It began life as a watch-repair store and then, in response to inquiries from customers, slowly inched into jewelry retailing. The second-generation owner had worked briefly for a commercial real estate developer after graduating from a small college—he always looked for an easy way to make a lot of quick bucks. Then, at the behest of his ailing father, he relocated to take over the family business; his father later passed on. At the time of our first engagement, OTJI reported total revenues of $2 million. "Gen2" told me that OTJI's biggest problem was declining area employment in the Big 3 U.S. car makers. We were retained for a valuation to facilitate the purchase of an equity stake by a member of the third generation (Gen3).

Metrics

1. Flat sales.
2. Annual financial statements only.

3. Un–bar-coded inventory.
4. $100,000 in cash in a safe.

Interviewees. Owner, would-be shareholder (who is vice president and a full-time employee), six employees.

V-M Findings

1. This engagement turned out to be one that falls under a category that I call "the Rattlesnake Syndrome." This syndrome occurs in companies that have internal weaknesses almost everywhere one looks. I think of it in terms of turning over a rock and finding a rattlesnake under it (a problem). I kill it (solve the problem), but the snake's tail stretches out to beneath another rock. I turn over that rock to pull the tail out, and zap! There is another rattler under there (another problem). I kill it, too, but its tail also extends to another rock, where, you guessed it, there is another rattlesnake. I have been in engagements where I felt like a herpetologist before I got done.

   In this situation, sales appeared to be flat. I say "appeared" because, frankly, I could not tell. Worse, neither could the owner. (The reasons why will be discussed later in this vignette.) Yes, the economy in the greater Detroit area was in decline, even in the mid-1990s. I suspect nearly every business there, except for pawn shops, therapists, and outsourcing firms, could blame the auto industry for *any trouble* it had, from revenues to gross margins to cash flow. The Detroit car guys are easy and deserving whipping boys. (**SPARC**)

2. I have seen more than a few businesses that get their financial statements once a year. To me, that is *always* a bad sign. No ifs, ands, or buts about it—it is a huge red flag. The reasons for this dreadful practice vary. Some owners want to "save money" (wow—that is *expensive!*). Others do not understand financial statements and figure that the less they see of them, the better they will feel. Still others are trying to beat the IRS. In this particular situation, I did not feel any better when I visited the company's outside accountant, shook his hand, and immediately looked for some disinfectant. (**SPARC**)

3. In *any* business that retails, wholesales, or rents products, inventory without bar codes or RFID (radio frequency identification) is a leading indicator of management malpractice. In a sector that has the kind of margins that jewelry retailing has *and* sells merchandise as fungible as diamonds and rubies, it is also reckless and self-destructive

behavior. OTJI's owner said, "You don't understand. Our business is different." OBID rocks again.[1] (SPARC)

4. As I watched Gen2 locking down the store after my site visit, he opened the safe and pulled out more cash than I had ever seen in one place. I raised an eyebrow and said, "Wow. How much you got there?"

"Over a hundred grand," he said.

"For what?"

"For whatever I need it for," he said.

That was the first time he and I had been in a situation where no one else was around and we were in no danger of being interrupted. I decided to pounce. The stars that night all pointed to the same thing, but I had to confirm it, just to make sure.

"You know," I began, "you have a wonderful business here. Your name is a household name in this community. You have civic awards that fill up two walls in your office. Yet you get your financials once a year, you draw a salary of fifteen grand, your inventory is not controlled in any way that I can see, and now you wave a hundred thousand bucks cash in my face. Why are you doing this?"

"Doing what?" He glared at me.

"Doing what you're doing. Running this business in a way that no sane owner would *ever* think of running a business that had high-margin, easily fungible inventory."

"You don't understand how real business is conducted," he snapped.

"And how is that?" I purred.

"This *is* real business. Everyone I know runs their business the way I do."

"I'll bet the inmates at Sing-Sing say the same thing," I said quietly."

"What the hell does THAT mean?" he said, raising his voice.

"You know as well as I do. I was born at night, but I wasn't born *last* night. You're skimming. We both know that."

"Yeah. So what? My dad did it. He taught me."

"Oh," I said. "The nuns at those parochial schools you went to never taught you any differently? Is that what you're trying to tell me?"

"I'm trying to tell you that this is the real world."

"I'll concede one point," I said. "This is *your* real world. But it's reckless, it's crazy, and, above all, it's really expensive."

---

[1] Our business is different.

"What do you mean, 'expensive'?" he thundered.

"Well, for starters, I assume that your employees know that you're doing this."

"Of course. They have standing orders to talk to me before selling anything for more than two grand in cold cash."

"That's terrific. The whole place knows you're crooked. I'd say that puts you in a pretty weak bargaining position anytime they need a raise or time off. If you ever try to fire someone, they have you over a barrel big-time."

"That's never happened," he said. "Besides, my turnover is low."

"Well, you don't know OTJI's inventory turn, so you're talking about employee turnover, right?"

"Yes."

"Well, have you ever thought about *why* employees don't often leave?"

"Of course. They like working here."

"That might not be the only reason," I said.

"Oh?"

"Maybe they have fringe benefits you haven't counted on."

"And what would those be?"

"Oh, nothing much. A few baubles each Christmas, when things are frantic."

"I'd know," he said.

"No kidding? Wow. That's some memory bank you have. Maybe you're in the wrong business. Ever thought about talking to Jerry Lucas?"

"The pro basketball player?" he said.

"*Former* pro basketball player. He wrote a best-selling book last year called *The Memory Book*.[2] Owns a company called Dr. Memory, LLC."

"You're joking," he said.

"Yeah, but not much. A few years ago, I saw a lawyer who owned a title agency go to prison for dipping into the escrow money. That's only a little nuttier than what you're doing, which is plenty reckless."

"I don't want to talk about it any more."

"OK," I said, "but I *am* going to talk to your would-be partner about this."

"He knows all about it."

"Good. But he hasn't heard it from my perspective."

---

[2] Lorayne and Lucas, *The Memory Book.*

"I don't know that I want you to do that."

"Well, it's either that, or this engagement is over. I'll refund all your money, including travel expenses. You can explain to him why I went back to Tulsa early."

He gulped. "Ummm, OK. Just don't screw up my relationship with him, OK?"

"I'm quite sure you don't need any help there," I said. (SPARC)

SPARC Elements

   People

   Routines

   Culture

V-M Solution.   Gen2 and I agreed to change the scope of the engagement. Instead of valuation, which was out of the question on anything other than a SWAG[3] basis, I agreed to prepare a memorandum for him and Gen3 on my recommendations for improvements in the business.

Postscript.   Gen3 bought in. According to the Web site, the two of them still work together. The jewelry store is chugging along, though with several fewer people than it employed when I was first there.

Several years later, I got a call from Gen2. Seems that he and a business partner were in a dispute over a restaurant they owned. (Another cash business.) Unfortunately, the partner, who had also been Gen2's close friend, also knew exactly how Gen2 ran his jewelry business. The partner emulated him in the booze/food venture—to the tune of $400,000; Gen2 went ballistic. He ended up paying us and an attorney over $100,000—*not* from OTJI's safe, I might add—to get a dreadful settlement because the other guy told him, through mutual acquaintances, that he would blow the whistle with IRS on Gen2's business practices.

Jewelry II

Overview.   Military Baubles Inc. (MBI) was a family-owned enterprise that catered to personnel in the U.S. armed forces; 90% of its eight-figure revenues came from active duty personnel in the 18 to 25 age bracket. It was a mature company with retail stores, a mail-order business, and a growing online presence. An outside accounting firm conducted an annual review of its financial statements. At the valuation date, which was in the wake of

---

[3] Scientific wild-arse guess.

9/11, it had no debt and was cash-flush. The purpose of the valuation was gifting.

Metrics

1. Inventory turn was three times its closest rival's.
2. Working capital was well into seven figures.
3. Gross margin increased by 8 percentage points in the five-year historical period and was 18 percentage points higher than its closest competitor.
4. Its revenues per full-time employee were two-and-a-half times those of its closest competitor.
5. MBI's rate of growth far exceeded that of the industry.
6. Four chains accounted for nearly 19% of U.S. jewelry industry sales yet enjoyed obvious economies of scale from having only 11% of retail stores.

Interviewees.   CEO, CFO, controller, sales director, two store managers, three retail sales professionals.

V-M Findings

1. Unlike OTJI, MBI's practices reflected its knowledge that jewelry styles were faddish *and* also that jewelry was fungible. It maintained tight control of its inventory through prudent purchasing; it also exercised tight security over it. Besides monitoring sales at the bar-coded SKU level (it had 10,000 of them in the typical store), it also had an elaborate security/loss prevention system that transmitted in-store video footage in real time to security personnel at corporate headquarters. Store managers had lucrative incentives to minimize inventory "slippage." (SPARC)
2. If a buyer was on active duty, MBI extended credit terms of 12 months with monthly payments. It ran that financing through a separate entity that it owned. The beauty of doing business with active-duty personnel is that monies can be withheld from paychecks via "allotments." Once the individual approves the allotment—MBI would not ship until the buyer did—the Marine Corps/Army/Navy/Air Force/Coast Guard withheld and then remitted the payments each month. Since MBI had differentiated itself with its customer base, it charged higher prices. The fact that the individual did not have to come up with the entire price at purchase and had access to easy credit, which is then converted to cash through the allotment system, is about as close as most enterprises get to a real live money machine. (SPARC)

3. During our on-site interviews, we learned that gross margin shot up for four reasons: (a) aggressive pricing by MBI, (b) strict loss-control measures, (c) well-conceived incentives for store managers, and (d) careful inventory management to avoid getting caught with faddish items when styles change. (**SPARC**)

4. At the time of the valuation, MBI's closest competitors did not have much of an online presence. That, plus the aggressive pricing, made for MBI's extraordinary productivity. Of course, the pricing works only if the firm is successful in differentiating itself, which MBI was (and is). (**SPARC**)

5. Judicious choices in new store locations was a major driver of MBI's revenue growth. Its growth in same-store sales also ran well ahead of the industry's. Some of that came from its higher prices, but a greater portion, in our view, came from its nimble-footedness in not having to sell at discounted prices by not getting stuck with obsolete inventory. (**SPARC**)

6. Ordinarily, we do not get much into domain-level metrics in our on-site interviews. However, in this case, it was worth noting. The obvious inference in the disparity between revenue concentration and store concentration is that there are scale economies in jewelry retailing. Indeed there are. Those arise from (a) advertising, (b) purchasing, and (c) training of new personnel. Successful chains get that. (**SPARC**)

SPARC Elements

Strategy
Architecture
Routines

V-M Solution.   What are the problems?

Postscript.   MBI was and is indeed a remarkable company. It was included to show the power of SPARC in "getting to what" for great metrics as well as not-so-great ones. It had reason to swagger, but it remained modest and low-key. When I went to MBI's headquarters for the first time, I would never have known it was a world-class performer had I not done my homework. The majority shareholder is a soft-spoken man, and the premises were a bit on the austere side. The CFO was not particularly strong, but, then, he did not need to be. The culture did not bowl me over, either. But all of the architecture that went into the design of MBI was something to behold. We wish we saw that aspect of SPARC more often.

Building Materials

Overview.   This small ($2 million) company in a rural setting was confronting the entry of Home Depot (HD) into its market. Most of us have heard of the "Wal-Mart effect." In smaller communities, HD and Lowe's often have a similar impact, though not so pronounced because they are specialty retailers. The client company was family-owned. Its founder had died owning a handful of commercial properties and Valley Building Materials Inc., a Virginia C corporation. Based on a referral from the family's accountant, the estate retained us to do the appraisal for estate-tax purposes.

Metrics

1. No fringe benefits, except two weeks' annual vacation.
2. Two active lines of business:
   a. Selling to do-it-yourselfers (DIYers)
   b. Doing remodeling and light commercial work
3. The founder never took a salary greater than $7,000 in any year.
4. The firm employed 12 full-time employees and issued 37 W-2s in the calendar year before the founder died unexpectedly.

Interviewees.   The decedent's widow, older son, younger son, two employees, and outside CPA.

V-M Findings

1. The decedent did not need health insurance because his spouse worked at a large manufacturing company where she had family coverage. She said that no one had ever mentioned to her or, presumably, to him that even high-deductible, wipe-out insurance might be a useful way to retain employees. (**SPARC**)
2. Valley Building Materials was a do-it-yourself retailer for most of its 20-plus years of existence. However, a few years before he died, the founder decided to "diversify" by taking on remodeling and light commercial work. It cost his company $200,000 a year in revenues from contractors because they were not about to buy their materials from a competitor. He enjoyed the work, so he reportedly said he did not care. (**SPARC**)
3. The decedent's older son, who had taken over the business in the wake of his father's death, first drew a blank when asked why his dad never took more than a seven-grand salary. Then he snapped his fingers and said, "Of course. Mom and Dad own a bunch of commercial real estate, including a couple of trailer parks. Those bring in over

150 grand a year. I'm sure he didn't need a salary from this business. Plus, Mom has always worked in that factory." (SPARC)

4. Employee turnover had been so high for so long that the family considered it to be normal. It seemed not to have occurred to them that a small company that sends three times as many W-2s as it has employees was probably missing quite a bit of revenue because few of its employees ever developed much knowledge of the business. That kept them from spotting opportunities to sell additional items that a DIYer had not asked for. The founder did not spend much time at either of the firm's locations. He played a lot of golf and looked after his real estate holdings. (SPARC)

SPARC Elements

Strategy
Architecture
Culture

V-M Solutions. We found the older son who ran the business to be pleasant and sociable. But he did not seem to have much energy, and he was not the go-getter that his dad was. We offered him suggestions to ramp up marketing, but he demurred. At our urging, he did start offering a low-cost, high-deductible health insurance policy. Turnover fell significantly, but the country also slid into a post–9/11 recession. There was no way to know how much of the lower turnover could be attributed to the insurance and how much to the economic downturn. As the economy began to rebound in 2003, however, Valley Building Materials' revenues dropped steeply. The son said he did not know why.

Postscript. In 2004, the company shut its doors. The family blamed HD. But no one could explain why another building materials concern almost right across the road from the new HD thrived after it opened up.

Pharmacy

Overview. Blue Ridge Pill Peddlers Inc. (BRPPI) had a long and colorful history as a community pharmacy in the Shenandoah Valley of Virginia. The owner was less than a decade from retirement when he was referred to us by his outside CPA. He thought he wanted to try to work out a deal with one of the two pharmacists working for him to buy the business. The would-be buyer was not so sure. Besides, her self-employed husband did not want her to have the responsibility of making payroll for eight full- time employees.

Metrics

1. Sales growth averaged 11% annually in recent years, and revenue approached $3.5 million.
2. Gross margin was 9 percentage points above the industry average.
3. No employee turnover.
4. Industry software for ordering pharmaceuticals and tracking prescriptions, QuickBooks for keeping accounting records.

Interviewees.   Owner, owner's spouse, five employees, outside accountant.

V-M Findings

1. The owner was an engaging and aggressive man who liked to sell. It did not matter if it was pills, high-margin durable medical equipment, patent medicine, athletic wraps, or electric thermometers. He had great rapport with children, greeted them and their parents by name, and always made it a point to spend a minute or two chatting with the kids; he strongly encouraged his employees to do the same, and some did. He also did "consulting" for herbal products, vitamins, and the like and claimed that it all made him feel better. I was skeptical. But one could not argue with the growth rate in revenues in a city where population growth had been flat to declining for many years. (**SPARC**)
2. BRPPI was the only pharmacy within a radius of 50 miles that did "compounding." Compounding is a process whereby the pharmacist custom-mixes pharmaceuticals prescribed by a physician, nurse practitioner, or veterinarian. The 2,000 members of the International Association of Compounding Pharmacists (www.iacprx.org) were less than 1% of the estimated 210,000 active pharmacists in the United States in 2002. Why so few? For one thing, compounding pharmacists risk being accused of manufacturing pharmaceuticals. For another, some have also been accused of practicing medicine by mixing over-the-counter, nonprescription medicines for patients who suffered nasty side effects from interactions with medications prescribed by physicians. When I asked the owner why he did compounding, he replied, "Simple. I make more money." (**SPARC**)
3. The newest employee had been with the store for eight years. All subordinates were women, as were most customers. To be sure, the owner was a serious control freak. Not a bad guy, just controlling and, at times, invasive in his inquiries about what his subordinates did outside of work. But he paid them well and lavished hefty Christmas

bonuses on them. His rationale was that his corporation was a C corporation, so he "might as well get the corporate taxes down." He said it never occurred to him that he could take out dividends and pay 15% income tax on them. (SPARC)

4. Like most industry-specific software packages, the one used by BRPPI was great on the operating side of the pharmacy and pathetic in its handling of accounting, so BRPPI used QuickBooks for its accounting records. We cautioned the owner that, before he put his business on the market or listed it with a broker, he should junk QuickBooks and install something less identified with "mom-and-pops." We mentioned MAS90 and the up-and-coming, refurbished Peachtree. His accountant advised him to stick with QuickBooks. I cautioned him that he was likely to leave money well into six figures on the table if he was still running QuickBooks when he exited. I hastened to reassure him that I did not think that QuickBooks was bad software, just bad for (a) his industry and (b) any multimillion-dollar business whose owner was looking at selling. We run QuickBooks in our own shop. It is great stuff. But we are not bringing in $3.5 million a year. (SPARC)

SPARC Elements

> **P**eople
> **A**rchitecture
> **R**outines
> **C**ulture

V-M Solutions. We were asked to come back several years later and do a valuation for his C corporation's election to S status. That was four years before he exited by selling assets.

We also encouraged him to instigate PDPs with his employees. We said that any buyer would find BRPPI's focus on helping its employees' professional development both useful and valuable.

Postscript. We could always tell this client, but we could never tell him much. We tried humor, cajolery, heart-to-heart conversations, and a bunch of other things, and none of them worked. When he finally did bail out, in 2009, he got less than we had valued the business for in 2002, even though sales and profits had continued to increase at a healthy pace. And he was still running QuickBooks when he exited.

CHAPTER

Services

O ur final chapter of vignettes is about the business services sector, plus two end-of-chapter segues into cases that are not SPARC-related, per se, but are worth your while nonetheless. The U.S. economy is heavily dominated by services now, yet the services space is miles behind manufacturing when it comes to productivity. The dominant cost in most services firms is human capital, not inventory or equipment, and people are not so susceptible to quick productivity tweaks as inanimate assets are.

In this chapter we deal with several services businesses. One is highly countercyclical and is booming today: outplacement services. (Some sectors root quietly for downturns: outplacement services, marriage counselors, consumer debt restructurers, and pawn shops, among others.) We follow that with profiles from executive recruiting, private equity, and investment banking. We end on an upbeat note with vignettes from two offbeat niches: dental laboratories and quick-lube services. These last two are not SPARC- related but they offer great lessons for those who might not yet appreciate the value of strong interviewing skills.

Outplacement Services

Overview. Recovering from Layoffs, Inc. (RFLI) grossed over $3 million with revenues growing at 15% to 20% annually. Its two principals were at loggerheads, so the purpose of the valuation was to establish a value so they could go their separate ways. There was no buy-sell agreement.

Metrics

1. Owners received financial statements annually.
2. DSO was 91 days.
3. There was no succession plan.
4. RFLI had no formal approach to governance.

Interviewees. Two owners (we were not allowed to speak with any other employee), outside accounting firm.

V-M Findings

1. and **2.** RFLI's sole financial person was a part-time bookkeeper. That was why the owners saw financial statements only annually. There were no budgets, no collections efforts, and no payment-related provisions in its contracts with its corporate clients. In addition, it was treading on thin ice by paying about 8% of its revenues to "independent contractors"; there were no written agreements backstopping those arrangements, either. (SPARC)
3. These guys were great therapists but not great businessmen. It turned out that one of the strains on the relationship between them was that the one who brought in over half of the revenue loved being in control. (Maybe a therapist needs one?) In addition, the control guy's dad had died when he was a teenager, so the notion of succession struck him as morbid. There was no life insurance, of course, because there was no buy-sell agreement, much less one that was funded. (SPARC)
4. Without a shareholders' agreement, there was no way to resolve 50-50 standoffs, which these two guys were having with increasing frequency. They did not even have cursory board minutes for the legally mandated annual meeting. (SPARC)

SPARC Elements

People
Architecture
Routines

V-M Solutions

1. At our suggestion, the outside accounting firm helped RFLI screen and hire a part-time accountant, a woman in semiretirement. She was delighted to have the job, and her age made her a bit intimidating to the 40-something owners.
2. She quickly brought DSO down to 44 days. Asked how she did it, she said, "I called and asked." Partners' distributions, already quite healthy, shot up as receivables fell by over $400,000.
3. Inasmuch as the principals were going their separate ways, they saw no need for succession. If anything, as sole practitioners, they needed something to reassure their corporate clients that there was

a plan for continuation. We even suggested that they adopt something similar to what we have at Beckmill Research—an understanding with another firm that, if something happens to me, they will wind down our business, and vice versa. That feature of our practice has reduced our malpractice premiums by almost 25% every year because the agreement is in writing.

4. Both principals rejected the idea of an outside council of advisors.

Postscript. They went their separate ways. The "surviving" principal went on to experience high turnover to the point that the only employee left on his payroll was the part-time accountant. He did manage to get some non-solicitation/nondisclosure agreements in place with his contractors, along with separate contractor documents that would keep him out of the "employee soup" if the IRS ever began questioning those relationships.

The "departing" principal formed a separate practice. Within a couple of years, he had nearly a dozen full-time professional employees and was doubt-less outgrossing his former partner, no longer the rainmaker but still in control.

Executive Search

Overview. At the time of our valuation, Careers4U.com (C4U) was a floun-dering firm that had suffered two straight years of major declines (from $9 million in 1998 to an annual run rate of $3.5 million in 2000). For reasons that will soon be obvious, the near-term outlook for the rest of 2001 and 2002, at least, looked dark indeed.

Metrics

1. Falling revenues.
2. Overreliance on a highly cyclical niche.
3. Rising overhead expenses relative to revenues.
4. Refusal to acknowledge a problem.

Interviewees. Owner, office manager, and the top-producing recruiter.

V-M Findings

1. and **2.** C4U derived over 85% of its revenues from permanent and temporary placements in the financial services niche. It was head-quartered in lower Manhattan with two small offices outside New York City that, we inferred from comments the owner made to us,

were seen as stepchildren in the C4U family. The valuation date was September 30, 2001. (**SPARC**)

3. C4U's overhead had risen from 17% of revenue to 29%, even though, in nominal terms, it had fallen. The owner never produced the details underlying the "Operating Expenses" category.

    For a firm specializing in the niche it did, it was remarkably unsophisticated in its financial practices. For instance, the owner could not recall seeing a balance sheet for C4U, perhaps because it filed as a "disregarded entity" (i.e., Schedule C). The owner kept the (Quick) books himself but was not a degreed financial guy. (**SPARC**)

4. The problem for C4U went beyond the obvious ones of its own making. The real obstacle it faced was the 9/11 attack and the recession that had begun in 2000 but would surely accelerate and decimate employment in financial services. (Of course, 2008 was yet to come.) Yet the owner, who was living pretty high on the hog, refused to believe, even in October 2001, that his firm faced undue risk from excessive dependency on financial services. He raved about rubbing elbows with the crème de la crème in his charitable activities in behalf of WNET/WLIW, the PBS affiliates in New York and Long Island, respectively. He cabbed it all the way from Downtown to the Four Seasons in Midtown for lunch most days but groused that he had not yet succeeded in getting the staff there to hold a special table for him. He appeared to think that a business that had turned $9 million in annual revenues into $3.5 million was a bucket of cash. It is nontrivial, to be sure, at 57th and Madison Avenue, a block from Trump Tower, it is chump change. (**SPARC**)

SPARC Elements

Strategy
Culture

V-M Solutions

1. and 2. Given the owner's singular resistance to the notion of diversifying his company's revenue stream, there was nothing more we could recommend to C4U.

3. We are not strong believers in cost-cutting as a way to future prosperity. However, in this case, C4U's revenues had fallen by almost 60%, and reducing overhead was essential. Even then, all it accomplished was to delay the inevitable.

4. As the old saying goes, "Denial ain't just a river in Egypt."

Postscript.   C4U staggered along living hand to mouth until the market implosion of 2008. Like Lehmann Brothers, it bit the dust that fall.

Private Equity

Overview.   A large local accounting firm in New England referred the valuation of one of its client companies, Invest-in-Power, LLC (IIP) to us. The enterprise was a niche private-equity firm specializing in a sector of the energy industry. IIP was funded by institutional investors, including the Harvard Endowment. The purpose of the valuation was to assist the firm's seven principals with estate planning.

Metrics

1. No consistent and documented process for analyzing prospective investments.
2. No credentialed valuation professionals on staff.
3. Ineffectual and low-performing finance function.
4. No transparency.
5. Dreadful Web site.
6. Sky-high profitability with carried interests worth well into seven figures for each principal.

Interviewees.   Six principals in person, plus one by telephone, CFO, four analysts, controller.

V-M Findings

1. **2, 3,** and **4.** A recurring theme at IIP was the absence of visible signs of management anywhere. There was an executive committee, but it was more secretive than the covert operations of the Central Intelligence Agency. IIP had enjoyed an extraordinarily successful run in its short three-year life. Bought out from a bank for a song by senior managers, IIP had compiled a remarkable record. Besides raising funds from investors (its latest one was $750 million), it did one thing really well: It knew how to buy high-performing assets on the cheap because its four most senior people had long experience in and around public utilities.

   Though most of its analysts had MBAs, not one held the CFA (Certified Financial Analyst) designation or the ASA (Accredited Senior Appraiser) credential. In fact, only one interviewee had ever *heard* of either one; he, with a law degree, was a Level 3 candidate for the CFA charter. He wanted to transition from legal work to portfolio management, probably in a different company.

The combination of IIP's very success and the egos that can attend seven-figure annual incomes made for an almost impossible situation. Everyone at the firm was overpaid. Conspicuous example: The CFO, who owned a small equity stake, took home over a million bucks a year, despite his meager accounting skills and financial acumen. His controller pulled down over $250,000 in a $90,000/year job. These inflated compensation levels muted dissent and discouraged candid communication. (**SPARC**)

5. In addition to overpaying every employee, IIP was abundantly over-staffed. That made the workplace a hive of amateur politicians. I do not think anyone worked a 40-hour week. IIP's principals' grasp of IT approached Luddite level, of Luddite, so it outsourced its Web site to a brother-in-law (literally) who might well have spelled byte b-i-t-e—that is how bad the Web site was. A half-dozen full-time employees were allocated to responding to information requests from investors. IIP could have put that information on the web for a fraction of the cost of the personnel involved. Why IIP's sophisticated investors did not demand that was a puzzle to me. (**SPARC**)

6. Despite overpaying, overstaffing, no visible management, and no disciplined investment analysis process, IIP was a stunning financial success. I valued it well into eight figures—guideline public company analysis and DCF came in within $200,000 of one another. Clearly IIP's strategy was dead-on. (**SPARC**)

SPARC Elements

Strategy

People

Architecture

Routines

Culture

V-M Solutions

1. **2, 3, 4,** and **5.** Even though we had been retained to provide some attenuated value-enhancement advice in addition to the valuation, IIP's key principals were so used to having everyone genuflect that any constructive criticism from me was met with an attitude of "If you're so smart, why aren't you rich?" The notion that their company

could be worth two or three times what I said it was worth never occurred to them. The irony was that the four sachems on the executive committee wanted to argue with me about how to do DCF and comparables analysis, even though none of them had a clue about how to do either one. It was a situation where a sane person surrounded by a sea of nut cases gets to thinking after a while that *he* is the crazy one and *they* are the normal people. Those inflated paychecks bought silence and loyalty that would be the envy of any family in organized crime.

6. As noted earlier, the one thing IIP did right was execute its strategy. It had no process and no discipline. It operated on industry knowledge born of years of experience and the unarticulated intuition that goes with it. I still shake my head when I ponder how much money these wealthy principals were leaving on the table. But they would never believe it.

Postscript.   With no leverage, IIP sailed through the 2008 meltdown with ease, scooping up energy assets at depressed prices. I hear that its next fund will be $1.5 billion.

Investment Banking

Overview.   We were called in to collaborate with another firm in the valuation of a sizable minority stake in an old-line investment bank, WeLuvBucks Inc. (WLBI), which also had retail brokerage operations. The holder was the company's largest, but he had run afoul of the compliance regulations that engulf securities firms and others that handle other people's money. Wanting to beat the regulators to the punch, his partners had decided he had to go. The fact that he was their rainmaker made theirs a gutsy call.

Metrics

1. No Web site.
2. Slow growth.
3. Excess overhead.

Interviewees.   Four members of the executive committee (the fifth was the departing holder), compliance officer.

V-M Findings

1. **2**, and **3.** The absence of a Web site was the giveaway: WLBI was clueless about technology. It still took orders to buy and sell stocks and

bonds by telephone, and it did not offer its clients any access to options or futures. It did have an aging mainframe computer system, but it also had old green-screen monitors.

One of my functions in the engagement was to do the guideline public company analysis. That experience was a revelation, one that cemented the final opinion of value. At the time, there were more than 30 publicly held brokerage houses. These types of firms, like other financial institutions, tend to be valued on a price-to-book basis. My analysis produced a bipolar distribution: firms such as E*Trade, Charles Schwab, and Scott Securities were in one group and such now-departed companies as J.B. Oxford, Research Partners International, and First Montauk Corp. were in the other. The former were high growth, and the latter were low growth. The multiples reflected that. In fact, in the no-name group, price-book multiples were *below 1.0.*

I decided to analyze the revenue streams in the two groups. They disclosed the components of their revenues: commissions, investment banking, principal transactions, clearing and execution, and net interest income. When I compared the results in the two groups, I saw that the no-names were heavily dominated by commission income. At least as important was the fact that almost all of them, like WLBI, had no Internet presence.

In contrast, all of the companies in the other group did. Some of their price-book ratios were over 3.0. Part of that was expected growth, no doubt. But that growth was facilitated by the *technology* that the no-names either did not understand or just denied the importance of. (**SPARC**)

SPARC Elements

Strategy
Architecture
Routines

V-M Solution.   There was nothing fancy here: WLBI needed to get with the technology program or, fairly quickly, go out of business because of its inability to compete. It turned out that the leading obstacle to the firm's embrace of web technology was the departing rainmaker. He also berated me for valuing his stake at 0.7x book. "You know NOTHING about this industry!" he bellowed. "NO COMPANY in financial services sells for less than book." I had data. He had bluster. When I showed him my data, his face turned beet-red, and he glowered at me.

Postscript.   Without the errant principal, WLBI is alive and well as this is written. Needless to say, it has a "Login" link for its clients. Its Web site emphasizes its use of "the latest electronic tools" to help its clients.

Dental Lab

Overview.   Crowns & Bridges Inc. (C&BI) grossed about $1.8 million per year serving a metropolitan market of higher-end dentists in the southwestern United States. It had four co-equal shareholders. One of the principals was getting divorced. Because of the adversarial nature of the engagement, value enhancement did not really come into play here. However, what I learned in the engagement was valuable and, I think, worth passing along to readers.

Metrics

(1) 17 full-time employees, including the principals.
(2) Pretax profits ≈ 20% of revenues.
(3) The nature of the business.
(4) Governance in an atypical SME.

Interviewees.   Four principals, plus the lead nonowner working in the lab.

V-M Findings

1. Size is a function of domain—I learned that when I contacted the National Association of Dental Laboratories. It turns out that dental labs are, like the dentists they serve (two-thirds of whom are sole practitioners) a fragmented industry. At the time of this engagement, a lab with 17 employees was in the twelfth percentile of labs nationally. The law firm equivalent then was about 22 attorneys, a fact that later got the judge's attention. (No SPARC here)
2. Dental labs are unregulated. They can charge whatever the market will bear. Relationships with dentists tend to be long-lived and comfortable with an emphasis on service. The longevity of those relationships is consistent with research on consumer products: the closer the use of a product is to the person herself, the more reluctant is the consumer to change to a competing product. That explains why most people use the same toothpaste, same make-up, same aftershave, same deodorant, etc., their entire adult lives.

   Except during recessions, patients show little pricing sensitivity. If what the dentist proposes will make them look good, they are for it.

The four shareholders also owned the building in which the lab was situated. They paid their real estate partnership rent that was about twice market. They also paid themselves well and made it a point to take nice vacations to attend professional conferences in exotic locations. Still, before normalization, profits were very high. (The rationale for normalizing, but with *no* discount for lack of control, is discussed in 4 below.) (SPARC)

3. The SIC code for dental labs is 8072; major group 80 in the SIC scheme is "health services." At the time of this valuation, there was exactly one publicly held dental lab company, a roll-up called National Dentex Corporation (NADX). If I was going to do guideline public company (GPC) analysis—which I thought the judge in question would understand more easily than DCF—I thought I needed more than one GPC.

   I did what most of us do: I first tried moving up the SIC code chain from 8072 and then down. That did not help. The first rung up was 8082 ("home health care services"), clearly a nonstarter, and the one after that was 8092 ("kidney dialysis centers"). Going down was 8069 ("specialty hospitals, except psychiatric"), followed by 8063 ("psychiatric hospitals"). I was left scratching my head.

   Late one night I thought of the first "factor to consider" in Revenue Ruling 59-60: "the nature of the business and its history since inception." What *was* the nature of this business? Sure, it was allied with healthcare, but what *technology* did it use to convert inputs into outputs? It was a manufacturing business, despite the 8072 SIC code. (The NAICS scheme remedied this anomaly.) And it was make-to-order, not make-to-stock, so it had no risk of obsolete inventory.

   The word "prosthesis" popped into my head. I grabbed my *American Heritage Dictionary of the English Language* and looked it up. Voila! "Dental crown or bridge" was the first example of a prosthesis.

   It was a short hop from there to prosthetics manufacturing (SIC 3842). I found dozens of public companies in SIC 3842 and size-adjusted their multiples, size-adjusted their multiples. My GPC analysis was off to the races. (No SPARC)

4. This dental lab was well-run. The four principals even conducted quarterly board meetings, usually to play poker and golf together a couple of hundred miles out of town. The minutes of their board meetings showed that, in the almost 20 years since they had started the company, there had not been a "No" vote cast on any issue, not even one. To me, that was evidence that the 25% holding of the propertied spouse enjoyed all of the rights and benefits of control

ownership. Therefore, I made normalizing adjustments for compensation and excess rent but took no discount for lack of control. It stood up in court, and the propertied spouse did not appeal. (SPARC)

SPARC Elements

Architecture

Culture

V-M Solution.   The principals were dumbfounded—and not happy—that my argument prevailed. It helped that the other appraiser was a tax guy who had done few valuations. My client's attorney was on him like hair on a bear. The fact is, this particular company was doing so many things right—it was large by industry standards, it was hugely profitable, and it had fine governance. It treated its people right, and employee turnover was low.

Postscript.   A few years later, one of the other principals decided he wanted a divorce. Although I was too busy to take the engagement, I heard later that the board minutes showed quite a few tie votes and even some comments about one or two members being irate on occasion. Those guys had learned their lesson about "the rights and benefits of control ownership."

Quick-Lube Services

Overview.   In 1995 I got a call from a CPA in Ohio who had attended a short course I had taught on valuation a few weeks before. He was having trouble understanding a new valuation client. It was in the quick-lube/ quick-oil-change business. Its narrow focus on two services delivered value by saving drivers' time. In return, customers paid a higher price than they would have to pay elsewhere. The client company had seven stores and had pulled in $2.8 million in revenue in 1994. After getting the client's permission, the accountant e-mailed me the financial statements of his client.

Metrics

1. Inferred four-firm concentration ratio was 90.
2. Pretax profit margin was 47.5%.
3. Higher price point than competitors.

Interviewees.   Outside accountant, company owner.

V-M Findings

1. ZapData (www.zapdata.com) did not exist in those days. Its predecessor, D&B MarketPlace did, however. I had data for over 10 million businesses on a CD-ROM. After some careful sorting, I found that, under SIC 7549 ("Automotive Services, Except Repair and Carwashes") in the metropolitan area where the client company had its 7 stores, there were 37 establishments dedicated primarily to quick-lube. Thirty-three of them had one of four names, including the client company's; the firm whose name showed up most often had 10 stores. Using the kind of leap of faith that is standard in valuation practice, I inferred a four-firm concentration ratio of 90. This domain had the makings of an airtight oligopoly. (No SPARC elements here)

2. At the Web site of the American Society of Association Executives (www.asaecenter.org), I found the Automotive Oil Change Association (www.aoca.org). I called and asked if they ever gathered financial information from their members and published composites. They said that they did and that they had just published their annual survey. I offered to buy the results, but they said they would overnight them to me. When they arrived, I compared certain of the client company's financial metrics with industry figures, looking for disparities. The one that really caught my eye was "Pretax Income as a % of Sales." The industry average was 8%. Obviously the client was doing some things differently. I asked the accountant to set up a conference call with him, the owner, and me on the phone. (SPARC)

3. The conference call began, and I asked the owner a few easy questions. I wanted to try to make him comfortable with someone he'd never met face to face and probably never would. After those softball queries, I picked up the pace and began throwing high, hard ones. He hung in there.

   I asked him why, in an industry where the pretax profit margin is 8%, his seven companies hit almost 48%. He had a pithy answer: "I take care of my people." I said, "I'll bet." We both laughed, and I asked, "Could you tell me a little more about that, please?"

   He warmed to telling stories about his business. He began with one about a consulting guy who dropped in to see him one day and managed to sell him on the idea of a customer satisfaction survey. The consultant designed a short but sophisticated survey that could be analyzed using multiple regression analysis. He also suggested that the survey be printed on a chartreuse- colored postcard so that customers would remember to mail it in. The return address was to a

Post Office Box that only the owner could access. Every customer whose car got a lube job or oil change was given a prenumbered card when they paid their bill. There was also a drawing from the numbers of the returned cards each quarter, and the winner got a weekend for two at a resort on Lake Michigan.

The owner used the survey results to motivate his seven store managers. Each one had to hit an overall satisfaction level of at least 6 on a scale of 1 to 7, or they were put on probation and given 90 days to get to 6. I then asked how much he paid the managers. "About $90,000 a year," he said.

I replied, "Phi Beta Kappas, are they?" He chuckled and said, "Nope, four of the seven are high school drop-outs." I said, "I'll bet you have low turnover among your managers." He laughed again and said, "Figured that out, did you? My most junior guy has been running a store for almost five years." "Wow," I said.

I then asked, "Besides holding your managers' feet to the fire where customer satisfaction is concerned, do you do anything else to either keep customers coming back or bring in new ones?" He allowed as how he had created a "frequent changer" program whereby after nine oil changes, the tenth one was free. After a couple of years, revenues at each store had increased by more than 25% accompanied by a 14% increase in the number of customers and about a 10% increase in prices.

The owner then volunteered that the consultant who had sold him the customer-satisfaction survey later suggested collecting customers' mailing addresses and odometer readings when they came in for service. He pointed out that automobile manufacturers no longer recommended an oil change every 3,000 miles (5,000 km). Most manufacturers now suggested an oil change every 5,000 miles (about 8,000 km). Some were even suggesting that every 7,500 miles (< 12,000 km) would be fine. The consultant rightly pointed out the impact that those recommendations could have on demand for oil-change services with the attendant effect on quick-lube services because the two were complements. The consultant then set up a spreadsheet template where data could be entered by customer number, date of service, and odometer reading. Using time-series analysis, the consultant helped the company see how to gauge when each car would have been driven about 3,000 miles. It didn't take a rocket scientist to figure out if customers came in every 3,000 miles, rather than every 5,000 or 7,500, revenues would go up. The company began sending out postcards when the 3,000-mile tripwire was approaching for each customer.

This same consultant asked the owner for access to financial data about each store. The owner agreed, and the consultant then asked to see daily sales figures by store. He looked at the numbers and asked, "Why are sales on Monday so much lower than the other days of the week?" The owner said he had wondered the same thing, but had no idea why.

The consultant suggested an experiment at two stores: sending out hot-pink postcards every Friday to customers whose cars should be approaching 3,000 miles since their last oil change and tell them that these two stores would stay open until 10 o'clock Monday nights. Now all seven stores are open until 10 on Monday, which became the biggest-grossing day of the week for the company. (Keeping them open until 10 p.m. on other nights of the week had no impact.)

Near the end of the interview, I asked the owner, "How do you increase market share—by cutting your prices?" (Remember the Five Rules of the Oligopolist in Good Standing.) The guy almost shouted at me through the phone when he replied, "Cut my price? Are you KIDDING? This is a small market. Word travels fast. If I cut my prices, everyone else would cut theirs, and we'd all be worse off. Why on earth would I do something THAT stupid?"

"You're right," I said. "Isn't it amazing that the airlines don't understand that?" We both had a good laugh, and the conversation soon ended.

I don't know if the guy knew what an oligopoly was or not, and I was not going to risk embarrassing him by asking. But he understood the market structure in which his company competed. He understood that price was not the way to fly. Compete on features, and motivate managers. Be different, but be different in ways other than price. (**SPARC**)

SPARC Elements

Strategy
People
Architecture
Routines
Culture

V-M Solution.   This owner did not need a value map!

Postscript.   The conversation shown here is a great example of the kind of Socratic process I have spoken about. One has to listen carefully, try to infer not only what is being said but what isn't, and then proceed with the next question. Incidentally, this owner now has 15 stores and is the leader in his market. His rivals can replicate every aspect of his business except one: the store managers. I would be surprised if the owner was not now focusing on hiring people without high school diplomas because he knows how to develop and retain them. Now THERE'S an example of `causal ambiguity.' How'd you like to quantify *that* intangible in an ASC 805 allocation of purchase price?!

PART IV

PRACTICE MANAGEMENT

CHAPTER

18

The Engagement Process

More than in most valuation-related engagements, practice management in value-enhancement services is crucial. It is essential to manage the client's expectations throughout the process. This applies in traditional valuation work, too, but it is the *sine qua non* of a successful value-mapping engagement.

In this chapter we deal with the engagement process from start to finish. We approach this process differently from many of our colleagues. More than other engagements, value-mapping work is collaborative. It requires the client company's active participation and buy-in. It is important to set the collaborative tone early. The process that we have developed does that.

When Can an Engagement Include a Value Map?

The short answer to this question is "Anytime there is no 'opposing counsel.'" The ideal situation for a value-map engagement is when an owner is several years away from an expected exit. That is because a business, like a house, requires fix-up expenses to get it ready to go to market. Those outlays are about the same, relatively speaking, for the business as they are for a decently maintained home. For the business, the time horizon is longer, and the outcome is less certain, especially in these volatile economic times.

An unfolding ownership transition is not the only time for a value map. It is a great tool for high-growth companies. It is superb for business planning. It can easily be part of value-based management (VBM).[1] And it is a nice tool for business owners and senior managers looking to increase the value of their businesses.

---

[1] VBM is a management approach that relies on maximizing shareholder value to create incentives for managers and owners. It has three components: value creation, value management, and value measurement. The best-known book on the subject is probably S. David Young and Stephen F. O'Byrne, *EVA and Value-Based Management: A Practical Guide to Implementation* (New York: McGraw-Hill, 2000).

We have also found it to be a great add-on for tax-related valuation work. In estate tax situations, for instance, heirs to a business might not know much about it. Rather than run it or hire someone to run it for them, they might want to cash out in a year or two. An owner's daughter or son who is the recipient of gifted equity can also learn much from an engagement that includes a value map.

Moreover, the value map is a natural extension of the knowledge that a capable and thorough professional can acquire in a traditional, nonadversarial engagement. The map works best for SMEs because it sees risk reduction as a primary tool for increasing value. SMEs are also easier client companies with which to work to effect widespread change. The intimacy of most SMEs makes political resistance to a value map much easier to overcome . . . assuming that the owner or CEO is not a conflict-avoider.

Finding Good Clients

Finding viable candidates for value maps is not difficult. The challenge is to find open-minded owners and managers. People like the cofounder of Military Gizmos, Inc. (see Chapter 11) are not what you're looking for. Big egos do not do well in this process. In fact, they often sabotage it, either overtly or indirectly. We seek thoughtful owners and managers with a tolerance for deferred gratification, the patience to deal with nuance, and an ability to keep their eye on the long-term ball, which is often a liquidity event involving the lion's share of their net worth.

Most owners of smaller businesses are usually too busy hanging on for dear life to try to focus on a longer-term process of value creation. A client company that has a majority or control owner is usually a better candidate than one with no one in control because control owners do not need to build a political coalition to achieve commitment to a process that can be wrenching and difficult for some participants. It is not that we are big fans of benign dictators. But they can get things done faster than those who have to massage personalities to build consensus.

We have also found that clients in lower-tech businesses are easier to work with and are more receptive to the demands that value enhancement places on participants. Consultants often ignore such businesses because they are not exciting enough or sexy enough for them. That works for us.

Good referral sources for these kinds of engagements include business lawyers and high-end insurance agents. We are particularly enamored of those associated with Northwestern Mutual Life, Mass Mutual, and New York Life. Good tax and estate lawyers can also be good sources. CPAs are a natural referral source for those of us in the valuation community who are ourselves CPAs.

Avoiding Problem Clients

We believe that there are some clients we cannot afford to have. In a business as personalized as ours, bad clients do not just ruin our day. They ruin our lives for a while. When we spot those clients during our own due diligence on them, we jack our prices into the stratosphere. Who says one price has to fit all?

We practice price discrimination in our business. High-maintenance clients, unreliable clients, deadbeat clients, and client companies in the middle of or facing a turnaround are not our value-map cup of tea. We want our closest competitors to have those clients, and we use price to get them there. It works.

Of course, we do have an occasional hiccup. One such occurred in the mid-1990s. We had a potential client referred to us by a trusted colleague. After several difficult telephone conversations, we went to see the prospective client one Saturday morning. Our face time reconfirmed our phone impressions of him. By prior agreement with Dorothy, I responded, when the prospective client asked me the price for the engagement, with a figure that was three times our usual fee. The guy said, "Great," and wrote us a check for the whole thing on the spot. I felt like someone who had a cash offer the first day her house was on the market.

Then there is the other extreme. An extremely good referral source sent us a prospective client in another town here in the Shenandoah Valley. The guy owned a couple of small convenience stores. He didn't know that I know a lot about C-stores. Dorothy usually goes with me on first meetings with prospective clients, but she had other commitments this particular day, so I went by myself.

He was one of those guys that even I knew instantly was pure trouble. I shook his hand and immediately wished I carried Lysol with me. He showed me his financial statements. Sure enough, gross margin was about 10 percentage points too low. To be sure, a high volume of gasoline sales relative to non–gas revenues will compress gross margins. But not down where this guy's were.

Then he started talking about all the real estate he owned that he had paid cash for. I nodded. In a cash business, figuring that one out wasn't rocket science. No need to get preachy about this stuff, though. I just raised the price.

The corker came when he did a rant about "all the crooks in the government" and about what an outrage big federal deficits are—this from a guy actively contributing to the level of those deficits. Well, to paraphrase Waldo Emerson: A foolish consistency really is the hobgoblin of small minds. But that one was too much, even for me.

When I got back to the office, Dorothy and I talked about it. We agreed that life was too short to deal with this guy. I called him back the next day and told him that we could appraise his convenience stores but that it was "probably going to cost a little more than [he was] expecting." I said that we had a lot of work in the house just then and that a slug of it was from repeat clients to whom we had committed firm deadlines. I noted that he wanted his appraisal done on a short timeline that was going to require us to push some of our long-standing clients back in the queue. I said that doing so would put us at risk of losing them and that, therefore, he needed to bear the risk of that happening.

He asked, "How much?"

"Forty-five thousand dollars," I said. This was in 1999.

There was silence at the other end of the phone. I suspect his face was as white as a sheet. I waited.

Finally, he sputtered, "I can't afford that!"

I thought, "Sell some real estate, dude." But I said, "I understand."

He then asked, "Do you know anyone else who does this work?"

"But of course," I said, and referred him to a guy up the road who fancies himself as a competitor of ours.

I didn't hear anything more and figured that all was well. We hadn't embarrassed our referral source, but we had ducked a bullet of sorts. The source continued sending work our way.

Six months later I was back in Las Vegas to attend the annual valuation conference of the American Institute of CPAs. I spotted the guy to whom I had referred the crazy client. Even though his face was about as long as the Mississippi River, I greeted him like a long-lost cousin and asked how he was doing.

"Oh, man, you wouldn't believe what I'm up against. I have the client from hell."

"Really?" I said.

"Yeah. You know anything about convenience stores?"

Marketing and Selling the Work

The work is actually quite easy to sell, once we find a business owner or manager who fits the "success profile." The perfect situation is when a point estimate of value is unnecessary, perhaps in a buy-sell negotiation between the existing owner and a minority holder buying in. We then combine a "calculations engagement" with the value map add-on. We confine the calculations side of the work to guideline public companies only and offer two deliverables: (1) a memorandum of five to ten single-spaced pages (plus exhibits) with a range estimate of value, and (2) a value map document. The primary focus of the value map is reducing risk to increase value.

We explain to the business owner that she is not paying for a big, thick valuation report mostly written from scratch because her business doesn't need that. Something short with limited scope will do the job just fine. We also say that the value map phase of the engagement is what she's paying most of the fee for, but that it is a document that will make her more money it costs her. If she seems doubtful, we guarantee the economics by including a money-back provision if she's not happy with the outcome. We have never had to give any money back.

The work almost sells itself. Get a 50% retainer up front and the balance when you produce a draft of your second deliverable, the value map. If you have extended a satisfaction guarantee and have *any* concern that you might not be paid, password the draft of the second deliverable so that it can be neither printed nor forwarded.

The "Shake-'n'-Howdy" Visit

We believe in sizing up a potential new client. We think that is best done in person. So, before we draw up an engagement letter (which is a nontrivial undertaking in our shop, as you will see later in this chapter), we like to look people in the eye.

We do enough due diligence to reassure ourselves that we are not confirming a reservation on the *Titanic*. That makes a pre–engagement letter visit to the business mandatory, just to get a feel for the place. By the time we show up for that first visit, which we keep to less than an hour, we have our standard ND&I (nondisclosure and indemnification) agreement in place. We will have received recent financial information, identified the outside CPA, clicked through the Web site, gotten a headcount, looked at an organization chart, noted the distribution of ownership, and so on. Basic stuff.

We will have also identified potential competitors through www .Zapdata.com; that enables us to get a first read on industry structure. One of our favorite questions in this get-acquainted visit is "How does your company compete?" If Zapdata tells us that headcount suggests the presence of an oligopoly, and the top gun answers our question with "We kill 'em on price," well, we just learned something really important.

On that initial visit we also take the measure of the lead financial person. As a former controller and ex-CFO myself, I can do that very quickly. When I walked into a CFO's office several years ago, the first thing I spotted was an adding machine with about ten feet of used tape cascading to the floor. With a smile and a wink, I said, "Does the Smithsonian know you have that?" He grinned and said, "Not yet." That was a leading indicator. It turned out later that the outside auditors had retired on the client's payroll, revenues per full-time employee were less than half the domain average, and allowance for doubtful accounts was $4.8 million, not $300,000.

Pricing the Engagement

For smaller companies (revenues ≤ $3 million), the price range in 2010 for one of these calculations-with-value-map engagements is $20,000 to $25,000. That range has risen briskly in the last few years. As the size of the firm increases, so does the price. Do enough due diligence to get an idea of what you are getting yourself into where the value map is concerned. If problems seem to pop up everywhere you look during that pre-engagement visit, raise your price enough to make you feel comfortable with what you are committing to.

Make sure you discuss the price with the owner or president *before* you start working on the engagement letter. This conversation is best done in person so you can look the person in the eye. Be sure to mention the 50% up-front retainer. If the prospect hesitates, poke around a little. You have to find out whether the retainer is the problem. If it is, that is usually, but not always, a bad sign. Our experience is that if a client cannot pay the retainer, our problems are just starting. It is usually better to back away from the engagement entirely. We don't mind working pro bono, but we want to know from the beginning that it's pro bono.

There is an occasional exception, though. For instance, a smaller company that is growing rapidly might find it hard to pay $10,000 to $12,000 in one pop. In that instance, you can space the payment for the *entire* engagement out over several months. Just make sure that you don't have more work in the job than you have been paid for. And include a provision in your engagement letter that permits you to stop working until or unless the client is current on what is due.

We send *all* of our invoices in Adobe PDF, and our engagement letter is explicit on that point. If a file transfer is problematic, chances are that a lot of other things will be, too. Take a closer look at the client.

Do not be so eager to get the work that you put a bunch of time into it without getting the retainer. That might sound as if I'm talking out of both sides of my mouth, but I'm not. Yes, you have to invest some hours in due diligence. You might end up not being paid for those. We believe that is better than getting a client that we wish we had steered elsewhere. Even if you do the requisite due diligence and conclude that you do want the client, don't get ahead of yourself. Don't start the heavy lifting until the retainer check has cleared.

Engagement Letter 1

This is likely the first of two or perhaps more engagement letters with this client. Make sure you get it right. Our standard engagement letter runs to about 13 pages, including three single-spaced pages listing information we need. As always, we manage the client's expectations. We are careful to inform the owner or CEO that the engagement letter "will be lengthy." We apologize for that, and then we blame the lawyers. Small businesses understand the burden that the legal profession imposes on them.

Our engagement letter has evolved over nearly two decades. We heard early on of valuation firms that routinely had to sue to get their money. We heard of others that got stiffed and did not sue. Our belief—which experience has confirmed repeatedly—is that those who have collection problems are not selling the work properly. There are three key aspects of that:

1. **A no-nonsense, soup-to-nuts engagement letter.** This is a serious legal document, not frou-frou. It is a contract. If you ever have to enforce it in court, you want to be sure you are bulletproof. Therefore, make sure that a good business attorney (or two) has vetted your engagement letter. That is cheap money compared to not being able to collect. Our engagement letter leaves nothing to chance. Nothing. And that's how we want it—no ambiguity, no winks, no wiggle room.
2. **Being up front with the client about the fee and the work to be done.** I remember the first time I asked for a retainer. I could hardly get the words out of my mouth. If the fee is hefty, rehearse how you will break the news to the client. Above all, look the client in the eye when you price the engagement. Before you get to price, of course, you will have spent a significant amount of time explaining the process to the client. Be sure to talk about the deliverables, especially the value map, and the benefits thereof. But do *not* disclose any of the specific content of the value map, even if you know what some of it is, which you probably will, or else you will risk not getting retained.
3. **Managing the client's expectations.** I know I sound like a broken record here, but I cannot emphasize this point strongly enough. If you run into problems later, tell the client immediately, and explain why. Most companies understand that things happen (e.g., sick spouse, ailing parent, etc.). They will not have a problem with that unless they perceive that you are being less than forthcoming.

We are not risk-averse, but we are also not reckless. We do not knowingly set ourselves up now to be a party to litigation later. We believe our engagement letter is airtight. We take the fact that we have had to write-off almost nothing over the past 19 years as market affirmation of our engagement letter. It contains these major sections:

- Purpose(s)
- Standard of value
- Premise of value
- Term
- Expertising
- Deliverables
- Use of deliverables
- No disclosure or right of reproduction
- Fee and retainer
- Out-of-pocket expenses
- Access
- Our responsibilities
- Client responsibilities
- Confidentiality and nondisclosure
- Use of third-party personnel
- Other appraisers
- Contingent and limiting conditions
- Privacy policy
- Death or physical impairment
- Management representation letter
- Conflicts
- Entire agreement
- Signature
- Document request list

We have the phrase "INCOMPLETE AGREEMENT—FOR DISCUSSION PURPOSES ONLY" plastered all over this document—in the watermark and in the headers. After all, this is a collaborative undertaking. We cement buy-in by inviting the engagement letter's signer(s)' to suggest modifications to it and ask questions about it. We emphasize that there are no dumb questions. We have never had to make any substantive changes.

Highlights of Engagement Letter 1

Because the length of our engagement letter can be intimidating, we prepare a one-page (and no more) "Highlights" document that details the salient aspects of the letter. We do not include every section, especially those that are boilerplate, but we do bring out the ones that strike us as really important. Everything about the fee is in there.

Rather than mess around with receipts for out-of-pocket expenses, we now just add 5% to our fee. That covers everything, including domestic travel, except for lodging for more than two nights. The 5% also helps us reclaim some of the overhead expenses that serious valuation professionals must absorb every year. All those subscriptions, association memberships, books, continuing professional education credits, and software run into real money real fast. Not a single client has complained about the 5%. We know of several other firms that do the same thing. None of them has gotten any pushback, either. Clients like the fact that we print and bind our reports in-house using solid-ink technology on 28-pound paper that is printed duplex and shipped for next-day delivery.

In the introductory paragraph of the "Highlights" document, we request that the client ask questions and feel free to suggest changes to the engagement letter. We reiterate that this is a collaborative undertaking, and we want things to feel right as well as be right.

The one-page "Highlights" note is bulleted with bold titles that coincide with those used in the "INCOMPLETE AGREEMENT" itself. We also include the page number(s) after each bold title. We close by stipulating that the "Highlights" document doesn't address every section of the draft, but it does cover what we believe are the most important features. If necessary, we use a smaller font, narrower margins, and less space between paragraphs in order to squeeze it on to a single page.

We do not let this draft-with-highlights phase remain dormant for more than 48 hours. As those reading this book can attest, pre-engagement dynamics tend to develop their own momentum. A draft engagement letter is a proposal of temporary marriage, and we do not want it to fester. If we do not hear back from the client within a couple of days, we call. We keep it light, but we do offer to try to resolve any questions the engagement letter might have raised. Again, though—and this is the important point here—we do not invest the time in preparing an engagement letter until the client company has agreed conceptually, including the fee, to "the deal." This is part of our overarching goal of avoiding surprises in the engagement. This work is tough enough without having to deal with such disruption.

Managing Expectations

It probably seems as if I have pounded my spoon on my highchair for long enough about this managing-expectations thing, but I think it bears both repeating and elaboration. It is just so crucial, and I have seen firsthand what happens when the client's expectations are *not* managed the way they should be. It is not pretty.

We maintain continual contact with the owner or CEO throughout the engagement. We often do so through her personal e-mail address. That relieves us of the need to worry about "prying eyes and inquiring minds." We can speak freely, and so can the owner/CEO.

Whenever we come across something that is even faintly negative, we pursue it until we are confident that what we are seeing is reality. At that point, we bring it up to the lead person. We do so casually and without being alarmist. If we can prod the owner into committing to biweekly phone calls just "for updates," that works best. Sometimes, however, and for whatever reasons, it is just not doable that way.

We do make it a point to take the owner/CEO and spouse out for supper about halfway through. Sometimes they will come to our home. If the couple cannot come here, we go there. We do like to see the inside of a client's residence because it tells us so much that either we didn't know or suspected but couldn't really be sure about.

That is not a negative, of course. We like to see books, furniture, and how clients live. It just helps us understand them better and deal with them more easily. Funny things happen sometimes.

In the late 1990s, for instance, a really weird thing happened when I was talking one morning to the second-generation owner of a sizable company in Virginia. When I say weird, I mean off-the-charts weird. You read about it in the vignette about the construction company that led off Chapter 13—you know, the industrial- strength conflict-avoider. As I tried to recover and gather my wits about me after that strange incident, I remembered that I was slated to go to his house for supper that night with him and his wife. Knowing that she has power over him that I can only dream of, I decided to wait until then to take on what he'd done.

Sure enough, after supper that night, I looked at him and said, "You know something? The next time you play your favorite little game— that would be 'Let's You and Him Fight'—things are going to get ugly fast."

He looked at me with a funny look on his face and said, "I did do that, didn't I?"

"Yes, sir, you did," I said.

"Did what? Did what?" his wife asked.

That was the opening I was looking for, and I grabbed it. I told her the whole gory story. I figured she'd grab him by the stacking swivel and read him the riot act.

She listened to me intently. When I was done, she snapped, "That's nothing, nothing at all. He's been doing that same thing in this marriage for 27 years!"

I stared at her in disbelief. Then I leaned forward, made a "T" (for time-out) with my hands, and said, "Whoa, Michelle. Kings' X. (*pause*) Marriage counseling is extra." The three of us erupted in laughter.

Nothing changed with him, then or since. He is still the greatest conflict-avoider I have ever met. However, I did stumble on someone in 2008 who could give him a real run for his money, unfortunately. I picked up on the conflict-avoidance early on and did double the price, but we got the work anyway. Drat. Sold too cheaply again.

Ours is an intimate business. We get close to our clients. They have invited us to bat mitzvahs, weddings, and funerals. We go. The relationships often endure long after the work is done. They may call us just to chat, and we might call them. We find that we can laugh about things that were not very funny when they happened. I find such conversations very affirming.

Engagement Letter 2

If a future exit event gave rise to the initial engagement and that project goes well, you will probably have an opportunity for a second one. It is unlikely that a company can execute the steps in a value map on its own. It needs an outsider—you, probably—to get it done. The details of the engagement to which you and the company then agree will depend on whether the exit event is the ultimate indicator of success or not.

If it is and you have risk tolerance, why not do it on a contingency basis the way investment bankers do? In 2008 we set up an affiliate, Beckmill Capital, LLC, to do just that. The purposes of the affiliate are capital raises (debt or equity), ownership transitions, and mergers and acquisitions; it is *not* a business broker because it does far more, and does it discreetly, than the typical business broker: It oversees for the client the fix-up work to be done before it takes the company to market, if that is the goal.

Even working on a contingency, you should get a nonrefundable retainer up front—something in the $25,000 to $50,000 range. That retainer is deductible from your share of the proceeds from whatever liquidity event the purpose of the engagement specifies. If the business does not raise the desired capital or change hands, as the engagement letter calls for, then you keep the retainer. That sounds better than it is because you will have far more time and out-of-pocket expenses invested in the engagement than any retainer can cover, and if not performing on the overarching purpose of the engagement becomes a pattern, then you won't have clients.

Be careful about how you draw the engagement letter. You *must* have complete control over how information is handled and dispensed. The saying in the U.S. Navy during wartime is "Loose lips sink ships." That applies in these kinds of engagements, too. For instance, the owner of Capital's first client company was a guy who had a hard time keeping his mouth shut. He thought everyone was his bosom pal. Worse, some of his "best buddies" were not the kind of people that I like. Each one I met struck me as a slippery quick-buck artist. I repeatedly told him that every time he opened his mouth and talked about his business with one of them, it cost him money. He said he would keep quiet, but he didn't. The gentleman was the ultimate case of insecurity. When he decided that we should part company, I learned a good lesson, but I doubt that he did.

In any event, it is likely that the sale or ownership transition will occur over a period of years. We are working right now with a client company whose owner has sold a minority slice of his company to one of his employees. We expect that there will be two more tranches. One will bring the employee up to just short of 1/3 ownership—Virginia is one of the 30-odd "supermajority" states in the United States. The last transaction will take the control owner out completely. It will be a lengthy process.

In the meantime, the (now) two shareholders and I are doing heavy lifting to increase the value of the firm. Among other options, we have considered small acquisitions that will pole-vault the firm into a related business activity that could complement its primary line of business to generate additional spill-off revenue for its primary line of business.

We have also worked with this client company to form a council of advisors. We identified particular skills and experience that the company needed—industrial (B2B) marketing, ownership transition experience, and skills opening ancillary locations for an existing business—and then recruited three guys with those skills and experience. I'm the ex-officio member who takes the notes and occasionally participates. The council meets quarterly. It follows an agenda to which everyone can contribute. One of the members is helping it move into a market segment—public utilities—that should be lucrative. That will reduce the firm's dependence on the building and housing cycle. Connecting with utilities during the federal stimulus spending should also be helpful.

There are many different ways that this phase of the relationship can work. It all depends on the dynamics between you and the client company as well as on what its ultimate objectives are. However it works out, plan on doing a lot of work over an extended period, perhaps several years. It is a nontrivial commitment for both you and the client company. If yours is a small firm, expect such an engagement to play a dominant role in your professional life for quite a while.

Summary

As noted several times in this book, managing clients' expectations is essential in valuation and value map projects. So much is, or will be, at stake. And, since we are seldom working with repeat clients, there is a learning curve of familiarity that happens quite quickly. That is why Dorothy and I are both involved at the beginning, and that is why we also spend personal non-business time with the owner(s) and spouse(s). We want to get to know them as people, too. That enables us to predict more accurately what they are likely to do in a given situation. That, in turn, helps us do a better job of helping them.

To recapitulate, we believe that there are clients we cannot afford to have. Bigger shops with more slack resources than we have might see that one otherwise. But, believing as we do, we conduct a fair amount of due diligence with a prospective new client. To the extent that a client has been referred to us by someone we know and trust, we can be a little more relaxed about due diligence. But we still want to look the person in the eye before we invest time in an engagement letter. Maybe it's a down-South thing, and maybe it sounds hopelessly old-fashioned, but we like that initial shake-'n'-howdy. It has saved us a lot of grief. This work is tough enough. Why make it harder by having to worry if the guy who signed the engagement letter and paid us a hefty retainer is telling us the truth or not?

We believe that more-difficult clients should pay more. On more than one occasion, I have picked up the phone and called the referral source to ensure that I was reading the referred client accurately. Such conversations can be highly illuminating.

Whenever we can, we combine a range estimate of value with a value map deliverable. The work is easy to sell. On occasion, we have offered a money-back guarantee, but we never have had to make good on it. Such a guarantee works only if we (and you) are dealing with an honest and forthright client. Anything less is stressful and miserable. Raise your price, refer them to a close competitor, and be glad you dodged a bullet.

Whenever practicable, we do a short, informal shake-'n'-howdy visit before we ever quote a fee or draft an engagement letter. We want to visit the prospective client company and get a sense of its people and their work environments. It takes time, but it works. We think that several hours of non-chargeable due diligence time is a small price to pay to get a sense of whether we are dealing with a person of honor and integrity.

A key aspect of managing clients' expectations is no surprise, including the period before they become clients. That goes in spades for the fee. We do not commit the time to drafting an engagement letter until we have a handshake deal on the fee and the deliverables. When we do draft it, clients find our one-page-only "Highlights" memo very helpful. Later, if we do our job right yet a client does get surprised, we had better end up flabbergasted ourselves. That transparency builds trust and helps keep the playing field level. It also makes for fewer problems, easier collections, more work, and more-interesting work.

19

Working with Clients

Value maps require close and intimate engagement with senior management, and sometimes with others as well, to get the job done. The good news is that the valuation process that preceded it gave at least the key players enough confidence in you, your judgment, and your knowledge that they wanted you to stay for a while. In a one-off business like valuation, it is nice to have an ongoing relationship or two. Or three. Or. . . .

But what is that relationship about? How is it structured? How does it work? And, since you have no real authority—unless the client gives it to you (get it in writing!)—what happens if you and they get crossways? What then? We will try to answer these and many more questions in this chapter. But you should realize going in that, by virtue of the fact that you are there, you have a lot going for you, and the odds are that you will be successful. And if you are, your client company will be, too.

A Few Words about Family Systems

Is the leadership of your client company committed to the stated end result of the value-mapping process? If you have a first-generation owner who says that she wants to sell out, look out. All of us in that boat, myself included, will be on an emotional roller coaster when it comes to selling what we have created and lived with every day for years.

For us, the firm is the kid that never left home. It is always there, tugging at our sleeve, demanding attention, wanting help. The emotional bond that adheres like Super Glue. And breaking that bond is like sawing off a limb without anesthesia: It hurts like hell. How do we mostly left-brainers prepare ourselves to deal with that?

Reading helps. If you are dealing with a family business but you have never heard of "family systems," you are missing essential information and knowledge. Let me illustrate.

In 1996 Dorothy and I attended the annual conference of the Family Firm Institute (www.ffi.org). It convened in Scottsdale, Arizona. I expected to see three groups of professionals there: (1) academics, (2) business owners, and (3) consultants like me. All three "ABC" cohorts were well represented. But we were outnumbered—dwarfed, if you will—by a fourth group: therapists. They owned the place. I was dumbfounded. Then, as I thought about it, it made sense. After all, if the American family unit is under some stress, as we have all read that it is, then can many, if not most, American family businesses be far behind? Or do crazies off the job change their spots on the way to work?

Nope.

Now, I am no armchair therapist, and I do not practice psychiatry without a license. But that 1996 conference taught me that I had better get my arms around some decent and workable psychology constructs if I intended to give sound business advice to owners and officers of family enterprises.

Until then, I had just assumed that when the behaviors of owners left me scratching my head, it did not matter much. After all, I thought, people are people, valuation is valuation, and ne'er the twain shall meet. I learned at that conference that I was dead wrong. I needed to try to understand those behaviors because not understanding them meant that there was more than a small chance that whatever counsel I gave would be wrong and could even make a bad situation worse.

I was not impeded by any courses in psychology during my long and undistinguished undergraduate career. I have since concluded that the vast majority of psychology majors and graduates I have met are less concerned about trying to understand others than they are about trying to understand themselves. So I turned to my cousin's wife, who was then a highly successful family systems therapist in California. At the time, I had no idea what "family systems" was. We spent some time on the phone talking about that construct, and then she recommended some reading, which I promptly undertook. It has made a big difference in the quality of our work.

We do not have the space here for a lengthy discussion of family systems. Let me just give a short synopsis: Its underlying premise is that, you guessed it, a family *is* a system of related individuals. Systems seek equilibrium, and families are no exception. So if, for instance, the family system is tilted steeply by the behaviors of one individual—an alcoholic, for instance—one or more units of that system will engage in behaviors that keep the system in balance. That explains why some long-suffering spouses of alcoholics dash to the liquor store to get the newly sober former drunk a bottle of his favorite hooch. The spouse just could not stand the shock to the system that her mate's new sobriety delivered. She hated the craziness of his drinking, but she hated the change more. I guess it's a case of better the devil we know. . . . I believe that a basic grasp of family systems will enhance the results of any valuation engagement, value added or not. If you want to do better valuations and understand phenomena that might otherwise be baffling, check out family systems. It is powerful stuff.[1]

Equally powerful is commitment on the parts of (a) the spouse of the owner or lead dog and (b) key senior managers. When push comes to shove, though, (a) usually steamrollers (b). Make sure that the spouse is on board. And do not take the lead dog's word for it. Take the two of them to supper, and make your own judgment.

Processes

Luckily for many readers, value mapping is a process. Those of us who are successful in valuation understand what I mean because we must follow *and trust* the valuation process. We know it works because each of us has made changes and tweaks to our own processes to enhance our trust and our fidelity to them.

As processes go, value mapping is valuation on steroids. Implementing a value map takes longer than doing a valuation. It is usually a couple of years rather than a couple of months. It is demanding, and it is difficult. In fact, as the work goes, it is at least as intellectually challenging as valuation for financial reporting (VfFR). That might help those who do VfFR get an idea of the nature of this process But I can also tell you firsthand: Value mapping is *the* most satisfying and gratifying work we do . . . and the most profitable.

The key to success in value mapping is commitment to the process, whether its ultimate goal is sale to an external buyer, an internal ownership transition, performance enhancement, or value-based management.[2] It is a rigorous, demanding process—*process*. Without the requisite commitment on both sides, it is unlikely to succeed. With it, it is unlikely to fail.

How Not to Do It

We learned about lack of commitment the hard way a while back. Our first clue should have been that the 100% shareholder was married and divorced three times. The second should have been that he was not on speaking terms with his two daughters . . . and their children—his grandchildren. So this guy, who had life-threatening health issues, was exactly the kind of owner with whom we should not have worked. Dorothy Beckert, my beloved bride, told me from the beginning that she did "not have good feelings" about the owner or about his primary internal advisor, about whom more shortly. I seldom go against my wife's judgment,

---

[1] See Additional Reading, Family Systems at the end of this chapter.
[2] See Additional Reading, Value-Based Management at the end of this chapter.

but every time I do, I end up asking myself why. This turned out to be no exception. Self-delusion helped.

I started by convincing myself that there were quite a few potential buyers out there, even though I had also advised the guy that he was selling too early. His company was growing fast. Smart buyers will not pay much for expected growth, even with earn-outs. Our workload had declined a bit, so I went ahead with the engagement anyway.

The owner relied unduly on the judgment of his lead financial person. I never understood why. This individual was a headstrong fountain of bad accounting ideas. She was nondegreed and had had no formal accounting training. It did not help that the outside accounting firm, to which I had referred the client in the first place to get its statements reviewed, was too spineless to stand up to her and tell her about some changes she should make in how she did things, which was what I had recommended. Of course, the fact that the accountants didn't do that helped them make more money because it added to their workload. She did not understand then, and probably never will, that an accounting system is—first, last, and always—an *information system.* Because it is, design, especially of the chart of accounts, determines the quality of information that can be gotten out of it. That can ease or torch the due diligence effort of a potential buyer. Which it does, in turn, requires clear choices by the people in charge. If they do not know, or they are inclined to let others make those calls, due diligence is going to be an even greater hassle than usual, and the owner will end up paying big-time with a lower price for the business.

But the accounting woman also had proximity. I learned a long time ago—the hard way, as usual—that I can never win a war of proximity. Close trumps right every time.

Instead, I tried to win her over. Somehow she sensed—rightly—that I might be a threat to her future, so she just worked on the owner until he threw up his hands and caved, just to end the badgering in his daily work life. He then told me that he wanted out of the engagement letter he had signed. Before I would agree to it, I asked him if he had a buyer for his company. He looked me straight in the eye and said he did not. It turned out he did have a buyer, but the deal didn't close. That is how it is with those with a track of record of no sustained personal relationships. That was something else Dorothy had pointed out to me.

It was a tough lesson, as hard knocks invariably are. So long as they do not become a pattern, an occasional whack upside the head like that one can be a good wake-up call. I had convinced myself that I could work with the guy. Maybe I could have. In the best of circumstances, though, it would have been very tough. But the crazy in-house would-be accountant doomed the value map engagement from the get-go, and I just could not, or would not—I think it was the latter—see that. It was a tough lesson, one that I hope you do not have to learn the way I did.

How (Else) Not to Do It

The single biggest no-no in a value map engagement is to try to change a company's culture. That goes in spades if the firm has been in existence for more than about a decade or has more than a dozen or so employees. By then, or with that headcount, the culture is pretty much set. The path dependence that we discussed in Chapter 5 will out. Maybe you can succeed in getting a few minor cultural tweaks done. But that is all. Therefore, do not waste time and effort on cultural change.

In contrast, the other four elements of SPARC are fair game. Of course, if you recommend changing the design of the organization or any of its major processes, expect opposition. Design changes can provoke visceral pushback because they mean a loss of power—maybe a big loss—for some and big gains for others. When the power goes down, the paycheck usually does, too. Those facing loss of power and pay figure they have nothing to lose by fighting like alligators.

Start at the Beginning

So you have a signed engagement letter for value mapping and a nice five-figure retainer check.[3] What is next? Oh, not much—just a bunch of heavy lifting that requires planning, social skills, flexibility, perseverance, finesse, and stamina. Especially stamina, because this intense process is going to unfold over many months. What comes first?

Start with planning the initial details of the engagement. Presumably you dealt with the big pieces back when you priced the fixed-fee work or took it on a contingency. Obviously, if it is a lead-in to a transaction, then, in essence, you have been paid all you are going to be paid until or unless the transaction closes. In that case, you need a bigger retainer because you might have to work with this particular client for a year or two before any more money, except for travel reimbursements, is going to come your way.

Whatever the ultimate purpose of the engagement, there is a sequence to it. The order is not driven so much by SPARC as it is by what you estimate

---

[3] I am assuming that the engagement letter for the value map was preceded by your conducting a business valuation or a calculations engagement. If it was not, then do one of those *first*. That is, you must know the client company well enough to know whether you even want that company as a value-mapping client. In addition, you have to measure the "before" and the "after." Start with a valuation or calculation.

to be the duration of the engagement. In general, you want to launch first those initiatives that you expect to take the longest. I say "in general" because that is not cast in stone. For instance, you might need to neutralize or co-opt some internal political opposition before you get to the super-heavy lifting.

You also want the people further down the economic food chain—especially middle managers in the case of the larger SME—to see your work with the value map as a plus for their careers. As with any other consulting gig, a significant part of their willingness to do that depends on their level of trust and confidence in you. Their assessment of what's in it for them can affect your work, too. A key piece of information you should have picked up in your on-site interviews was whom the people in the company trust the most with sensitive information. Such individuals will have influence beyond their titles and job responsibilities. You want these people on your side. Court them.

That individual—and there might be more than one, though you hope that, if there are, they are not rival power centers within the firm—is likely to be a key ally in your work. You want to do whatever you can to get that person on your side as early in the engagement as possible. You should not shy away from asking the owner or CEO for some political horsepower to get you off on the right foot. Your work is unlikely to be fruitful—either for the company or for you—if you raise hackles early on and inspire a near-unanimous wall of opposition.

Think Like a Buyer

To do right by client companies trusting you to help them enhance value, nothing is more important, in my view, than *thinking like a buyer*. Nothing. Every project in a value map, along with the phases and tasks that comprise it, must be viewed through the piercing gaze and skeptical perspective of a savvy buyer of the firm you are helping. This requirement has much in common with being the skunk at the garden party. While your client's employees are dislocating their shoulders patting themselves on the back, you are the one saying "Yeah, but. . . . "

Thinking like a buyer will be a lot easier if you have done some buy-side due diligence. Even if the engagement will culminate in the sale of the client company, you should be thinking like a smart buyer. The due diligence crowd comes in with one objective: no postclosing surprises. That means finding bad things, risky things, wrong things. Negative, negative, negative.

Those people are hired guns for the buyers they represent, just as surely as you are a hired gun for the sellers you represent. The two sides are natural opposites, just like opposing sides in a war. Great generals will tell you that one of the keys to their success was being able to see themselves, their troops, and their situations through the eyes of their enemies. Those who can do that can then take the steps necessary to protect themselves. It is a matter of doing right by your clients.

Yes, you are an advocate for your client. But to be an effective advocate, you had better be able to find the holes and the weaknesses in what you will be asking the checkbook-carriers to believe. They will use every hint of weakness in the target firm—your client—as an excuse to pound down the price. In SMEs, that means they are looking for risk. If they can increase the perception of risk, they will have succeeded in reducing the price. They win their spurs by helping their clients avoid surprises. You win yours by eliminating surprises before those guys show up.

Planning the Engagement

In at least one respect, the plan for implementing a value map is like a battle plan: It will change early and often. So do not think that the map you construct will be the path you take maybe, wand maybe not. That is unlikely because there is high complexity and many moving parts, especially people, involved in one of these engagements. Unexpected things happen, and those delay or cause a reshuffle in the plan. Swing with it. Be flexible.

Review Your Valuation (Again)

I know you have read your valuation report a dozen times at least, but read it again. Better yet, print a copy your key staffers to read. They often can sense the nuances of sequencing and planning better than we who have been involved in it. Many times we are just too, too close to the company to be able to see things as clearly as we might.

Review Your Rationale for Pricing (Again)

When you read the valuation and the rationale back to back, you will see ties between them. Those are as they should be. We would be worried if there were nothing in common.

Consider the Politics of the Situation

Because of the changes you will be working to help the company bring about, there is likely to be internal opposition, perhaps a lot of it. Size it up. Talk to the CEO or owner about how best to convert the opponents into supporters who are constructive and helpful, rather than the opposite. Be sure to noodle with the lead person about how the power of incentives might help accomplish that conversion. Political redemption is a good thing, too.

The best public example I know of about the high cost of ignoring incentives played out early in the Iraq War. After receiving strong advice to the contrary, the U.S. ambassador there, L. Paul Bremer, made the twin decisions to (1) disband the Iraqi army and (2) lay off Baathists in senior government posts. With two strokes of his pen, Bremer created two large groups of people who had lost all the status they used to have and now had plenty of time on their hands. Why not start an insurgency?

Break the Value-Mapping Process into Discrete Projects

This step goes back to the old line about how to eat an elephant: one bite at a time. Reexamine each of the negative aberrant metrics you uncovered in your valuation and ponder their underlying causes. Write down what you think the steps will be, along with a timeline, to turn each metric into a positive or, at a minimum, neutralize its damage. For now, do not worry about sequence.

Organize each project into phases and each phase into tasks. Then apply a bottom-up timeline to each set of tasks and phases. Add up the projects' timelines as if you were going to do them consecutively. The sum will tell you if the engagement's expected duration is long enough. If it is not, think about overlapping or running parallel tracks; even if there is time to do them consecutively, it still might make sense in some cases to have overlaps and parallels.

Finally, do not put anything in concrete without getting a reality check with the owner or CEO and her most trusted lieutenant(s) to see what ideas and suggestions they have about how best to proceed. That is crucial for the initial project.

In fact, we have found it useful to take the owner or CEO off-site for a couple of days at the beginning of the value map engagement. Go someplace nice, remote, and quiet. This one is not reimbursable; you soak it up. Do not pick anything too tony, just a nice quiet place that is relaxed, clean, and comfortable.

In this situation, spouses can be real pluses. It depends on how your relationship with the owner evolved during the valuation phase of your relationship. These engagements tend to become very intimate relationships in terms of the personal information, background, and experiences that are shared with us and that we share, in return, with the owner or other principals. Greater transparency inspires greater trust if those doing it are well-adjusted human beings. And they better be, or you should have never gotten into this undertaking in the first place. The work to be done is incredibly difficult. The last thing you want is to do it alongside a lunatic of some kind. If that is the case, failure is almost a lead-pipe cinch. Don't forget *family systems.*

The First Project

Let me be blunt: You need a win here. Anything less is totally unacceptable because it lays down a predicate for what follows. You cannot afford *not* to finish this first segment of the value map satisfactorily, on time, and with the key players all pulling in the same direction. That is why you must choose carefully.

Pick a project about which there is a consensus on the need for action. Make sure *you* understand where the land mines, booby traps, and trip wires are. Do not be in a hurry to make a mistake. You *must* get this right. The success of the entire engagement and, ultimately, the owner's objective(s) rest, in part, on how this first project turns out. Your choice should not be a slam dunk. It should be a stretch but doable. The stretch builds confidence in those participating, and they will pass their good feelings along to their coworkers who are not yet involved in the work.

Be 100% certain that you and the owner/CEO designate a project leader who (1) will champion the project, (2) is used to succeeding, and (3) is respected and trusted by other participants. The whole company will watch every move you make at this point in the engagement. Take all the time you need, and do not go forward until you have it nailed down. A deliberate choice to do nothing is, in fact, a form of action. Too many people cannot sit still for very long. You must sit still for as long as it takes.

Once you are ready to pull the trigger and are certain that you are not in your own gun sights, then circle back to the owner/CEO. Confirm with him the sequence, time line, start date, project leader, other key players, and everything else you have laid out. Put yourself in the position of an internal opponent and ask yourself what it looks like. Ask your colleagues to do the same. A clear-eyed business owner who is also a friend can be an invaluable sounding board both now and later on in the process. Make sure the people you choose to tear your ideas apart can and will do that.

Finally, before you go public with the first project, sleep on it for a couple of nights. Do not obsess about it, but do muse. Navel-gazing and chin-stroking can help. Make sure you have every move in the first phase as scripted as you can make it. If anyone gets surprised, it better not be you.

As the Process Unfolds

Remember, this is going to be a lengthy undertaking. Eat the value map elephant one small morsel at a time. Do not get ahead of yourself, and resist looking too far into the future. The mountain of work staring you down will be daunting. You will feel better and do better if you follow your plan, tacking in whatever direction is required to get the job done, plug the holes,

322   Working with Clients

convert bad metrics to good ones, help increase the value of your client company, and measure, measure, measure.

You will need at least one full-time senior person on-site with the client company at all times. That individual needs to be smart enough to avoid going through minefields on a pogo stick, and she needs to be tough enough to say no every time, if that is what it takes. He needs to be astute enough to read people and situations and then walk whatever political tightropes are necessary . . . without any net below. She needs to be able to disagree without being disagreeable. He must know how to be tactful and stand his ground in the most difficult situations. She must have the stamina of a marathoner and the spine of Nelson Mandela.

Obviously this process is expensive for your firm. That is why (1) you get a hefty nonrefundable retainer, (2) you screen your clients with the greatest caution, and (3) you keep your own finger on the pulse of the situation. Make it a point to speak with your on-site person at the beginning and end of each day.

Winding Up the Value-Mapping Process

When the projects are done and your client company is ready to go to market, begin that internal ownership transition, do the first transaction in that employee stock ownership plan (ESOP), or continue its value-based management process, you must go back to the beginning. Pull that first valuation out again. Go through the aberrant metrics and their underlying causes with a fine toothed comb. Then review the projects constituting the client's value map. Make sure that each completed project resulted in decreased risk, higher revenue, lower costs, or some combination thereof. If it did not, revisit it and rework it until it does.

Then, and only then, are you ready to take another run at the client company's valuation. You should be working on a contingency that will pay out with monies either from a transaction or from the increase in value of the firm ("after" minus "before"). The valuation arm of your client's outside accounting firm will be there to advise the client on the goodness—or, heaven forbid, the not-goodness—of your firm's work. If the accounting firm is too small to have a valuation arm, it is your job to introduce the firm to two or three competent valuation professionals. It can then if it wants to.

If your company and your people have done the job you committed to do months or years before, going to market or engaging in some other transaction will be fun. It will *not* be easy. But your firm will have improved the lives of many people, including the owners of your client company. Everyone involved will have learned a lot.

You and your team will then be ready for some well-deserved time off, maybe climbing mountains in Tibet, surfing the Australian coast, or fly-fishing in Patagonia. This work is high-pressure and relentless, and everyone needs time to decompress between assignments. You should not care how hot the market is. You and your troops need the break. If you and they do not get it, you will find out that not even a great market will keep them with you.

Summary

Working with clients to reduce risk and increase value is the hardest, most intense, most rewarding work I have ever done. It is humbling to be trusted with the mantal of value mapping because of the difference it makes in people's lives. Here are a few closing bullets:

- Know your client company and its owner(s).
- Never agree to be engaged if you are hesitant about the client.
- Understand family systems.
- Think like a buyer—no surprises.
- Work like a dog.

Additional Reading

Family Systems

Gilbert, Roberta M. *The Eight Concepts of Bowen Theory*. Falls Church, VA: Leading Systems Press, 2006.

Hazell, Clive. *Family Systems Activity Book*. Bloomington, IN: AuthorHouse, 2006.

Papero, Daniel V. *Bowen Family Systems Theory*. Boston: Allyn & Bacon, 1993.

Schwartz. Richard C. *Internal Family Systems Therapy*. New York: Guilford Press, 1997.

Titelman, Peter. *Triangles: Bowen Family Systems Theory Perspectives*. Boca Raton, FL: Haworth Press, 2007. Web site: www.thebowencenter.org/pages/theory.html.

Value-Based Management

Arnold, Glen and Matt Davies. *Value-Based Management: Context and Application*, New York: John Wiley & Sons, 2000.

Dermine, Jean. *Bank Valuation and Value-Based Management: Deposit and Loan Pricing, Performance Evaluation, and Risk Management*. New York: McGraw-Hill, 2009.

Jönsson, Peter W., and Beau Bassin. *Value-Based Management: Positioning of Claimed Merits and Analysis of Application*. Mauritius: VDM Verlag, 2009.

Knight, James A. *Value Based Management: Developing a Systematic Approach to Creating Shareholder Value*. New York: McGraw-Hill, 1997.

Martin, John D., and J. William Petty. *Value Based Management: The Corporate Response*. New York: Oxford University Press, 2000.

Pohlman, Randolph A., Gareth S. Gardiner, and Ellen M. Heffes. *Value Driven Management: How to Create and maximize Value over Time for Organizational Success*. New York: AMACOM, 2000.

Young, S. David, and Stephen F. O'Byrne. *EVA and Value-Based Management: A Practical Guide to Implementation*. New York: McGraw-Hill, 2000.

CHAPTER

20

IFRS, IVSC, and Value Maps

Where International Financial Reporting Standards (IFRS), the International Valuation Standards Council (IVSC), and value maps are concerned, there is the proverbial good news and bad news. The good news is that IFRS will not be a problem, at least as it is currently constituted. There are differences between IFRS and U.S. GAAP (generally accepted accounting principles), of course, but if you know how IFRS works in your country, then the valuation *process* that is the essential first step in creating a value map should not be much different where you are from the way it works in the United States.

For U.S. readers, it is important to note that IFRS is *not*—repeat, *not*—the principles-based system that those with vested economic interests in converging the two systems would have us believe. IFRS, too, is rules-based and will become only more so if there is convergence. If nothing else, the U.S. tort bar will see to that. But do not be seduced by the siren song of "principles-based."

Moreover, the IVSC (www.ivsc.org) is not an issue for those interested in value maps. For one thing, there is even less consensus about international valuation standards than there is about international financial reporting standards. For another, no government has thrown its weight behind the IVSC. Finally, most membership organizations, while paying lip service to the need for something like international valuation standards, will fight like alligators for their own organization's standards to be the model for the international version. Though the IVSC has been around for 25 years, it has not gotten very far.

The bad news is that the underlying data for the first step in the process—a rough-cut estimate of business value—might not be as accessible or as accurate as they are in the United States. That is no knock on other countries, mind you. The availability and accuracy of data are, I think, a function of a country's institutions and the level of senior management's appreciation for actionable information. To the extent that those embed transparency and a commitment to accurate data, there are few problems. But no country of which I am aware has the traditions of disclosure and of balance of powers—among executive, legislative, and judicial branches—that the United States has. While there is, even here, a certain coziness between government and many big corporations, the relationships are not incestuous the way that they are in some countries. In those, business is an extension of government.

The Valuation Process Outside the United States

The *process*, if not the work itself, in your country should be about the same as it is here. There are the usual phases of defining the engagement, gathering data, analyzing data, arriving at a tentative opinion of value, and report-writing. If your client is a small or medium-sized enterprise, then your focus should be on its risk profile. You should think about unsystematic risk outside the United States the same way we think about it here: size, macroenvironment, domain, and company.

For lack of anything better, we have used the sum beta for the tenth cohort in the Morningstar/Ibbotson data set as the proxy for the size premium in international engagements. So far, auditors have not pushed back.

You should then analyze, top down, the other three components of unsystematic risk. Follow the process we discussed in Chapters 8 through 11. At the domain level, be sure to zero in on government policy as a barrier to entry. That hurdle is more common in other countries than it is in the United States. That might be changing here, though.

The Cost of Capital Outside the United States

As appraisers who work in international engagements know, Morningstar/ Ibbotson publishes the *International Cost of Capital Report* (ICCR) annually in PDF.[1] The 2009 version of this report covered 177 countries. (NB: This report is prepared from the perspective of a U.S. investor.) The major difference between this data set and the U.S. version is that the international perspective includes a country-level credit-risk component that originated in a 1995 research paper.[2] This factor is a proxy for the lack of market data in most countries in the world.

The ICCR has six models for estimating a country's cost of equity capital:

1. Country risk rating (log model)
2. Country risk rating (linear model)

---

[1] http://corporate.morningstar.com/ib/asp/subject.aspx?xmlfile=1423.xml.
[2] Erb, Harvey, and Viskanta, "Country Credit Risk."

3. Country spread model
4. International CAPM
5. Globally nested CAPM
6. Relative standard deviation model

In general, the less developed the country, the fewer models the ICCR uses. Each of the 177 countries uses at least two models—1 and 2. Three countries—Mexico, Argentina, and Brazil—use all six, while Chile uses five. The United States and the European Union countries all use four.

Besides the ICCR, Morningstar/Ibbotson also publishes the *International Equity Risk Premia Report* in PDF. This report contains historical equity risk premium data for 16 countries going back to 1970. These 16 are developed countries in North America (United States and Canada), Europe (11 of the 27 European Union members), and Asia (Australia, Japan, and New Zealand).[3]

A prominent academic, Professor Cam Harvey of Duke University, has done extensive research in the international cost of capital arena.[4] Much of his work and research papers are accessible at no cost via the Internet. In particular, we commend your attention to his "Country Risk Analysis" page, subtitled "A Chronology of Important Financial, Economic and Political Events in Emerging Markets";[5] it covers 55 countries. Unfortunately, it has not been updated since mid-2004. For a fee (not including support), Professor Harvey also offers an Excel-based "international cost of capital and risk calculator."[6]

Gathering Data Outside the United States

It should surprise no reader that the quality and availability of data are uneven around the world. In general, the more developed the country, the better are its data. That spells trouble for most of the countries in Africa, some in the Balkans, and a few in Asia and South America. Fewer than half of the 27 member countries of the European Union have usable data, however.

It is crucial to emphasize here that comparing data between or among countries is hazardous duty at best. For one thing, what a given phrase means in one country might not be what it means to another. Then, too, how the data are gathered, and how often, will affect such comparisons. Even within a country, the same term might have different meanings.

---

[3] http://corporate.morningstar.com/ib/asp/subject.aspx?xmlfile=1424.xml.
[4] www.duke.edu/~charvey/.
[5] www.duke.edu/~charvey/Country_risk/couindex.htm.
[6] www.duke.edu/~charvey/applets/iccrc.html

Therefore, it is crucial in non-U.S. valuations to know not only the "what"—the measures—but also the "how"—how they are created. For instance, before one can determine if a country has an analog to the U.S. fed funds rate, one must know how the central bank in that country works.

The deeper one gets into these kinds of ambiguities, the more one realizes that such analysis involves at least as much—and maybe more—of the qualitative stuff which has to be a strong suit in any firm valuing closely held businesses. The ambiguities are especially dicey in emerging markets where institutions are volatile and agencies may have their charters rewritten, their missions redone, and their managements replaced often, and sometimes every year for several years running.

A comprehensive list and discussion of Web sites and sources of data outside the United States is well beyond the scope of this book. However, with the help of my good friend, valued colleague, and world-class subcontractor, Professor Peter Klein of the University of Missouri,[7] data sources and comments follow.

The International Monetary Fund's (IMF's) International Financial Statistics (www.imfstatistics.org/imf/) site has a host of macroeconomic, financial, demographic, and trade indicators for nearly every country. Variables include measures of each country's money supply, interest rates, stock market indexes, price levels (Producer Price Index and Consumer Price Index), industrial production, employment, and exchange rates.

The World Bank also maintains a massive database of national economic, financial, and demographic indicators (www.worldbank.org/data and http://econ.worldbank.org/). Economic and financial measures include country and regional measures of output, employment, prices, debt, exchange rates, and so on. The Bank also collects data (less standardized from country to country) on education, poverty, and the like.

Two major commercial data aggregators specialize in international data: Bureau van Dijk (www.bvdep.com) and Global Insight (www.ihsglobal insight.com). These providers charge hefty subscription fees (but also offer free trials) to collect, standardize, and organize country-specific economic and financial data for hundreds of countries. The data are retrieved from government agencies, other commercial providers, and nongovernmental organizations (NGOs) such as the IMF and World Bank. N.B.: Web site addresses change often, so we do not guarantee that what follows will work; however, they all did as of April 3, 2010. Sample modules include:

---

[7] www.petergklein.com. He can reached at pklein@missouri.edu. Peter's research and industry analysis are first-rate in every respect. He is also a well-known intellectual force and highly respected scholar in Austrian economist circles.

- **Global Economic Data** (www.ihsglobalinsight.com/ProductsServices/ ProductDetail895.htm). According to Global Insight, it includes "key indicators and broad economic data for more than 200 countries world-wide covering balance of payments; cyclical indicators; finance and financial markets; government finance; housing and construction; output, capacity, and capacity utilization; merchandise trade; national accounts; labor market; population; prices; [and] wholesale and retail trade." (Note: URL provides a list (without links) of country-specific government agencies and other entities from which the raw data are extracted.)
- **Global Financial Data and Financial Indicators** (www.ihsglobalinsight .com/ProductsServices/ProductDetail897.htm). This site has "key financial indicators for more than 75 countries and broad financial data coverage for over 200 countries covering: commodities/futures, derivatives, equities, money markets, exchange rates, fixed income, indexes, [and] stock markets."
- **Industry and Sector Data** (www.ihsglobalinsight.com/Products Services/ProductDetail900.htm). This site has data from "over 70 countries, including major economies from North America, Latin America, Europe, Asia, Eastern Europe, the Middle East, and Africa. A wide range of concepts both historical and forecast, consist[ing] of total sales and all its components, sources and uses of production, production prices, producer price indices, consumer price indices, [and] labor cost indices."
- **Bureau van Dijk's Country-Specific Databases** (www.bvdep.com/en/ Company%20data%20-%20national.html). These contain mostly firm-level financials from many countries and regions around the world.
- **Economist Intelligence Unit** (http://store.eiu.com/product/60000206 .html). Like the usual work from the Economist Intelligence Unit (part of the London-based magazine, the *Economist*), this site has impressive reach and information. From the site itself: "Comprehensive two-year forecasting service that monitors risks in 120 key markets. It is designed for commercial bankers, institutional investors and corporate executives who invest in both emerging and developed markets. The service measures political, economic policy and economic structure risks as well as currency, sovereign debt and banking sector risks. In-depth forecasts are provided for up to 180 macroeconomic variables for each country, as well as a free call-up facility to our country experts."
- **Bureau van Dijk's EIU Market Indicators & Forecasts** (www.bvdep .com/en/EIU_Market_Indicators___Forecasts.html). This site provides "[d]etailed data and forecasts on a full range of industries,

including: Comprehensive coverage of consumer demographics, income, expenditure and housing; Key macroeconomic forecasts, including gross domestic product, inflation, investment, trade, foreign direct investment, and the overall EIU Business Environment Rating; risk ratings covering both country credit risk and business operational risk, ranging from economic structure and currency to regulatory and security risk; competitiveness ratings such as a labour market rating, labour costs, levels, and assessment of technology, education and productivity levels."

- **Bureau van Dijk's Bankscope** (www.bvdep.com/en/BANKSCOPE. html). This site provides "[r]atings, rating reports, country risk ratings and reports—ratings are provided by 4 agencies and a total of 18 ratings are available."

- **Bureau van Dijk's ISIS** (www.bvdep.com/en/ISIS.html). This site provides "a comprehensive database of detailed reports on public and private insurance companies around the world. ISIS contains information on 5,250 non-life companies (back to 1992), 2,400 life companies (to 1995), and 610 composites (to 1995) in over 120 countries. Each company report typically contains the following: income statements and balance sheets, ratios, shareholders, and subsidiaries."

Bureau van Dijk also offers firm-specific data from which Herfindahl-Hirschman Indices, CR4s, and the like can be constructed:

- **Bureau van Dijk's Amadeus** (www.bvdep.com/en/AMADEUS.html). This site says it has "financial information on over 11 million public and private companies in 41 European countries."

- **Bureau van Dijk's Bankscope** (www.bvdep.com/en/BANKSCOPE. html). This site provides financials on 29,000 banks around the world; "detailed consolidated and/or unconsolidated balance sheet and income statement totaling up to 200 data items and 36 pre-calculated ratios per bank."

Here are some other providers:

- **Euromonitor's Global Market Information Database** (www.euromoni tor.com/). This site's "Countries and Consumers" module is a collection of consumer lifestyle reports, including information on population, consumer segments, regional development, income, health, education, eating/drinking habits, leisure, savings, and home ownership rather than economic, historical and political comment.

- **Organisation for Co-Operation and Development (OECD)** (www
  .oecd.org/statsportal/0,3352,en_2825_293564_1_1_1_1_1,00.html).
  The 30-member OECD has information on countries and regions. It
  includes the OECD country Web sites (statistical profiles) and OECD
  economic surveys (in-depth reviews of member countries' economies
  and those of selected nonmember countries). Chapters include the economic situation, fiscal policy issues, product market competition, and
  growth) and *OECD Regions at a Glance* (regional economic indicators
  such as dispersion of population, GDP, industrial concentration,
  employment growth, patents).
- **Food and Agriculture Organization of the United Nations** (www.fao
  .org/waicent/st/level_1.asp?main_id=10). Under Geographical and
  Regional Information, this site contains data on development, trade,
  and agriculture.

Following are links to government agencies, publishers, and NGOs that
provide detailed national data:

- **MarketNewZealand.com** (www.marketnewzealand.com/).
- **European Union** (http://europa.eu/index_en.htm).
- **Organization of American States** (www.oas.org). The Organization of
  American States consists of 35 countries in North/South/Central
  America, plus the Caribbean.
- **United Nations** (www.un.org). There are 192 member states in the
  United Nations.
- **North Atlantic Treaty Organization** (www.nato.org). There are 28 mem-
  ber countries in NATO.
- **Instituto Brasileiro de Geografia e Estatística** (Brazil) (www.ibge.gov
  .br/english/). Note: Some links go to sites in Portuguese.
- **World Trade Organization** (www.wto.org). At the beginning of 2010,
  the WTO had 153 members.
- **World Almanac** (www.worldalmanac.org). The 2010 edition of what the
  St. Louis Post-Dispatch calls a "desk reference superstar" has population
  stats for every city in the world that has more than 10,000 people as well
  as a nifty feature entitled "Decade in Review."
- **Statistics South Africa** (www.statssa.gov.za/).
- **Asian Development Bank** (www.adb.org). Headquartered in Manila
  and now with 67 members and more than 2,500 employees, the Asian
  Development Bank is a regional version of the World Bank, though the
  two are not directly affiliated.
- **National Bureau of Statistics of China** (www.stats.gov.cn/english/).
  As I mentioned earlier in this chapter, be careful with data from

developing countries. They usually have a political dimension that understates bad economic news and overstates (or outright fabricates) good news. Don't be surprised by inconsistent or wildly varying data from period to period. Use it with the utmost skepticism and with explicit caveats.

- **Ministry of Commerce in China** (http://english.mofcom.gov.cn). This is the English-language version of the ministry's homepage. The usual caveats about emerging markets apply here, too.
- **Statistics of Russia** (www.infostat.ru/). Then there's Russia's version of economic statistics, which is called the Information & Publishing Centre.[8] I checked the Excel price list; it might well have come from Madison Avenue.
- **Federal State Statistics Service** (www.gks.ru/eng/). The fact that this Romanian Web site's copyright says "1999–2004" telling.
- **Central Intelligence Agency** (www.cia.gov).

Summary

For the process of creating value maps in countries around the world, we have barely scratched the surface of data sources. What this chapter contains will only get you started. In most cases, your primary hurdle is going to be accessing quality data. However, you should also be careful about employment laws in other countries. Those in the United States are complicated, but elsewhere they are often more so, especially where an employee's right to privacy is concerned. For example, in a purchase price allocation in 2008, we were not even allowed to see the names of employees of a subsidiary in Germany.

If you are not a resident of the country in which you are working with your client company, we strongly recommend that you team up with a knowledgeable professional who is. This individual need not be a member of the valuation community, although it will certainly help if she is. If networks of which you are a member are unable to help you, check with the International Association of Consultants, Valuators, and Analysts (www.iacva.org). IACVA has global reach, and its chairman, Jim Catty of Toronto (jimc@iacva.org), has been doing valuations around the world for more than 40 years.

---

[8] Note the choices in the "Voting" section top-right on the homepage: "Good," "Satisfied," and "Could Be Better."

Epilogue: The Future for Value-Mapping Services

Value-mapping services are a game-changer for clients and a register-ringer for a special cadre of professionals. To be sure, we are not the most objective sources in town on this subject, of course, but we have strong reasons to believe the future is bright. In this wind-up to the book, I want to talk about that future, especially as it relates to valuation, how I see the future, and why I see it the way I do. I will devote a chunk of this chapter to marketing issues, and I want to elaborate on why that "special cadre" is so special.

The Future for Valuation Services

The near-term future for valuation services remains as bright as it ever was. Longer term, however, there are potential threats; I will address those shortly. And there are trends in valuation services that might disturb some and thrill others. The community of valuation professionals is nothing if not a rowdy group—distinctly and uniquely American, in my view—so I doubt that all or most, and perhaps not even some, will agree with what I have to say here. But those who know me know that I worry when I am in the majority on nearly any issue. I always think I must be overlooking something.

With low barriers to entry and plenty of demand, the number of valuation professionals continues to grow. As I have written elsewhere, some membership organizations are more interested in jacking up their membership rolls than credentialing knowledgeable professionals.[1] We cannot tell if increases in supply are keeping pace, running about even, or trailing the increases in demand. During the 2008–2009 economic decline, some valuation enterprises and large accounting firms laid off staff. We suspect

---

[1] Miller, "Valuation as Craft," 253–254.

that is more a function of either poor marketing or overstaffing in the first place than anything else.

One thing is not speculative: Valuation services must be marketed. Many professional services firms—attorneys, accountants, architects, engineers, physicians—eschew marketing. Some think it is beneath them. Others think a Web site is all they need. Still others cannot differentiate between marketing and selling. But good marketing is a formidable weapon when it comes to value-mapping services. One look at most firms' Web sites will tell you whether they appreciate the benefits that good marketing creates.

Another trend is specialization. Part of that is driven by the experience of those who offer litigation support services: Courts increasingly demand industry-specific knowledge and expertise, or else an expert witness can be on the receiving end of a legal challenge. The move toward specialization accelerates with the prospect of estate taxes going away in 2010. We doubt that the politicians will allow that to happen, but we do expect the threshold for estate taxes to eventually be set at about $5 million, with annual increases indexed. That will eliminate most valuations for estate purposes while still capturing the big bucks from those with estates north of $5 million.

How will that affect gifting? One political compromise might be a trade-off among politicians that ups the threshold for estate taxes while eliminating discounts for fractional interests. At a minimum, it would dampen demand for services valuing fractional interests in family limited partnerships and limited liability companies. Certainly those annual "Discount for Lack of Marketability seminars" would dry up.

A major impact on specialization has come from valuation for financial reporting (VfFR). The December 2009 issue of the monthly newsletter from malpractice insurer CAMICO was all about VfFR. A mini–case study highlighted violations of the American Institute of Certified Public Accountants (AICPA) Code of Professional Conduct, Rule 103-2. We have seen those ourselves. Some accounting firms, it seems, would rather game the system than do the right thing. One of these days, the tort bar will trip over business valuation, and life in our profession will get ugly fast.

As those of us who offer the service can attest, VfFR is unlike any kind of accounting we ever saw in college.[2] It is demanding, exacting work with lots and lots of opportunities for error. It is not an area in which one can dabble. If you are going to offer VfFR services, you will not make any money doing it just once or twice a year. It has to become a deep specialty, complete with its own templates in Excel and Word/WordPerfect.

---

[2] We hope this changes as new graduates enter our community in the coming years.

At least four other venues are already deep specialties in the valuation catalogue: (1) auto dealerships; (2) medical practices and hospitals; (3) pharmaceuticals and biotech; and (4) any volatile technology area with products or services that have short half-lives. In our view, one must work almost full time in any of these niches in order to be competent.

We stay away from all four of those domains. The knowledge required to serve them with even minimal competence is deep, complex, and time-consuming to acquire. We have resisted specializing, if only because, even though industry specialists usually make a lot more money than we mere mortals, we like the variety that valuing lower-tech SMEs offers. To be sure, we have valued an ambulatory surgical center, and we would not be reluctant to value either an Internet service provider or a managed services provider. Each of these abuts a domain that we do not enter, but each is an operating business that is relatively easy and straightforward to appraise because of its similarity to trade publishing.

The message here is simple: The days of generalists may be winding down. Certainly the scope of specialization is increasing. The paradox is that we consider each of these negative trends in valuation to be *positive* for value-mapping services. Why? Because value enhancement, like other specialties, offers another opportunity to differentiate service offerings. Unlike other types of valuation services, the value of value mapping far exceeds its costs.[3]

Moreover, the value proposition for value enhancement and related services is not driven by compliance (which clients tend to price-shop because they fail to perceive value) or by fat, jargon-laden, dust-gathering reports (which most clients read once, at most). We combine calculations with a mini–value map anytime we can because the work is lucrative and fun. Besides, clients understand value. When they receive it, they cannot get their checkbooks out fast enough.

Marketing Matters

Even if every ASA and CFA chartholder (www.cfainstitute.org/cfaprog/charterholder/index.html) offered value-mapping services, the market for them would exceed the supply of professionals available to deliver them. But value-mapping services, like their traditional valuation counterparts, *must be marketed.*

Unlike gifting or value-based management, value mapping is not an annuity service. It is complex. It is expensive. It is not required. For all of those reasons, clients must be educated about what value-mapping services can

---

[3] If you think it doesn't, please send a note to me at wmiller@beckmill.com.

do for their companies. If you can conduct seminars through your local chamber of commerce or offer in-house continuing legal education (CLE) courses to law firms with a captive audience over lunch, you will be miles ahead of your competitors.

Writing

But it is not just the in-person public pitches that count. Writing for publication is a big plus. You need to have a jazzy Web site, but it need not cost a fortune. A quarterly newsletter is really important, too. Try to buy one where you can pick the content, or, if you have the bandwidth or the staff, produce it in-house. Most important, in my view, are an icon (logo) and a tagline. If you can do a great job of devising those yourself, you might be in the wrong line of work. Most of us do not have that talent.

Ad Agencies

You are apt to find the services of a small advertising agency well worth the money. We have worked with two of them, and both, in their own ways, have helped us a lot. Our current ad-visor is Charlottesville-based Birch Studio Graphics Inc. (www.birchstudio.com). I cannot toss enough kudos to these talented professionals. In addition to redoing our existing Web site, Birch also takes care of our business cards and hosts our web site.

Some valuation firms produce what the ad business calls "portfolios." You know, loose papers of different sizes with different headings sticking out of the pockets of a two-pocket paper folder. Besides being really expensive, we find them annoying. The papers fall out unless the ad agency bites the bullet and takes steps to ensure that they do not. We have always thought that the only people who come out ahead on those contraptions are paper recyclers and the public relations/ad firms that put them together.

Branding

Until we changed our logo three years ago, we had a brochure that fit snugly into a #10 envelope. Our then-logo was embossed on the front, and several small pages were stapled along the spine. On the right inside was a pocket that was die-cut to hold a business card. We also had a number of different inserts from which we could choose, depending on the nature of the engagement. Each one had a short blurb and then testimonials with real names and business affiliations. This getup was not cheap, but it helped open the door to quite a few engagements. The design was ingenious, and the appearance was striking.

Barbara, the one-woman shop that put that together for us, suggested late in 2005 that our logo and tagline were "long in the tooth, Warren—it's time to get something new, something jazzy." I instantly became the most anal-retentive, left-brain guy on the planet and dug in my heels. I *liked* that brochure. I *liked* the logo we had then. I *liked* our tagline.

But I also knew that Barbara really knew her stuff. Her business was neither down nor struggling, and she was not trying to shake some work out of thin air. She cared enough to butt heads with me (just as we do on occasion with our own clients), and that meant something to me. So we set a spending ceiling and off she went to do her stuff. It took a lot of back-and-forth in file transfers, but finally we had a logo that channeled our trilevel framework of unsystematic risk. Then she made a watermark out of it. Two of them, in fact. One was for everyday use, and the other had **DO NOT COPY** going around the perimeter of the inside triangle. It is on every page of our reports now.

Business Cards

Barbara and I also worked together to create a tagline that reflected our unusual strategy-based approach to valuation. I chose the custom maroon color of my high school, Culver Military Academy, and Barb did the rest. Then she designed a "vertical" business card. That is, the printing on the card ran laterally when the card was in "portrait" mode. She managed to hang the tagline along one of the vertical edges, so it was perpendicular to everything else on the card. On the back of it are bullet points for each of the services we offer. We have never understood why so many companies leave the backs of their business cards blank. That is valuable real estate. Use it. But on both sides, practice that old adage, "White space is your friend. White space is your friend." Do not do what we first did, and that was fill up every square millimeter of the card with verbiage of some kind. It looked intimidating. It *was* intimidating.

Speaking

Speak to any audience that will listen to you. I mean that. For one thing, most of us can use the practice. For another, public speaking sharpens your platform skills. If you do litigation support, the public speaking will be a boon to you. If speaking to a group or, even better, a crowd, intimidates you, check out Toastmasters International (TI, www.toastmasters.org). That is one of the best educational organizations I know of. Besides improving your ability to deliver prepared remarks, it does something much more important: It teaches you to think on your feet. We can all benefit from doing that better.

TI does that through a portion of each meeting called "Table Topics." The Table Topics Master (TTM) for a given meeting prepares a topic ahead of time. He gets up, talks for two minutes about it, poses a question, and then calls on someone to answer it. The respondent stands and holds forth on whatever he was directed to speak about, and then, after two minutes, sits down. Anytime anyone in a meeting says "Uh," someone with a noisemaker will set it off. That alone can throw you off-stride. The TTM then poses another question and calls on someone else. And so it goes. TI is a remarkable group of fun people. It is also a great venue for developing inexperienced or shy staffers. The tariff is low, the meetings last an hour, and they are held all over town in any big city at different times of the day and night. You can shop them until you find a group with which you are comfortable. You will *not* regret joining TI.

Sponsorships

Sponsorships are a little dicier. However, if your firm can sponsor a project or a fundraiser for a nonprofit organization in your community, the resulting goodwill can bring clients. We know. We do that.

Convention Booths

If you have expertise in a particular industry, go to its annual convention. Pay for a booth. Meet-and-greet until you are blue in the face. Hand out brochures or DVDs. Collect business cards as if you are addicted to it. Add them to your newsletter's mailing list.

Articles of Interest to Potential Clients

When you find an article that may be of interest to a potential client, business-related or not, send it out using a "Business Reply Card." Ours is on heavy stock that fits into a #10 envelope. It has our logo, tagline, service portfolio, contact information, and, in the upper right corner, the logo of the CFA Institute (permission is required). We scribble a note on that card, fold up the article we are sending, clip our reply card to the article, and slide them into an envelope with our logo and return address on it. We bang an address into our labeling software, and our little Brother QL-500 spits out a nice, crisp mailing label for us. On goes the stamp, and we're done. Because of the obvious personal touch, we prefer snail mail to electronic delivery.

Postage Meters

No, we do not use postage meters or www.stamps.com. The research shows that envelopes with brightly colored stamps, preferably of wildlife or with patriotic themes, are more apt to get opened and read. Who says research does not matter?!

Electronic Media

Valuation professionals are beginning to use DVDs, streaming video (.mp4 or .wav), and downloadable audio (.mp3/.wav) files to get their message out. Production costs are coming down, and we know clients who have played them on their laptop's DVD player on a cross-country flight. That is a one-on-one for which most of us would kill.

And there is YouTube (www.youtube.com). If you want to inject a little humor into electronic media, test it first on people who will tell you if it stinks. Well-placed humor is unbeatable, but it is awfully hard to do it well. Even for those of us who can tell a great joke, humor in electronic media often falls flat. Once it is on YouTube, it is forever. Be careful. And if you want to see a hilarious video about Austrian economics, go to www.econ stories.tv and click on the icon.

Social Media

Use all available social media. Twitter and LinkedIn are the most widely used by professionals. However, we are seeing increasing use of Facebook.

A Newspaper Column

If you can write—and most of us cannot—then you might be able to talk your way into a weekly or monthly column in your newspaper. If you do take on a column, be willing to work for free, at least to start with. Hold it to 800 words, and do not submit them on the installment plan just because you could not say anything of note in a mere 800 words.

Write on topical subjects, but *tie them* to valuation. Stay away from politics, unless its valuation-related (e.g., a Financial Accounting Standards Board (FASB) pronouncement or the issue of converging or not converging with IFRS). Most important, use simple English. No jargon, no eye-glazing sentences.

Developing Continuing Education Courses

These are difficult and time-consuming. They are also great credentials for a C.V. for anyone doing litigation support, though. Do not figure on making a fortune in royalties. However, if you teach what you develop, you can find peers who might want to hire you on a project basis. That is especially true if they are one- or two-person shops. The time you spend developing a course might come back to you many times over.

Webinars

If you can conduct these under the auspices of Business Valuation Resources, LLC (www.bvresources.com) or NACVA (www.nacva.com), do not miss the opportunity; beware the political games and chicanery at AICPA and other membership organizations, though. Better yet, if you can devote the time to doing a monthly webinar yourself and promote it to your mailing list, so much the better. You can even charge a few bucks for it if you are registered with the National Association of State Boards of Accountancy (www.nasba.org); your attendees will get CPE credit. Most people will gladly pay a few bucks for a webinar that helps them get CPE credit without leaving their offices. If you can make the webinar available on demand in streaming video 24/7, so much the better. Your Web site will need to take credit cards, though.

Blogs

If you have the discipline to write a blog, do it. Be sure to include a syndication "star" in your browser window so folks like me can syndicate new material in your blog to our Google home pages. (And if you do not have one of those, you are missing one of life's productivity-enhancing experiences.)

Good blogging requires commitment, whether you do it Monday through Friday or once a week. If you do not have the time or the discipline, recruit guest bloggers; make sure you trust them, and then turn them loose. Like the newspaper column, neither their posts nor yours should run on forever. Some retirees do that. Even though they have great things to say and share, many of us do not have the time in one sitting to read a 5,000-word essay on the evils of IFRS.

Learn to use some basic HTML in your blog. That way your readers can click on a link, or their attention will be drawn to something you **bolded**, and the like. Above all, try to get links to your blog on the "blog rolls" of others, and make sure you reciprocate. Do not be afraid to post to someone else's blog and then link it to yours. The other blogger will appreciate your help in trying to broaden his audience, and you never know when the phone will ring.

One closing thought about blogging: Do not make it 100% business. Show the human and family side occasionally, too. Subscribers like that.

That Special Cadre Dedicated to Delivering Value to Clients

As some readers know, I have talked publicly about add-on value enhancement services for nearly a decade now. Until recently, I got mostly man-from-Mars stares from colleagues whenever I brought up the subject. Now the notion of such services seems to be becoming almost mainstream. It will never be the sweet spot of the valuation community because it is complex and multidisciplinary. That is why those who do it now and will do it in the future are such special people.

For starters, the approach, perspective, and tools I have described and tried to demonstrate in this book go far beyond the traditional tools of finance. In fact, I do not know how anyone does traditional valuation services well without the benefits of the toolkits from, at a minimum, strategic management and industrial organization. I know that I could not. I would be lost without those arsenals. But there are several dozen world-class appraisers out there who do wonderful work without strategy and industrial organization. Their reports are different from ours, of course, but they still practice the craft of valuation on a very high level. More power to them.

But those who do make the commitment to taking the path I have laid out in these pages will not regret it if they persevere and stay with it. I am intent on launching a movement of sorts because I am passionate in my belief that most appraisers cannot possibly be getting decent results in traditional valuation services, much less anything as multifaceted and demanding as value mapping. I have read enough reports prepared by such appraisers to marvel that they can make even a modest living doing what they do the way they do it.

But serious valuation professionals—and that means you if you have read this far—know that too many of our colleagues get away with egregious cases of malpractice simply because clients do not know any better. Some of this will begin to come to light as the implementation of the Pension Protection Act of 2006 begins to take root. There will be appraisers sanctioned and barred from practicing in front of Internal Revenue Service for at least five years and maybe as many as eight. That is a step in the right direction. All of us who are committed to this craft are dragged down by the part-timers, the hacks, the charlatans, the quick-buck artists, and the scammers.

I had one of those in a valuation class recently. He is a partner in an accounting firm in the eastern time zone. This guy parachuted into the second day of a three-day class, announced that his firm specializes in a particular industry, put his world-class ignorance about valuation on display in a most impressive way (even though he carried some valuation "credentials"), and then vanished before the lunch break. We never saw him again. Guys like him are Public Enemy #1 in our fight for respectability. If we do not self-regulate responsibly—and get these undesirables out of our profession, loudly and publicly—then, sooner or later, we will be dealing with the heavy, over-reaching, overreacting, and heavy hand of the federal government.

All of this is why readers of this book are indeed a special cadre. You are committed to practicing this craft on a very high level. You are not part of the boilerplate/report-writing-software crowd that is so much in evidence. You are serious professionals who are committed to producing the best possible deliverables for your clients. You are also interested in learning new ways to add value to your client companies and to your services for them.

Readers know that we who have climbed the rungs of the business valuation ladder have invested thousands and thousands of hours—tens of thousands in more than a few cases—in learning, practicing, and improving how we do our craft. We know that we live better lives than most of us ever thought we could. We know that without the Shannon Pratts, the Roger Grabowskis, and the Aswath Damodarans of the world, we would not practice anywhere near the high level at which we do our craft. No way.

You and we have traveled to conferences, read, devoured new books and new ideas, and embedded leading-edge practices into our existing processes and templates. We have done this even though we know that most of our clients would probably not know the difference if we failed to elevate how we, as craftswomen and craftsmen, do what we do. But we are about our craft, and we are committed to doing it the best we can, so we do it. We have to. Our integrity demands it.

For that is what craftspeople do. Every engagement is a new opportunity to extend what we know, what we do, and how we do it. Every deliverable to a client is a personal statement about how we do our craft. Every client gives us the opportunity to learn, to experiment with new learning and new tools, and to be well paid for having as much fun as we do. And it *is* fun. I spent many years on the not-fun side of the occupational ledger, and, for me, it was not the best of times and the worst of times. Except for my tenure at Union Pacific Corp., it was only the worst of times. Every day.

That I now am privileged to live in a country that allows me to do this craft at the highest level I can and do it for clients willing to pay our firm a more than decent sum for doing what we love to do—well, I cannot imagine how my professional life could ever be any better. But though I, like you, have said that for a few years, somehow that same professional life continues to improve. There are times when I have to pinch myself to believe that what I do and how I feel are real.

Closing Words

That you have done me the honor of reading this far is high praise indeed. Thank you. For at least a decade, colleagues have asked me when I was going to write a book. "When I think I have something to say that is worth hearing" was my constant response. I hope that you believe that I have had something to say that is worth reading. Please drop me a line any time. And thank you for supporting our work by buying and reading this book. There will be others.

We end now with an anecdote from more than 35 years ago. It taught me a life lesson that we practice to this day. It came from a sign I saw in the window of a "Junque Shoppe" (that was the name of the business) in a ghost town in Nevada in May 1974:

NOTICE: Price Subject to Change According to Customer's Attitude

We believe it. We practice it. To the extent that your circumstances allow, do your craft for clients that are deserving of your effort, your commitment, and your professional integrity. Always look for ways to add value to the client company. If you can add more than you were paid, well, the client got you for free, didn't it?

Now think about that in terms of your value-enhancement service being a "complement" (see Chapter 3, p. 165) to your basic valuation service. The best complements are free. That is why IBM has pushed the Linux operating system. If it's free—or if close to it—then the potential for IBM to sell a lot more hardware (which is NOT free!) skyrockets. With a free good or service, demand is unlimited. So, if your client gets your services for free on a "net basis," then the demand for those services is likewise unlimited. Raise your prices, and enjoy the ride.

Bibliography

Alchian, Armen. "Uncertainty, Evolution, and Economic Theory." *Journal of Political Economy.* 58, No. 3 (June 1950): 211–221.

Andrews, Kenneth R. *The Concept of Corporate Strategy.* Homewood, Ill.: Irwin, 1971.

Bain, Joe S. "Relation of Profit Rate to Industry Concentration: American Manufacturing, 1936–1940." *Quarterly Journal of Economics* 65 (1951): 293–324.

Barnard, Christian I. *The Functions of the Executive.* Cambridge, Mass.: Harvard University Press, 1938.

Barney, Jay B. *Gaining and Sustaining Competitive Advantage,* 3rd ed. Upper Saddle River, NJ: Pearson/Prentice-Hall, 2007.

Barney, Jay B. "Strategic Factor Markets: Expectations, Luck, and Business Strategy." *Management Science* 32 (1986), 1231–1241.

_____. "Firm Resources and Sustained Competitive Advantage." *Journal of Management* 17 (1991), 99–120.

Barney, Jay B., and William G. Ouchi, eds. *Organizational Economics.* San Francisco: Jossey-Bass, 1986.

Blattberg, Robert, Thomas Buesing, Peter Peacock, and Subrata Sen. "Identifying the Deal-Prone Segment." *Journal of Marketing Research* 15 (August 1978): 369–377.

Bower, Joseph L. *Managing the Resource Allocation Process: A Study of Corporate Planning and Investment.* Boston: Harvard Business School Press, 1970.

Bracker, Jeffrey. "The Historical Development of the Strategic Management Concept." *Academy of Management Review* 5 (1980): 219–224.

Brandenburger, Adam M., and Barry J. Nalebuff. *Co-Opetition: A Revolutionary Mindset That Combines Competition and Cooperation.* New York: Currency, 1996.

Burton, Richard M., and Borge Obel. *Strategic Organizational Diagnosis and Design: The Dynamics of Fit,* 3rd ed. New York: Springer Science+Media, 2004.

Caves, Richard E., and Michael E. Porter, "From Entry Barriers to Mobility Barriers: Conjectural Decisions and Contrived Deterrence to New Competition." *Quarterly Journal of Economics* 91 (1977): 241–261.

Child, John. "Organizational Structure, Environment, and Performance: The Role of Strategic Choice." *Sociology* 6 (1972): 1–22.

Christensen, C. Roland, Kenneth R. Andrews, and Joseph L. Bower. *Business Policy: Text and Cases* (3rd Ed.)Homewood, Ill.: Irwin, 1973.

Clark, Kim B., and Takahiro Fujimoto. *Product Development Performance: Strategy, Organization and Management in the World Auto Industries.* Boston: Harvard Business School Press, 1991.

Cyert, Richard M., and James G. March. *A Behavioral Theory of the Firm.* Englewood Cliffs, NJ: Prentice-Hall, 1963.

Daft, Richard L. *Organization Theory and Design*, 10th ed. Florence, KY: South-Western, 2009.

Dolan Edwin G., ed. *The Foundations of Modern Austrian Economics.* Kansas City, MO: Sheed & Ward, 1976.

Ehrbar, Al. *EVA: The Real Key to Creating Wealth.* New York: John Wiley & Sons, 1998.

Erb, Claude, Campbell R. Harvey, and Tadas Viskanta. "Country Credit Risk and Global Portfolio Selection." *Journal of Portfolio Management* 9 (Winter 1995): 74–83.

Fahey, Liam, and V. K. Narayanan. *Macroenvironmental Analysis for Strategic Management.* St. Paul: West Publishing, 1986.

Galbraith, Jay R. *Designing Organizations: An Executive Guide to Strategy, Structure, and Process.* San Francisco: Jossey-Bass, 2002.

_____. *Designing the Customer-Centric Organization: A Guide to Strategy, Structure, and Process.* San Francisco: Jossey-Bass, 2005.

Garvin, David A. "The Processes of Organization and Management." *Sloan Management Review* 39, No. 4 (Summer 1998), 33–51.

Grant, Robert M. *Contemporary Strategy Analysis: Concepts, Techniques, Applications*, 6th ed. Malden, Mass.: Blackwell Publishers, 2007.

Grove, Andrew S. *Only the Paranoid Survive.* New York: HarperCollins, 1996.

Hamel, Gary, and C. K. Prahalad. "Strategic Intent." *Harvard Business Review* 67, No. 3 (May-June 1989): 63–76.

Hawkins, George C., and Michael Paschall. *The CCH Business Valuation Guide*, 9th ed. Chicago: CCH, 2008.

Hitchner, James R., ed. *Financial Valuation: Applications and Models*, 2nd ed., Hoboken, NJ: John Wiley & Sons, 2006.

Hitt, Michael A., R. Duane Ireland, and Robert E. Hoskisson. *Strategic Management: Competitiveness and Globalization*, 8th ed. Cincinnati: South-Western, 2009.

Ibbotson Associates.*Ibbotson 2010 "SBBI" Yearbook.* Chicago: Morningstar, Inc., 2010.

Jacobson, Robert. "The 'Austrian' School of Strategy." *Academy of Management Review* 17 (1982): 782–807.

Kaplan, Robert S., and David P. Norton. "The Balanced Scorecard: Measures That Drive Performance." *Harvard Business Review* 72, No. 1 (1992): 71–80.

Kerr. Steven. "On the Folly of Rewarding A, While Hoping for B." *Academy of Management Journal* 18 (1975): 769–783.

Kirzner, Israel M. *Competition and Entrepreneurship.* Chicago: University of Chicago Press, 1973.

Knight, Frank H. *Risk, Uncertainty, and Profit.* Chicago: University of Chicago Press, 1921.

Koller, Tim, Marck Goedhart, and David Wessels. *Valuation: Measuring and Managing the Value of Companies,* 4th ed. Hoboken, NJ: John Wiley & Sons, 2005.

Lawrence, Paul R., and Jay W. Lorsch. *Organization and Environment: Managing Differentiation and Integration.* Boston: Harvard Business School/ Division of Research, 1967.

Learned, Edmund P., C. Roland Christensen, Kenneth R. Andrews, and William D. Guth. *Business Policy: Text and Cases.* Homewood, Ill.: Irwin, 1965.

Lockett, Andy, Rory P. O'Shea, and Mike Wright. "The Development of the Resource-based View: Reflections from Birger Wernerfelt." *Organization Studies* 29 (2008): 1125–1141. Available at: http://papers.ssrn.com/sol3/ papers.cfm?abstract_id=957031.

Lorayne, Harry, and Jerry Lucas. *The Memory Book: The Classic Guide to Improving Your Memory at Work, at School, and at Play.* New York: Ballantine Books, 2000.

Mahoney, Joseph T. *Economic Foundations of Strategy.* Thousand Oaks, Calif.: Sage, 2005.

Makadok, Richard. "The Competence/Collusion Puzzle and the Four Theories of Profit: Why Good Resources Go to Bad Industries." Unpublished working paper, Goizueta Business School, Emory University, 2004.

March, James G. "Exploration and Exploitation in Organizational Learning." *Organization Science* 2 (1991): 71–87.

McGahan, Anita M. *How Industries Evolve.* Boston: Harvard Business School Press, 2004.

Menger, Carl. *Principles of Economics.* Vienna: Wilhelm Braumiller, 1871.

_____. *Investigations into the Method of the Social Sciences with Special Reference to Economics.* Leipzig: Verlag don Duncker & Humblot, 1883.

Mercer, Z. Christopher, and Travis W. Harms. *Business Valuation: An Integrated Theory.* Hoboken, NJ: John Wiley & Sons, 2007.

Miles, Robert H., and Kim S. Cameron. *Coffin Nails and Corporate Strategies.* Englewood Cliffs, NJ: Prentice-Hall, 1982.

Miles, Raymond E., and Charles C. Snow. *Organizational Strategy, Structure, and Process.* New York: McGraw-Hill, 1978.

_____. "Fit, Failure and the Hall of Fame." *California Management Review* 3 (Spring 1984): 10–28.

Miller, Danny. "Stale in the Saddle: CEO Tenure and the Match between Organization and Environment." *Management Science* 37 (1991): 34–52.

Miller, Warren D. "The Grim Reapers of High Growth and Internal Focus." *CPA Letter.* New York: American Institute of Certified Public Accountants, September 2000.

_____. "Valuation as Craft." *Business Valuation Review* 27 (Winter 2008): 252–255.

Mintzberg, Henry. "Structure in 5's: A Synthesis of the Research on Organization Design." *Management Science* 26, (1980): 322–341.

_____. *Structure in Fives: Designing Effective Organizations.* Englewood Cliffs, NJ: Prentice Hall, 1983.

Mises, Ludwig. *Social and Economic Evolution.* New Haven, Conn.: Yale University Press, 1957.

Montgomery, Cynthia A., ed. *Resource-Based and Evolutionary Theories of the Firm: Towards a Synthesis.* Boston: Kluwer, 1995.

Nelson, Richard R. "Why Do Firms Differ and What Does It Matter?" *Strategic Management Journal* 12 (1991), 61–74.

Nelson, Richard R., and Sidney G. Winter. *An Evolutionary Theory of Economic Change.* Boston: Belknap Press, 1982.

North, Douglass C. *Institutions, Institutional Change and Economic Performance.* New York: Cambridge University Press, 1990.

Penrose, A *Theory of the Growth of the Firm* 3rd ed. New York: Oxford University Press, 1995.

Peteraf, Margaret A. "The Cornerstones of Competitive Advantage: A Resource-based View." *Strategic Management Journal* 14 (1993), 179–191.

Peters, Thomas J., and Robert H. Waterman, Jr. *In Search of Excellence: Lessons from America's Best-Run Companies.* New York: Harper & Row, 1982.

Porter, Michael E. "How Competitive Forces Shape Strategy." *Harvard Business Review* 59, No. 2 (March-April 1979): 137–145.

_____. *Competitive Strategy: Techniques for Analyzing Industries and Competitors.* New York: The Free Press, 1980.

_____. *Competitive Advantage: Creating and Sustaining Superior Performance.* New York: The Free Press, 1985.

_____. 2008."The Five Competitive Forces That Shape Strategy." *Harvard Business Review* 88, No. 1 (January 2008): 78–93.

Prahalad, C.K., and Gary Hamel. "The Core Competence of the Corporation." *Harvard Business Review* 68, No. 3 (May-June 1990): 79–91.

Pratt, Shannon P. *Valuing a Business: The Analysis and Appraisal of Closely Held Companies*, 5th ed. New York: McGraw-Hill, 2008.

Richardson, George B. "The Organisation of Industry." *Economic Journal*, 82 (1972): 883–896.

Roberts, John. *The Modern Firm: Organizational Design for Performance and Growth*. New York: Oxford University Press, 2004.

Roberts, Peter W., and Kathleen M. Eisenhardt. "Austrian Insights on Strategic Organization: From Market Insights to Implications for Firms." *Strategic Organization* 1 (2003): 345–352.

Rumelt, Richard P. *Strategy, Structure, and Economic Performance*. Boston: Harvard Business School Press, 1974.

Scherer, F.M. "Technological Innovation and Monopolization" American Antitrust Institute Working Paper No. 05-07, 2005.

Scherer. F.M., and David Ross. *Industrial Market Structure*, 3rd ed. Boston: Houghton Mifflin, 1990.

Schumpeter, Joseph A. *Capitalism, Socialism, and Democracy*. London: Allen & Unwin, 1942.

Selznick, Philip. *TVA and the Grass Roots: A Study in the Sociology of Formal Organization*. Berkeley, Calif.: University of California Press, 1949.

_____. *Leadership in Administration: A Sociological Interpretation*, Berkeley, Calif.: University of California Press, 1957.

Shaw, Arch Wilkinson. *An Approach to Business Problems*. Cambridge, Mass.: Harvard University Press, 1916.

Sobel, Russell S. "Entrepreneurship" in *The Concise Encyclopedia of Economics*, www.econlib.org/library/Enc/Entrepreneurship.html, accessed on March 7, 2009.

Solow, Robert M. "Technical Change and the Aggregate Production Function." *Review of Economics and Statistics* 39 (1957): 312–320.

Stern, Joel M., John S. Shiely, and Irwin Ross. *The EVA Challenge: Implementing Value-Added Change in an Organization*. Hoboken, NJ: John Wiley & Sons, 2001.

Stewart, G. Bennett. *The Quest for Value*. New York: HarperBusiness, 1991.

Stowe, John D., Thomas R. Robinson, Jerald E. Pinto, and Dennis W. McLeavey. *Equity Asset Valuation*, 2nd ed. Charlottesville, VA: CFA Institute, 2007.

Teece, David J., Gary Pisano, and Amy Shuen. "Dynamic Capabilities and Strategic Management." *Strategic Management Journal* 18 (1997): 509–533.

Therrien, Lois. "Want Shelf Space at the Supermarket? Ante Up." *BusinessWeek*, August 7, 1989, 60–61.

Thompson, Arthur A. Jr., A.J. Strickland, III, and John E. Gamble. *Crafting and Executing Strategy: The Quest for Competitive Advantage—Concepts and Cases*, 17th ed. New York: McGraw-Hill, 2009.

Thompson, James M. *Organizations in Action.* New York: McGraw-Hill, 1967.

Uttal, Bro. "The Corporate Culture Vultures." *Fortune,* October 17, 1983, 66–72.

von Neumann, John, and Oskar Morgenstern. *Theory of Games and Economic Behavior.* Princeton, NJ: Princeton University Press, 1944.

Waldman, Don E., and Elizabeth J. Jensen. *Industrial Organization: Theory and Practice,* 3rd ed. Boston: Addison-Wesley, 2007.

Wernerfelt, Birger. "The Resource-Based View of the Firm." *Strategic Management Journal* 5 (1984): 171–180.

Williamson, Oliver E. *The Mechanisms of Governance.* New York: Oxford University Press, 1996.

Winter, Sidney G. "The Satisficing Principle in Capability Learning." Chapter 18 (275–295) in *The SMS Blackwell Handbook of Organizational Capabilities: Emergence, Development, and Change,* Constance E. Helfat, ed. Malden, Mass.: Blackwell, 2003.

Wrigley, Leonard. *Divisional Autonomy and Diversification.* Unpublished doctoral dissertation, Harvard Business School, 1970.

Index

The italicized phrase "in vignettes" refers to concepts and issues addressed in the case studies that constitute Chapters 13-17; sectors shown under Domains do not repeat those in the Table of Contents; an italicized page number refers to the Exhibit on that page